THE FLETCHER JONES FOUNDATION
HUMANITIES IMPRINT

The Fletcher Jones Foundation has endowed this imprint to foster innovative and enduring scholarship in the humanities.

The publisher and the University of California Press Foundation gratefully acknowledge the generous support of the Fletcher Jones Foundation Imprint in Humanities.

MESSIANISM AND SOCIOPOLITICAL REVOLUTION IN MEDIEVAL ISLAM

MESSIANISM AND SOCIOPOLITICAL REVOLUTION IN MEDIEVAL ISLAM

Saïd Amir Arjomand

 UNIVERSITY OF CALIFORNIA PRESS

University of California Press
Oakland, California

© 2022 by Saïd Amir Arjomand

Library of Congress Cataloging-in-Publication Data
All rights reserved. First Paperback Printing 2025.
Names: Arjomand, Said Amir, author.
Title: Messianism and sociopolitical revolution in medieval
Islam / Saïd Amir Arjomand.
Description: Oakland, California : University of California
Press, [2022] | Includes bibliographical references and index.
Identifiers: LCCN 2022001022 (print) | LCCN 2022001023
(ebook) | ISBN 9780520387584 (hardback) | ISBN
9780520387591 (ebook) | ISBN 9780520425163 (pbk)
Subjects: LCSH: Mahdism—Political aspects—History. | Islam
and state—Islamic Empire—History. | Messianism—Islamic
Empire—History. | Revolutions—Islamic Empire—History.
Classification: LCC BP166.93 .A75 2022 (print) | LCC BP166.93
(ebook) | DDC 297.2/72—dc23/eng/20220223
LC record available at https://lccn.loc.gov/2022001022
LC ebook record available at https://lccn.loc.gov/2022001023

28 27 26 25
10 9 8 7 6 5 4 3 2 1

GPSR Authorized Representative: Easy Access System Europe,
Mustamäe tee 50, 10621 Tallinn, Estonia,
gaps.requests@easproject.com

The Hour is near and the moon is split.
—Qur'an 54:1

CONTENTS

Acknowledgments   *xi*

Introduction   1
   The Apocalyptic Motivation of Revolutionary Action: The Process of Revolution as Realization of Messianism and the Structural Models of Its Outcome   3
   Historiography of the Rise of Islam and the Abbasid and the Fatimid Revolutions   16

1. **The Emergence of Apocalyptic Messianism from the Maccabean Nativist Revolution**   33
   The Authority Structure of the Seleucid Empire and the Religious Background of the Nativistic Rebellion in Judaea   34
   Revolutionary Power Struggle under Dual Sovereignty and the Second Maccabean Temple-State and the Emergence of Messianism   51
   The Institutionalization of Apocalyptic Messianism in the Judaean Desert   69

2. **Muhammad's Constitutive Revolution and Its Apocalyptic Roots**   74
   The Religious Conditions of Arabia on the Periphery of Three Empires   75
   Apocalyptic Messianism and Muhammad's Revolutionary Motivation   88
   Muhammad's Call and the Formation of Islam as Realized Messianism   101
   The Mobilization for Holy Struggle (jihād) and the Unification of Arabia   105
   The Succession to Charismatic Leadership and the Suppression of Rival Messiahs   111

3. Civil Wars and the Emergence of Apocalyptic Mahdism — 116
   The First Civil War and the Umayyad Victory — 117
   The Second Civil War and the Failed Revolution of the Mawālī in Kufa — 131
   The Reemergence of Apocalyptic Messianism in the Figure of the Qa'im-Mahdī — 139
   The Marwanid Counterrevolution and the Development of Sunni Orthodoxy — 144
4. The Self-Destruction of the Umayyad Empire — 148
   The Structure of the Umayyad Imperial State and the Caliphate of al-Walīd II — 149
   Yazīd III and the Failed Revolution from Above — 156
   The Rebellion of 'Abdallāh b. Mu'āwāyia and the First Hashemite State — 163
   The Internal Collapse of the Marwanid Regime — 169
5. The Process of the Hashemite Revolution — 173
   The Outbreak and Process of Revolution in Khurasan — 173
   Revolutionary Power Struggle from Multiple Sovereignty to Dual Power — 192
   Ibn al Muqaffa' and his Manifesto for the Caliphate of the House of 'Abbās — 200
6. The Integrative and Centralizing Consequences of the Abbasid Realized Mahdism — 206
   The Reactivation of Millennialism in the Rebellions of Abu Muslim's Followers in Iran — 206
   The Defeat of the 'Alid Mahdī and the Closure of the Hashemite Apocalyptic Messianism — 211
   The End of the Hashemite Revolution and the Abbasid Autocracy as Realized Mahdism — 216
   The Integrative Consequences of the Abbasid Revolution — 219
7. Apocalyptic Messianism in the Fatimid Revolution — 224
   Nomads and Intellectuals in the Process of the Fatimid Revolution — 228
   The Routinization of Revolutionary Charisma and Its Resacralization into Autocracy in the Fatimid Empire — 252
   Apocalypse and the Great Resurrection in Mountain Fortresses of Northern Iran — 258
8. The Almohad Revolution of Mahdi Ibn Tumart and the Berbers — 262
   Dress Rehearsal for Revolution: The Almoravids' Turn in Power — 263
   Mahdism and the Revolutionary Power Struggle — 266
   The Establishment of Patrimonial Monarchy and the Almohad Hierarchy — 281
   The Consequences of the Berber Revolution of the Mahdi b. Tumart — 289

9.	The Islamicate Conceptions of Revolution	291
	The Apocalyptic Idea of Transfer of Sovereignty in Antiquity	292
	Islam's Social Revolution and Its Persianate Self-Conception	295
	The Mahdist Revolutions of North Africa and the Maghrebi Conception of Revolution	302
	Concluding Remarks	309
	Abbreviations	315
	References	319
	Index	345

ACKNOWLEDGMENTS

I have worked on this book for a quarter of a century and am indebted to too many colleagues and friends for its development to remember and thank. As beginnings and ends are what the memory retains best, let me thank my colleague and friend Björn Wittrock for his input and encouragement as the principal of the Swedish Collegium for Advanced Study, Uppsala, throughout my long association with SCAS, which began with a fellowship in fall 1998, when the project was conceived and continued through another in spring 2019. I am also grateful to the Hungarian Institute for Advanced Study and its director, Nadia al-Baghdadi, for a fellowship in January and February 2019 that enabled me to put the final touches on the earlier chapters. Lastly, in the production stage, I am most grateful to John E. Woods, my teacher at the University of Chicago in the 1970s and friend since then, for his help with the historical maps included in this volume, and to my son, Noah Amir Arjomand, for drawing them.

Introduction

The goal of this study is to enrich political theory and the sociology of revolution by a historicized analysis of messianism. It examines messianism as a major source in the motivation of revolutionary social action with the aim of reaching a comparative sociological understanding of its Islamic variant, Mahdism, in relation to the pattern of revolution in the Islamicate civilization. To this end, the structural models of the sociology of revolution provide the societal context for the analysis of the motives of the historical agents of revolutionary action and channels its unfolding along structural paths that are independent of their will. Explaining the transition from the charismatic, apocalyptic motivation—motives that set the process of revolution in motion—to the instrumentally rational motivation aiming at winning the power struggle is the thorniest conceptual problem we need to solve.[1] This challenge is the crux of the analytical integration of millennial motives, as they unfold in the process of revolution, with the societal structure of domination as it is being transformed under their impact. If we meet it successfully, we will have integrated the theory of apocalyptic politics or political messianism with the sociological theory of revolution. The broadening of analytical horizons resulting from such theoretical integration will in turn solve some major problems in the historiography of the rise of Islam and its sociopolitical revolutions.

---

1. It is this instrumentally rational motivation that makes the outcome of the process dependent on structural conditions and thereby partially independent of the will of the messianic actors.

This original undertaking is indeed timely. A leading sociologist of revolution concluded in a recent survey of the field: "If Marxism-Leninism was the dominant revolutionary ideology of the last century, Islam may be the dominant revolutionary ideology of the present."[2] A century and a half earlier, Alexis de Tocqueville (d. 1859) considered the political religion born of the French revolution of 1789 a new Islam that terrified contemporary observers by its missionary fervor. The Great French Revolution had indeed "developed into a species of religion ... This strange religion has, like Islam, overrun the whole world with its apostles, militants and martyrs."[3]

Yet, there is no substantial theoretically informed study of revolutionary movements in the richly documented Islamic history. Nor do we have a comparative study of religion and revolution that significantly includes Islam. The modern myth of revolution was born of the French Revolution of 1789. As a noted historian of the French revolution has put it recently: "revolution was revolutionized in 1789 when the notion of revolution as fact gave way to the conception of revolution as an ongoing act."[4] The concept of revolution generated a transportable script as its agenda that was then given a sociological inflection by Karl Marx during the European Revolution of 1848 and was propagated into the rest of the world by Marxism-Leninism in the twentieth century. For long, the Marxist-Leninist variant of the myth served as an ersatz theory of revolution. As the number of Muslim revolutionaries in the Afro-Eurasian landmass in the first quarter twenty-first century far exceeds that of the Marxist-Leninist revolutionaries a century earlier by any reasonable estimate, is it not time for a fresh look at the alternative conception of revolution from the perspective of Islamic history and its Mahdistic political messianism?

---

2. Goodwin 2005, 422.

3. Tocqueville 1955, 13. Tocqueville (1959, 114) further finds that the "character of the revolutionary conquests ... has something in common with the early Islamic period"—namely, that of the Arab conquests.

4. See Baker 2013, 189: It follows that "there were no 'revolutionaries' before revolution was revolutionized."

THE APOCALYPTIC MOTIVATION OF REVOLUTIONARY ACTION: THE PROCESS OF REVOLUTION AS REALIZATION OF MESSIANISM AND THE STRUCTURAL MODELS OF ITS OUTCOME

Max Weber, a founding father of sociology, proposed the understanding of the motivation of meaningful social action as its major task and distinguished between the subjective and objective meanings of social action. He called the motives of social action its subjective meaning.[5] Revolutionary action is meaningful for the historical actors themselves, and its subjective meaning consists of the motives of the revolutionaries. The objective meaning of revolutions, which is determined by theorists and not the actors themselves, consists in the significance of consequences in world history and in terms of the value-ideas that set them in motion and that are further defined in the course of revolutionary action.[6]

The apocalyptic view of politics can supply a powerful stimulus to agency by generating a pattern of politics driven by uncompromising ethics of absolute ends that can be called "absolute politics." It is apt for describing political action during the great opening and the freedom that occurs with the collapse of the old regime and at that moment of revolutionary liminality, when the sociopolitical rules and conventions are broken, and a new beginning can be made. The apocalyptic vision is a powerful means for transcending the normative order. True order is no longer identified with this world but requires a radical break with it; the existing reality is radically rejected, indeed destined for cataclysmic destruction. By holding up the vision of the imminent destruction of the current cosmic and normative order and its radical sociopolitical transformation, political messianism generates powerful motivation to innerworldly absolute social action aiming at the destruction and reconstruction of the world, including its political order. It thus establishes a transcendent cultural form that can grow autonomously and be transplanted and potentially universalized in world history. This is how Weber saw it in the preface to his unfinished study of ancient Judaism, whose significance in world history he attributed to the "conception of a future God-guided political and social revolution" that it generated.[7]

---

5. Weber 1978, 1:4.
6. Arjomand 2019, 12–28.
7. Weber 1952, 4.

In absolute politics, no boundaries are set to political will, and everything social is seen as transformable by politics. The revolutionary impact of absolute politics on preexisting social alignments and interests follows from the transformation of identity and values of the historical actors in the course of action. Absolutization of the ends of political action makes it constitutive of the identity of the participant. Absolute ends do not stop at moral sentiment but lay claim to reality itself and thereby to the radical transformation of the world that is found to be at variance with it. The ideologies of absolute politics are born of the claim to possessing the truth and to changing the world congruently. The goals of political action are set accordingly. The politics of absolute end thus justify the claim to converting others to the cause and giving political action a universalist and proselytizing character. This is typical of the missionary world religions of salvation.[8]

The claim to the possession of cosmic reality itself made messianism fundamentally religious: it thereby made revolutionary politics heteronomous. The apocalyptic vision of messianism was by no means confined to political order, and its political impact was therefore variable. Apocalyptic texts can be read very differently, and they can be compatible with categorical pacifism, as in the mainstream Christian interpretation, or with militancy, as we shall see was the case with the Essenes of the Qumran community as Muhammad's messianic predecessors. If absolute politics are the result rather than the cause of messianism, it follows that apocalyptic messianism must sociologically be analyzed in terms not of its political causes but its sociopolitical consequences.

The political revolutions motivated by messianism remained subordinate to millennial religious ends for two millennia. Then the French Revolution secularized old messianism into political messianism in the form of Jacobin revolutionary action driven by the modern myth of revolution made into the social revolution by Karl Marx. The modern idea of revolution thereby become an autonomous political phenomenon, being conceived as a redemptive, people-guided, social and political revolution, acquiring a strong, albeit hidden, religious dimension. The apocalyptic vision, thus secularized, became a major source of motivation to revolutionism in modern history. Revolution consequently became the engine of history as long as the modern myth of revolution was accepted as a secular, political religion.

---

8. Pizzorno 1994, 16–19.

While Marxism as secular religion attained its climax in the twentieth century, the inadequacy of the Marxian idea of revolution as a theory became apparent to the more perceptive observers of Communism and Fascism. Already in 1920, Fritz Gerlich wrote on "Orthodox Marxism as chiliasm" (millennialism) and a "religion of salvation for this world."[9] In 1929, Karl Mannheim compared the "spiritualization of politics" (*Vergeistigung der Politik*) in the twentieth-century revolutionary movements to the chiliasm of the Peasant Wars and the Anabaptists in early modern Germany. He emphasized the qualitative difference between the sacred, kairotic time of chiliasm, when the here and now is pervaded by eternity, with the routine, chronological conception of time in the post-Enlightenment, nonrevolutionary modern politics.[10]

Mannheim's distinction between kairotic and chronological time was associated with his more general conceptions of "utopia" and "ideology" as the respective cognitive/normative worldviews of chiliastic versus secular politics. The distinction was in fact the tip of the iceberg of the contrasting motivational patterns prevailing in spiritualized and routine political action. In contrasting these distinctive patterns of motivation, I call the first messianic or apocalyptic, instead of using Mannheim's term *utopian*, and I further qualify it as charismatic in order to highlight the pervasion of charisma in a new community of fellow believers, which made them live in the kairotic time set by the new revelation.[11] The second pattern of motivation comprising the routinized, chronological conception of time, I shall discuss presently as a consequence of "realized messianism."

In the following decade, Eric Voegelin coined the somewhat unfortunate term, "modern Gnosticism," to refer to the so-called spiritualization of politics in Europe; later, however, in *The New Science of Politics* (1952), he developed the more suggestive idea of "political religions" with reference to twentieth-century revolutionary Communism and Fascism.[12] In the same year, Jacob

---

9. Cited in Cattaruzza 2018, 212.
10. Mannheim 1978, 184–96.
11. This follows the original collective conception of charisma as the inherence of the holy spirit in the church in early Christianity by the Protestant theologian, Rudolph Sohm (1888) in preference to its unduly individualistic conceptualization by Max Weber as "charismatic leadership."
12. This was very much in line with Tocqueville's above-cited description of the French Revolution. The term is nevertheless ambiguous, as Voegelin himself finally concluded. (Cattaruzza 2018, 218n41)

Talmon published *The Origins of Totalitarian Democracy* (1952), which he followed up with *Political Messianism: The Romantic Phase* (1960). He equated the terms he coined, "totalitarian democracy" and "political messianism," and he made the Jacobinism of the French Revolution the modern sources of both. The messianism of Antiquity and the Middle Ages, our subject and the source of their metaphor for modern totalitarian movements, was not studied directly by either Voegelin or Talmon any more than it had been by Weber.

Weber had nevertheless put forward a compelling conceptualization of "world religions" as grand solutions to the problem of the meaning of life with far-reaching ethical implications for social action in the economic and political spheres that could lend itself to the comparative analysis of the total ideologies of the twentieth century as equivalent secular meaning systems giving urgent purpose to sociopolitical action. In the mid-1950s, Manuel Sarkisyanz showed the Bolsheviks' harnessing to the Marxian scientific socialism of Orthodox Christian themes in Russia and of Islamic and Buddhist millennial beliefs in Asia, and shortly thereafter Norman Cohn published his study of Christian revolutionary messianism and its bearing on twentieth-century political religions.[13]

It goes without saying that world history did not stand still after Fascism and Communism, whose days were in fact numbered. Roughly coinciding with the collapse of Communism, the last quarter of the twentieth century witnessed a revolution that combined the technical, ideological advances of the century's political religions while emphatically retaining the promise of otherworldly salvation—namely, the Islamic revolution of 1979 in Iran. "Rather than creating a new substitute for religion, as did the Communists and the Nazis, the Islamic militants . . . fortified an already vigorous [world] religion with the ideological armor necessary for battle in the arena of mass politics. In doing so, they have made their distinct contribution to world history."[14] Furthermore, what should become evident as we proceed is that it was not accidental that the Islamic revolution of 1979 was born of Shi'ite Islam, which preserved the heritage of its pristine apocalyptic messianism, and not of Sunni Islam, which developed largely from the historical memory of the realized messianism of the last eleven years of Muhammad's prophecy in Medina.

13. Sarkisyanz 1955; Cohn 1957.
14. Arjomand 1988, 210.

The spectacular and unexpected Islamic revolution in Iran notwithstanding, the insights drawn from these works on secular Western revolutionary movements in relation to religion have not been applied to the revolutionary movements in the Islamicate civilization.[15] Nor has Weber's assertion about the revolutionary potential of ancient Judaism ever been critically examined in light of the sources discovered since his death. Our goal in the present study is to rectify the long neglect of a world religion that can lends itself to revolutionary interpretation and can motivate revolutionary action more readily than any other. In pursuing this goal, the opportunity will also be taken to supply an analysis of the developments in ancient Judaism not known to Weber that may justify his assertion.[16] In fact, one of the main findings of the present study is the transmission of the Danielic and Qumran apocalyptic ideas to Arabia through the Jews of Medina, and this finding provides us with a unique opportunity for beginning our analysis of messianism where Weber left off.

Chapter 1 accordingly examines the emergence of apocalyptic messianism and the motivation of the idea of a revolution guided by God with an extensive analysis of the roots of political messianism in the Maccabean revolt against the Seleucids in the second century before the Common Era. Ancient apocalyptic messianism is the root of the motivation for revolutions in the Judeo-Christian and Islamicate civilizations as well as those of the modern world in the secular age. Certain key elements of ancient apocalyptic messianism will be shown to have been transmitted to Arabia indirectly through Manichaeism and directly through the Dead Sea Scrolls of the nonrabbinical Qumran sectarians.

The world-historical significance of Muhammad's messianism is much greater than that of the Danielic and Qumran messianism in which it was rooted. This is because Muhammad succeeded in realizing his messianism through a political revolution in seventh-century Arabia. The progressive realization of the Meccan apocalyptic messianism after his migration to the oasis

---

15. Marshall Hodgson published *The Order of Assassins* on millennium and revolution in medieval Iran in 1955 but it did not attract any general attention.

16. Weber died before completing his study of ancient Judaism. Had he advanced as far as the book of Daniel and the two Maccabees, he may have given us a sense of the source of motivation to the apocalyptic vision that motivated God-ordained revolutionary sociopolitical action, but it would have been narrowly based. The Dead Sea Scrolls of the Qumran community, by far the richest set of apocalyptic texts in world history, were discovered long after his death.

of Yathrib meant the creation of a protostate in Medina that achieved the political unification of Arabia within a few years of his death. This dramatic transition already requires a sharp analytical distinction between the two stages of Muhammad's prophecy, but the radical change resulting from the impact of realized messianism was particularly profound after the death of the Prophet. The charismatic community under a living messianic leader ceased or was rather transfigured as the Prophet's disciples became authoritative narrators of the memory of the kairotic years, conceived as the sacred history of the charismatic community when heaven and earth were joined through the revelation of God's last Messenger. Meanwhile, the Prophet's successors, the first caliphs, engaged in the rational management of the war of unification and subsequent statebuilding for conquest in measured chronological, secular time as they routinized Muhammad's prophetic charisma into the institution of the caliphate. With the death of the Prophet Muhammad the Messenger of God, the kairotic time of liminality thus collapsed into the chronological time of political unification and empire of conquest. Islamic history as we know it began.

It was with good reason that the decisive migration of Muhammad from Mecca to Medina, marking the inception of eleven years of progressively realized messianism, was chosen as the beginning of the Islamic era, and the years of Medina conceived as its sacred, protohistory. Since I consider apocalyptic and realized messianism the two stages of Muhammad's prophecy separated by a change in the pattern of motivation, a few analytical remarks on the realized messianism in Islamic protohistory seem in order. Muhammad began to enhance his authority as an invited arbitrator (*hakam*) and a holy man, Muhammad the "Prophet" (*nabi*), with a view to building his own polity in his chosen "abode of migration" (*dār al-hijra*). Within some two years of his arrival in Yathrib, which was renamed the "City of the Prophet" (*madinat al-nabi*), Muhammad instituted a pact of brotherhood between the Muslim migrants from Mecca who followed him and the new local converts, and he signed a number of pacts (most probably three) with the Jews of Yathrib. Shortly thereafter, he assumed the unwonted and non-Abrahamic title of "the Messenger of God" (*rasul Allāh*) and as such led the Islamic Constitutive Revolution that unified Arabia and established Islam. The sober, instrumentally rational and at times ruthless statesmanship he displayed in realizing his messianic mission and the apocalyptic vision of his Meccan preaching was indeed remarkable—so much so that it gave birth to a realistic mainstream historiography that minimized the liminal apocalyptic breakthrough of the initial revelation, or rather compartmentalized and insulated it within an increasingly otherworldly religious sphere. However, as an apocalyptic repository in the Islamic scriptural tradition, its record constituted a reservoir to be tapped by Shi'ite Mahdism in subsequent centuries.

As for the (Sunni) mainstream Muslims, the apocalyptic preaching about the End of Time (ākhir al-zamān) by God's last messenger was still read charismatically but as a nonapocalyptic, routinized, universal, sacred history of the divine guidance of humankind through a series of prophets. The Muslim community of the empire of conquest was no longer living in kairotic time, and although it cherished the memory of the Prophet and his disciples, it even forgot about their new identity and new sacred names given to them under the new revelation. Muhammad was the one exception whose postrevelation identity was congealed into a new name. Muhammad (the praised one), and his messianic designation as the Paraclete, Ahmad, was awkwardly relegated to commentaries that claim it to have been his given name![17]

It was indeed the very "conception of a God-guided political and social revolution" that motivated Muhammad to carry out his Constitutive Revolution in Arabia; realized messianism was, if anything, a revolution in world history. The apocalyptic vision that set this divinely guided Constitutive Revolution in motion is examined in chapter 2. Muhammad's Constitutive Revolution occurred on the periphery of the Persian (Sasanian) and the Ethiopian empires, as well as on that of the Byzantine Empire. Apocalyptic ideas received through Manichaeism, transmitted through the vassal state of Hira in Sasanian Mesopotamia, nonrabbinical Judaism, and partly through Ethiopia, I argue, constituted an important ingredient in Muhammad's revolution in Arabia, and were thus major influences in the elaboration of Islam. The career of Islam therefore began as an apocalyptic messianism that created and cemented Muhammad's charismatic community of the faithful. The believers' revolutionary struggle in the path of God in kairotic, sacred time under a charismatic messianic leader and in accordance with God's continuing revelation, marked the onset of the period of realized messianism and the creation of a new political order. With the realization of the messianism of Muhammad as the Messenger of God came the routinization of the prophetic charisma of Muhammad and the institutionalization of Islam as a new world religion. First and foremost, there was

---

17. Ibn Sa'd, 1.1, 66–67, 103–11.

the arrangement of recorded divine revelations into the Qur'an as the book of God. Thereafter, Muhammad's Constitutive Revolution in Arabia set the distinctive pattern for millennial revolutionary action in the Islamicate civilization in the form of struggle in the path of God (*jihād*).

The origins and history of Muhammad's Constitutive Revolution are one thing; its historical memory that can motivate the revolutionary social action of Muslims in the following generation is quite another. The memory of the Messenger of God was modified into the messianic figure of the Mahdi in the utopias of heterodox sects that challenged the basis of the status quo, just as the script of the French Revolution in the historical memory of subsequent generations of revolutionaries created the myth of revolution that produced a cycle of modern revolutions in the ensuing two centuries. And just as was to be the case with the modifications of the modern myth of revolution, each modification of the myth of the Mahdi could motivate an epicycle of Mahdistic revolutions. As the remaining chapters of this book will show, the myth of the Mahdi, forged as Muhammad redivivus, served as the inexhaustible resource for subsequent generations living in routinized, chronological, and secular times to reverse the routinization that was consequent on realized messianism.

Both revolution and messianism are defined typologically in this study. Political messianism is defined in terms of a cluster of beliefs we may call the "messianic syndrome"—beliefs that are present to varying degrees in all the movements included in the category. There is a strong family resemblance among the cases of Mahdist revolution studied in the Islamicate civilization, a less strong family resemblance between them and ancient apocalyptic messianism, and a categorical affinity with modern revolutions as well as with a broader variety of millennial experience in world history.[18] Even though our definition is typological, etymology is our inevitable beginning, and the Messiah (the anointed one) was the title of the king of Israel under the monarchy of the House of David. Some "protomessianic" dimension may have been built into the Judaic notion of the ideal king even before its collapse.[19] But, as the Davidic monarchy was never restored after the Babylonian captivity, the messianic trait was greatly strengthened during the Second Temple period, and the conventional wisdom places the origins of messianism in this period. This

---

18. Landes 2011.
19. Schaper 2007.

messianism, however, was particular to the Jews, and it did not develop out of the ancient Jewish historical experience into what Talcott Parsons called an "evolutionary universal" until the double civilizational encounter with the Persian and the Greek culture in the earlier and later chapters of the book of Daniel.[20] The importance of Israel as a seedbed society for the universalist development of messianism as a general religiocultural form that was inherited by Muhammad can thus be dated to this period.

The generic and universalistic form of apocalypticism, inspired by the "God of heaven" and containing all the elements of the messianic syndrome in a variable configuration, thus emerged from the revolutionary conflict between the religion of Yahweh and the imperialism of the Seleucid successors of Alexander the Great in the third quarter of the second century BCE.[21] Foremost within this generalized messianic syndrome or cluster is apocalypticism, as epitomized much later in John's book of Revelation (Apocalypse), which is the revelation of the scenario for the End of Time. Apocalypticism can therefore be defined as a cluster of belief concerning the nearness of the End of Time, the signs of which make for a time of unprecedented cataclysmic disaster, an age of gloom and doom marked by unimaginable trials and tribulations that can only be ended by divine intervention and finally, by the appearance of a charismatic leader sent by God to end the world as we know it.

What happens the day after is a consequential part of the messianic syndrome. It could be of renewal of the world (*frašo kereti*), as in Mazdaean Iranian religions, or it could be an "apocalyptic theodicy" that is later routinized and rationalized into an otherworldly eschatology, taking the form of the theological idea of the end (*eschaton*) as the Day of Resurrection and Last Judgment in the Abrahamic religions.[22] The charismatic leadership of the Messiah, as etymologically implied by messianism, is only one of these three components of apocalyptic messianism that can together generate an intensely charismatic and emotional tenet that propels revolutionary social action here and now that is made into kairotic time. The unfolding of the millennial motive in Mahdism as the Islamic variant of political messianism is here analyzed with a view to its long-term consequences in a small number of cases of

20. Parsons 1966.
21. See chapter 1, below.
22. Landes 2018, 3.

sociopolitical transformation that are important enough to be called revolutions. Centuries later, with the French revolution, the religiocultural messianic form was secularized into the modern myth of revolution.

This brings us to the sociopolitical theory of revolution that began with the analysis of the revolution as a process conceived as its "anatomy."[23] The process of revolution was seen as the revolutionary power struggle among the contenders in the competition engendered by political mobilization that was in turn caused by the breakdown of the old regime. On closer inspection, the process of revolution is more complex and can heuristically be thought of in two phases, the short and the long terms. While the short-term outcome of a revolution is the result of the process of power struggle among the contenders, the long-term consequences of major revolutions, their teleology, unfold through a different process that takes longer to end. This second process I call constitutional politics; it is driven by disagreements over the principles of the new political order and involves the resolution of differences about the proper institutionalization of fundamental values implicit in the motivating apocalyptic vision. The *consequences* of revolution are the outcome of this long-term struggle for the constitution of a new political order. These consequences set the direction of sociopolitical transformation and depend on the power coefficient of the contending groups and forces in the first process of revolution but also on what Weber called their "ideal interests." The ideal interests of the winners of the revolutionary power struggle set the parameter of the constitutional politics in each revolution. Constitutional politics, in other words, is the politics of postrevolutionary political and social reconstruction through the institutionalization of competing principles of order.

In both phases of the process or revolution, the constitutional politics of a millennially motivated or Mahdist revolution is inflected distinctively by the routinization revolutionary charismatic leadership of the claimants to Mahdihood in the struggle for the reconstruction of the political order of realized messianism. The messianic myth in Mahdistic or any other modified form, however, can reverse this routinization and motivate the regeneration of revolutionary liminality and with it the resacralization of the motivation to revolutionary absolute politics in kairotic time. The goals of revolutionary

---

23. Edwards 1927; Brinton 1938. The process of revolution was conceived as the rotation of "moderates" and "radicals" in the Reign of Terror and the final return to the moderates with the passing of the revolutionary fever and the return of the body politic to normalcy.

absolute politics differ from case to case, directing each Mahdist revolution along different paths in the face of historical contingencies and thus giving it a distinct and historically unique teleology.

In Mahdist uprisings, social action in expectation of the Hour (*al-sāʿa*) of cosmic cataclysm ushering in the Day of Judgment, was soon conceived as the End of Time (*ākhir al-zamān*) and can be categorized as millennial. The belief in the End of Time tends to be associated with the advent of a messianic savior figure to prepare the world for the Last Judgment. Muhammad inherited the belief in apocalyptic messianism from various channels: the book of Daniel, the Dead Sea Scrolls through the nonrabbinical Jews of Arabia, Manichaeism, and, lastly through Christianity, which probably supplied the Paraclete with the Gospel of John, but only through Manichaean Christology. Within a generation after Muhammad's death, the notion of the Qaʾim (*qāʾim*), meaning the riser/redresser, had entered the radical, oppositional heterodoxy of the Islamicate civilization as the supreme messianic figure. The Qaʾim was before long assimilated to the Mahdi (*al-mahdi*, meaning the rightly guided) as Muhammad redivivus reshaped into the savior of the End of Time. Millennialism, then, takes on the distinctive form in the Islamicate civilization that we here call Mahdism.

It goes without saying that the unfolding of millennial motive does not occur in a vacuum but takes place in a historical context with its particular contingencies and in a society with a definite sociopolitical structure This study presents a distinctive pattern of revolution in the Islamicate civilization illustrated by a detailed comparative analysis of the cases. In other words, the pattern of motivation that sets a Mahdist revolution in motion is complemented by a typological analysis of the structural changes derived comparatively from major revolutions in world history. Elsewhere, I have proposed a typology of ancient and medieval revolutions that shifts the analytical focus from the causes to the consequences of revolutions.[24]

The main ideal types of revolution found in the ancient and medieval world, I called Integrative Revolution, since this term captures the relation between revolution and the enlargement of the political community. It is divided into

---

24. See Arjomand 2019, 315, table 3. The causes are reconsidered in the light of this shift, and the causes and consequences of revolutions are combined to build a small number of heuristic ideal types for comparative analysis.

three subtypes. The ideal type, which I call "Constitutive Revolution," models the revolutionary construction of an integrated political community from segmentary tribal societies or self-contained city-states.[25] The social revolution of Islam is known as the Abbasid Revolution and it is covered in chapters 4, 5 and 6. Its structural model fits the two other subsidiary ideal types of Integrative Revolution, each highlighting a different aspect of it: the Aristotelian-Paretan revolution of disposed counter-elites;[26] and the Khaldunian revolution from the tribal periphery of empires.[27]

The ideal type of revolution, which I call Tocquevillean, captures the centralization of power in the modern state and is thus the main ideal type of

---

25. According to the ideal type of Constitutive Revolution, radical change in the political order may result from the incongruence between cultural and political integration. This can arise in a culturally unified society, where the structure of authority remains segmented—confined to tribes or city-states. The larger society is culturally unified while political authority is segmented, except under martial emergency, and political integration remains either intermittent, in the form of ad hoc confederations of tribes and city-states, or weak, based solely on networks of personal ties among patrons and clients across the segments. Such societies, including the "segmentary states" that are found to be prone to rebellions, can be restructured through revolution. The type of revolution that belongs to these societies is an Integrative Revolution that constitutes a new political order by institutionalizing central political authority and unifying the segments into a more integrated political community. See Arjomand 2019, ch. 1.

26. Aristotle's idea of revolution as the enlargement of the political community in oligarchies and aristocracies can serve as the starting point for this model. According to Aristotle (*Politics* 1305a–1307b), oligarchies and aristocracies are prone to revolution because of those they *exclude* from the political society. Impoverished members of the governing class in oligarchies become revolutionary leaders; the regime is undermined by persons who are wealthy but are excluded from office; and sedition in aristocracies arises when the circle of government is too narrow and "the masses of a people consist of men animated by the conviction that they are as good as their masters in quality." Among the moderns, Pareto's theory of revolution comes closest to Aristotle's idea. Put simply, his theory is as follows: If access to the political class, the ruling elite, is blocked to energetic and resolute individuals—lions—from the lower classes; and if the elite ruling by cunning—foxes—become weak and incapable of stern repression because of an increase in the proportion of foxes over lions in its composition, a revolution is likely to occur. In this situation, socially upwardly mobile individuals who are excluded from power develop into a revolutionary counterelite that eventually seizes power and makes history the graveyard of yet another aristocracy. The leadership of the revolutionary counter-elite often comes from politically dispossessed aristocracies. See Arjomand 2019, ch. 1.

27. The model is described in chapter 9 as the Maghrebi conception of revolution.

modern revolutions. Nevertheless, it can capture important aspects of ancient and medieval revolutions—namely, the centralization of power as a consequence of the revolutionary power struggle. As such, it can throw considerable light on the centralization of power after the Second Civil War and the Abbasid Revolution. The model of centralization of power as both the cause and the consequence of revolution is therefore used in chapter 3 to interpret the cycle of civil wars of the seventh century that culminated in the Abbasid Revolution in the mid-eighth; these can therefore all be considered the long-term consequences of the rise of Islam as a Constitutive Revolution. The Tocquevillian focus on the concentration of power and its dysfunctional results highlights the importance of the breakdown of centralized power, the state, as a cause of revolution. This draws our attention to the self-destruction of the Umayyad state in 744 CE as the beginning of the Hashemite Revolution analyzed in chapter 4.

The modified Tocquevillian model also highlights another consequence of the concentration of power in the state prior to the revolution.[28] This requires a systematic treatment of the revolutionary role of the groups that are dispossessed by the growing state. The considerable revolutionary role of *declining* classes, and of cohesive social groups with strong solidarity that are dispossessed by the centralization of power or threatened by socioeconomic change, is generally neglected. The chapters on the Abbasid Revolution in this study highlight the leadership of the dispossessed aristocracy of Medina belonging to the clan of the Prophet, the Banu Hāshim, in the revolution against the Umayyads.

Finally, the Tocquevillian model helps us focus on the formation of a new political class as a consequence of postrevolutionary centralization of power in the process of state building under the early Abbasids itself, a process described as the rise of caliphal absolutism.[29] The other important Iranian social group consisted of the bureaucratic elite integrated into the new political community for the purpose of state-building by the early Abbasid caliphs— that is, the secretaries (*kuttāb*), who had played an increasingly important role in the late Umayyad administration, but who nevertheless suffered the degradations and disabilities that pertained to the status of the *mawāli*.

28. Arjomand 1988.
29. Hodgson 1974, 1.

HISTORIOGRAPHY OF THE RISE OF ISLAM AND THE ABBASID AND FATIMID REVOLUTIONS

Islamic historiography never recovered from or modified the lapse in memory of the charismatic community of the apocalyptic messianism of the Meccan birth of Islam, since its reading was heavily influenced by the protohistorical narrative of realized messianism in Medina, leaving the recovery of the apocalyptic origins of Islam to modern scholarship. Modern critical historiography of the rise of Islam by Orientalists began at about the same time as the scientific study of the Bible (called "higher criticism") in the latter part of the nineteenth century. Higher criticism of the Old Testament began as part of the movement in German historical hermeneutics, and it was eagerly embraced by W. Robertson Smith in Britain.[30] The higher criticism or scientific study of the Qur'an and hadith (traditions or reports of the sayings and deeds of Muhammad) began during the same period. In fact, some of the key figures of the biblical higher criticism were also interested in Islam. Robertson Smith wrote about kinship in Arabia and his thinking about sacrifice as the key institution in Semitic religion was clearly influenced by his knowledge of ancient Arabia.[31] The pathbreaking higher criticism of the Qur'an came from the German Orientalist, Theodor Nöldeke, in *Geschichte des Qorans* (1860), a work later significantly dedicated to Ignaz Goldziher, his Jewish Hungarian contemporary.[32] Goldziher had broken his analytical teeth on a study of Hebrew mythology (1877) and had published his major critical studies of the Qur'an and hadith in 1888.[33] He demonstrated that many of the traditions attributed to the Prophet belonged to a different period, reflecting concerns of the major contending groups in later Islamic history, and he completed his career with a critical study of the Qur'an commentaries (Goldziher 1920), fundamental historical sources that are totally neglected by the trendy hyperdeconstructions of the last quarter of the twentieth century to be discussed presently. In the next generation, Joseph Schacht drew critically on Max Weber's sociology of law in a pathbreaking article published in 1933. Using its

---

30. He translated Wellhausen's *Prolegomena to the History of Ancient Israel* ([1878] 1957).
31. Robertson Smith (1889) 1972.
32. Its subsequent volumes were completed by other Orientalists—namely, Friedrich Schwally, G. Bergsträsser, and O. Pretzel—in 1909 and 1938, respectively.
33. Goldziher 1971.

theoretical framework, Schacht followed Goldziher's work on the hadith as the basis of Islamic law and published his classic *Origins of Muhammadan Jurisprudence* in 1950. Schacht took a more extreme position than Goldziher, maintaining that Islamic law in fact reflected the legal practice of the first century of the Islamic Empire during the Umayyad period, and was strongly colored by legal variations among those of Medina, the formerly Persian Iraq, and the formerly Byzantine Syria. The hadith, he argued, were fabricated by the schools of jurisprudence in the second century of Islam to give religious legitimacy to the local, practically based legal traditions.

Goldziher's criticism of the traditions as the basis of Islamic law was systematically extended to historical traditions by his German contemporary, Julius Wellhausen (d. 1918), a leading proponent of the higher criticism of the Bible and the author of *Prolegomena to the History of Israel* (1878).[34] In the early 1880s, Wellhausen adopted the methodology of higher criticism to the history of the rise of Islam and the early caliphate with great sensitivity to source-critical problems. He considered many traditions, such as those concerning the central control of the conquests, land, and fiscal measures attributed to the second caliph, 'Umar, unreliable, and he more generally divided the primary sources into Medinan, Iraqi, and Syrian schools, each with its distinctive biases and tendentious fabrications that needed to be carefully checked. But he also made ample use of the early hadith he considered well-authenticated in his concise discussion of the rise of Islam out of Arab paganism.[35]

Wellhausen had turned from the religion of ancient Israel, with which he had begun his career, to the far better documented study of early Islam. His substantive contributions to the historiography of the rise of Islam and the Abbasid Revolution are noteworthy and remain relevant. He traced the emergence of Allāh as a transtribal, higher god tending to universality and a god without a cult in pagan Arabia to the One God of the Qur'an. The rise of Islam was a religious revolution that found expression in a polity and thereby underwent change "from being an individual to being a political religion," making the pristine mosque its "drilling ground."[36] As for the rise of the Abbasids as the social revolution of Islam, the aspect of revolution captured by both our

---

34. Rudolph 1983.
35. Wellhausen 1899; Noth 1994, 4–14, 59–62; Wellhausen 1887, 234–42.
36. Wellhausen 1883, 553.

Integrative and Tocquevillian models of revolution were highlighted by Wellhausen, who began his account with the breakdown and collapse of the Umayyad state and considered the revolution that of the Persian clients (*mawāli*) of the Umayyad Empire. Both these features were largely ignored in the later historiographical controversy between the Arabists and the Persianists to be considered presently.

Wellhausen's study of Arabian pagan religion has more recently been taken up by Aziz al-Azmeh, who suggestively labels the emergence of Islam under Muhammad as "Paleo-Islam." He renews Wellhausen's search while maintaining the latter's insistence on the primacy of ritual and the cultic sodalities organized around the sacred enclaves (singular, *haram*) centered on the shrines of deities in Late Antique Arabia. Al-Azmeh emphatically excluded any overarching theological template that might derive from Judaism or Christianity, and meticulously traces the evolution of Muhammad's conception of God from the Lord (*rabb*) of the sacred Meccan enclave along the path of monolatry and henotheism through what he later called "Muhammad's henotheistic diplomacy of the divine" to the pure monotheism as the worship of Allah as the One and only God, whose description he leaves to others.[37]

Among the first generation of critical Orientalists, however, only Paul Casanova (1911) emphasized the apocalyptic messianism of Muhammad, but his work had little impact and the apocalyptic dimension of the rise of Islam received no attention until recently.[38]

Two generations later, Wellhausen's source-critical approach was refined by Albrecht Noth.[39] Noth rejected the critical approach to the historic traditions as representing regional biases as too totalistic, and advocated instead painstaking formal and substantive microcriticism of individual traditions further broken down into component elements, maintaining that source-criticism in Islamic historiography must focus on their "editorial manipulation" and not ascribe falsification "to the politically biased reworking of authentic news, but to the assembling of heterogeneous pieces of tradition, rather like a photomontage." Noth's ultimate aim was constructive scholar-

---

37. Al-Azmeh 2014; Al-Azmeh 2018a, 358.

38. Shoemaker 2014.

39. It is interesting to note that he is the son of Martin Noth, a notable representative of the higher criticism of the Old Testament in the generation after Wellhausen.

ship, however, and he concluded that "while source criticism repudiates some accounts, it vindicates others."[40]

In 1977, Noth's source-critical approach ignited an explosion of deconstructionism, avant la lettre, across the North Sea in England by the heirs presumptive to the higher criticism of Goldziher, Nöldeke, Wellhausen, and Schacht. This first found expression in *Qur'anic Studies* by John Wansbrough and *Hagarism* by Patricia Crone and Michael Cook. Wansborough published a second book, *The Sectarian Milieu*, in 1978. With these books a scholarly storm broke out, emanating from the School of Oriental and African Studies of the University of London (SOAS), and the old constructive higher criticism and its source-critical successor studies were suddenly discarded and replaced by a deliberately destructive higher or rather *hyper* form of deconstruction. Wansbrough has two major arguments. First, he extends Schacht's rejection of the hadith to the Qur'an itself, assuming its text to have been generated in sectarian controversies over two centuries and projected back as the revelation of a fictitious Arabian prophet. Secondly, he argues that the Islamic doctrine and the figure of the Arabian prophet are applications and mere perpetuations of Jewish prototypes. Early Islamic history is a mythic construction; it is mere "historicization" of the pericopes and myths of Jewish "salvation history" (*Heilsgeschichte*)—possibly the only German word he deigns to translate. One of the curious points made by Wansbrough is that Qumran and the Islamic community are the only two communities whose existence for two centuries was attested only by internal textual evidence. He goes on to say that at least the Qumran community has been identified with the Essenes, implying the Islamic community remains unidentified![41]

In *Hagarism*, Crone and Cook took Wansbrough's ideas and ran with them, arguing that the whole accepted version of the history of the rise of Islam in the seventh century is a later fabrication. This argument was used to justify their rejection of all later Islamic sources for scraps of near-contemporary information such as hearsay reports by the bishop of Armenia about the agitation of Ishmaelites in the Arabian desert.[42]

---

40. Noth 1994, 24; Noth (1968) 2008, 260.
41. Wansbrough 1977, 3; Wansbrough 1978, 52–53.
42. More reliable Syriac sources, by contrast, have been painstakingly shown to corroborate the Arab conquest of Khuzistan. See Robinson 2004.

All this was challenging, provocative, and refreshingly welcome at the time, given the uncritical and sanctimonious attitude of Muslim modernists toward Islam and its history. The ferociously hostile and often deliberately offensive tone of the *hyper*deconstructionists was, however, problematic, and it did not have a parallel in early higher criticism and source-critical studies. More fundamentally, provocation, desirable or not, should not be mistaken for serious scholarship.

Inspired by Wansbrough, another SOAS deconstructionist, G. R. Hawting constructed comparative parallels to the Kharijite revolutionary slogan in light of the Jewish oral law that seem arbitrary and ignore the sociohistorical context altogether.[43] The last exemplar of the SOAS hyperdeconstruction worth mentioning is N. Calder's study of Islamic law; this makes the development of Islamic law during the half-century following the Abbasid Revolution entirely a literary fiction.[44]

The ripples of the wave of hyperdeconstruction set off by the tremor at SOAS reached Israel and Germany.[45] The SOAS storm subsided, however, as its two leading enfants terribles matured and crossed the Atlantic in the opposite direction from John Wansbrough (formerly Weinstein). Michael Cook produced a monumental compilation of Islamic ethics based entirely on classics in Muslim jurisprudence.[46] Patricia Crone continued for a while in her hyperdeconstructionist mode but increasingly combined it with more solid higher criticism of the Qur'an and the rise of Islam, albeit without being able to resist showing off by making improbable provocative assertions.[47] The trend she had helped set in motion and was identified with, however, continued unabated.

---

43. Hawting 1978.

44. Calder 1993. Just because the historicity of the *Kitāb al-Umm* by Muhammad b. Idris al-Shafi'i (d. 814) cannot be established, absolutely anything goes for Calder, and the entire corpus of early Islamic law is said to have been fabricated. Even after pages of breathless textual deconstruction, Calder does not consider it his responsibility to explain what in the historical circumstances of the mid-ninth/third century might possibly account for the sudden outburst of the alleged feverish fabrication and forgery.

45. For Israel, see Sharon 1988; Nevo and Koren 1990; Nevo and Koren 2003. In Germany, hyper deconstruction produced a most chillingly arid source-critical exemplar, *The Biography of Muhammad* (2000) under the editorship of H. Motzki.

46. Cook 2000.

47. Crone 1987; Crone 2007; Crone 2010.

Many scholars remained impervious to the charms of the passing storm of hyperdeconstructionism, however. Some explicitly refuted the contentions of the hyperdeconstructionists from the 1990s onward. Convincing evidence and arguments for early codification, historicity, and stability of the Qur'anic text and its priority over the traditions about the life of the Prophet were produced in the United States.[48] In Europe, Jacqueline Chabbi demonstrated the historical value of the Qur'an while adhering strictly to the higher-critical standards. Robert Hoyland, using a much larger fund of non-Muslim sources to reach opposite conclusions from those of the narrowly biased *Hagarism*, proceeded to find plausibility in some Arab narratives of the conquests.[49] M.J. Kister, and Michael Lecker in Israel, continued the tradition of solid critical scholarship; while Uri Rubin produced a remarkably constructive biography of Muhammad.[50]

More recent scholarship has rejected the main revisionist argument of the hyperdeconstructionists that the Qur'an is a later plagiarized composition as unconvincing and not substantiated.[51] Most decisively, Behnam Sadeghi and his associates have established that the Companion codices taken from the Prophet's own dictation show very minor differences owing to semi-orality but prove that he fixed the content of the suras include ordering and division of the verses. These "codices indeed existed at the time of the Companions." Furthermore, the correspondence between the two best known companion codices and the San'ā' palimpsest from the first half of the seventh century is striking.[52]

It is therefore not surprising that Al-Azmeh, who had been sympathetic to the deconstruction movement, now calls it "hyper-scepticism" and has written a scathing criticism of its slapdash treatment of Arabic sources. He considers the biblical paralellomania built into the hypersceptics' paradigm implausible, and their arbitrary and illegitimate dismissal of the Arabian evidence unreliable or irrelevant. He complains more generally that it has made limitless skepticism "a creed, not a canon of method," and has

---

48. Whelan 1998; Donner 1998; Donner 2008b, 42–43.
49. Chabbi 1997; Hoyland 2001; Hoyland 2006.
50. Rubin 1995.
51. Neuwirth 2003, esp. 1–11; Neuwirth 2006, 100; Hilali 2010; Al-Azmeh 2014b.
52. Sadeghi and Bergmann 2010, 413–14; Sadeghi and Goudarzi 2012.

characterized the recalcitrant resistance of this hyperscepticism to evidence as "cognitive filibuster."[53]

Meanwhile, Islamic modernists, too, had embarked on systematic studies of the Qur'an. Following the lead of Toshihiko Izutsu in the semantic analysis of the Qur'an, Fazlur Rahman published his *Major Themes of the Qur'an* in 1980.[54] Mehdi Bazargan, who was to serve as the provisional prime minister of the Islamic Republic of Iran in 1979, was completing his *Sayr-e tahavvol-e Qur'an* (course of evolution of the Qur'an), a monumental work that has found striking stylometric corroboration. By emphasizing the coherence of the Qur'an, these studies substantively show that Muhammad's religious reconstruction of Arabian religion already created the last world religion in his lifetime. A quantitative study of Bazargan's chronology of the Qur'an establishes the Qur'an as a self-consistent historical source independently of the hadith collected on the life of the Prophet or the *Sira* literature. Thus, contrary to Wansbrough's contention, the Qur'an and the *Sira* literature are two independent and at times mutually supportive sources for the study of early Islam.[55]

---

53. Al-Azmeh 2014a, xii, 99, 518; Al-Azmeh 2014b; Al-Azmeh 2018a, 360–63; Al-Azmeh 2018b; Al-Azmeh 2019. Nevertheless, Al-Azmeh still shares the higher deconstructionists' uncritical assumption that Islam is a post-Muhammadan invention by considering the transition from Paleo-Islam to Islam under the Umayyads as a move in the direction of Late Antique Hellenistic rationality, as "theological sublimation" required by "the vast change of scale from the Arabian beginning to empire." Although Muhammad's revolutionary break with Arabian cultic practice by ending the intercalation in Arabian ritual calendars is properly noted by him, Al-Azmeh has little, if anything, to say about the reconstructive rationalization of beliefs that preceded and went along with the ending of intercalation. His otherwise impressive analysis leaves out entirely Muhammad's new revolution in the Abrahamic religious tradition that used Arabian pagan religion as a springboard. He implies that any such rationalization was later and was aimed at bringing the Arabian religion into line with the Hellenistic rationalism under the unspecified but allegedly imperative requirements of empire. Empire acts as the *telos* in this explanatory framework, contradicting the claim that nowhere will the end product be used to color his interpretation of the emergence of Islam (see Al-Azmeh 2018a: 262–63). In my view (Arjomand 2019, ch. 8), by contrast, empire, far from being an explanatory deus ex machina, is itself a consequence of the centralization of power characteristic of one ideal type (the Tocquevillian) of revolution. The Umayyad empire was a long-term consequence of Muhammad's Constitutive Revolution in Arabia.

54. Izutsu 1964. Izutsu was a leading Japanese champion of Eastern spirituality.

55. Sadeghi 2011, 289.

Here we should add a third independent and mutually supportive fundamental source that had given rise to Islamic historiography in the first place: the Qur'an commentaries. As the science of *tafsir* emerged among the early generations of Muhammad's companions and their followers, the concern to historicize the revealed verses of the Qur'an through an examination of the causes of their revelation (*asbāb al-nuzul*) was at least as important as the so-called mythological interpretation (*tafsir bi'l-ra'y*). And it should further be noted that the first and last great medieval Qur'an commentaries, those of Tabari (d. 923) and Ibn Kathir (d.1373), are works of the greatest Muslim historians of their respective epochs, both of whom rejected the mythological interpretations and formulated historically oriented exegetical methodologies.[56] To dismiss the monumental historicized Muslim exegetical tradition as mere "fabrication" or to deny its value as a historical source, just because it also had interpretive and legalistic functions, is a petty and unforgivable arrogance.[57]

So now that the hyperdeconstructionist storm in the teacup has passed, let us calmly turn to the critical study of Islamic history and boost it with some state-of-the-art comparative-historical theorizing. To do so in this study, I draw on the Qur'an as the key contemporary historical source and on early *tafsir* as the attempt at its historicization by the pious first generations of Muslims, while also using as my second primary source the early biographies of the Prophet, a few crucial hadiths that have passed modern critical scrutiny, and finally a very few of his letters that can be considered authentic.

A word may also be in order here on a different historiographic issue—namely, the interpretations of the rise of Islam in world history. Foremost among the interpretations of the world-historical significance of Islam put forward by general historians was that of Henri Pirenne. His thesis was that the rise of Islam in the seventh century split the unified world of Late Antiquity into two different cultural worlds, thereby ending the Greco-Roman civilization and opening the Middle Ages.[58] The Pirenne thesis encountered much criticism,[59] but it was not shelved until the emergence of a contrasting Late Antiquity

---

56. Leehuis 1988.
57. Wansbrough 1977, 141–42, 177–85; Rippin 1988.
58. Pirenne 1925, 1937.
59. Donner 2008a, xiii–xiv.

thesis that highlighted the common features of the Late Antique ecumene that had given birth to Islam.[60] The Late Antiquity thesis, by implication, minimized the distinctiveness of the emerging Islamic civilization and denied the revolutionary breakthrough it constituted in world history. The implication that Islam made little or no difference in the world of Late Antiquity is disturbing. This study considers the rise of Islam as the great apocalyptic revolution of Late Antiquity in chapter 2 and thus rejects this unwarranted implication.

The Late Antiquity approach, however, helps us understand that we are dealing with one civilization of the tripolar imperial (Iran, Rome, and Ethiopia) ecumene growing around the core of a bipolar (Abrahamic and Mazdaean-Zoroastrian) religious traditions as the civilizational context of the rise of Islam. As the political and social revolutions that created the distinctive Islamicate civilization unified the eastern and southern shores of the Mediterranean with Iran and further east with Central Asia and the Sind, this study can be considered implicitly and broadly supportive of the Pirenne thesis.

We can now move from the rise of Islam to its revolutions. In his last major historical work,[61] Wellhausen wrote: "The Abbasids called their government the *dawla*, i.e., the new era. The revolution effected at this time was indeed prodigious."[62] The Abbasid Revolution marked the end of the *Arab* empire and was prodigious in its effects—the creation of an integrated *Islamic* society in which the hitherto disprivileged non-Arab Muslims, the *mawāli* (clients), especially the Iranians, played the crucial role in the evolution of a common culture based on Islam and the Arabic language. He had earlier offered a penetrating analysis of the uprising of Mukhtār in Kufa during the Second Civil War as a rebellion of the *mawāli* (non-Arab clients) that foreshadowed this great revolution.[63] The term *dawla* originally meant "revolution" or the "turn [in power]," and contemporaries saw the Abbasid Revolution undoubtedly in such a way, and indeed in apocalyptic terms.[64]

---

60. Brown 1971; Fowden 1993; Al-Azmeh 2007; Saleh 2010, 38. Fowden (2014, 189) however, acknowledges that "the notions of spirituality and apostolicity may owe more to Manichaeism than has been recognized."

61. After that, Wellhausen turned to a comparative study of Judaic and Arab penal law, following Theodor Mommsen's study of the Roman penal law. See Rudolph 1983, 26–27, 52n84.

62. Wellhausen 1902, 556.

63. Wellhausen 1975b.

64. The revolutionary connotations of the term quickly receded, and it acquired the meaning of (rule by a) dynasty and thus of "the state." See chapter 9 below.

Although *The Abbasid Revolution* (1970) by M. A. Shaban popularized the idea, there was little theoretically informed discussion of the causes, process, and consequences of that prodigious revolution. Instead, scholarly debate took the form of a controversy between the Persianist and the Arabist interpretations of the Abbasid Revolution. The Persianist interpretation had already been put forward around the turn of the twentieth century, notably by Wellhausen, and was restated periodically. It emphasizes the role of the Iranians, their millenarian beliefs as well as their disprivileged status as clients.[65] The Arabist interpretation[66] was elaborated on the somewhat narrow basis of the hitherto unknown *Akhbār al-Dawlat al-'Abbāsiya* published in 1971.[67] The *Akhbār al-Dawla* (Record of the revolution), in fact, referred to the revolutionary movement it recorded not as Abbasid but as Hashemite.

Differences between the two sides in the controversy over the Abbasid Revolution narrowed with the admissions by the Arabists that the revolutionary partisans, referred to as the "people of Khurasan" (*ahl khurāsān*), included the early Arab settlers who had mingled with the villagers and had spoken their own dialect (*lugha, lisān*), which could not be understood in Baghdad. They constituted a distinct ethnic category and were regarded as such even after they moved to Iraq.[68] This is an understatement, as the Abbasid themselves, as we shall see, are recorded as giving the critical military command, "strike!" (*dahid*), in Persian. The revisionist thesis, furthermore, claimed the major role in the revolution for the Arabs and correctly underlined the decisive contributions of the Arab tribesmen settled in Khurasan to the defeat of the Umayyad armies in 749/131. It should not be forgotten, however, that "while the revolutionary army was led by Khurasanian Arabs, it had the backing of the Persian populace, Muslim and non-Muslim. The Umayyad armies might not have collapsed so quickly if they had not been operating in enemy country."[69] The more general claim of the Arabists concerning the Arab ethnicity of the revolutionaries must now be firmly rejected as its alleged factual basis was utterly destroyed by the painstaking examination of the biographies of

---

65. Van Vloten 1894; van Vloten 1898; Wellhausen 1902; Zarrinkub 1964; Zarrinkub 1975; Daniel 1979; Daniel 1996; Daniel 1997.
66. First put forward by Omar 1969 and Shaban 1970.
67. Lassner 1980; Sharon 1983; Sharon 1990.
68. Sharon 1986, 129, 141–42; Lassner, 1989, 251–55.
69. Madelung 1988, 8.

the Abbasid missionaries mentioned in *Akhbār al-Dawla* by Said Salih Agha who showed that the great majority of them were *not* Arabs but mawāli.[70] After this devastation of the Arabist interpretation, there seems little justification in discussing it further.[71] Wellhausen's interpretation was by contrast amply vindicated by Agha's findings.[72] Wellhausen's analytical scope as sociology of revolution is also more comprehensive, and it covers the self-destruction of the Umayyad state in Syria and Mesopotamia that was left out in this controversy by the Arabists and the Persianists alike.

Moving from historiography to historical facts, the most important fact established by the *Akhbār al-Dawla* is that the anti-Umayyad revolutionaries called themselves the Hāshimiyya, the partisans of the clan of the Prophet, Banu Hāshim. The clandestine leader or imam of the Hashemite movement was never named but repeatedly proclaimed in the Iranian cities that were opened by the advancing revolutionary army in 749 as "the one agreed upon (*al-ridā*) from the House of the Prophet."[73] The Hashemite Revolution was no more Abbasid than it was Arab. The later Abbasid fabrication of history of the Hashemite revolutionary movement to prove their continuous and uncontested leadership has been deconstructed by recent scholarship. The Hāshimiyya as a movement identified itself in reference to the Banu Hāshim, the clan of the Prophet, and any of its members of the Hāshemite could become the revolutionaries' leader. In fact, other Hāshemites had served as possible

---

70. Agha 2003. To be more precise, seventy-four of the 401 missionaries, or under 19 percent were Arabs, while 150, or over 37 percent, were non-Arab *mawāli*, and 177, or over 44 percent, were non-Arab new converts. Since its launching by the Persian client, Bukayr b. Māhān, the Khurasanian movement in Khurasan recruited secretly among the *mawāli* who gradually outnumbered the Arab settlers. The latter groups became conspicuous in military leadership as the revolutionary armies marched from the periphery toward the center of the Umayyad Empire. Abu Muslim's revolutionary mobilization greatly increased the number of local converts, thus making them the largest group. With the recruitment of ninety-three new local converts for revolutionary mobilization by Abu Muslim, the converts made up 46 percent of the 340 Abbasid missionaries in Khurasan. See Agha 2003, 257–58.

71. Nevertheless, for a latter-day attempt to shore up the Arabist interpretation, see Elad 1995; Elad 2000.

72. Barthold, in the same generation of critical Orientalists, adds to Wellhausen's interpretation a dense analysis of the revolutionary power struggle between the Abbasids and the 'Alids and their respective allies among the native nobility in Khorasan. See Barthold 1928, 180–201.

73. *Akhbār D*, 335, 340, 355.

leaders of uprisings—notably, Yahyā b. Zayd, who rose in Khurasan, two years after the suppression of the uprising of his father Zayd b. ʿAli in Kufa, and ʿAbdallāh b. Muʿāwiya, to whom, as we shall see, the future second Abbasid caliph Abu Jaʿfar and his two uncles had indeed sworn allegiance during his rule in Fars and Isfahan. Furthermore, the clients who led the organization of the Hashemite clandestine movement in Kufa and Khurasan supported two different branches of the Hashemite clan, one the ʿAlid and the other the Abbasid; the revolution was highjacked by the latter.

Two analytical shortcomings seriously impair the value of modern historical scholarship on the Abbasid Revolution sketched above. The first is the lack of macrosociological perspective, which results in separating the Abbasid mission from the Hashemite movement and the Hashemite movement from the revolutionary movement of the Kharijites while neither movement is put in the context of the breakdown of the Umayyad state and the disintegration of its authority, as has been done in this study. The second is the lack of attention to periodization. To rectify these shortcomings, our study is premised on both the sociological and the temporal coherence of the trends and events that convulsed the Umayyad Empire from North Africa to Central Asia from 744 to 763 CE.

Periodization is not a matter of empirical observation but of theoretical analysis. It involves the important theoretical task of conceptualizing revolution as an event with a beginning and an end. This task, in turn, involves "aggregating occurrences into conceptual events," and in fact determines *what* we want to explain.[74] By collocating a set of events as constitutive of a revolution, we are already explaining the connection among them, and the most significant contribution of the comparative historian may in fact be the presentation of a systematic rationale for these connections with the help of theory.

The Hashemite self-conception of the revolutionary movement has important theoretical implications. It enables us to define the Abbasid Revolution, named after the winners of the Hashemite revolutionary power struggle, as an event to be periodized. A number of hitherto unconnected episodes would have to be colligated. These include the movement of the above-mentioned ʿAbdallāh b. Muʿāwiya, who set up the first Hashemite state in Fars and Isfahan. The murder of the caliph Walid II in the Syrian desert in 744 as the starting point

---

74. Abbott 1992, 76.

of the revolution must thus be connected to the rebellion of the chiliastic palace guards in the early Abbasid capital Hāshimiyya in 758–59 CE and the rebellion in the same year of the governor of Khorasan, 'Abd al-Jabbār b. 'Abd al-Rahmān, who had been a Hashemite revolutionary and had appointed the first Abbasid chief of police and who now counted on the support of the Persian *Mubayyida* (whites) in the province he was governing. The end of the Hashemite Revolution would finally have to be the rebellion in 762 of the early 'Alid rival of the Abbasid victors, Muhammad b. 'Abdallāh b. al-Hasan as the Mahdi of the house of Prophet, whom Caliph Abu Ja'far al-Mansur had recognized as such back in 744. The suppression by February 763 of this fundamental challenge to the Hashemite legitimacy of Abbasid rule then appears as the most plausible end point. Only after the suppression of the rebellion of Muhammad b. 'Abdallāh, the Pure Soul (*al-nafs al-zakiyya*), and his brother Ibrāhim, did Abu Ja'far's anxiety about survival abate, enabling him to proceed with building the City of Peace (Baghdad) as the new center of the empire, and at last to definitively appropriate the titles of Mansur and Mahdi for himself and his son and heir. The connection among these temporally and spatially separated events by mostly unconnected groups of historical actors is implied by a Hashemite conceptual reconstruction of the history of the period as "the Abbasid Revolution: 744–63." The medieval Muslim historiography is, incidentally, decidedly superior to modern scholarship as regards the periodization of the Abbasid Revolution. The Muslim historians instinctively understood the Hashemite self-conception of the revolution and coherently presented their concatenation and collocation of events in this light. They also gave the revolution greater significance by according it far greater attention than the events preceding and succeeding it.[75]

Our typological approach outlined above can offer a solution to some of the historiographic controversies under discussion. Viewing the Abbasid Revolution in the light of the "Integrative Revolution" ideal type, the Arab-Persian dilemma can be seen to be a false one anyway. It presents the role of the Iranians in the Abbasid Revolution in a new light. The core of mobilized

---

75. Tabari's coverage of the dozen years of centralization of power and state building by Abu Ja'far al-Mansur is very thin compared to his coverage of the eighteen revolutionary years. The twelve years (146–158/763–785) are covered in merely 140 pages in Arabic and 169 pages in the English translation, as compared to the eighteen years (127–145/April 744–January 763) that require 460 pages in Arabic, and 521 pages in the English translation. Each year of the revolution receives twice as much attention as each succeeding year.

Iranian subjects of the Umayyad Empire participated in the revolution not as an ethnic group or as nationalists but as militant clients and recent converts to Islam who demanded inclusion in the political community (and were followed in this respect by non-Muslim subjects). The role of the Arabs, too, is better understood within the frame of the integrative strategy of the Hashemite revolutionary movement from the beginning. Not only did the Abbasid partisans exploit the alliance of the Yaman and Rabi'a tribes against the Qaysite tribal dominations under the last Umayyad caliph, Marwān II, but they also recruited any tribesman belonging to the dominant (Mudar) tribes who may have been dissatisfied and disaffected with government. they also recruited among the Arab rabble (*suqāt al-'arab*). Like the Khawārij (secessionists) before them, they also recruited women into the movement. Slaves, too, were recruited and had their own camp, though they were apparently not fully armed. The seventy-one known Abbasid missionaries represented twenty-five tribes, or the entire range of Arab tribes settled in Khurasan; and the tribal partisans are even credited with having healed tribal factionalism.[76] The recruitment of the disgruntled northern Arabian tribes (Mudar), such as some of the members of the Tamim, was opportunistic; the latter were soon eliminated. Such, indeed, is the fate of many revolutionary bedfellows.

Once the Abbasid Revolution is examined in the light of the integrative model, it becomes clear that more than one social group among the vast *mawāli* and non-Muslim subject population of the Umayyad Empire was pressing for entry into the political community and for access to power. The victory of the revolution was achieved "only through the union of the most heterogeneous elements."[77] Furthermore, the focus on the integrative dimension of the Hashemite Revolution suggests that different groups of Iranian supporters of the revolution that ended with the victory of the Abbasids might have had different motives and outlooks. In fact, it would be a mistake to think that the Iranian population was either homogeneous or acted as a unified group. Among the Iranians who contributed to the overthrow of the Umayyad regime and/or joined the new Abbasid rulers to help them rebuild the state, we must minimally distinguish between

---

76. *Akhbār D*, 248; Omar 1969, 98; Sharon 1990, 54–55; Bolshakov 1998, 28. The term used in *Akhbār al-Dawla* for factional tribal partisanship, *'asabiyya*, was to be made into a major sociological concept by Ibn Khaldun, as we shall see in chapter 9.

77. Barthold 1928, 194.

two very different groups. The first and more numerous group consisted of the masses of Iranian subjects, courted by missionaries from various Islamic and syncretic religious movements who were joined by an increasing number of *dehqān*s from the landed nobility. They were prone to neo-Mazdakite and millenarian beliefs; they became the followers of Abu Muslim and his partisans; and, as we shall see, they rebelled after his death and formed a host of religiopolitical movements that have been comprehensively surveyed.

Last but by no means least, we have the Khaldunian Integrative Revolution. It too helps us understand the success of the Abbasid Revolution as a revolution from the periphery, whereas the uprisings in Kufa, a garrison city at the center of Umayyad Iraq, had failed repeatedly. Its rise in the periphery of the Umayyad Empire in the first place, and the infusion of tribal solidarity by a religious mission in the second also fit the Khaldunian type of Integrative Revolution. These features of the Abbasid Revolution were highlighted by Ibn Khaldun himself. The Khaldunian model is also crucial for the last two revolutions examined in this volume—namely, the Fatimid Revolution (chapter 7) and the Berber Revolution of Mahdi Ibn Tumart (chapter 8) These revolutions, especially that of Mahdi Ibn Tumart, were most closely studied by Ibn Khaldun, and the latter was most likely the historical case on which he built his theory.

The one area where the SOAS source-critical higher deconstructionism has had a beneficial effect has been the study of the Fatimid Revolution. Despite their scholarly distinction, the line of twentieth-century students of Ismāʿili Shiʿism remained trapped in the hadith-based typology of the seventy-two sects in the tenth- and eleventh-century Muslim heresiography and accepted the existence of the Ismāʿili Shiʿa as an organized clandestine sect throughout the ninth century anachronistically. The same typological bias has separated the study of Ismāʿili, or for that matter Zaydi Shiʿism from the Imamiyya in the first centuries of their development, when the Shiʿa primarily meant the *shiʿat ʿAli* (party of ʿAli). It was appropriately in the Wansbrough Festschrift that Michael Brett first exposed the source-critical naïveté of this approach to the study of the origins of Ismāʿilism and of the Fatimid Revolution and placed the latter in the broader context of Shiʿite trends in the last quarter of the ninth century.[78] The positing of the undetected existence of a well-organized clandestine sect as one of the seventy-two into which the

---

78. Brett 1994.

Prophet was said to have predicted the division of his *umma* intrudes a stereotypical and anachronistic bias into the accounts of the rise of Ismāʿilism and makes them insular, since they "excluded both the elaboration of Islam and the Islamization of the Maghrib from consideration."[79] Brett subsequently identified and separately analyzed a number of different movements in the East that eventually came together under the rubric of Ismāʿilism and that the Fatimids sought to appropriate and control decades after their revolution in the Maghreb.

Brett also sought to remedy the exclusion of the Berbers from analysis by putting the rise of the Fatimids in the contexts of the Islamicization of the Berbers of Ifriqiyya.[80] The Berber character of the Almohad Revolution may not have had lasting consequences comparable to the Persianate consequences of the Abbasid Revolution, but they were not negligible.[81] The Almohad Mahdist Revolution, however, has not received nearly as much attention as the Fatimid Revolution, and it has no historiography to speak of.

The present study goes beyond solving the above-mentioned specific problems raised in the historiography of Islamicate revolutions and seeks to integrate the political theory and sociology of revolution and to historicize messianism as the subjective meaning representing the motivation of revolutionary social action. The final chapter (9) on the Islamicate conceptions of revolution accordingly aims at understanding the meaning of the revolutionary transformations for their historical agents.

---

79. Brett 1996, 433; Brett 2001, 47–72.
80. As he points out, the Ismaʿili revolutionary missionary to Ifriqiyya, Abu ʿAbdallāh, was known simply as "the Shiʿite" (d. 911); he was neither identified as Ismāʿili nor as Fātimi.
81. Fromherz 2013.

CHAPTER 1

The Emergence of Apocalyptic Messianism from the Maccabean Nativist Revolution

Of the manifold long-term consequences of Alexander the Great's conquests and the Hellenistic domination of the Near East, the most important from our point of view is the emergence of the apocalyptic political mentality. We have discussed the function of apocalyptic mentality as a source of motivation for revolutionary action in political messianism.[1] Apocalypticism, it is true, is a fundamental religious perspective that transcends and cannot be reduced to politics, revolutionary or otherwise. For the millenarian, political action in the world to be destroyed, far from being the means for attaining the sovereign common good, as Aristotle had taught Alexander, aims at combatting the evil to be eradicated. The creation of the new world after the destruction of the old is not conceived as the result of deliberative human action but of divine providence. From the apocalyptic viewpoint, the political theory of the Greeks was therefore incomprehensible, since the political as such was completely heteronomous and religiously determined.

Messianic yearnings and the apocalyptic vision they are embedded in can be triggered by any short-term political crisis or breakdown in the authority structure, such as the overthrow of the Achaemenid Empire by Alexander in second half of the fourth century BCE, or the Antiochene crisis in the

---

1. See the section titled "The Apocalyptic Motivation of Revolutionary Action: The Process of Revolution as Realization of Messianism and the Structural Models of Its Outcome" in the introduction.

Seleucid Empire that demonstrably precipitated the Maccabean revolt in the mid-second century BCE. Such crises or breakdowns, however, cannot be considered its efficient cause. It is now generally agreed that the earliest apocalyptic texts, especially the early parts of the book of Enoch, considerably predate the Maccabean revolt.[2] The Aramaic version of Enoch found among the Dead Sea Scrolls had in particular been important for proving that the origins of the apocalyptic "are previous to and independent of the Antiochean crisis, and underline the priority of the cosmic apocalypses over the historical ones," which date from the Maccabean revolt.[3] In all likelihood, the Zoroastrian ideas of the glorious renewal of the world (*frašo-kereti*) at the End of Time—with the fall of what the book of Daniel called the fourth empire at the end of the final millennium—are older still.[4] Nevertheless, once the apocalyptic religious perspective is culturally available, one would certainly expect it to be drawn on by revolutionaries whenever the space for extraordinary political action is opened by political crisis or state breakdown.

THE AUTHORITY STRUCTURE OF THE SELEUCID EMPIRE AND THE RELIGIOUS BACKGROUND OF THE NATIVISTIC REBELLION IN JUDAEA

The authority structure of the Judaean province of the Seleucid Empire was to a large extent the heritage of the Achaemenid Empire before it. The return from the Babylonian captivity under the terms of the decree of 538 BCE issued by Cyrus,[5] the gentile king who was Yahweh's Anointed One (Messiah),[6] ended that captivity and established an elite group of returnees in Jerusalem that saw itself as the "holy race" (*golah*) in distinction to the natives, "the peoples of the land" (*'amme ha'aretz*). It was the first step in the process of the organization of the Jews into a province of the Achaemenid Empire founded by him. In 520, the second year of the reign of Darius I, who was chiefly responsible for the administrative and legal organization of the empire, the prophets of God, Haggi and Zechariah, appeared in the company of the

---

2. Collins 1987.
3. Garcia Martinez 1992, 71.
4. Boyce 1984; Widengren, Hulgård, and Philonenko 1995.
5. Ezra 1:2–11.
6. Isaiah 45:1.

governor Zerubbabel and the high priest Joshua to sanction the rebuilding of the Temple, but had no further role in the new regime of the Jewish province, Yehud.[7] The building of the Second Temple was subsidized by the Achaemenid treasury, and the organization of Yehud as a province of the Achaemenid Empire was consolidated under the governorship of Ezra and Nehemiah. The fiscal organization of the new polity assured the centrality of the Temple. The Levites themselves were authorized "to collect the tithes from all the towns of our religion. An Aaronite priest will accompany the Levites when they collect the tithe." Furthermore, supervisors were "appointed whose business it was to collect in [the Temple treasury] those portions from the town lands awarded by the Law to the Levites and the priests."[8]

Ezra, an Aaronite priest and "a scribe versed in the Law of Moses," was commissioned by Artaxerxes I (465–423 BCE) "to investigate how the Law of your God, in which you are expert, is being applied in Judah and Jerusalem," and to execute sentences swiftly "on anyone who will not comply with the Law of your God and the Law of the king."[9] Ezra played the crucial role in shaping the hierocratic polity of the province of Yehud, in which the priestly class controlled access to the Temple and elaborated extensive legislation, much of which ("Priestly source [P]") was included in the final redaction of the Pentateuch generally dated from this period.[10]

The exclusion of prophets from the regime appears to have been made definitive during the first year of Nehemiah's governorship (445 BCE). On the other hand, "the priest-scribe Ezra and the Levites who were instructing the people" made the corpus of laws, "the Book of the Law of Moses which Yahweh had prescribed for Israel," the essence of Judaism. Thus, standing on a wooden dais erected for the purpose at the Water Gate on the southeastern side of the Temple, "Ezra read from the book of the Law of God, translating and giving the sense; so the reading was understood."[11] The supreme judiciary authority among the Yehud had presumably been given to the temple court, which included both the Temple priests and the lay aristocracy. To offset the power of this body, which may have resisted some of their policies, especially

---

7. Ezra 5:1–2; von Rad 1965, 253.
8. Nehemiah 10:38–39, 12:44.
9. Ezra 7:6, 14:26.
10. Berquist 1995, ch. 10.
11. Nehemiah 6:7–14, 8:1–9.

Nehemiah's, Ezra and Nehemiah appear to have set up a second tribunal that took root. This tribunal eventually presented itself as the heir to the pre-exilic tribunal of Jerusalem, a high court instituted by Jehoshaphat with jurisdiction over both civil and religious cases, which came to be known as (the Men of) the Great Synagogue.[12]

Soon after Alexander's overthrow of the Achaemenid Empire in 333 BCE, the Jewish temple-state came under Hellenistic rule, and it remained under the Ptolemies of Egypt throughout the third century BCE. In the first decade of the second century BCE, the Seleucids of Syria replaced the Ptolemies of Egypt as Judaea's rulers. There can be little doubt about the major disruption between the fifth and the second century BCE as the Achaemenids' centralized empire was replaced by the fragmented successor empire of the Seleucids. Even though the historical evidence we have is indeed meager, the Achaemenid regime in Judaea underwent drastic change.

The empire founded by Alexander's general, Seleucus, extended over Syrian and Iran, but with the failure of Seleucus to incorporate Macedonia and the entombment of its founder-king in Northern Syria, that region became its important epicenter. Shortly after the year 200 BCE, Antiochus III (219–187 BCE), who had won his war against Egypt with Jewish help, granted a charter to Jerusalem under Seleucid rule.[13] The "diasporic imperialism" of the Seleucids, however, made it prone to rebellions of religious elites who derived their oppositional legitimacy from local traditions, which were arguably strongest in Judaea in Syria and Persis (Fars) in Iran.[14]

Meanwhile, apocalyptic beliefs spread widely in the Hellenistic era and gave rise to a particular oracular form of resistance to Hellenistic domination that was absorbed into intertestamental religious literature. The earliest of these was the oracle of the Persian Sibyl who foretold the destruction of Alexander's Macedonian empire by the Persians:

> But Macedonia will bring forth a great affliction for Asia
> ... at a certain time there will come to the prosperous land
> of Asia a faithless man clad with a purple cloak on his shoulders,
> savage, stranger to justice, fiery ...

---

12. Deuteronomy 17:8–12; 2 Chronicles 19:5–7; Finkelstein 1989a, 229, 237–38.
13. Eckhardt 2016, 60–63.
14. Kosmin 2014, 93–119.

... Asia will bear an evil yoke, and the earth, deluged, will imbibe much gore.
But even so Hades [i.e., Ahriman] will attend him in everything though he knows it not.
Those whose race he wished to destroy, by them will his own race be destroyed.[15]

A century or more later, and as an expression of resistance to Hellenistic rule in the heartland of the Achaemenid Empire, Persis, we have the appearance of the fire altar as a defiant Zoroastrian symbol on the governors' coins in the latter part of the third century BCE, and the oracles of Hystaspes were put into circulation. In these oracles, Hystaspes (Vishtaspa, the patron king of Zoroaster) foretells that a great king will be sent from heaven to liberate the righteous and to destroy the wicked in a cosmic fire. The influence of the oracles of Hystaspes lingered for centuries as other political oracles followed suit.[16]

The empire created by Alexander had the strongest assimilative and universalist tendency to date. Alexander's order after defeating the Achaemenid Darius III to his generals and soldiers that they take Persian wives signaled the beginning of the trend toward universalism under Hellenistic cultural domination that continued under the successor empires. It resulted in the spread of Greek philosophy and forms of political organization in the Near East and Central Asia and the appearance of a number of privileged poleis in a vast and variegated but nevertheless distinctly Hellenistic world. By the third century BCE, this universalist Hellenizing tendency can be seen unfolding through the agency of the native upper classes of the Seleucid Empire that included a much greater variety of subject peoples than did Ptolemaic Egypt. The diasporic imperialism of the Seleucids gave rise to nativistic local movements that they sought to control by compromising with them and that could be expected to make for both assimilation and nativistic reaction of different segments of the subservient native nobilities from its various regions.

15. *Sib. Or.* 3:381–95 = OTP 1:370–71. See also Eddy 1961, 10–14. According to the Zoroastrian priests, Alexander was the agent of Ahriman/the Evil Spirit. See Henning 1944, 136–37, 141; Boyce and Grenet 1991, 1.

16. Cumont 1931, 64–96; Hengel 1974, 1:184–86; Hinnells 1973; Colpe 1983, 832–33; Sellwood 1983, 299–302 and plate 10. A first-century BCE fragment of Nigidius Figulus similarly attests to the Magis' expectation of the coming Kingdom (*regnum*) of Apollo (i.e., Mithra, the sun god) and the cosmic conflagration, equated with the Stoic *ecpyrosis*. See Cumont 1931, 44.

Antiochus III had been killed in Susa in southwestern Iran when despoiling a temple, and there are several reports of Antiochus IV despoiling temples as well. There was a nativistic revolt against Antiochus IV in Persis parallel to the Maccabean revolt in Judaea. Putting together the evidence from undated coins of the *fratarakā i yazdān* (commanders of the gods)[17]—that is, the dynasty of the semi-autonomous rulers of Persis—with undated references to Persia in 2 Maccabees 1:9, as well as rebellions against the Seleucids mentioned in Greek and Roman sources, Paul Kosmin considers a rebellion of the *fratarkā* and their defeat of Antiochus IV (175–164 BCE) before his death very likely. One may further speculate that the above-quoted Sibyl inspired by Zoroastrian millennialism was generated during this or a similar nativistic event.[18]

Under the Seleucids, a royal supervisor (*epistates*) oversaw the fiscal administration of all temples in Coele-Syria, including the Temple in Jerusalem, and he had authority over their priests, including the high priest (*archiereus/kohen gadol*). The political organization of their empire was rather complex, and it allowed for three basic modes of integration of the subject populations. The latter could be organized as a polis, a city-state with municipal self-government by its citizens as represented by an assembly (*boulé*) and with the right to strike bronze coins; an *ethnos*, a people that lived its traditional way of life and could still be a distinct polity (*politeuma*) with a council of elders (*gerousia*) but without any citizenship; and finally, princedom under indigenous rulers.[19] The charter granted to Jerusalem by Antiochus III in 198 BCE established the Jewish temple-state as a special *politeuma* by giving tax exemption to "the council of elders (*gerousia*), the priests, temple scribes, and the temple singers," and above all, by giving the Jews permission to live "according to their ancestral laws," which meant Ezra's "Book of the Law of Moses."[20]

Simon, son of Onias, the Just, from the hereditary line of the Zadokite high priests, ruled the new hierocratic polity and carried out the constitutional

---

17. Especially one that depicts a ruler in Achaemenid costume killing a colonist in hoplite armor.

18. Kosmin 2016, 48–49. Kosmin cautions against "overemphasizing the distinctiveness of the Jewish reaction to Seleucid imperialism." We have, however, no evidence of messianic militancy from other nativist rebellions.

19. Tcherikover 1959, 88, 297–332; Hengel 1989, 159–60.

20. Bickerman 1935; Tcherikover 1959; Momigliano 1975, 98; Eckhardt 2016.

reconstruction of Jerusalem promised in the 198 charter. His contemporary, Ben Sira, captured the political culture of the hierocratic regime of the temple-state well when he enjoins his audience: "Fear God with all thy heart, and reverence for His priest." He also complained of "sinners who foregather in the haunts of the godless," however, and he spoke of the "godless people who have forsaken the Law of God Most High, . . . [and] were born to be accursed."[21]

The loss of Asia Minor to the rising Roman power in 188 BCE resulted in a severe fiscal crisis, forcing Antiochus III to plunder the temple in Susa; this resulted in his death in 187. The attempt by the Seleucids to despoil the Jewish Temple around 180 was also fiscally motivated.[22] The Seleucid rulers sought to alleviate this fiscal crisis by offering the native aristocracies the option of obtaining a charter and becoming citizens of a Hellenized polis in exchange for an appropriate payment to the royal treasury. Stronger evidence of Hellenization is provided by the large number of attested Greek first names in the first quarter of the third century BCE.[23]

Like some other Hellenized Greco-Syrian upper classes, the aristocracy of the Jewish temple-state seized the opportunity offered by the accession of Antiochus IV (175–164 BCE), Epiphanes (god made manifest), who saw Alexander as his model, his "stereotypical Hellenism betray[ing] the exaggerated compensation of a colonial Mimic Man," and who displayed great nostalgia for his ancestral homeland.[24] He was eager to secure the honor of being the founder (*ktistēs*) of cities—to adopt the most advanced form of constitution and become a polis. The conversion of the Jewish polity from ethnos to polis would mean a fuller integration of a peripheral political island into the imperial ecumene through purchasing its most privileged category of political constitutions. One could not ask for a clearer expression of the desire to join the Hellenistic imperial commonwealth integrally than the slogan of the reformist party who supported him: "Come," they said, "Let us make a covenant with the gentiles surrounding us, for since we separated ourselves from them

---

21. Ecclesiastes 7:29, 41:5, 8–9.
22. 2 Maccabees 3; Momigliano 1975, 98–99. The Seleucid chancellor, Heliodorus, was allegedly stopped from despoiling the Temple by a supernatural horseman.
23. Hengel 1989, 177, 217.
24. In contrast to the earlier generation of Seleucid emperors who had shed their Macedonian identity and considered themselves primarily as heirs to Achaemenid Mesopotamia Great Kings. See Kosmin 2014, 118.

many misfortunes have overtaken us."[25] Knowing full well the hunger of the crisis-ridden Seleucid treasury, Jason, the ambitious younger brother of the high priest, embarked on Hellenization at full speed with the support of a reformist party of Hellenizers "and a number of the people eagerly approached the king, who authorized them to practice the gentiles' observances."[26]

The reformist Hellenizers petitioned the king "to abandon the ancestral laws and *their own constitution* [i.e., the charter of 198 BCE], and instead to follow the royal laws and to obtain *a political constitution in the Greek style*."[27] The covenant with the gentiles thus set up a new polis of Antioch-at-Jerusalem, which Antiochus IV as its founder visited, most probably in 172 BCE. He was "given a magnificent welcome by Jason and the city, and escorted in by torchlight with acclamation." Hand in hand with the citizenship of a polis went Hellenistic culture and education centered around the gymnasium. Eager to impress the king with the success of his Hellenistic educational reform, Jason sent a team of "Antiochenes of Jerusalem" to compete at the quadrennial games at Tyre.[28]

The conversion of the Jewish polity from ethnos to polis, however, was far from simple, and the clash of the underlying cultural premises of these two constitutional forms generated considerable political tension. The Jews, needless to say, had a monotheistic religion and a transcendent God, and a divine rather than man-made law. The authority of the high priest was derived from this sacred law. The religion of the Graeco-Roman ancient cities, by contrast, was quintessentially an immanent and civic religion, which by this time required a public cult of the founder as the divine guardian of the city and which made the high priest no more than a municipal official. The "ancestral laws" would also be subject to alteration by the legislation of the assembly. Furthermore, cultural prerequisites of citizenship had serious religious consequences. To appear naked in the athletic games at the gymnasium, many Jewish youths "disguised their circumcision," and the athletes sent to the games at Tyre took with them "three hundred silver drachmas for the sacrifice

---

25. 1 Maccabees 1:11.
26. 1 Maccabees 1:12–13. "Godless wretch that he was and no true high priest, Jason set no bounds to his impiety; indeed, the Hellenizing process reached such a pitch that the priests ceased to show any interest in serving the altar [as] they esteemed Hellenic glories best of all" (2 Maccabees 4:7–15).
27. Antiquities 12:240, as cited in Bickerman 1979, 49 (emphasis added).
28. 2 Maccabees 4:18–19:22.

to Hercules." None of this was lost on the opponents of political reform and Hellenization who thought Jason had "suppressed the liberties which the kings had graciously granted to the Jews ... and, overthrowing the lawful institutions, introduced ways contrary to the Law."[29]

The tension created by political reform was exacerbated by personal rivalry, as well as family and faction feud within the Jewish upper class in the broader context of the fiscal crisis of the Seleucid state. Jason was deposed and "obliged to take refuge in the land of Amman," which was under the rule of his relatives belonging to a rival branch of the Tobiad family, the most powerful family in the lay aristocracy.[30] Menelaus of the Bilga family became the high priest and was summoned before the king. He took much gold and silver from the Temple with him back to Syria and bribed a high official to lure out and assassinate his rival, Onias III, probably in the fall of 170 BCE. Menelaus also sent instructions to his brother and deputy to intensify the spoliation of the Temple. When the urban populace noticed the removal of sacred gold and silver objects from the Temple, "some snatched up stones, others cudgels, while others scooped up handfuls of ashes [of sacrifice] . . .; the sacrilegious thief himself they killed near the Treasury."[31] Civic violence thus broke out in Jerusalem, with the upper class deeply divided by family and faction feud. As the crisis deepened, the family feuds within the Zadokite high priestly family between the two brothers, and between the Tobiads of Transjordan and those of Jerusalem who were backing Menelaus, the upstart high priest, were increasingly cut across by the clash between Hellenizers and traditionalists.

Menelaus returned to Jerusalem as high priest against the wishes of the council of elders, and in the fall of 169 BCE, Antiochus IV visited Jerusalem, where, guided by Menelaus, he plundered the Temple, taking back 1,800 talents of silver as the arrears of tribute undertaken by Menelaus.[32] In the late summer or early fall of 168 BCE, the deposed high priest Jason, having believed false reports of the death of Antiochus IV, returned from his exile in Transjordan and attacked Jerusalem with "at least a thousand men." He took the city and Menelaus fled to the citadel. Bloodshed was much greater in this second round

29. 1 Maccabees 1:15; 2 Maccabees 4:11, 19.
30. 2 Maccabees 4:26.
31. 2 Maccabees 4:42; Goldstein 1983, 114.
32. 2 Maccabees 4:44–47, 5:11–21.

of civic violence (2 Maccabees 1:8, 5:5–9). Antiochus IV "concluded that Judaea was in revolt," (2 Maccabees 5:11), and marched from Egypt and stormed the city, taking "furious action against the holy covenant and, as before, [favoring] those who forsake that holy covenant" (Daniel 11:30). Forty thousand inhabitants of the city are said to have been massacred and as many sold into slavery. The killing, however, was selective and restricted to the presumed supporters of Jason. Others were spared and co-opted by Antiochus IV,[33] who then departed for Antioch, "having shed much blood and uttered words of extreme arrogance ... and the whole House of Jacob was clothed with shame."[34]

Menelaus barely survived, sustained by of an army of 22,000 men under the heavy hand of its commander, the *mysarch* (collector of tribute), who was ordered to pillage Jerusalem, tear down its walls, and rebuild the City of David as a citadel (Acra). The Acra was constituted as a polis, the Antioch-at-Jerusalem, where "they installed a brood of sinners, of renegades, who fortified themselves inside it." In fact, the Acra was built for the permanent settlement of a cleruchy (military colony) of Syrian and Phoenician soldiers, "men of an alien race" making it "a lodging for gentiles," even though the collaborating Hellenizers assumed the rights of citizenship as "Antiochenes of Jerusalem." The creation of this military settlement imposed a heavy burden on the inhabitants of a devastated Judaea, as soldiers had to be quartered with the inhabitants, taxes raised, and land confiscated for redistribution to military colonists.[35] Population flight was the predictable and sociologically typical response to expropriations and heavy taxation, and the religious typification of this response as "flight into the desert" became a powerful motif in the subsequent revolutionary propaganda, and thence in the apocalyptic lore.[36]

The worst, however, came with the decision to open the Temple to the Syrian soldiers settled in the Acra, which resulted in the introduction of the cult of their supreme deity, Baal Shamim, and of the rite of temple prostitution. The infamous Antiochene persecutions soon accompanied this violation of the Temple with the ill-fated decree of 167 BCE: "the king issued a proclamation to his whole kingdom that all were to become a single people, each

---

33. Daniel 9:26; Collins 1993, 357.
34. 1 Maccabees 1:24, 28.
35. 1 Maccabees 1:24, 3:37, 45; 2 Maccabees 5:24–26; Daniel 11:39.
36. Tcherikover 1959, 189–93.

nation renouncing its particular customs. All the gentiles conformed to the king's decree, and many Israelites chose to accept his religion . . . "[37]

The Antiochene persecution was in full force at the end of 167 BCE, making the clash with the Jewish religion the central element of politics. The Law of Moses was abolished, circumcision and observance of the Sabbath were prohibited and made punishable by death. Antiochus appointed a special commissioner for persecution, and on December 7, 167 BCE, "the abomination of desolation," an altar to the Syrian Baal Shamim, was officially inaugurated "on top of the altar of burnt offering." Sacrifices on the king's birthday were offered every month on the new altar, and Dionysiac feasts were observed. Nevertheless, the immediate reaction of many of the Jews was that of the new but loyal citizens and subjects of the imperial commonwealth, "sacrificing to idols and profaning the Sabbath."[38] Resistance, however, must have begun when the commissioner for persecution sent agents to Jerusalem and the towns of Judaea to enforce the pagan sacrifice of pigs and unclean animals, even at people's doorsteps, and to force them to eat the meat.

The revolutionary coalition against Hellenization included traditionalists and protomessianists, consisting of different social groups. By the time of the persecution, the Pharisees appear as the best entrenched opponents of the Hellenizing reforms. They controlled the high court of Jerusalem, the so-called Men of the Great Synagogue, which was also called the Great Tribunal of the Pharisees and included the Hasmonian family (the Maccabees). A decree issued by the Pharisee tribunal stated that even death could not atone for the Hellenizers who led others astray, and their official prayer condemned them as renegades. The word Hellenizer (*meshummad*) used in this condemnation soon acquired the meaning of "apostate."[39]

---

37. 1 Maccabees 1:41–43. The imperial response to political turmoil in Judaea was in line with Antiochus's attack on religion in Persis that provoked the rebellion that cost him his life.

38. 1 Maccabees 1:54–61; 2 Maccabees 6:1–9; Tcherikover 1959, 196.

39. Finkelstein 1989a, 241–44; Finkelstein 1898b, 259–60. Another tradition preserved in the Mishnah suggests that the Pharisees justified the killing of a certain Lysimachus as an outlaw for stealing vessels from the Temple (Goldstein 1983, 241). Menelaus, with the help of his family, implemented the Seleucid policy of Hellenization and the desecration of the Temple. The Pharisee opposition eventually responded to the high priest and his relative by excluding the clan of Bilga from performing priestly functions for ever. See Goldstein 1975, 119–23; Goldstein 1983, 459–63; Hengel 1974, 1:225–26, 279.

One important consequence of the Hellenistic reform movement was the relaxation of the high priest's control over the religious life of the Jews; religious and protosectarian groups became vocal in their opposition to Hellenization and recruited among the younger generation, which returned to the Torah and reproached "their parents and their elders on account of... forsaking the covenant."[40] The Pharisees formed a community of fellows (*habirot*) with Jose b. Joezer as its first president (*nasi*), and a rival one as there were two pharisaical schools. Other oppositional groups did likewise, and they constituted themselves into religious associations according to Hellenistic law. These included the pious (*hasidim*), who probably formed several "Hasidic synagogues" and their offshoot, the Essenes, who later formed a community, *yaad* (= *koinon*) and moved to Qumran.

The pious intellectuals who produced the Epistle of Enoch or parts thereof shortly before the persecution and the second half of the book of Daniel during that time were heirs to a wisdom tradition in the third century BCE to which God's mystery was revealed. They were mantic virtuosi, divinely inspired experts at divination and at knowing and pronouncing the predetermined events past and future as inscribed in the Heavenly Tablets. As these texts are our only source for identifying them we shall divide them accordingly as the Enochic and the Danielic circles in our account of the struggle against the Hellenizing prosecution that also set in motion the Maccabean revolt.[41] Enoch was the antediluvian prototype of this new medium of revelation of God's mysteries through dreams and visions, and Daniel was its representative among the Babylonian diaspora.[42] Revelation of divine mysteries to the wise through dreams and visions, increasingly with the help of an interpreting angel, was the means of salvation. Salvation was redemption of mankind from its sinful nature. It meant the salvation of the soul of the individual, and was no longer a collective matter, as had been the case in the ethical prophecy of the axial age. The salvific function of revelation was essential. Salvation came with the knowledge of God's design for nature, history, and the eschaton,

---

40. Jubilees 23:16.

41. This was the early stage of the apocalyptic movement that was organized into the Dead Sea sect by the Teacher of Righteousness. See Collins 1997, 28–29.

42. VanderKam 1984, 151–52. There is now scholarly consensus "that *1Enoch* rather than *Daniel* contained the earliest full-blown apocalypses, and there was obvious discontinuity between this material and Hebrew prophecy" (Collins 1991, 25).

which was communicated by the wise recipient of revelation to the chosen circle of individuals, the elect. Central to this view was the astral determination of natural and human affairs, in which "the movements of heavenly bodies are a Torah that is foundational for correct calendrical observance." This new religious lore produced its own form of religious authority that stemmed directly from the religious virtuoso's direct reception of revelation through dreams, and from his mantic power of divination. This mantic authority was verified and authenticated by ritual mourning, fasting, and deprivation as preparation for the reception of revelatory wisdom by the virtuoso.[43] Mantic calculation of the end thus became a function of the professional seer, and one likely to draw him into propagandist activity in political crisis. What is pertinent at this point was the belief that the events of the End of Time were determined at the beginning of creation, and the saving event at the end-time.[44] From the viewpoint of motivation to revolutionary action, it should be emphasized that the new apocalyptic outlook involves considerable departure from Weber's ideal type of "ethical prophecy," so much so that we may typify it as "apocalyptic prophecy."

In the third quarter of the second century BCE, the followers of this mantic wisdom tradition provided many of the traditionalist opponents of Hellenistic reform with intellectual ammunition. This was the group that developed an apocalyptic vision that engendered political messianism. The book of Daniel designated them as the *maskile 'am* (wise teachers of the people) on the model of the Babylonian Daniel and his circle who were the "*maskilim*, skilled in all wisdom."[45] Unlike the Maccabees and their Pharisaical and proto-Essene militant supporters, the Maśkilim were not militant and did not take up arms against the Hellenistic persecutors and their Jewish allies. Indeed, an argument can be made that the intellectual revolution they wrought was premised on theoretical detachment from physical violence and practical politics. Nevertheless, persecution made them populistic; as their self-designation indicates, they turned to the masses/the many (*rabbim*) to instruct them, thereby removing the barriers that hitherto surrounded the

---

43. Daniel 10:2; Reid 1989, 111–12, 118. The new wisdom acquired prophetic features, and the prophets were seen as inspired men of wisdom revealing divine mystery, subject to mantic interpretation for predicting events of the inexorable end of history. See Hengel 1974, 1:206.

44. Nickelsburg 1991, 61; von Rad 1967, 273.

45. Collins 1985, 132–34.

circle of the elect. The Maśkilim's new role in the time of Antiochene tribulation was thus to "lead the masses to [salvific] righteousness."[46] The pious author who compiled the old Aramaic material on the Babylonian seer, Daniel (chapters 1–6) and who added the fundamental apocalyptic reading of the Antiochene persecution to produce a complete booklet in Aramaic, belonged to a class of educated Jews that exemplified Mannheim's category of "socially unattached intellectuals." The Danielic group considered Onias III, the last Zadokite legitimate high priest who was dismissed at the onset of Hellenization and who was later murdered, "the prince of the covenant." But they do not appear to have had any connection with Jerusalem; nor do they seem to have had any particular interest in the priestly politics of the temple-state.

The intellectual orientation of the Maśkilim was not centered on the Temple in Jerusalem but was rather toward Persian Babylonia and the East, as is reflected in the content of the stories, the unusual influx of Persian vocabulary, and the imperial Persian mode of designation of Yahweh as "the God of heaven." Like the Enochic circle, they at first wrote in Aramaic, the lingua franca of the peoples of the Seleucid Empire, and their interest in dreams and vision was cosmopolitan.[47] It was the cosmopolitan, universal "God of heaven" (and not Yahweh), who revealed (*apokalypto*—th first appearance of this term in the Septaguint) to Daniel the mysterious secret (*raz*, a Persian loanword). The revealed mystery is the future of world history: the End of Days that features so conspicuously in Daniel.[48] The Qumran literature shares these features of Daniel.[49] The certain knowledge of this future

---

46. Daniel 12:3; Hengel 1974, 1:209–10.

47. Daniel 11:22; Collins 1993, 18, 35, 38, 159, 382.

48. In a later Zoroastrian apocalyptic text, the sun god of war Mithra divulges the hidden secret (*rāz-e nehān*) of the great battle of the End of Days. See the text and translation in Shaked 1969, 209.

49. The great majority of the apocalyptic texts, by far, were written in Aramaic, even though Aramaic texts constitute only 13 percent of the total recovered collection (Dimant 1995). Turning to the Hebrew apocalyptic texts at the Qumran, by contrast, one is struck by their paucity and the overall different style. "Whereas the Aramaic works treat their biblical models with considerable freedom, the Hebrew pseudepigrapha slavishly reproduce their model sources" (Dimant 1994, 179, 188). Aramaic gave the apocalyptic writers easy access to the religious literature of the common Aramaic Babylonian and Persian milieu beyond the constrictive paradigms of the Hebrew prophecy; they, in turn, draw on notions of mantic wisdom and the succession of the empires/kingdoms. See Flusser 1972; Collins 1993, 162–75.

gave unshakable hope to the wise and emboldened them to undertake cosmically significant action.

What were the components and character of the Maśkilim's apocalyptic vision? In the later Christian and Muslim contexts, apocalypticism acquired a strongly antinomian character that has deeply colored the modern sociological understanding of the phenomenon.[50] It is therefore necessary to be reminded that in the context of Second Temple Judaism the observance of the sacred law and eschatological, apocalyptic expectations were mutually supportive. The postexilic Jewish identity, including such sectarian self-definitions as the remnant, the Lord's planting, and the like, was linked to the observance of the Law and was the lasting result of the mode of restoration of the returning "holy race" (*bene haggolah*), which had, according to the chronicler, "separated themselves from the uncleanness of the peoples of the land."[51] This heritage explains both the basic fact that differences over the observance or nonobservance of the rules of the sacred law constituted the natural basis for divisions within the Jewish community and the corollary ethicolegal rigorism of the sectarian dissidents. The spread and politicization of the apocalyptic tradition in the course of its struggle against Hellenization was superimposed on this orientation of Second Temple Judaism toward the observance of the sacred law and in fact accentuated it.

In the pseudepigraphal book of Jubilees and Epistle of Enoch we have indications of the rapprochement among various religious groups as their differences were gradually appearing less important than their common opposition to Hellenism. This opposition gave birth before long to the contrasting term "Judaism," which appears for the first time in the second book of Maccabees to describe the set of beliefs subjected to persecution and crystallized into a common commitment to the cause of the Torah. The Epistle uses the terms "the righteous and the pious" for the group to which it is addressed, most likely the circles ancestral to the Essenes. These terms, and in particular "pious" (*hsyd* in Aramaic; later *hasid* in Hebrew), could be used for self-designation by any group opposed to Hellenization. The term *hasidim* (the pious) was thus current in a broadly descriptive way, rather than specific

---

50. Mannheim 1929; Cohn 1957.
51. Cited in Blenkinsopp 1981, 4.

to any group.⁵² This makes good sense in the light of the sociology of social movements, corresponding to the reality of a movement at its initial stage when the boundaries are loosely set and the degree of organization is minimal. We will therefore use the notion of Hasidism as the original, minimally structured movement of the 170s BCE, which, within a quarter of a century, solidified into two or the three organized and distinct sectarian offshoots recorded by Josephus: the Pharisees and the Essenes—the third being the Sadducees. Furthermore, it so happens that the Hasidic groups deviated from Second Temple orthodoxy by their shared belief in resurrection of the dead.⁵³

The book of Jubilees (23:14–19) refers to the Hellenizing Jews as the evil generation that sins in the land:

> Pollution and fornication and contamination and abomination are their deeds... Behold, the land will be corrupted on account of all their deeds.... because they have forgotten the commandments and covenant and festivals and months and sabbaths and jubilees and all the judgments.

Then comes the imminent time of redemption:

> And in those days children will begin to search the law, and to search the commandments and to return to the way of righteousness... And then the Lord will heal his servants, and they will rise up and see great peace.... And you, Moses, write these words because thus it is written and set upon the heavenly tablets as a testimony for eternal generations.⁵⁴

In a similar vein, the Epistle of Enoch speaks of the holy warfare of the righteous against the wicked. The righteous of the last generation, recognizing Enoch, the wise primordial author of the Epistle, as the divine agent of salvation, will be in possession of sevenfold wisdom revealed through him and can instruct "the sons of the earth." The same Epistle also contains evidence of

---

52. 1 Enoch 103:9, 100:4–5, 102:4, 104:12; Nickelsburg 1982, 347–48; Goldstein 1983, 479.

53. Archaeological excavations in the Qumran cemeteries have confirmed the common eschatology of the Essenes and the mother Hasidic movement: the elect of the Qumran buried their dead "facing toward the north, ready to enter the paradise of justice" (Puech 1994, 254). Furthermore, the original Hasidic movement was a "penitential movement" (Hengel 1974, 1:79), since the common goal of the sundry elements was repentance from the sins of the Hellenizers, which many had abetted.

54. Jubilees 23:26–32.

diversity within the pious anti-Hellenistic movement that was gathering momentum with the removal of the high priestly control over the religious life of the Jews. Its complaint of the sinners who "will alter and distort the words of truth, and speak evil words, and lie, and concoct great fabrications, and write out my Scriptures on the basis of their own words."[55]

The Apocalypse of Weeks, the oldest surviving historical apocalypse, which was written shortly before the persecution edict in the Enochic circle of the Epistle, contains no reference to a messianic figure or to any overt political opposition to Hellenistic rule.[56] Nevertheless, the struggle between the righteous and the wicked is depicted in a fully apocalyptic form. This form contains the two basic elements in the apocalyptic motivation of absolute political action: the investment of the present with intense salvific import, and a rigid historical determinism capable of inspiring total confidence by assuring *certitudo salutis* in the last days. In the Apocalypse of Weeks, Enoch communicates "that which was revealed to me from the heavenly vision, that which I have learned from the words of the holy angels and understood from the heavenly tablets." It is no other than the predetermined history of mankind in ten stages or "weeks of years." The present time of distress is placed in the seventh week, when "an apostate generation shall arise; its deeds shall be many, and all of them criminal. At its completion, there shall be elected the elect ones of righteousness from the eternal plant of righteousness, to whom shall be given sevenfold wisdom . . . " This indeed is the threshold of the eschaton, "the eighth week—the week of righteousness. A sword shall be given to it in order that judgment shall be executed in righteousness on the oppressors, and sinners shall be delivered to the hands of the righteous . . . A house shall be built to the Great King in glory for evermore." The intensive salvific investment of the present time is the result of its firm connection to primordial and eschatological times in this divinely predetermined plan. The last two stages are purely eschatological, being placed in an abstract future devoid of apocalyptic intensity per se; they end with "the eternal judgment" and the appearance of "a new heaven": "there shall be many weeks without number forever; it shall be

---

55. 1 Enoch 104:10, 105:1; Nickelsburgh 1982, 342–43; OTP 1:85 (translation modified in line with Knibb 1978, 2:242). This can be taken as a reference to the tendentious promulgations of new divine legislation and the dispensation of rival groups such as the followers of Jubilees and the proto-Essene Temple Scroll.

56. VanderKam 1984, 146–47, 160.

(a time) of goodness and righteousness, and sin shall no more be heard of forever."[57]

The persecution edict and the desecration of the Temple supplied the shock necessary for bringing the pious closer together; it integrated the inchoate Hasidic movement and sharply politicized it. This is not to say that militancy was a uniformly inevitable response. Some of the pious took to the desert and refused to obey the king's orders; even Judas Maccabee is said to have done so at the outset. Some of those pious who had fled to the desert refused to fight on the Sabbath even in self-defense, and accepted martyrdom instead in expectation of God's miraculous intervention.[58] Notable among these pious martyrs was the leader of a religious group, a Levite whose title, rendered as Taxo, was probably the teacher (*moreh*) of the Essene lawgiver (*meoqeq*),[59] whose nonmilitant position is recorded in the pseudepigraphal Testament of Moses. According to this pious group, the rule of "destructive and godless men" had roused the wrath of God. God punished them by stirring up "against them a king of kings of the earth."[60]

All this the original author of Daniel wove into an apocalyptic vision of history in which the Antiochene tribulations marked the threshold of the eschaton and the advent of the eternal kingdom of God. The vision, recorded in Daniel 7, combines two distinct elements from the lore of the common Aramaic milieu: the view of history as the succession of the four empires propagated by the anti-Hellenistic political oracles, and the Canaanite myth of chaos and creation.[61] The four empires are assimilated to the four beasts of the primordial chaos. God appears as an Ancient of Days on the heavenly throne with wheels of burning fire. The first three beasts are "deprived of their empire." The fourth beast, with ten horns representing the Greek kings, and a sprouting eleventh little one standing for Antiochus IV, is "put to death and

---

57. 1 Enoch 93:2, 9–10, 12–13, 17.
58. Testament of Moses 10:3–7; OTP 1:931–32.
59. Goldstein 1976, 39–40n7.
60. That king "will crucify those who confess their circumcision. Even those who deny it, he will torture and hand them over to be led to prison in chains. And their wives will be given to the Gods of the [gentile] nations [in sacred prostitution instituted at the Temple for the settled soldiers of the Acra] and their young sons will be cut by physicians to bring forward their foreskin" (Testament of Moses 8:1–3; OTP 1:930–31).
61. Mosca 1986; Collins 1993, 286–94.

its body destroyed and committed to flames." An angel interprets the vision for Daniel. The eleventh horn "will insult the Most High and torment the holy ones of the Most High... But the [divine] court will sit, and he will be stripped of his royal authority which will be finally destroyed and reduced to nothing. And kingship and rule ... will be given to the people of the holy ones of the Most High, whose royal power is an eternal power ... "[62]

REVOLUTIONARY POWER STRUGGLE UNDER DUAL SOVEREIGNTY AND THE SECOND MACCABEAN TEMPLE-STATE AND THE EMERGENCE OF MESSIANISM

As some recent models of revolutionary outbreaks show, the threshold from widespread discontent to overt rebellion must be crossed conspicuously and in exemplary fashion.[63] The man who set the example in the small town of Modein early in 166 BCE was a dispossessed old priest, Mattathias, who belonged to a family of traditionalist Pharisees and had left Jerusalem, presumably because of Hellenistic reforms. Claiming to be acting in the age of wrath with the same zeal for the Torah as Phineas, who had shown his outrage against mixed marriages among the Israelites by killing a couple "under the very eyes of Moses," he attacked and killed the king's commissioner sent to enforce apostasy. Mattathias fled to the hills with his five sons but rejected the stand of the nonmilitant groups among the pious concerning the prohibition of fighting on the Sabbath. Before long, he and his friends "were joined by a company of Hasideans [*synagog Asidain*], stout fighting men of Israel, every one of them a volunteer in the cause of the Torah."[64] Pious volunteers who had been organized into a fighting force and called themselves the Hasidim thus accepted the Maccabees' leadership and joined the armed struggle in the cause of the Torah against the apostasy of the Hellenizers.

The socioreligious movement of various discontented Jewish groups and individuals who considered themselves "the pious and the righteous" was beginning to define itself in the course of an anti-Hellenistic struggle, and its most politicized and militant wing appropriated the designation of Hasidim.

---

62. Daniel 7:11–12, 25–27.
63. Granovetter 1977; Kuran 1989.
64. 1 Maccabees 2:42.

Mattathias and his zealots then "made a tour, overthrowing the [new] altars and forcibly circumcising all the boys they found uncircumcised in the territories of Israel." In what purports to be the testament of Mattathias and can be taken as the first political manifesto of the Maccabean party, Mattathias championed the cause of the Law (Torah) for the disenfranchised religious elite. Invoking Phineas once more, he reclaimed as granted by God's covenant the priestly authority lost as a result of Hellenistic reforms. Mattathias died in the year 166BCE. Meanwhile, the task of mobilization and recruitment in the countryside had been taken up by the most energetic, though not the oldest, of his sons Judas, who "raised a mixed force of believers and seasoned fighters by the Seleucid army."[65] Thus began the nativist revolutionary struggle in Judaea to preserve the heritage of Moses against the Greek ruler and his Hellenizing Jewish supporters. A revolutionary situation of dual power was thus created with an insurgent counterstate engaged in guerilla warfare against the Seleucids. It lasted for six years and ended with the killing of Judas.

The story of Judas Maccabee's failed revolution is told sympathetically and in fascinating detail in the two books of Maccabees, which the interested reader is strongly encouraged to read. As his revolutionary struggle failed to achieve what he and his fighters had set out to do, I will only highlight the aspect of the process of revolution in those six years that had lasting implications for the emergence and growth of apocalyptic messianism.

The collaborators from the Hellenized aristocracy and their estates were an early target of the Maccabean guerilla warfare. Maccabean guerrillas soon felt strong enough to attack local Seleucid forces and captured some of their fortifications, forcing the Seleucid governor to dispatch an army—probably in the spring of 165 BCE. A Maccabean propaganda bureau also produced books clearly aimed at religio-national mobilization, some of which have survived among the apocryphal/deutero-canonical books of the Bible. Judith (Jewess), the virtuous widow who beheaded Holophernes (evoking Antiochus's commissioner for persecution), is one such product of the Maccabean religio-national mobilization.[66] The Maccabean party also co-opted sympathetic Hellenized

---

65. 1 Maccabees 2:25–42, 46, 50, 54. Only about half his fighters, three thousand in number, were the core of his regular fighting force. See 2 Maccabees 8:13, 16.

66. The important role of women in religio-national mobilization is also reflected in the widely circulated story of the godly and fearless mother of the seven martyrs in 2 Maccabees 7.

elements, including two defecting Hellenized officers with Greek names from mixed settlements in Transjordan, as their militant movement was becoming an insurgent counterstate.[67] The Maccabees' traditionalist politico-military organization of the insurgent state deviated from the structure of the Hellenistic armies and followed biblical models. Judas must have borrowed this traditionalist model from the Sons of Zadok among the Hasidim who were prominent partners in the revolutionary coalition.[68] In December 164 BCE, the Maccabean holy warriors under Judas captured Jerusalem, pushed the high priest Menelaus and the council of elders into the citadel (Acra), and purified the sanctuary. Heeding the widespread apocalyptic expectations, Judas had the defiled altar of burnt offering dismantled, "and deposited the stones in a suitable place on the hill of the Dwelling *to await the appearance of a prophet* who should give a ruling about them." On the third anniversary of the abominable sacrifice to Zeus (December 167), a lawful sacrifice was offered to Yahweh on a new altar of burnt offering. "Judas, with his brothers *and the whole assembly of Israel* made it a law that the days of dedication of the altar should be celebrated yearly..." The unacknowledged appropriation of Hellenistic constitutionalism here is also brought out in the statement on the institution of the eight-day Feast of Dedication (Hanukkah): "They also decreed by public edict, ratified by vote, that the whole Jewish nation should celebrate those same days every year."[69]

Once drawn into the deadly power struggle as a partner in the revolutionary coalition led by the Maccabees, there can be no doubt that the Hasidic participants began to see it in apocalyptic terms while revolutionary mobilization extended beyond women moved by the example of Judith. The book of Jubilees was redacted to celebrate the unity of the armed revolutionary coalition and to exhort steadfastness in a long struggle:

> And they [the righteous] will stand up with bow and sword and war in order to return them [the wicked] to "the way," but they will not be returned until much blood is shed upon the earth by each group.[70]

More significantly, when the Enochic circles joined the Maccabean revolutionary coalition, they wrote the Animal Apocalypse—undoubtedly in Aramaic.

---

67. 2 Maccabees 12:19, 24, 35; Hengel 1974 1:189.
68. See Temple Scroll 57:4–5; Vermes 1995, 174.
69. 1 *Maccabees* 4:46, 59 (emphasis added); 2 Maccabees 10:8.
70. Jubilees 23:20; Davenport 1971, 42–43.

The apocalypse celebrates the unity of the revolutionary coalition by placing its rise of a distinct movement led by a horned ram (Judas Maccabee) at the critical stage of the schematic sacred history on the threshold of the eschaton.[71] Enoch, at least as the mantic interpreters of his wisdom in the Animal Apocalypse saw him, thus fully sanctioned the Maccabean revolutionary movement:

> I saw thereafter the shepherds coming; and those vultures and kites cried aloud to the ravens so that they should smash the horn of that ram. . . . I kept seeing until the Lord of the sheep came unto them and took in his hand the rod of his wrath and smote the earth . . . Then I saw that a great sword was given to the sheep . . . I went on seeing until the Lord of the sheep brought about a new house, greater and loftier than the first one. . . . All the sheep were within it.[72]

The group that made the most lasting ideological contribution was the one in the most uneasy position in the revolutionary coalition: the Danielic wise teachers of the people. The initial publication of the seven-chapter Daniel in Aramaic must have had a considerable impact, as Mattathias quotes from it in his testament.[73] The Maśkilim, encouraged by this success, sought to coordinate their public instruction with the traditionalist revolutionary movement that had fast gathered momentum in reaction to the desecration of the Temple. A different hand in the circle then added chapters 8–12 in Hebrew, the language favored by the traditionalists.[74] The enlarged Daniel was an even greater success. It can safely be assumed to be foremost among the contemporary works collected by Judas Maccabee to constitute the canonical scripture, and it was incorporated into the Old Testament.

Two major innovations of the author of the Hebrew Daniel help us understand its enormous immediate appeal to the anti-Hellenistic revolutionaries.[75] The first innovation is the enlistment of the heavenly host led by the archangel Michael as the prince of Israel in the holy warfare of the righteous against their Hellenistic persecutors. For the author of the Hebrew half of Daniel, it

---

71. Goldstein 1976, 41–42; Collins 1993, 69; Garcia Martinez 1992, 74–78.
72. 1 Enoch 90:13–19, 29; OTP 1:70.
73. 1 Maccabees 2:59.
74. In all likelihood, chapter 1 was also translated into Hebrew in order to produce a coherent new bilingual edition for "the people who know their God [and] will stand firm and take action" (Daniel 11:32; Collins 1993, 24, 385).
75. 2 Maccabees 2:14; Wacholder 1978, 123–25.

not Yahweh himself but "Michael, your Prince," who is the heavenly warrior, introduced in the Bible for the first time in Daniel's great vision. It is Michael, the angelic ruler of Israel, who is introduced into the vision of world history as the predetermined succession of empires subject to astral divination, with the ram (Ares) and the he-goat (Capricorn) as the signs of the Zodiac dominating Persia and Syria respectively.[76] Having completed his apprenticeship in the overthrow of the prince of Persia, Michael bides his time during the empire of "the Prince of Javan [Greece]," and will appear on earth for the apocalyptic termination of the struggle between the kings of the north and south. The suggestion in the older Aramaic part that God, "the King of heaven,"[77] "disposes the army of heaven" is thus elaborated into the idea that the final battle in the succession of empires on earth will be won by Michael and the angelic army who will establish the eternal kingdom of Israel as "the people of the holy ones [i.e., angels] of the Most High."[78]

The second innovation is the full apocalyptic development of the notion of "the Time of the End" and its precise mantic calculation. The biblical term "the Time of the End" (*qetz akhrin*)—as well as its equivalent, "End of Days" (*akrit ha-yomim*)—only acquire their definitive apocalyptic sense by being integrated into this conjunction of the heavenly and earthly dramas at the fall of the last historical empire. The author assures us that despite setbacks and reversals in the revolutionary power struggle, the Maśkilim will persist "until the time of the End, for the appointed time is still to come ... At that time Michael will arise—the great Prince, defender of your people. That will be a time of great distress, unparalleled since the nations first came into existence. When that time comes, your people will be spared—all those whose names are found written in the Book." There follows immediately the resurrection of the dead, and the Maśkilim will join the angels of the Most High and will shine brightly in the heavens. Although Daniel is told by the angel Gabriel to "keep these words secret and [to] keep the book sealed until the time of the End," its coming was an infamously well-publicized secret, and the Danielic

---

76. Daniel 8:1–14; Cumont 1909, 265, 273; Hengel 1974, 2:124n514. This is a complete departure from the position of the Hasidim of Jubilees who had declared the following: "over Israel he did not appoint any angel or spirit, for he alone is their ruler" (Jubilees 15:31–32; Collins 1993, 376).

77. This is the only instance of the expression in the Hebrew Bible. See Collins 1993, 232.

78. Daniel 4:31, 34; 7:27; 10:13, 21.

mantic virtuosi set it within three and a half years of the desecration of the Temple.[79]

There can be no doubt that Judas Maccabee welcomed Danielic innovations, claiming on one occasion that "victory in war does not depend on the size of the fighting force: Heaven accords the strength"; while on another occasion, just before his greatest battle, he prayed, "Sovereign of heaven, send a good angel before us to spread terror and dismay."[80] Nor was the calculation of the imminent end without considerable mobilizational value to the Maccabean revolutionaries. The Maśkilim for their part, however, were extremely uneasy about the revolutionary coalition. The Maccabean party was "little help," and like other parties, it would court the Maśkilim as an act of "slippery treachery."[81] The wise teachers evidently felt they had been double-crossed and taken advantage of in the revolutionary power struggle:

> Of the wise leaders some will stumble [from sword and flame, captivity and pillage], and so a number of them will be purged, purified and made clean. . . .[82]

With the redaction of the book of Jubilees and the Animal Apocalypse, as well as the book of Daniel, we thus have the first instances of "that apocalyptic interpretation of contemporary struggles which was to become an ordinary feature of the later rebellions of the Jews against foreign rulers."[83] But the advocates of the Jubilees' calendrical reform, the Enochic circles, the followers of the Maśkilim, and those in the Maccabean party who appropriated their ideas and techniques were not the only ones to adopt the apocalyptic interpretation of the revolutionary power struggle. The proto-Essenes among the Hasidim did likewise. Indeed, they collected the apocalyptic writings of other groups that later found a cherished place in the library at Qumran. The exhortation at the beginning of the Damascus Document on the history of the Essene sect, which branched off from the Hasidic movement and later abandoned the Maccabean revolutionary coalition to found the Qumran community in the Judaean desert near the Dead Sea, points to the era of

---

79. Daniel 9:27; 11:35; 12:1, 4.
80. 1 Maccabees 3:19; 2 Maccabees 15:23.
81. Daniel 11:21.
82. Daniel 11:33–35.
83. Momigliano 1975, 112.

Hellenistic reform, called the "age of wrath," as the time of the emergence of its first leader among the Hasidim, when God "caused a root for planting to spring from Israel and Aaron to inherit His Land . . . and He raised for them a teacher of righteousness to guide them."[84]

We can hypothesize that the Teacher of Righteousness (*moreh ha-tzedek*) among the Hasidim began to organize his followers into the proto-Essene sect of "the Sons of Zadok," which remained within the Hasidic movement, opposing the Hellenizers, "the latter generation, the congregation of traitors, who . . . departed from the way," and joined the Maccabean revolutionary coalition, probably as part of the "company of Hasideans" in 166 BCE. It is also very probable that by that date, the Teacher of Righteousness, who is also referred to as the Interpreter of the Law (Torah), had delivered "the rules which the legislator [*meoqoq*] legislated for walking in all the ages of wickedness" in what purported to be new divine legislation: "the sealed book of the Law which was in the ark [of the Covenant]," unread by David, and had remained hidden "and was not revealed until the coming of Zadok."[85] This book of law can be no other than the Temple Scroll in which God at times promulgates his new ordinances, often in the first person. The Teacher of Righteousness was, like Mattathias, a dispossessed priest who, furthermore, belonged to the high-priestly Zadokite line, and adopted the designation, "the sons of Zadok," from Ezekiel 44:15 for his sectarian followers: "The sons of Zadok are the elect of Israel, the men called by name who shall stand at the End of Days."[86]

In his youth as an educated priest, the Teacher of Righteousness appears to have been susceptible to the charms of Hellenism, but he repented and turned to God:

> For I remember my sins and the unfaithfulness of my fathers. When the wicked rose against Thy Covenant . . . I said in my sinfulness, "I am forsaken by Thy Covenant." But recalling to mind the might of Thy hand and the greatness

---

84. CD 1:5–13, 6:9–10; Vermes 1995, 97–100, 152. The identification of the "root" in this passage with the Hasidim and the "planting" with the Essene community is acceptable. See Jeremias 1963, 162.

85. CD 1:5–13, 6:9–10; Vermes 1995, 97, 152; Collins 1995, 62–63, 148. "Legislator" is a play on the "staff" (*meoqoq*) of Numbers 21:18, which explains the use of these rules for "*walking* in all the age of wickedness." More typical English translations of this phrase in the literature fail to convey the fact that all the key words in it are derivatives of the same Hebrew word, *hoq* (statute).

86. CD 4:4–5, 5:4–5; Vermes 1995, 99–100.

of Thy compassion, I rose and stood, and my spirit was established in face of the scourge.

Then he became convinced of God's confirmation:

Thou hast shed Thy Holy Spirit upon me that I may not stumble ... Thou hast not permitted that fear should cause me to desert Thy Covenant ... Thou hast placed me, O my God, among the branches of the Council of Holiness...[87]

His teachings suggest familiarity with the ideas of the angelic presence in the assembly of the faithful, and conversely, the entry of the wise "amidst the spirits of knowledge into the congregation of the Sons of Heaven," as well as with the Zoroastrian apocalyptic notion of the destruction of sinful men by a cosmic fire emanating from the source of light and the eternal fountain of bright flames. Furthermore, he rested his authority as teacher of "the elect of righteousness" on his claim to be a "discerning interpreter of wonderful mysteries." Under his instruction, however, the Sons of Zadok (צדוק בני) gave the cosmic, wisdom apocalypticism of the Enochic and Danielic circles a distinctly prophetic and legalistic (halakhic) form. They maintained that "God told Habakkuk to write down that which would happen to the final generation," and that the inspired interpreter of the prophet Habakkuk's words was "the Teacher of Righteousness, to whom God made known all the mysteries of the words of His servants, the Prophets."[88]

We do not know if Judas had a program for postrevolutionary government, but his partners in the revolutionary coalition, the Sons of Zadok, did. As their Teacher of Righteousness organized his following into a political faction, the Sadducees, he developed a messianic program for government. This project for theocratic monarchy was contained in the same divine legislation he delivered. There is no reason to think Judas would have disputed it at this stage (before seizing power) because it was impeccably traditionalist. Drawing on the biblical account of the institution of monarchy by Samuel for its model, the Temple Scroll recorded a divine ordinance according to which, on the promised land, just like other nations,

---

87. 1QH 4:34–37, 7:6–9; Vermes 1995, 202–3, 210–11.
88. 1QH 2:13–14, 3:20–22, 6:13–18; Vermes 1995, 193, 198, 208; 1QpHab 7:1–5; Schiffman 1989, 50.

you may surely appoint over you the king whom I choose. It is from your brothers that you shall appoint a king over you. You shall not appoint over you a foreigner who is not your brother... When he sits on the throne of his kingdom, they shall write for him this law from the book which is before the priests.[89]

The so-called Halakhic Letter claimed in its final exhortation that what was written in the book of Moses of the ancient kings of Israel who were "the seekers of the Torah" was that in this End of Days, "they will return forever..."[90] The expansionist goals of the Zadokite (Sadducee) militant future state, too, fit well with those shortly to be exhibited by the Maccabean insurgents:

> When you approach a city to fight it, [first] offer it peace. If it seeks peace and opens [its gates] to you, then all the people found in it shall become your forced laborers and shall serve you. If it does not make peace with you, but is ready to fight a war against you, you shall besiege it and I will deliver it into your hands. You shall put all its males to the sword, but the women, the children, the beasts and all that is in the city, all its booty, you may take as spoil for yourselves.... But in the cities of the peoples which I give you as an inheritance, you shall not leave alive any creature.[91]

The tortuous revolutionary power struggle during the short reign of the young Antiochus V who succeeded his father in 164 BCE and was killed by a Seleucid pretender supported by Rome in the fall of 162 need not concern us except for the appointment of Alcimus (Jakim) to the high priesthood in Jerusalem to replace Menelaus. The choice of Alcimus (Jakim) made good sense as a conciliatory move from the Seleucid monarchy's position of weakness, even though it turned out to be a mistake. Alcimus has plausibly been identified as the nephew of the president of the association of the Pharisees, and his appointment may have aimed at securing the defection of the Pharisees from the Maccabean coalition. In any event, though not of Zadokite descent, he was clearly acceptable to many pious Jews as a priest of the stock of Aaron. In choosing Alcimus, however, the Seleucid king and the regent had passed over one obvious candidate: Onias IV, the son of the last legitimate Zadokite high priest, Onias III, who had been murdered at the instigation of

---

89. Vermes 1995, 173–74 (11 QT 56:12–20).
90. 4QMMT C21, 24; translation on 61.
91. Vermes 1995, 177–78 (62:6–16).

Menelaus.[92] Not surprisingly, the Maccabees refused to recognize Alcimus, and ousted him from Jerusalem after a temporary withdrawal of the Seleucid army, and he went to the Seleucid court in Antioch.

For reasons that remain obscure to us but are consistent with Saturn's devouring his own children in the revolutionary power struggle, when Alcimus was reinstated after a compromise between the Pharisees and the Seleucid army under the conditions of continued dual power/sovereignty, he embarked on a bloody purge of the Hasidic defectors whose loyalty he must have suspected. The purge claimed the lives of sixty of the Hasidim who had switched to his side, and probably of Alcimus's own uncle, Jose b. Joezer, who was the chief Pharisee jurist. Once the Seleucid army left, the Maccabean rebels were no gentler than Alcimus. "Judas went right round the whole territory of Judaea to take vengeance on those who had deserted him."[93] Nevertheless, Onias IV, who had been passed over for the high priesthood by the Seleucid government, now defected to the Maccabean revolutionary coalition. This defection must have been facilitated by the fact that the Sons of Zadok among the Hasidim were partners in the revolutionary coalition,[94] and their leader, the Teacher of Righteousness, belonged to the Zadokite high priestly family. The Sons of Zadok fell out with Judas, however, probably because the excesses of the export of revolution and looting of the estates of the Hellenized aristocracy seemed unnecessary or unprincipled to them. Judas was the first person they called the "Wicked Priest." He "was called by the name of truth when he first arose. But when he ruled over Israel . . . he robbed and amassed the riches of the men

---

92. We know nothing of the activities of Jason, son of Simon the Just, the architect of the failed Hellenizing reform, but it is safe to infer that Egypt took him in as a protégé, and may even have allowed him to organize a counterrevolution in exile in the 160s BCE. Jason's disastrous second attempt to regain Jerusalem must have devastated his Hellenizing partisans, who "had revolted against the rule of God" (2 Maccabees 1:7) and doomed their political future. By contrast, the traditionalist support for Zadokite legitimism among dispossessed priests and Levites, including some Hasidic leaders, must have grown, and some of them rallied behind Onias III. Onias III, once a refugee in a pagan shrine, was now glorified as a martyr, "the anointed one" who was "cut down" (Daniel 9:26); the Zadokite legitimists could rally behind his son, Onias IV.

93. 1 Maccabees 7:24.

94. The decisive evidence for the adhesion of the Zadokite legitimists to the revolutionary coalition consists of the use of Zadokite legitimist propaganda in a dream by Judas in March 161 about "Onias [III], the former high priest, that paragon of men" (2 Maccabees 15:11–16).

of violence who rebelled against God, and he took the wealth of the [Gentile] nations."[95]

The Maccabean revolt failed and was crushed in 160 BCE. The situation of dual sovereignty thus came to an end and Seleucid rule over Judaea was reestablished. Eight years later, in 152 BCE, Jonathan and what had survived of his seasoned band of outlaws were drawn into Seleucid dynastic politics as their rule was critically threatened by the Parthian Mithridates I, who was soon to conquer Ecbatana in western Iran and then move the center of his empire alarmingly close to Antioch, the Seleucid capital. In desperation, the hard-pressed Seleucid king, Demetrius I, authorized Jonathan to raise troops; in a counterbid, a Seleucid pretender went further and offered him the office of the high priest. Jonathan's fantastic rise to power can reasonably be said to have ushered in "a chapter in the history of the Maccabees which, except for the identity of the family, has little in common with their destiny." While Judas's had been the anti-Hellenistic cause of the Torah, under Jonathan and Simon and the latter's descendants "Judaea became a Hellenistic principality."[96]

The Maccabees had no reason to disown their revolutionary past, however, and naturally drew on some of their former partisans and partners in the revolutionary coalition in the political reconstruction that began with Jonathan's contingent takeover. The former coalition partners excluded from power would appeal to the ideals of the rebellion to protest their exclusion and back their claims to entitlement. In this fashion, the dynamics of the revolutionary process would resume despite the eight-year interruption, and the Maccabean revolution could be conceptualized as an extended sequence consisting of two sets of events. The embers of both the traditionalist and the protomessianic anti-Hellenism in the ashes of the extinguished Maccabean fire indeed flared up again under the contingencies of international and intradynastic conflict, which had put a premium on Jonathan's mobilizational and military capacity as a condottiere. Under him, the old power struggle resumed between the traditionalist party and the protomessianists, who increasingly appeared as an organized sect. We can therefore say that the Essene sect became clearly differentiated from the Hasidic movement at this stage. For this reason, the

---

95. 1QpHab 8:9–12; Vermes 1995, 344 (with slight modification); Garcia Martinez 1988, 128.
96. Bickerman 1947, 64.

revolutionary power struggle in which the losers invented political messianism needs to be considered in some detail.

The Essenes developed their distinctive monikers in the course of the revolutionary power struggle and saw the enemies of the sect as the apocalyptic enemies of God. "The Wicked Priest," whose application to Judas Maccabee we have accepted, was given regular currency later to denigrate Alcimus, Jonathan, Simon, and possibly the latter's descendants. The same labeling also occurs in the intra-Zadokite sectarian schisms, where the arch enemies are termed "the Spouter of Lies" and "the Liar" (*daggāla*). Both groups are subject to dire apocalyptic punishment. The political opponents would be punished "in the last days" by the Gentiles chosen as instruments of God's design. The sectarian opponents, the Liar and his followers who were "outraging the elect of God," will be punished by fire and "shall perish by the sword and famine and plague." Finally, the same revolutionary mentality saw the opponents engaged in conspiratorial plotting: "they dissemble, they plan devilish schemes..."[97]

Alcimus survived Judas Maccabee as the high priest and the official head of the restored Seleucid temple-state in Judaea until his paralytic stroke and death in May 159 BCE.[98] The attitude toward Alcimus is the most likely cause for the split between the two Zadokite groups, but even without it, there would probably be enough tension and rivalry in their partnership in the revolutionary coalition to cause a split.[99] In any event, whatever its causes, the Habakkuk Commentary (*pesher*) enables us to assert that a split did in fact occur:

---

97. 1QpHab 8:13, 9:6; 4Q171 2:1, 4:15; Vermes 1995, 344–45, 348; 1QH 4:13; Vermes 1995, 200; Qimron and Strugnell 1994, 118–20. The habit persisted, and the leader responsible for a later schism, after the sectarian separation of the Essenes from Hasidism, is called "the Scoffer" (CD 2:10–14; Vermes 1995, 104–5).

98. Goldstein 1989, 311–12.

99. We know that Onias IV went to Egypt when he lost hope of becoming a high priest, and that he was well received by the Egyptian king, Ptolemy VI Philometor (180–145 BCE). Using a prophecy of Isaiah (19:19), he set up a temple in Leontopolis with Ptolemy's support. Onias IV and his circle adopted the techniques of their former partner. When Alcimus's double-crossing of the Hasidim and his bloody purge produced bitter recrimination within the Pharisaic and Zadokite branches of the Hasidic movement, the Sons of Zadok under the Teacher of Righteousness were bound to dissociate themselves from him, and they very probably labeled him a wicked and identified him as "the Priest who rebelled [and violated] the precepts [of God] ... And they inflicted horrors of evil disease and took vengeance upon his body of flesh." It is reasonable to deduce that the proto-Essene Sons of Zadok and the legitimist followers of Onias IV broke violently with each other over Alcimus. See 2 Maccabees 1:10–2:18; 1QpHab 8:16–9:4; Vermes 1995, 344.

"Woe to him who builds a city with blood and founds a town upon falsehood..." [Habakkuk 2:12–13]. Interpreted, this concerns the Spouter of Lies who led many astray that he might build his city of vanity with blood and raise a congregation on deceit, causing many to perform a service of vanity...[100]

It follows from the above hypothesis that the Spouter of Lies, also called the Liar, is Onias IV,[101] who persuaded many of the followers of the Teacher of Righteousness to defect to the Zadokite legitimist party and who thus "outraged the elect of God." The Habakkuk Commentary seems to throw additional light on this schism. It tells us that

> the House of Absalom and its council... were silent at the time of the chastisement of the Teacher of Righteousness and gave him no support against the Liar who flouted the Law in the midst of their whole [congregation].[102]

It appears from this passage that Absalom, who had represented the Hasidim in the first round of negotiations with the coregent Lysias, was an important member of the Sons of Zadok who broke with the Teacher of Righteousness and, at the time of the intra-Zadokite schism, gave him no support against the Liar, Onias IV. It also suggests that the House of Absalom and its organized followers may have been the linchpin of the Hasidim-Maccabean revolutionary coalition but were forced to choose the latter side when Jonathan "chastised" the Teacher of Righteousness and drove him out of Jerusalem. If so, Absalom's sons, Mattathias and Jonathan, were rewarded for their defection, and were given important posts in the second Maccabean temple-state.[103]

What was most likely seen as particularly deceitful about the Liar/Spouter of Lies by the Teacher of Righteousness was the apocalyptic propaganda put out by Onias IV and his circle of Jewish émigrés in Egypt. Evidence of messianic political propaganda, however, is preserved in the *Sibylline Oracles*. A

---

100. 1QpHab 10:6–11; Vermes 1995, 345. The city of vanity would, according to this hypothesis, be Leontopolis, and the "congregation of deceit" would be the Zadokite legitimists and the Egyptian Jews who joined them and performed prayer services of vanity.

101. Onias IV is the best candidate among the known historical figures for being (or having a senior advisor who is) "the Liar who has led astray many by his lying words so that they chose frivolous things and heeded not the interpreter of wisdom [i.e., the Teacher of Righteousness]" (4Q171 1; Vermes 1995, 348).

102. 1QpHab 5:10–13; Vermes 1995, 342.

103. 1 Maccabees 11:17, 13:11; Vermes 1995, 37.

set of political oracles dated to the middle of the second century BCE shares the Danielic concern with the rise and fall of empires, and furthermore resembles the Second Isaiah "in endorsing a Gentile king as the agent of deliverance." Onias IV's hope was that Ptolemy Philometor could act as a latter-day Cyrus, a gentile Messiah, who would restore him in Jerusalem. One such oracle predicts the apocalyptic era in the reign of "the young seventh king of Egypt . . . numbered from the line of the Greeks," who is hard to identify with anyone other than Ptolemy Philometor. Another oracle foretells of a savior king: "the heavenly God will send a king," and possibly makes a reference to the temple Onias built at Leontopolis: "[Onias]will begin to raise up a new temple of God."[104] As one would expect, the Hellenistic Egyptian political oracles served as a source for Onias IV's propaganda office:

> then God will send a king from the sun, who will stop the entire earth from evil war, killing some, imposing oaths of loyalty on others; and he will not do all these things by his private plans but in obedience to the noble teachings of the great God.[105]

But the Persian influence is also evident in the last two sets of oracles. The Zadokite legitimists in Egyptian exile, no less than the Danielic Maśkilim, drew on the Persian anti-Hellenistic current in the ecumenical Near Eastern Aramaic milieu, adopting the general Zoroastrian apocalyptic ideas of the transfiguration/renovation of the world and the signs of the end, as well as some of the specific details of the Oracle of Hystaspes:

> But when the wrath of the great God comes upon you, . . .
> All the souls of men will groan mightily and stretch out their hands straight to broad heaven and begin to call on the great king as protector and seek who will be a deliverer from the great wrath.[106]

In the end, however, Onias IV had no more luck in being restored by a foreign power than the typical counterrevolutionary émigré, and he became the general of a Jewish cleruchy set up at Leontopolis in the vicinity of the Temple.

---

104. *Sib. Or.* 3:286, 290, 608–9; Collins 1995, 38–39; OTP 1:355, 375.

105. *Sib. Or.* 3:652–56; OTP 1:376. There is just a hint of legitimist propaganda for the restoration of the Zadokite line in one Aramaic Pseudo-Daniel fragment from the Qumran that speaks of "the holy ones, and they will return" (4 QpsDanar [4Q245]). The text and translation are courtesy of Flint 1995.

106. *Sib. Or.* 3:545–656 and 657–808.

His following in Judaea must have gradually broken their ties with the former high priest-turned general, and according to some scholars, later became the group known as the Sadducees after making their peace with the Hasmonians.[107]

Jonathan Maccabee came to power not by revolutionary seizure but through royal appointment. For this reason, among others, the victory of revolutionary traditionalism in Judaea was incomplete. The Acra remained a Seleucid polis independent of the jurisdiction of the high priest, and the Hellenized Jews lived there freely. It was not until seven years later, in 145 BCE, that Jonathan set siege to the Acra in the context of yet another contest for the Seleucid throne that occurred after the serious loss of territory to the Parthians in the East. As soon as the contest for the imperial throne was won by Demetrius II, however, "some renegades who hated their nation made their way to the king." Jonathan took the deliberate risk of competing with them, "himself taking silver and gold, clothing and numerous other presents" to the new king. The risk came off and, in an edict to "the nation [*ethnos*] of the Jews," Demetrius II confirmed Jonathan as the high priest and the head of the Jewish temple-state.[108]

The program of the Sons of Zadok for revolutionary reconstruction was completely different, and it clearly envisaged a dual system of authority: a Jewish king, and an Aaronite high priest who would act on the model of Samuel and determine the constitutional position of the monarch according to the Torah. Given this dualistic conception of authority in the law for the age of wickedness in the Temple Scroll, which later developed into the dual messianism of the Essenes, it is very plausible to assume that in this period, when the office was up for grabs, the Teacher of Righteousness expected the high priesthood as the reward for his part in the revolutionary struggle. The divine ordinance in the Temple Scroll, as we have seen, forbids appointing as king "a foreigner who is not your brother." When his brother and erstwhile revolutionary partner Jonathan suddenly came to power in Jerusalem, he was admissible and very probably accepted as king. The Teacher of Righteousness had very good reason to expect the high priesthood by the same token. In any event, he and the Sons of Zadok were in principle committed to the separation

---

107. Tcherikover 1959, 276–80; Hengel 1989, 141; Goldstein 1975; Hengel 1989, 141.
108. 1 Maccabees 11:21–30.

of temporal and religious authority and could therefore only regard the assumption of the high priesthood by Jonathan as usurpation. Jonathan was indeed the quintessential Wicked Priest, "the Wicked Priest whom God delivered into the hands of his enemies[109] [in fact, the Seleucid general Tryphon] because of the iniquity committed against the Teacher of Righteousness and the men of his Council."[110]

The details of the Teacher of Righteousness's clash with Jonathan during the resumed revolutionary power struggle between 152 and 143 BCE remain obscure. The Teacher of Righteousness appears to have posed as the champion of the poor who shall possess "the whole world as an inheritance"—an implicit accusation of their betrayal by the Maccabean ruler.[111] But what left no room for compromise between the two was the clash of their respective religious convictions. Jonathan was a traditionalist and a proto-Pharisee, whereas the Teacher of Righteousness had a conception of the Law that was diametrically opposed to its literal reading by the Pharisees. He was most likely the founder of religious interpretation/commentary (*pesher*), notable commentaries on Habakkuk and the Psalms, which formed the cornerstone of his synthesis of the Jewish scriptural religion and the ecumenical wisdom of the Maśkilim.[112]

Consequently, Jonathan's authority was specifically challenged at least one more time by the Teacher of Righteousness in a letter on his "legal precept/injunction and the law [Torah]."[113] The Zadokite teacher does, however, appear to have made an effort to persuade Jonathan as a fellow Hasid from the old days to follow the example of David, "a man of righteous deeds [*ḥasidim*]," and accept his interpretation of the law.[114] Jonathan, however, was not only unwilling to learn the correct interpretation of the Torah; he sought to liquidate his

---

109. The commentary on Psalms has him delivered "into the hand of the violent of the [Gentile] nations" (4Q171 4:10–11; Vermes 1995, 351).

110. 1QpHab 9:8–10; Vermes 1995, 30–36, 247, 345; Jeremias 1963, 139; Garcia Martinez 1988, 127.

111. 4Q171 4:10, see also 1QH 5:14–15; Vermes 1995, 350, 204.

112. According to the commentary on Psalm 37, "The mouth of the righteous utters wisdom, and his tongue speaks justice. The Law (Torah) of God is in his heart, his feet do not slip." Cited in translation in Grossman 2002, 76.

113. Grossman 2002, 69–70.

114. "We have (indeed) sent you some precepts of the Torah according to our decision, for you welfare and the welfare of your people, for we have seen (that) you have wisdom and knowledge of the Torah" (4QMMT, C25–28; translation on 63).

opponent in the power struggle: "The Wicked [Priest... watched the Teacher of Righteousness] that he might put him to death [because of the ordinance] and the law which he sent him . . . "[115] What is clear, despite the murkiness of our detailed information, is that the clash with Jonathan was decisive for the withdrawal of the Essenes from Jerusalem and their separation from other sectarian groups. The Teacher of Righteousness and his followers withdrew to the Judaean desert and founded a new community for "the converts of Israel who depart from the way of the people" and "enter the New Covenant."[116]

Another group whose claim to historical memory as revolutionary coalition-partners was ignored by Jonathan was the Jubilees circle of calendrical reformists. The group's disappointment with the consolidation of power and concentration of wealth in the hands of Jonathan as the high priest is evident from the following passage:

> Those who escape [the suppression of Judas's rebellion] will not be turned back from their evils to the way of righteousness because *they will lift themselves up for deceit and wealth . . .; and they will pronounce the great name but not in truth or righteousness.* They will pollute the holy of holies with their pollution and with the corruption of their contamination.[117]

The fundamental preoccupation with the Law, shared by all the elements of the Hasidic movement, supplied readily available *differentia* for setting the new Essene community apart from the rest of Judaism, and thus added a sectarian dimension to the Essenes' split with the Maccabean party under Jonathan. The Halakhic Letter thus affirms, "we have separated ourselves from the multitude of the people [and from all their impurities]." On the basis of a creative (mis)reading of Amos 5:26–27, the new location in the desert, very probably Qumran, was identified with "the land of Damascus." Elsewhere, it is Lebanon that is interpreted as "the Council of Community," while "the city [of Habakkuk, 2:17] is Jerusalem where the Wicked Priest committed abominable deeds and defile the Temple of God."[118]

Furthermore, Jonathan himself could not resist playing the sectarian card. Not only did the Wicked Priest pursue "the Teacher of Righteousness to the

---

115. 4Q171 4:8–9; Vermes 1995, 351.
116. CD 8:16, 21; Vermes 1995, 104.
117. Jubilees 23: 21 (emphasis and explication added).
118. 4QMMT C7, translation on 59; CD 7:20; 1QpHab 12:4–9; Vermes 1995, 346.

house of his exile that he might confuse him with his venomous fury." But he did so with the clear purpose of making an issue of religion in order to split the Essenes: "And at the time appointed for rest, for the Day of Atonement, he appeared before them to confuse them, and to cause them to stumble on the Day of Fasting, their Sabbath of repose." Jonathan seems to have had some success as "the violent of the Covenant ... plotted to destroy those who practice the law, who are in the Council of the Community." Jonathan may also have instigated the other Jewish sects, the Pharisees (Ephraim) and presumably the Sadducees (Manasseh) who opposed the Essenes on religious grounds to "seek to lay hands on the Priest [i.e., the Teacher of Righteousness] and the men of his Council."[119]

With this sectarian crusting of the break between the Teacher of Righteousness and Jonathan, we thus have the division of the Jews, as reported by Josephus, during the reign of Jonathan into the Pharisees, the Sadducees, and the Essenes.[120] All three had at some point been affiliated with the Hasidic movements and had been partners in the Maccabean revolutionary coalition. Of the three, the Pharisees are the only ones never to leave the Maccabean side. They continued their support for Jonathan and his successors during the period of postrevolutionary reconstruction. The Sadducees wavered toward Egypt in the 150s BCE but then came to an understanding with Jonathan. The Essenes, by contrast, remained excluded from power. Their shibboleths called the Pharisees as "the seekers of smooth things," and the "(sons/wicked of) Ephraim," while it is probably the Sadducees who were symmetrically called the "(sons/wicked of) Manasseh." After the last brother who had led the Maccabean guerilla bands, Simon, had established the Hasmonian dynasty—the House of Hashmonay, at first probably a derogatory reference[121]—the Essenes described them as "the last Priests of Jerusalem, who shall amass money and wealth by plundering the people," and affirmed the apocalyptic expectation that "in the last days, their riches and booty shall be delivered into the hands of the Kittim ... "[122]

The Teacher of Righteousness survived the rigor of the reign of Jonathan to see further concentration of power and wealth in the hand of Jonathan's brother Simon (143–134 BCE), as well as the latter's son, John Hyrcanus

---

119. 4Q171 2:14–19; 1QpHab 11:5–9; Vermes 1995, 346, 349.
120. *Commonwealth*, 68–69.
121. Goldstein 1976, 17–19.
122. 1QpHab 9:5–8; Vermes 1995, 344–45.

(134–104 BCE), during whose reign he "gathered in." The ups and downs, both of the revolutionary power struggle and of the sectarian fissures, have left some clear traces in the confessional verses of the thanksgiving hymns specifically attributed to the Teacher of Righteousness. He speaks of his political opponents as "violent men who have sought after my life because I have clung to Thy Covenant." His opponents among the Jewish sectarians are "lying interpreters," "congregations of those who seek smooth things," "teacher of lies and seers of falsehood," and the worst, the Essene defectors, are "the members of my [Covenant] [who] have rebelled and have murmured round about me; they have gone a tale-bearers before the children of mischief concerning the mystery which Thou hast hidden in me." With unusual humility, the Teacher of Righteousness appears to have taken the blame for some of the reversals, considering it the cause of God's "just rebuke." He also bemoans the return of Hellenization under the Hasmonians among those who seek smooth things or who "have exchanged [his teachings] for lips of uncircumcision, and for the foreign tongue of a people without understanding."[123]

THE INSTITUTIONALIZATION OF POLITICAL MESSIANISM IN THE JUDAEAN DESERT

The most important consequence of the Maccabean revolt that accounts for its significance in world history was due not to the winners but to the losers of the Maccabean uprising as a failed revolution—those who lost the power struggle and withdrew from Jerusalem to the Judaean Desert to form the Qumran community. The same Halakhic Letter in which the Teacher of Righteousness announces the sectarian separation of the Essenes from the rest of the Jews contains a striking apocalyptic affirmation: "And this is the End of Days when the [kings of Israel] will return to Isra[e]l [forever . . .], but the wicked will act in wickedness."[124] Elsewhere, God's promise to the Branch of David (2 Samuel 7:14) to "establish the throne of his kingdom" is explained

---

123. 1QH 2:18–22, 32–33, 4:10, 5:24–25, 9:20–34; Vermes 1995, 194–95, 200, 205, 214–15; Jeremias 1963. The Qumran commentaries on Isaiah, too, condemn the latter-day Hellenizers in the same vein as the Teacher of Righteousness had done—namely, as "the scoffers in Jerusalem" and "the congregation of those who seek smooth things in Jerusalem" (4Q162–4Q163; Vermes 1995, 322).

124. 4QMMTC21–22 (pp. 60–61).

as referring to "the Branch of David, who will arise with the Interpreter of the Law who [will rise up] in Zi[on in]the Last Days."[125]

From the very beginning, the Teacher of Righteousness considered the world-rejecting sect he had formed an apocalyptic community of salvation, a community for "the penitent of the desert who, saved, shall live for a thousand generations and to whom all the glory of Adam shall belong, as also to their seed forever."[126] Exclusion from power and rejection of the world of Jerusalem reinforced the apocalyptic perspective on politics the Sons of Zadok had shared with other anti-Hellenistic groups. The Teacher of Righteousness did set a date for the End of Days and lived to face the embarrassing task of explaining that "the final age shall be prolonged and shall exceed all that the Prophets have said, for the mysteries of God are astounding." The revised date for the time of the End was later adjusted to about forty years after the death of the Teacher of Righteousness—that is, to the first quarter of the first century BCE. Such adjustments, however, rarely prove fatal to millennialism.[127]

Once the sect of Essenes withdrew to the Judaean Desert and started to live in preparation of the expected dawning of the eschaton, the dualistic system of authority adumbrated in the Temple Scroll was buttressed by a systematic, Persian-inspired, dualistic demonology, which increasingly referred to the wicked as the people of Belial and the sons of darkness in contrast to the pious elect as the sons of light. The dualistic normative model of authority itself was progressively transposed into an apocalyptic perspective that became specifically *messianic* as the Davidic notion of the anointed king, the Messiah, was counterposed to the Hasmonian usurpation and mingling of priestly and kingly authority. This messianic transposition resulted in the crystallization of the distinctly Essene dualistic form of "Messiahs of Israel and Aaron"—an anointed king and an anointed high priest, respectively. The expression is first attested in manuscripts dated to around 100 BCE, and later, in the first century BCE, it also appears in the form of the Branch of David and the Interpreter of the Torah. The development of the notion of the Davidic Messiah, however, was not adversely affected by this dualism.[128]

---

125. 4Q174 as cited in in van Henten 2007, 27.
126. 4Q171 3:1–2; Vermes 1995, 349.
127. 1QpHab 7:8–9, also 14–15; CD (B II) 8:14; Vermes 1995, 105, 343–44.
128. 4Q174 1:10–13; Schiffman 1989, 69; VanderKam 1994, 214, 227; Horbury 1998, 59–63.

We have ample documentation of the far-reaching institutionalization of messianism in the most famous and fantastically detailed example from the Dead Sea Scrolls: *The War Rule* for the apocalyptic battle at the final days that is recognizable by the Persian loanword, *nakhshir* (Middle Persian *naxčēr* [hunting]) as the *ardig-e buzurg* of the Zoroastrian apocalyptics. The Hebrew *milhamah* in the *War Rule* was a rendering of the Middle Iranian apocalyptic term, *ardig-e buzurg* (the great war), and should be counted as one of the indicators of the well-documented Persian influence on the Qumran community. Messianism is explicitly institutionalized in the *Messianic Rule* for the apocalyptic congregation and the apocalyptic banquet with the two Messiahs, Israel and Aaron. The military aspects of political messianism, too, were thus legalized in precise detail in the *War Rule*.[129]

Furthermore, the messianic syndrome proved expansive and its emotive appeal was strengthened by the addition of Gog and Magog as the foes of the Messiah.[130] The great battle of the End of Time and the participation of archangels in it were established with the giving of the sword to the righteous as the people of God. The *War Rule* also drew considerably on the book of Daniel and elaborated a systematic integration of earthly and heavenly armies in the holy war of the last days, and an apocryphal fragment on Daniel (4 Q246) offers details of the calamities preceding the final victory of the "people of God" whose "domination will be eternal" (4 Q246), protected and aided as it is by God Most High and his angels.[131]

The Qumran settlement was destroyed by the Roman army of Vespasian, but the messianism it had sustained in institutionalized form for two centuries survived and was passed on to Christianity, nonrabbinical Judaism, and Islam. Many instances of political messianism in the first century of the Common Era are reported by Josephus. The Enochic circles effected the otherworldly transposition of political messianism in the Similitudes of Enoch (1 Enoch 37–71), as did the Christians gradually after the destruction of the Temple in 70 CE. Other apocalyptic notions, too, survived and coalesced with messianism and its extensions and elaborations. The prophet, for example, so

---

129. Vermes 1995, 123–50 (1QM); Vermes 1995, 119–22 (1 Qsa); Rabin 1957, 119; Winston 1966; Shaked 1972; Schiffman 1989; Shapira 2013, 40.

130. Horbury 1998, 61; Horbury 2003, 337–39.

131. Collins 1975, 604–7; Wacholder 1983, 80–81; Puech 1996, 183.

inconvenient from the Maccabean point of view and at best uneasily accommodated in Essene thought, reappears in the apocalyptic reconstruction of Elijah as the returning prophet of the End of Time. The apocalyptic perspective of the book of Daniel was especially privileged, as the Maccabean winners of the revolutionary power struggle, through only "a little help" to the losing Maśkilim, had appropriated their ideas and effected its inclusion in the Old Testament canon. Thence, Daniel, and especially its Aramaic chapter 7, exercised an enormous influence on the New Testament.[132]

The older Aramaic portion of the book of Daniel (chs. 1–6) shows the cosmopolitan intellectual source of the later political messianism. There we find the heavenly transposition of the idea of empire to the kingdom of God the Most High—a notion that was to pass to the apocrypha (1 Esdras 4:46) and thence to Islam. ("His kingdom is an everlasting kingdom" [Daniel 3:33]— the only instance of the phrase "king of heaven" in the Old Testament occurs in Daniel 4:34). The Danielic circle (the Wise) introduced this perspective to Judaism in relative detachment from armed struggle and in dialogue with the ecumenical Near Eastern religious culture expressed in its Aramaic lingua franca.

The apocalypticism of the Danielic circle was developed into messianism by the Essenes only after the Maccabeans had finally captured Jerusalem. As the losing party in the revolutionary political struggle, they left Jerusalem and formed the Qumran community in the desert. Their cultural creativity had no immediate impact, but it greatly influenced Christianity, Manichaeism, and Islam in the long run.

The Maccabean revolt not only upheld the Torah as the Law of God for his chosen people against Hellenism but it also gave the ecumenical apocalyptic view of politics a perpetual and definitively universalistic cultural form. Whereas the cause of the Torah and of the exponents of the Mosaic Law in Hebrew supplied the traditionalist goals of the revolution through the agency of the Pharisees, the political messianism of the vanquished Essenes was ecumenically inspired and therefore expressed primarily in Aramaic, and it became an autonomous cultural form available for adaptation by future generations of revolutionary millenarians in the Aramaic ecumene. Political messianism thus became a permanent form in the ecumenical religious culture

---

132. Flusser 1982; Frend 1984, 253–57; Collins 1995, 112–23.

of Late Antiquity, in part through appropriation by the victors and in part through sectarian institutionalization by the vanquished themselves. Either way, the credit for this major contribution to world history goes not to the winners but to the losers of the Maccabean revolution.

The development of Qumran messianism was thus fundamental to the future of Judaism, Christianity and Islam. As a noted historian of Rome put it, "If there ever was an identifiable 'turning point in history' it was the years 167 to 164 B.C. in Palestine."[133] Eight centuries separates the apocalyptic chapters of Daniel from the Qur'an, and yet, as we shall see in chapter 2, the apocalyptic Danielic vision, transmitted through the Essenes to the Gnostic Christians and Manichaeans of Mesopotamia as well as to the heterodox Jewish and Judeo-Christian communities of Arabia over the intervening centuries, resurfaced in the oldest Qur'anic suras that record the earliest stage of the new revelation that motivated a political revolution in seventh-century Arabia and the rise of Islam as a world religion.

133. Millar 1978, 1.

CHAPTER 2

Muhammad's Constitutive Revolution as Realized Messianism and Its Apocalyptic Roots

The rise of Islam in Arabia was a revolution by any reasonable definition of the term. It was stimulated by a strong apocalyptic vision that accompanied the new revelation and by the pervasive expectation of the imminent Hour (*al-sā'a*) of reckoning that is described in the earliest Meccan verses of the Qur'an. This new revelation invested its recipient with messianic charisma—first as the Prophet (*nabi*) and then as the Messenger of God (*Rasul Allāh*). Already in the lifetime of the Prophet, however, the coming of Islam was seen as the realization of the messianic expectation of the advent of a new Prophet of the Gentiles (*nabi al-ummi*) and the Paraclete (Ahmad).[1]

In 622, a decade or so after receiving and reciting his first revelation in Mecca, Muhammad moved to the oasis of Yathrib, later called Medina (city [of the Prophet]), and he began to translate his apocalyptic vision into a religious movement under his charismatic leadership and thus to realize his messianic mission. There, as God's Messenger and his latest prophet, Muhammad created a community of believers engaged in the struggle (*jihād*) on the path of God, which produced a political revolution that began with the unification of Arabia and continued through the creation of an empire of conquest. The expectation of the cataclysmic destruction receded to allow the construction of a new, divinely sanctioned order. The realization of his messianic mission consisted in the construction of a new sociopolitical order that was

---

1. Q. 3:20, 75; 7:157–58; 62:2.

completed by Muhammad's first two successors as caliphs (singular, *khalifa*) and can be called a Constitutive Revolution in seventh-century Arabia. It entailed first the creation of a community of believers (*umm*a) in Medina and then the unification of the tribes of Arabia based on the submission to the One God (Islam).

This Constitutive Revolution was, however, a byproduct of a religious revolution. Its transcendental monotheism shaped the inspired—in Aristotelian terms, poetic—construction of a new order and of a world religion with a novel cosmogony and ethos expressed in "clear Arabic tongue" that was eventually presented as the religion of Abraham, the ancestor of the Arabs who was "neither a Jew nor a Christian but one who submitted to God [*muslim*]."[2] The unification of Arabia, where the language of the new revelation was the *koiné*, was itself the political consequence of Muhammad's religious revolution and of his "realized messianism."

THE RELIGIOUS CONDITIONS OF ARABIA ON THE PERIPHERY OF THREE EMPIRES

The religious conditions of Arabia on the periphery of the Persian, Roman, and Ethiopian empires provided the historical context of this Constitutive Revolution. Among these neighboring empires, the penetration of Arabia by the Persian Empire was the greatest; this was followed by that of the Ethiopian Empire (the kingdom of Aksum). The Sasanian Khosraw I conquered the Yemen in the latter part of the sixth century. The capital of the Sasanian Empire, Ctesiphon, was in Mesopotamia, close to their Lakhmid vassal state in al-Hira, which, while dominating Medina politically, was arguably the most important trading partner of Mecca in the early seventh century.[3] It was also particularly important as a channel for the transmission of religious ideas to Arabia through its flourishing Syriac literature. Yet the transmission through the city of Hira of religious beliefs that convulsed the Sasanian Empire in the late sixth century has received very little attention compared to the transmission of Judeo-Christian religious concepts presumably through the Roman

---

2. Q. 20:113; 26.195; 3:67.

3. The king of Hira, Nuʿmān III, regularly sent a caravan of spices to the ʿUkāz trade fair near Mecca (Tora-Niehoff 2011, 323n3, citing *Aghānī*).

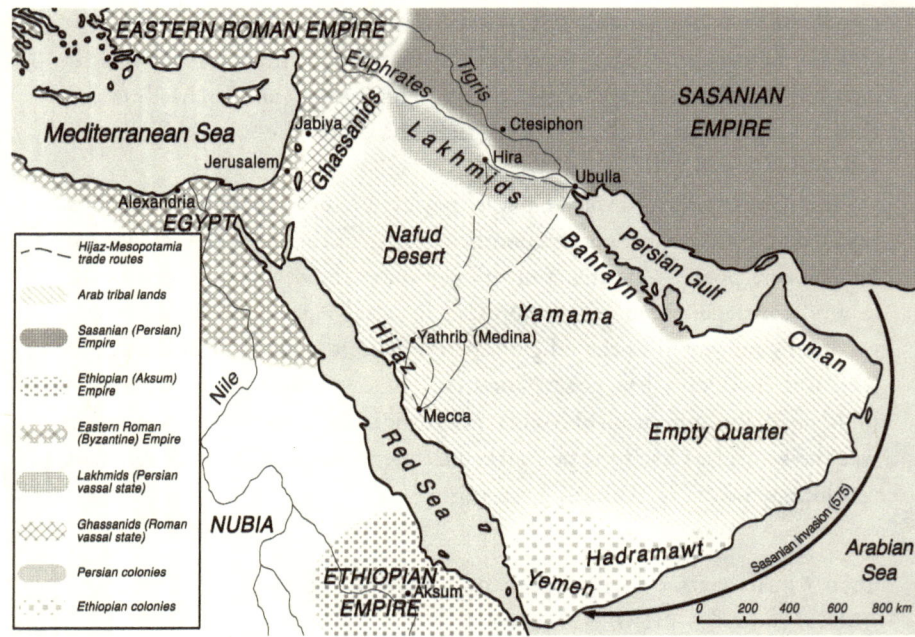

MAP 1. Arabia on the periphery of the three empires ca. Muhammad's birth (575).

Empire, which also had the Jafnid vassal tribal state in Syria. The influence on Islamic beliefs of the Ethiopian Empire, which had an extensive colony in the Yemen under a viceroy or king for half a century until the Sasanian invasion in 575, has received even less attention.

Zoroastrianism was the religion of the Sasanian imperial state, and it was not proselytizing or exportable, even though there were some Arab converts to it around the Persian Gulf.[4] It was otherwise with Manichaeism, which was proselytizing. It had developed out of the dualist Mazdaean religion of Iran during the Sasanian Revolution in the mid-third century in a radically different direction from the official Zoroastrian orthodoxy.[5] Manichaeism interacted vigorously with rival Mesopotamian gnostic Christian sects, which had already been deeply influenced by the Iranian dualism of light and dark-

---

4. Monnot 1975, 29; de Blois 1995, 49. The Qur'an (22:17) only once mentions them as the Magi (*majus*).
5. Arjomand 2019, ch.6.

ness. Manichaeism was as missionary as it was universalist. Furthermore, it was quintessentially a religion of the book, as its monastic elite, the Elect, emphasized the primacy of scriptures for guarding distortions of revelation by priests.

Māni (216–77 CE), the Messenger of Light, rose in Mesopotamia, where he was raised in a (Judeo-)Christian Baptist sect of Elkasaites and was familiar with the Gnostic Christian trends identified with Marcion and Bardaisan, which he synthesized with Mazdaean Iranian dualism to create his own world religion. He sent out missionaries from Kushan to China and was emphatic that his religion should be expressed in all languages and spread to all countries. The Manicheans gained a foothold early on in the Nabataean colonies, and they directed a successful missionary program from Babylon and the not-too-distant al-Hira, whose king, 'Amr b. 'Adi, became a Manichaean, vying with the Christian Mesopotamian sects into the first quarter of the fourth century. The mutual influence and interpenetration of the Mesopotamian Gnostic communities and Manichaeanism continued in the subsequent centuries, and many ideas traceable to the former were absorbed and systematized by the latter by the seventh century. That Manichaeism survived in Mesopotamia into the tenth century is clearly demonstrated by Ibn al-Nadim's ample and first-hand knowledge of their history, beliefs and community leadership.[6]

In the sixth century, the ruling dynasty of Hira were Nestorian Christians, but the population may have been predominantly Manichaean.[7] Meanwhile, there had been another major heresy in the Persian empire, that of Mazdak, whose followers were properly called *zindiq*. The Sasanian Kawād had supported the Mazdakites before the ferocious suppression of Mazdak's rebellion by his son Khosraw I in the 530s, and he had reportedly ordered the king of Hira to convert to Mazdakism and replaced him when he refused. Mazdakism was an offshoot of Manichaeism, and, after its suppression in Iran, many Mazdakites took refuge in Hira and intermixed with the Manichaeans of that city. Western Arabia had not been as attractive to Manichaean Nabataean traders in the fourth century as Aksum, but, as the kingdom of Hira extended

---

6. Ibn al-Nadim 2010, 507–23.
7. Ibn 'Abbās sees those Christians as instructors of the Manichaeans (Gill 1992). See also Van Reeth 2016.

its penetration of Hijaz with Sasanian backing in the mid-fifth century onward and the Ethiopian influence grew, the heterodox Manichaean-Mazdakite ideas emanating from Hira thus reached Mecca by the time of the rise of Islam as the most coherent late-antique universalist religion and were later correctly identified as *zandaqa* (interpretation [of the Avesta]).

The Quraysh had well-established commercial activities with Hira, and the Manichaean-Mazdakites of that city could easily have converted some of the Quraysh merchants. Mazdakite exiles were also found in the Sasanian colonies on the southern shore of the Persian Gulf and could have spread their influence to Mecca from there. Furthermore, the kings of Kinda in southern Arabia, who challenged those of Hira from time to time, converted to Manichaeism and later proved very receptive to the Mazdakite religion. According to Ya'qubi, one group of Arabs joined the religion of the Jews and another joined Christianity, "and yet another group became *zindiq* [*tazandaqa*] and were called the dualists." We also hear of the "Mazdakites/Manichaeans [*zanādiqa*] of Mecca" by the time of Muhammad's mission.[8]

The presence and recent missionary activity of the Manichaeans coming from Hira to Mecca during the life of Muhammad is attested both by the great antiquarian of Arab paganism, Ibn al-Kalbi (d. 820), who had been a *zindiq* before converting to Islam, and by his follower, Ibn Qutayba, in the ninth century. With the appearance of Arab Manichaean traders and missionaries from Hira and Babylon, conversion from polytheism to the Manichaean faith had increased in Mecca. As for Medina, we hear of a group of *hanifs* who refused to convert to Islam and who were led by the monk (*rāhib*, one of the ascetic Manichaean Elect) Abu 'Āmir, who had himself fought against the Muslims in the Battle of Uhud; they remained opposed to Muhammad in Medina in the last years of the Prophet's life.[9]

The Ethiopian Empire was also an important presence in Arabia. The Ethiopians had a garrison and settlements in Tihama, and, as is attested by the Qur'an's Elephant Sura, they had attacked Mecca under the viceroy of the emperor of Aksum, Abraha. The Muslim tradition claims that after establishing his state in Medina, Muhammad sent letters to the Roman caesar and the Persian khosraw and the Ethiopian negus (*najāshi*). The authenticity of these

---

8. Ya'qubi, 1:257.
9. Watt 1956, 189–90; Gil 1987; Gil 1992; de Blois 1995, 48–49.

letters is doubtful, but we have much firmer historical evidence that during the earliest persecution of his followers in Mecca and long before he may have thought of the other emperors, Muhammad tried to convert the emperor of Aksum. Some eighty-two early Muslim converts who emigrated to Ethiopia during what is called the first *hijra* were in fact Muhammad's first missionaries.[10] It is possible that Muhammad spoke some Ethiopic, and he took his young wife, 'Ā'isha, to see Ethiopians dance in Medina. He also married Umm Habiba b. Abu Sufyān, who had been among the emigrants to Aksum with her first husband. A number of Ethiopian loanwords entered the Qur'an itself in the Medinan Verses and presumably after the return of the first Muslim emigrants from Ethiopia. Notable among these are *"mā'ida"* (table), *"al-munāfiqun/nifāq"* (the hypocrites/hypocrisy), used to designate the Prophet's opponents after the disastrous Battle of Uhud in 625, and the phrase, *Shaytān al-rajim* (from the Ethiopic *rəgem*) (the accursed Satan).[11] One prominent disciple of Muhammad who stayed long in Ethiopia and had an interview with the emperor, was his cousin Ja'far b. Abi Tālib (whose later nickname, *al-tayyār* [the diviner of birds; entrails] may indicate his pre-Islamic religious status as well as his familiarity with Enochic mysteries). Ja'far told the negus that God had sent Muhammad as the messianic Gentile prophet to the ignorant people of Arabia, and he may well have brought back some Enochic notions, or even the book of Enoch, which was translated into Ethiopian by or in the sixth century and has survived only in Ethiopic. Its apocalyptic notions may even have penetrated South Arabia before the first migrants through the twenty-two Christians from Ethiopia or Najran among other early converts.[12]

In contrast to the three surrounding empires, the Arabian Peninsula on their triple periphery was primarily one of the last reservoirs of ancient paganism. The religious map of pagan Arabia was preserved in Ibn al-Kalbi's *Book of Idols*. Let us consider some of its key beliefs and practices that were carried

---

10. *Life*, 148. The number given by Ibn Sa'd 1904–28 (vol. 1, part 1:136, 138) for the two waves of migrants is smaller. Of these, thirty-three, including his daughter Ruqiyya and her husband 'Uthmān b. 'Affān, returned while Muhammad was still in Mecca; the rest remained in Ethiopia much longer—until 629.

11. Kropp 2008, 210–11.

12. *Life*, 146–48, 179–80; Tabari 1:1194–95 (translation 6:110–11); Nöldeke 1910, 47–48, 59; Watt and Bell, 1970, 120; Kropp 2008; Gilliot 1998, 120n231.

over, altered, or contradicted in Muhammad's religious revolution. It is tempting to downplay the significance of beliefs and to focus on rituals, especially on sacrifice.[13] Nevertheless, one could speak of an Arabian religion (*din al-'arab*) whose beliefs and rituals were centred on a pantheon of interrelated tribal gods. These gods had their sanctuaries in the territory of a tribe, and they were usually shared by allied tribes or those in the vicinity who were able to visit them. Cultic associations were formed around sacred enclaves of sacred stones, betyls/baetyls, and their shrines in the Arabian Peninsula. The sacred enclave was called a *hijr*, where common rituals of initiation, as well as pilgrimage to and circumambulation of the sanctuary shrine with shaven heads were performed.[14] Such sharing of the divinities, and the participation in common fairs and festivals around their sanctuaries, made for religiocultural unity. The most important divinities were Manāt, the goddess of the tribes of Aws, Khazraj, and Ghassān, the Lāt, the goddess of the Thaqif, whose shrine in Tā'if rivaled the Ka'ba as a pilgrimage center, and the 'Uzzā, the goddess of Muhammad's tribe, the Quraysh, as well as of the Kināna, the Khuzā'a, and the entire Mudar tribal confederacy. She was worshipped alongside several other deities. The three goddesses were considered the daughters of the paramount god, Allah, the creator of the world who did not have any specific cult or shrine.[15]

The Qur'ān is by far the best historical source for tracing the development from associationist polytheism (*shirk*) to Islamic monotheism in the early and doctrinally formative period, since it is our only record of Muhammad's debates with the pagans of Mecca. Muhammad's starting point in these debates was the predominant position of Allah in the associationists' pantheon, or more precisely in the congeries of gods and demons that were variously shared, as well as in the overlappingly named betyls and astral deities that were acknowledged by his pagan opponents.[16]

The Qur'ān also mentions the major religious groupings in Arabia in two verses. Beside "those who believe [*āmanu*]," "those who recognize divine partners [*sharaku*]," and the Zoroastrians (*majus*), Q. 22:17 enumerates the three

---

13. Al-Azmeh 2018a, 355; Al-Azmeh 2018b, 29–30. The latter follows Wellhausen's insistence on the primacy of cult and ritual in Semitic religion.
14. Chelhod 1955; Chelhod 1962; Retsö 2003, 587, 624.
15. Q. 33:19–21, 37:149; Wellhausen 1887, 24–45.
16. See Chabbi 1997.

cosmopolitan faiths, only one of which is given a name: the Nazarenes (*nasārā*). The other two are "those who Judaize [*hādu*]," and the "converts/converters [of religion] [*sābi'un*]." Another verse, Q. 2:62, identifies the religious communities entitled to salvation, later to be designated Peoples of the Book:

> Verily those who believe [*āmanu*], those who Judaize [*hādu*], the Nazarenes [*nasārā*] and the converts [*sābi'un*] are those who believe [*āmana*] in God and the Last Day.[17]

The identity of these three religious groups was evidently clear to the Qur'anic audience, but who were they? "Those who believe [*āmanu*]" are of course the *mu'minun*. They are "the believers" according to the concept of *imān* (faith) as the defining attribute of the *mu'minun*, developed in the Meccan Verses of the Qur'an and before Islam partly replaced it in Medina.[18] By this definition, the other peoples entitled to salvations (*man āmana*) would also be the *mu'minum*, however, but they are not. As the term can alternatively be derived from *amān* (pact), it can be argued that in Medina, it acquired a compound meaning as those who have "put themselves under the security/protection of God."[19]

"Those who Judaize" belonged to the Jewish sects, either those enumerated by Josephus or their later offshoots. The evidence that they belonged to heterodox Judaism—that is, the offshoots of the Essenes, including Judaizing Christian sects—is as strong as it is neglected. There can be little doubt that the apocalyptic notions of the Enochic and Danielic circles discussed in chapter 1 were known to the Jews of Arabia in the seventh century. It is certain that the Karaite Jews of the ninth century were called Sadducees by their opponents, while considering themselves the Righteous (*saddiqin*) and the sons of Righteousness (*sādōq*), and that their missionaries called themselves the wise

---

17. A slight variant of this verse is repeated in Q. 5:69, with the ordering of the last two groups reversed.

18. Donner 2010, 57. Lecker (2014) remains agnostic as to who, as distinct from the Muslims, they were precisely in the so-called Constitution of Medina. Following my suggestion that the Constitution of Medina is in fact a covenant of federation among the *mu'minun* (covenanters) and the *muslimun* (Arjomand 2009), Al-Azmeh (2014, 362–63) argues for understanding the latter as the "submitting [Bedouin] [*a'rāb al-muslimin*]," which in the Medinan period refers to the Bedouin who submitted to Muhammad without making the *hijra*.

19. "Those who believe in God and the Last Day" (Q. 2:62) is elsewhere replaced by "those who believe/put themselves under God's protection with him [*āmanu ma'ahu*] [i.e., Muhammad] . . . , verily God's help is near" (Q. 2:210).

(Maśkilim) in the Danielic tradition, and that they carried the religious tradition of the Essenes in the Islamic era. The Karaites and the Zadokites, both of whom rejected the oral law of the rabbis, are the same group separated by a few centuries.[20] It is thus more than probable that the Essenes, or unorthodox Jewish sectarians influenced by them, were present in seventh-century Arabia. The religious leaders of these sectarians were evidently not called rabbis but *aḥbār* (*ḥaberim* in Hebrew),[21] the designation that was distinctive of the members of the Qumran community; incidentally, quite a number of them converted to Islam.[22] The Prophet's cousin and expert of the Qur'an was known as the *ḥabr al-umma*, and the greatest authority on the apocalyptic lore who converted from Judaism was called Kaʿb al-aḥbār. Many apocalyptic notions of early Islam can be traced to Jewish sectarian sources, either directly or through the Manichaeans whose Elect called themselves the *saddiqin*, just like the latter-day Sadducees/Sons of Zadok. The Enochic pseudepigrapha were absorbed into Manichaean literature, and the Manichaeans must have translated their Enochic *Book of the Giants* from Parthian into Syriac, and possibly also into Arabic. Their influence in seventh-century Arabia thus commingled with that of the nonrabbinic Jews of Arabia.[23]

Among the Enochic ideas spread among Mesopotamian Gnostics and hence among the Manichaeans/Mazdakites of Hira, was that of the consubstantiality of God and his names, the foremost of which was Matatron—who has, according to 3 Enoch, seventy hidden names.[24] This may well have served as the key idea in Muhammad's monotheistic diplomacy for establishing the supremacy of Allah over other gods, who, as we shall see, despite being said to be mere names, were nonetheless also appropriated as some of Allah's own most beautiful names.

The other religious grouping, and the only one given a proper name, were the Nazarenes (*nasārā*). They were most probably the Nazoraeans (Ναζωραῖοι),

---

20. The Zadokite/Sadducee identity of the Qumran leaders was highlighted in chapter 1, and it can be argued that the name of the Karaite sect, *qārā'im*, was derived from *qĕri'ĕ ha-šem* associated with "the Sons of Sâdôq" in the Damascus Covenant. See Erder 1994, 197, 210–12.

21. The alternative plural is *ḥubur*—as in Kaʿb b. Mālik. See Imhod 2011, 400, line 1.

22. Rabin 1957, 116, 123, 126, citing Q. 3:110, 7.156–57, 17:108, 26:197; Newby 1988, 86; Erder 1990, 349–50.

23. Reeves 1994; Arjomand 2021.

24. Stroumsa 2003, 238n34.

who were described in the last quarter of the fourth century as the hated enemies of the Pharisees but who were also strict adherents to the Jewish law while accepting Jesus as the Christ and the son of God. The distinct combination of messianism and the Law in the Halakhic Letter of the Essene Teacher of Righteousness mentioned in chapter 1 comes to mind. The Qur'an's most likely referent is at any rate the Nazorean Jewish Christianity with which Muhammad very probably became acquainted in Mecca, as he briefly adopted their ritual of praying toward Jerusalem.[25] Although the sixth-century persecution of the "martyrs of Najran" by the Jewish king of Himyar, Yusuf, in the first quarter of the sixth century is on record, caution may be required in identifying the referent simply as Christian in view of the lack of archaeological evidence for the presence of Christianity in western Arabia.[26] In northeastern Arabia, the term *nasārā* referred to different groups of followers of Jesus of Nazareth, groups that Muhammad probably did not know.[27] As was mentioned above, the so-called first *hijra* to Christian Ethiopia may have acted as a stronger channel of transmission than that of the Arab Christians.

And who, finally, were the last group among the people [of the Book] "who believe in God and the Last Day?" Just before his conversion, 'Umar b. al-Khattāb burst into a gathering of some forty Muslim men and women with his sword unsheathed, saying "I am making for Muhammad the convert [*sābi'*] ... to kill him!" This was his very last pagan outburst, however, and a few days later, 'Umar himself "suddenly converted [*qad saba'a*]!" This must have been clearly understood by contemporaries and was not lost on the Qur'an commentators. A tribe accused at sword's point of idolatry by Khalid b. al-Walid similarly cried out *sabana, sabana!* (we have changed our religion/converted)! The earliest Muslims themselves were called *sābi'a* "converts" by their pagan opponents.[28]

Ibn al-Kalbi identifies the three cosmopolitan religions as Judaism, Christianity, and *zandaqa*, and he gives the regions where they were practiced. The *zandaqa* were indeed with the people of Quraysh; they came from Hira and

---

25. De Blois 2011, 622–23.
26. Nebes 2011.
27. They consisted of splinter communities of dissident Nestorians around the Persian Gulf heading southward to Yamāma, to Jacobites and Melkites. See de Blois 2002; Widengren 1955, 60–62; Villeneuve 2010, 227–29.
28. Ibn Ishāq, 225; *Life*, 156; Wellhausen 1887, 234–38; Widengren 1955, 135.

were merchants.[29] Hira, as was pointed out, had been the refuge of the Manicheans and the Mazdakites since the sixth century. *Zandiq*, a Persian loanword not found in the Qur'an, refers to Māni, Manichaeans, and the Mazdakites in Muslim sources. A strong case can be made for Manichaeans as the *sābi'un*, since their ritual prayer, alms-giving, and fasting were to become the pillars of Islam.[30] Even stronger evidence in support of this intended and understood meaning of the term *sābi'un* comes from the Persian translation of the Qur'an, along with the Great Commentary (wrongly) attributed to Tabari, as well as from Biruni, who attests that the Manichaeans formed a large community in Samarqand in his time, and they called themselves the *sābi'un*. The Samanid doctors who composed the Great Commentary from 961 to 975, translated *sābi'un* in Q. 22:17 as "those who turned from one religion to another [*dini be-dini shodand*]"; this is glossed in one manuscript as "*naghushgān* [Manichaeans]."[31] It is not translated at all in Q. 2:62; rather, it is simply replaced by *khorram-dinān* (Mazdakites)! This testimony supports the identification of the Mazdakites/Manichaeans as "the converts." The tenth-century Muslim doctors in Central Asia understood the term *sābi'un* in its Qur'anic sense. If we accept their rendering of *sābi'un*, we must at least include the Manichaeans as the main component.[32]

This brings us to the presumption of the existence of a distinct group of Arab monotheists called the Hanifs (hanifiyya/hunafā') whose beliefs included the foundation of the Ka'ba by Abraham and the settlement in Mecca of his son Ishmael, the ritual of *hajj*, and the sacrifice of animals consecrated to the Ka'ba. The term *hanif* is etymologically puzzling and controversial.[33] Before the rise of Muhammad, one of the Hanifs, Zayd b. 'Amr b. Nufayl, accused

---

29. See Ibn al-Kalbi as translated in Monnot 1975, 29. Muhammad's cousin, Ibn 'Abbās, must have known them and he attests that they were Hira merchants.

30. Ballamy 1996. De Blois (2002, 6–7) shows that the Aramaic word for the righteous/just, *zaddiq*, which was used to designate the Elect as the highest rank of the Manichaean hierarchy, is the cognate of the Middle Persian *zandiq* (*mzaddeq*, the one who justifies/makes righteous, which is itself the cognate of Mazdak!) and the Arabic *siddiq*.

31. The term *naghushgān* technically means "auditors," the lowest rank in the Manichaean hierarchy to which St. Augustine belonged in his youth; however, in this case, it must be taken to mean Manichaeans generically.

32. *Tarjuma* 1:65; 4:1054; Biruni, 191; Al-Azmeh 2014, 363–64.

33. De Blois (2002, 23) translates this word as a gentile, while Al-Azmeh opts for a possible literal meaning as "the bent."

the Quraysh of abandoning the religion of Abraham (*din/millat Ibrāhim*), whose image hanged in the Ka'ba: "Oh Quraysh, by Him in whose hand is the soul of Zayd, not one of you follow the religion of Abraham but I!" The *hanif tabliya* formula for the ritual of *hajj*, however, was significantly monotheistic, and unlike those of the other tribes mentioned above, it did not identify any partners for God. There is clear indication that the Hanif community expected a new prophet as two of their poets claimed prophecy: Abu Qays b. al-Aslat, the leader of the Aws Allāh tribe in Medina, and Umayya b. Abi'l-Salt in Tā'if, where some dissident Jewish merchants had been banished by the leaders of Yathrib Jewish community. The identification of the Hanifiyya with Abraham was easy, as he and his son Ismael were already considered the ancestors of the Quraysh at the time of Josephus. With the biblicizing outlook of the Qur'an in Medina, the ancestral significance of Abraham and his sons increased.[34] Muhammad would successfully identify with the hunafā' and, as we shall see, adopted their core Abrahamic tenet and ritual for Islam. In the course of this adoption, Muhammad corrected one pious returnee from Ethiopian, who had evidently converted to ascetic Manichaeism and thus qualified as a *hanif*, by urging him to follow the approved, nonascetic or simple, Abrahamic Hanifiyya, which he called *al-hanifiyya al-samha*.[35]

The evidence from the Qur'an itself only partly supports this picture. The word *hanif* occurs twelve times in the singular, almost exclusively in connection with Abraham, and twice in the plural—and in all these cases it is used adjectivally. Indeed, *hanif* is the religion (*milla*) of Abraham (Q. 6:161). It is this religion of Abraham that is then generalized into the *hanif* religion (*al-din al-hanif*) in the late Medinan portions of the Qur'an (10:105).[36] The term never occurs as a noun describing a group. This means there is no evidence for the existence of a distinct group of monotheists other than the five above-mentioned Peoples of the Book who are entitled to salvation. On the other hand, the virtually exclusive association of the term with Abraham strongly suggests that the group it came to designate is none other than the Sabaeans (*sābi'un*), who believed in Abraham and claimed to be in possession of his scriptures (*suhuf*), which were acknowledged in the Qur'an (53:37; 87:19). The

---

34. Sinai 2011.
35. *Life*, 98; Rubin 1990, 89–96, 100–104; Rubin 1995, 72–75; Gil 1992, 43; Bashear 2004.
36. This is duplicated in Q. 30:29.

author of a ninth-century commentary on the Sabaean Book identifies the two groups: "the *hunafā'* are the Abrahamic Sabaeans." Ibn al-Nadim calls them Chaldeans, "the nation who is called the Abrahamic *hanifiyya* and have the Book of Abraham to which they swear." The great al-Mas'udi in the mid-tenth century categorically identifies the same people with the *hunafā'*.[37] In short, the *hunafā'* are none other than the *sābi'un*.

The one question remaining is why was the meaning of the term *sābi'un* lost in the rest of the Muslim world? The identity of "those who Judaize" became quickly fixed after Muhammad's clash with the Jews of Medina, as did that of the Nazarenes with the conquest of Roman Syria and the movement of the Umayyad caliphate to Damascus. Of the rest of the dissident Peoples of the Book, some opponents of Muhammad who left a historical memory of their opposition to him contested his appropriation of the designation *hanif* are recorded as such in our sources. Others, who were inspired by Persian heresies but had no imperial protections from the very beginning, became more and more scattered, and the blanket term that serves best to designate them pejoratively is the non-Qur'anic *zindiq*. The *sābi'un* thus became an empty verbal residue. The term was taken as the designation of the "Sabaeans" as a specific People of the Book whom nobody could identify![38]

---

37. Ibn al-Nadim 2010, 495 (citing al-Kindi); Haddad 1974, 117; de Blois 1995, 42 (citing al-Mas'udi's *Tanbih*).

38. The author was Ahmad b. 'Abdallāh b. Salām, a client of the caliph's father, Harun al-Rashid; he showed that the Sabaeans "believe in Abraham and attribute to him the Scripture (*suhuf*) God revealed to him." They further believed that the Creator's messengers, beginning with Adam, incarnated the Law (*nāmus*; the term used for Gabriel by Muhammad's mentor, Waraqa b. Nawfal). See Ibn al-Nadim 2010, 35, 495–532; Widengren 1955, 63, 101. The origins of the book are explained by an anecdote according to which Caliph al-Ma'mun (d. 833) wanted to convert the star-worshippers of Harran at sword point when a learned jurist advised them to claim to be the vanished Sabaeans, and thus a People of the Book entitled to God's protection! They made their claim stick, and they were followed by some other Mesopotamian minority groups that successfully claimed to be the Sabaeans. See de Blois 1995, 42–48. This is not to say, however, that their claim was baseless. Just like the Manichaean Sabaeans of Central Asia, the Sabaeans of Harran had a good claim to be one of the Peoples of the Book as heirs to the Manichaeanized Mesopotamian Gnostic tradition. Ibn al-Nadim presents the (Christian) Chaldeans, the Sabaeans, and the Manichaeans in the same chapter (9.1).

Self-references in the Qur'an to the "Arabic Recitation (*qur'ān*)" (Q. 20:113, 42:7, 43:3) and an "Arabic judgment" (Q. 13:37), and to "Arabic tongue" (Q. 16:103, 26:195, 46:12) effectively present Islam as an alternative to foreign religions.[39] "When Muhammad brought the Qur'ān in Arabic," as Newby puts it, "Judaism and the various forms of Christianity were already hopelessly compromised by the strong identification with foreign domination, taxation and warfare."[40] Muhammad therefore began his prophetic career in Mecca as God's messenger to the Arabs, "a people [*qaum*] to whom no warner came before thee" (Q. 32:3); or "And so We have revealed to thee an Arabic Recitation [*qur'ān*], that thou mayest warn the Mother of Cities and those who dwell about it . . ." (Q. 42:7).

As the divinely inspired gentile prophet of the "Arabic Recitation," Muhammad fully appropriated the other imported religions. He reshaped the identity of the Judaizers into the followers of Moses, and that of the Nazarenes into the followers of the Anointed Jesus (al-Masih). Even more crucially, the Hunafā'/Sābi'un were Islamicized and Arabized simultaneously as the followers of Abraham.[41] The appropriation of Abraham and Ishmael in the late Medinan period ends with the assertion that Abraham and his descendants were neither Christian nor Jews but Muslims (Q. 2:125–40), and it marks the affirmation of Islam as both the pristine and recovered and the perfected monotheistic religion of the One God.

To summarize our analysis of the last two nonpagan religious categories, I have proposed considering the Hanifiyya-Sābi'a as one single category of literate Arabs in the Hijaz acquainted with the world religions of Late Antiquity who shared the same salvation-oriented religious outlook but did not form any fully differentiated religious community or sect. Muhammad created two separate categories from this composite group, making the Hunafā' into pristine monotheists by linking them with Abraham as the ancestor of the

---

39. The adjective *'arabiy* (Arabic) is said to occur for the first time in the Qur'an.
40. Newby 1988, 47–48.
41. Before the conquest of Palestine from the Byzantines, the Arab commanders demanded: "God gave this land to our father Abraham and to his posterity after him. We are the children of Abraham. You have possessed our land for long enough. Cede it to us peacefully, and we shall not invade your territory. If not, we shall take back from you with usurious interest what you have seized" (Kaegi 1992, 214, citing Bishop Sebēos).

Arabs and the founder of the Ka'ba, while leaving the Sabaeans as a "People of the Book" without further identification.[42]

Our analysis thus demonstrates that Muhammad drew two critical components of Islam from the ecumenical culture of Late Antiquity: apocalyptic messianism and the belief in revelation through God's messengers both angelic and human. Apocalyptic messianism supplied the key factor in the causation of the revolutionary break with the embedded religion of the clans in Arabia. The first component explains Muhammad's motivation to revolution in Arabia, and it was drawn from the belief of the Jews of Arabia in the coming of the Gentile Prophet of the End of Time and from the Manichaean/Mazdakite idea of the Paraclete (Ahmad) promised by the last messiah. The second was derived from the Manichaean belief in a series of divine messengers as agents of the progressive salvation of humankind and goes some way in explaining the spread and global consequences of Islam, notably the Muslim imperial expansion and the axial civilization it gave birth to.

APOCALYPTIC MESSIANISM AND MUHAMMAD'S REVOLUTIONARY MOTIVATION

Apocalyptic messianism, as we have seen in chapter 1, was the contribution made not by the winners but by the losers of the Maccabean Revolution who withdrew to the desert to form the Qumran community. Although the Qumran settlement was destroyed by the Roman army of Vespasian, the messianism they had sustained in institutionalized form for two centuries survived them. The broader apocalyptic frame of messianism was carried by them and by other sectarian groups through the intertestamental period and was taken up by the Christians and the Manichaeans. The Enochic circles effected the otherworldly transposition of political messianism in the Similitudes of Enoch (1 Enoch 37–71), as did the Christians gradually after the destruction of the

---

42. Medieval and modern scholars have consequently erred in searching for two distinct sects as the referent of these alternate designations for what must have been a distinct but vaguely defined, salvation-oriented, religious milieu consisting of a congeries of literate individuals who held some or all of a cluster of beliefs. There were doubtless shades of difference and subcategories of individuals partaking in this common, salvation-oriented, religious outlook in the same small urban milieus of Mecca and Medina that are impossible to determine given our meager body of evidence.

Temple in 70 CE. Other apocalyptic notions survived and coalesced with messianism—notably, that of the prophet of the End of Time, which informs the apocalyptic reconstruction of Elijah as the returning prophet. The apocalyptic perspective of the book of Daniel was especially privileged by its inclusion in the Old Testament canon. The Manichaeans, whose scriptures include the *Book of Giants*, were probably the main transmitters of Enochic notions from the Qumran and other ancient sources to Arabia. Māni's claim to be the "Seat of the Prophets," and the Paraclete Jesus Christ had promised to send were doubtless transmitted to Arabia through the Aramaic translations of the Manichaean scriptures.[43] The specific channel of transmission cannot be reliably determined but at any rate matters little as sectarian identities were imprecise and many religious communities shared a common, ecumenical pool of semiotic ideas and sacred symbols.

The apocalyptic worldview found a forceful statement in the early-seventh-century, Meccan verses of the Qur'an on the coming of the Hour. Indeed, the purpose of the revelation in this earliest period is to confirm Muhammad's mission as the Warner (*nadhir*) of the imminence of the Hour. The warning may initially have been that of a pagan *nadhir* concerning a ritual transgression punished by the god/betyl of a sanctuary ("betylic wrath")![44] But it was soon coupled with *bashir* (the bringer of good news) to align it with the Qumran-Manichaean conception in the course of Muhammad's monotheistic revolution. By holding up the vision of the imminent and complete destruction of the prevalent order, apocalyptic messianism generated a powerful motivation to absolute political action aiming at the destruction and the reconstruction of the political order, as evidenced in the inception of some two decades of revolutionary "struggle (*jihād*) on the path of God") in the remote Arabian periphery of the ancient empires, a struggle that changed the course of world history.

Muhammad was an orphan (Q. 43:6) from an important Quraysh family; his father ('Abdallāh) is said to have been a worshipper of the predominant God, Allah. He lost both his parents in infancy (Q. 93:6) and was raised by his uncle Abu Tālib. One day in the month of Ramadan, at the end of the first decade of the seventh century, Muhammad, now a trader in skins and about forty years of age, was in seclusion for expiation according to an ancient custom

---

43. H.-Ch. Puech 1972, 538; Stroumsa 1986.
44. Rubin 2001, 442; Al-Azmeh 2018b, 355.

of the Quraysh, when he received the call to prophecy.[45] Muhammad was shaken until he was reassured by Waraqa b. Nawfal b. Asad b. 'Abd al-'Uzza, a cousin of his former employer and current wife, Khadija, from the family of worshippers of 'Uzza who, however, read scriptures in "the barbarian ['ajami]" languages. From what we have said above, we suspect the "barbarian" language in question was Syriac or Aramaic and that the scripture was Manichaean.[46] Waraqa had reportedly taken an interest in Muhammad since the latter's childhood, and he now told Khadija the following: "Verily Muhammad is the prophet of this people. I knew that a prophet of this people was to be expected; his time has come!" Another trope on prophecy that could have had currency in the literate milieu of Mecca is attributed to another relative of Khadija, the Meccan *hanif*, Zayd b. 'Amr b. Naufayl, who had earlier learned the religion of "Abraham, the friend of the Rahmān" from a monk (presumably one of the Manichaean Elect). Zayd predicted the coming of a new prophet, though he did not expect to live long enough to see one: "I expect a prophet from the descendants of Ishmael ... who has the seal of prophecy between his shoulders. His name is Ahmad." The Qur'ān was to confirm that God sends to the "Gentiles [*ummiyyun*] ... a messenger, (one) of themselves, to recite to them His signs ... " (Q. 62:2). And Muhammad was indeed "the gentile prophet" (*al-nabiyy al-ummi*), whom they find "written down with them in the Torah and the Gospel ... Believe then in God, and in his messenger, the gentile prophet ... " (Q. 7:156, 158). As such, he was the expected messianic figure predicted by the Torah, and by the good news of the last messiah, Jesus the son of Mary. Like Māni, who made the same claim but is nowhere named, he was also "the Messenger of God and the Seal of the Prophets." (Q. 33:40)

---

45. The custom of *tahannuth* involved an expiatory seclusion on Mount Hirā'; it was followed by feeding the poor and it ended with the circumambulation of the Ka'ba. See Kister 1968; Al-Azmeh 2014, 235–36.

46. *Life*, 83, 107; Tabari, 1:1144; translation in 6:64; Gilliot 1998, 102. The evidence of the Qur'an itself (16:103)—namely, that the informer did not speak a foreign tongue but good Arabic—leaves Waraqa b. Nawfal as the only viable candidate for being the Prophet's informer. The early commentaries, however, identify a number of foreigners, mostly slaves, as Muhammad's "informers," and they consider these informers either Jewish or Christian. The Ethiopian connection of a few and the familiarity of one of them with the stories of the Persian epic heroes, Rostam and Esfandiār, however, suggest that Manichaeans/Mazdakites must at least be included.

The Qur'an asserts that Jesus had the "knowledge of the Hour" at his calling (Q. 43:61) and brought the good news of the coming of a messenger (Q. 61:5). Taken together, these Qur'anic verses gave rise to the belief in the Second Coming of Jesus as a sign of the Hour in Islamic apocalyptic lore. In Qur'an 61:6, Jesus the son of Mary tells the children of Israel "I am the Messenger of God to you . . ., the bringer of good tidings [*mubashshir*] of a Messenger who shall come after me and whose name shall be more praised/Ahmad [*ismuhu ahmadu*]." This statement is a reasonable paraphrase of the promise of the coming of the Paraclete in John 16:13–14. Ibn Isḥāq quotes John 15.23–26 verbatim, rendering the term *Paraclete* by the Syriac *al-Munhammanna*, which he takes to mean Muhammad! In a poem addressed to the hostile leaders of the Quraysh, Abu Tālib, Muhammad's uncle and protector in his early days in Mecca, identifies him as "a prophet like Moses described in the oldest books" and the promised *ahmad*. The identity of Ahmad as the Paraclete (Comforter) is confirmed by the oldest extant commentary on Qur'an 61:6.[47]

The Hebrew cognate of the word for the bringer of good tidings, *mubashshir* (מבשר), is found in the Qumran fragment, 11QMelchizedek13, to describe Melkizedek, the apocalyptic high priest and savior of the righteous, as the bringer of the good tidings of salvation indicated in Isaiah 52:7. Melkizedek is he who is anointed by the Spirit of God (see Psalm 11:1 and its Qumran commentary). The Qur'anic statement, however, is even closer to Manichaeism—both etymologically, as *b-sh-r*, the root of *bashir* and *mubashshir* is a Persian loanword; and substantively, as a paraphrase of a Manichaean prophetological trope.[48] Biruni gives us a striking presentation of the prophet Māni as the forerunner of Muhammad: "In his gospel . . . he says that he is the Paraclete announced by the Messiah, and that he is the seal of the prophets (*i.e.*, the last of them)."[49] Melkizedek served as the archetype of Christ and the Paraclete in the Mesopotamian Gnostic literature down to the fifth or sixth centuries, and he was adopted by the Manichaeans.[50] The notion of divine epiphany in Melkizedek, Christ, and the Paraclete is echoed in the

47. *Life*, 160; Rubin 1995, 23.
48. Jeffery 1938, 79–80. The term is translated by van Henten (2007, 23) as "the messenger of good." *Bashir* occurs nine more times adjectivally to describe prophets and messengers, but in those cases the term is accompanied by the words "and warners [*mundhar*]." See Kassis 1983, 339.
49. Biruni, 190.
50. Van Reeth 2012b.

Qur'an, where "the Anointed, Jesus son of Mary" is called "the Messenger of God and His word [as in John's Gospel] and a spirit from Him [*ruḥunminhu*]" (Q. 4:171), in line with the Melkizedek/Paraclete inspiration.[51] Just like in the case of Mānī, we may conclude, simply replacing Ahmad for Mānī, that Muhammad claimed to be the Paraclete Jesus had promised to send.

The influence of the Gospel of John must thus have been reinforced through the more immediate Manichaeism of the Hanif/Sābi'i community. To this historical evidence for the presence of Manichaeans in Arabia at the time of Muhammad's mission mentioned in the previous section, we must add the strong evidence for the influence of Manichaeans on Muhammad from the striking typological similarity between Islam and Manichaeism as world religions of salvation, and between their architects as systematic religious thinkers. We have Mānī's extant words that "this revelation of mine ... and my living books, my wisdom [*khrad*] and knowledge [*dāneshn*] are above and better than those of religions of earlier generations." They demonstrate that the coupling of wisdom (*ḥikma*) and knowledge (*'ilm*) to describe divine revelation is frequently found in the Qur'an. This notion was appropriated, alongside the Manichaean prophetology that God sends messengers bringing his revelation to different generations of mankind.[52]

Muhammad, who called himself the Seal of the Prophets as Mānī had most probably done. We see, for example, in Biruni's eleventh-century translation/citation of the opening passage of Mānī's *Shāpuragān* that Mānī calls himself the successor of the earlier prophets Zoroaster, the Buddha, and Jesus, as God's envoy to the last generation and their Seal.[53] The striking notion of the Seal of the Prophets has been examined by many since Biruni, but not the new designation of Muhammad in the Qur'an as the Messenger (*rasul*) (instead of prophet [*nabi*]) in the same verse. This term has never been properly explained.

Mānī called himself the "Messenger [*šelikhā*] in Aramaic-Syriac, *apostelos* [Greek] of Jesus Christ," alongside his primary self-designation as the Messenger

---

51. The variant in Q. 3:45 is "a word from Him" (*kalamatin minhu*).
52. Widengren 1955, 130–31; Widengren 1974; Asmussen 1975, 12 (M5794I, translation); Arjomand 2021b. The Iranian-inspired coupling of wisdom and knowledge, however, is also found in the Dead Sea Scrolls (Shaked 1972, 440–41) and in 4 Ezra 14:47.
53. Biruni, 190. This is cited in Rodinson (1971, 63).

of Light (*rwšny fryštg*).⁵⁴ The Qur'an never uses *rasul* for the Apostles of Jesus Christ, for whom the term *hawāriyun*—a loanword from the Ethiopic New Testament is used.⁵⁵ The Avestan term *fryštg/freštag* used by Mānī' was readily available in its Syriac rendering as *šelikhā* in the small, religiously literate milieu of Mecca to be discussed presently. The term *fryštg/freštag* (literally, the sent one) was used by Mānī not only for himself and the prophets before him but also for angels as well as. The Qur'an likewise often speaks of God's angels and his messengers in the same breath (e.g., Q. 22:75). In a late Medinan verse (Q. 2:98), the archangels Gabriel and Michael are included among God's "angels and messengers." This late verse became the basis for the identification of the unnamed but high-ranking heavenly messenger of Qur'an 69:40 and Qur'an 81:19–21 with Gabriel as the conveyer of revelation. There is ample evidence in the Qur'an (17:96–97, 25:8, 25:23) that God's sent ones/messengers were primarily heavenly and not human.⁵⁶ It was in response to this Manichaean-derived notion spreading among Muhammad's opponents that God instructed him thus: "Say, Glory be to my Lord! I am but a man, a messenger" (Q. 17:95).⁵⁷ The term *rasul* had been used fourteen times, at least twice as often in its passive participle form, *mursal* (sent), usually in the plural and with reference to the messengers sent by God, including angels. *Fryštg* is a past participle that means "sent/the sent one" in Middle Persian and corresponds linguistically to *mursal* (the sent one) and substantively to *rasul* (messenger).⁵⁸ It was chosen by Muhammad, in preference to *nabi* (prophet), as his formal title in Medina: God's Messenger (*rasul Allāh*).

---

54. Mānī is also the messenger from the paradise of light, as well as the messenger sent by Vohu Manah of Light (*whmn rošn*). See Widengren 1945, 13, 29–33.
55. Widengren 1955, 15.
56. Widengren 1955, 15, 96–102.
57. It is highly significant that the above-mentioned affirmation of the humanity of the Messenger of God who was not an angel occurs in the Meccan sura on Muhammad's heavenly journey (Q. 17), which he evidently saw and recited as the vindication of his prophetic claim. The Prophet's night journey (*mi'raj, isrā'*), during which he met God, is itself proof of his familiarity with the Mazdaean notion of the heavenly journey, which is attested for both Mānī and his Zoroastrian nemesis, Kartir, and was known in Arabia through the 1 Enoch and 4 Ezra of heterodox Judaism and from Iran through Mesopotamia. Equally well-known is the Iranian provenience of the eschatological bridge (*chinvat, sirāt*), and the apocalyptic trumpet (*sur*) of the angel Isrāfil. See Busse 1991; Widengren 1950, 59–76; Widengren 1955, 107; Duchesne-Guillemin 1979; Rabin 1957.
58. The term goes back to the Gathic (Yasna 49.8), thus demonstrating Mānī's knowledge of the Old Avesta and his adoption of the archaic term for his own purposes. See Arjomand 2021.

I submit that the Qur'anic "Messenger," *rasul*, is none other than the Arabic translation via Syriac of Māni's *freštag*.

Muhammad's messianic title is more directly relevant to our purpose. It is never *messiah*, that term being exclusively reserved for Jesus despite the evident inconvenience of having to admit his Second Coming as a sign of the Hour (Q. 43:61). Jesus Christ is called the Anointed, Jesus the son of Mary (*al-Masih 'Isā*), four times in the Qur'an.[59] We should recall that Māni, facing the same problem four centuries before Mohammad, made the divine epiphany (not incarnation) in the historical Jesus of Nazareth distinct from the divine hypostasis he called the Jesus of Splendor (*Ishō' ziwā* in Syriac). At the same time, he appropriated an apocalyptic Christian term found only in the Gospel of John (14:16, 15:25–26), the Paraclete (comforter, *prqlt/paraqlitā* in Syriac). After Jesus, the Paraclete as divine epiphany appeared in Paul as the messenger of light. After Paul, Māni was sent as the Paraclete according to the prophecy of Jesus himself (John 14:16). This made Māni, among other things, the "Messenger of Jesus Christ."

The Qur'an paraphrases the same Johanine prophecy of Jesus giving the good news of the one Ahmad coming after him has been mentioned. In four other Qur'anic verses, however, the prophet is named Muhammad. This adjectival epithet, Muhammad, is a plausible Arabic rendition of Manuhmed/Manvahmed, the Manichaean variant of Wohu Manah (Intellect, the Manichaean Living Spirit).[60] According to Ibn Ishāq, Muhammad is Munahhemanā in Syriac and Paraclete (Barqalitus) in Latin. This coupling of Ahmad and *Munhammanna* suggests that both the Greek and the Syriac terms for the Paraclete were semiotically ecumenical and generally understood. I consider this evidence sufficient to establish that the Qur'anic Ahmad is the Paraclete of Māni.[61]

Ibn Ishāq's statement also throws light on the provenance of Muhammad's very unusual and adjectival proper name to which we can now turn.[62] Whatever his personal name might have been, it left no trace in the Qu'ran, which calls him Muhammad four times only—once Muhammad, the Messenger of God (Q. 48:29) and once the Messenger of God and the Seal of the Prophets (Q.

---

59. See Q. 3:45 and 4:171. Jesus is referred to twice as "the Anointed son of Mary" in Q. 5:17.
60. Van Reeth 2012a, 437.
61. Arjomand 2021.
62. *Life*, 104 (see also Guillaum's note on p. 1). In fact, even more intriguing than the Syriac *al-Munhammanna* is the "praised Lord of the Jews" (*rbhd b-mhmd*), which is found in a sixth-century Najran inscription. See Al-Azmeh 2014, 313.

33:40). The charismatic community Muhammad created on the basis of his new revelation required a new identity for those admitted to it. For himself, he thus assumed a sacred name, Muhammad—sacralized as he was praised by God's angels. Later commentators were at great pains to explain the fact that neither Muhammad nor its equivalent, Ahmad, could be found during pre-Islamic paganism (*jāhiliyya*), and offered no explanation for his prohibition of adding his patronymic (*kunya*) to his name. Sacred names were also given to his closest disciples. Unlike his own given name, which was thus forcibly condemned to oblivion, the historical sources have retained faint memories of those as epithets—Abu Bakr al-Siddiq, 'Umar al-Fāruq, and above all, 'Ali al-A'lā' as the epiphany of God Most High on the model of Melkizedek.[63] As shown by Ibn Sa'd and our other early sources, Muhammad gave new names to his other disciples and their wives and children as well. Equally significant was his disallowing of pagan theophoric or otherwise offensive names associated with the prohibited rituals of Arabian paganism. He typically changed theophoric names that indicated the worship of the pagan gods, such as 'Abd al-Shams, 'Abd al-'Uzza, and 'Abd al-Muttalib, to names like 'Abd Allāh and 'Abd al-Rahmān. He also encouraged the use of his own name, Muhammad, and to a lesser extent, Ahmad, as well as those of a number of prophets, notably Abraham.[64]

The attestation of messianic expectations among the Jews of Arabia in Muslim traditions cannot be dismissed as an Islamic version of *praeparatio evangelicorum*, since this attestation is corroborated by both Jewish and Syriac sources.[65] One particular tradition, doctored to suggest that the Jews of Yathrib (the future Medina), expected their city to become "the sacred enclave/place of migration (*muhājar*) for a prophet from the Quraysh," retains the significant apocalyptic phrase, "at the End of Time" (*fī ākhir al-zamān*).[66] Furthermore, it is clear from the Qur'an that the acceptance of Muhammad's prophetic claim by the few converts among the "People of the Book" was of

---

63. Van Reeth 2012b, 11–14, 25. Amir-Moezzi (2016) insists that the early Shi'ite tradition has as equal a claim to historicity as the Sunni, and plausibly speculates that 'Ali al-A'lā' was, to some extremists (*ghulāt*)—members of the early charismatic community of believers—the expected Messiah to act as the Riser (*qā'im*) of the Resurrection and that Ahmad was his Paraclete.

64. Benkheira 2013.

65. *Life*, 197–98, 240; Ibn Sa'd 1904–28, vol. 1, part 1:103–4; Lewis 1953; Crone and Cook 1977, ch. 1.

66. Ibn Ishāq 1858, 13–14, my translation; Guillaume's translation in *Life* (7) is misleading.

great psychological importance to his early career. To those who accepted him, Muhammad was indeed the gentile prophet sent to the people of Arabia, and he was the prophet of the End of Time.

In the earliest Meccan period, as Muhammad encountered mounting opposition from his own oligarchic clan of Quraysh, he was repeatedly told in the Qur'an to distance himself from them and to seek confirmation from the people to whom "the Book and the Knowledge" had already been given (Q. 3:158, 4:57). The recognition of Muhammad as the prophet of the End of Time by literate (heterodox) Jews clearly meant a lot to Muhammad, since they were the ones who knew the Book sent down by God and since they could read the signs (*āyāt*) of the new revelation now sent down as a "recitation in Arabic" (*qur'ān 'arabī*) (Q. 12:1).[67] Indeed, the Qur'an contains evidence of their acceptance of his messianic claim:

> Say to them [i.e., to the recalcitrant Meccans], "O Muhammad, Whether you believe in [the Qur'an] or not, those who have been given the Knowledge before it, when it is recited to them, fall upon their faces in prostration." And they say, "Glory be to our Lord! Our Lord's promise has been fulfilled." And they fall upon their faces weeping ... (Q. 17:107)

As for the apocalyptic dimension of messianism, there is ample evidence of the imminent cataclysm expressing divine wrath in the early, Meccan, verses of the Qur'an, which speak of the coming of the Hour: "The Hour has drawn near and the moon is split" (Q. 54:1); "The Hour is coming, no doubt of it" (Q. 22:7 and 40:59[61]); "Haply the Hour is near" (Q. 33:63 and 42:17[16]); and "surely the earthquake of the Hour is a mighty thing" (Q. 22:1). The apocalyptic Hour is the hour of calamity that precedes the Resurrection. Such cosmic cataclysms as the smoke (*dukhān*) (Q. 44:44, 9), the rolling-up (*takwīr*) of the sun (Q. 81), the darkening of the stars and the movement of the mountains (Q. 81:2–4), the splitting of the sky (*infitār* [an Ethiopian loanword]—Q. 82), and the scattering of the stars and the swarming over of the seas (Q. 82:2–4) are given as the signs of the Day of Resurrection, "when the tombs are overthrown" (Q. 82:5) The Qur'an also speaks of "the day the earth shall be transformed to other than the earth" (Q. 14:49). The mountains will be pulverized into dust (Q. 56:4–6) or become like plucked tufts of wool (Q. 70:9, 101:5). But

---

67. *Life*, 240–41; Ibn Sa'd 1904–28, vol. 1, part 1:104, 108; Wellhausen 1883, 550; Rahman 1976, 11–12; Retsö 2011, 289.

the final day has no precedent. It is indeed "the day when the earth is split asunder about them as they hasten forth" (Q. 50:43).

To these generic and pagan signs of the catastrophe of the End of Time can be added signs of Judeo-Christian-Manichaean derivation through the Hunafā'/Sābi'un. There are also signs drawn from the Iranian religious notions of the Hanif-Converts: The appearance of the Beast (Q. 27:82). At the Hour, "the Trumpet [*sur*] shall be blown; that is the Day of the Threat.... And listen thou for the day when the caller shall call from a near place. On the day they hear the Cry [*sayha*] in truth, that day is the day of coming forth" (Q. 50:19, 40–41).[68] "The day the Trumpet [*nāqur*] sounds shall be a hard and joyless day for the unbelievers" (Q. 74:8). "For the Trumpet shall be blown, and whosoever is in the heavens and whosoever is in the earth shall swoon, save whom God wills. Then it shall be blown again, and lo, they shall stand, beholding. And the earth shall shine with the light of its Lord ..." (Q. 39:69–70). Among the few signs of social disorder accompanying cosmic cataclysms, at least one clearly derives from the Mazdaean religion—in all likelihood through Manichaeism: "And when the Blast shall sound, upon the day when a man shall flee from his brother, his mother, his father, his consort, his sons" (Q. 80:33–36). More importantly, this final transfiguration of the Earth ushered in by the Hour is presumably "the new creation" (Q. 14:22), which corresponds to the Avestan notion of *frašo kereti* (renewal of the world) adopted by Mānī.[69]

The Enochic idea of the heavenly tablet (1 Enoch 90), multiply transmitted through Manichaeism and heterodox Judaism, providing the archetype of all revealed books, is crucial in informing the Qur'anic conception of revelation according to which the heavenly archetype and eternal source of all revelation is "the preserved tablet" or "the Mother of Books" (Q. 22:69, 43:1–3, 57:22, 33:6). The conception was transmitted to Arabia through Mesopotamia as well, and it was known to Muhammad through his frequenting the Hanif/Converts milieu in Mecca.[70] The Qur'an (19:57–58, 21:85–86) mentions Enoch twice as

---

68. The Cry (*saiha*) is not unprecedented, however. It is a portent of God's physical destruction of the nations that had disowned their prophets in sacred history. See Q. 11:67, 94.

69. MacKenzie 1979, 503, 510–11.

70. Windegren 1955, 116–19. It may be worth noting in this connection that in his *History of the Church* (6:37–38) Eusebius mentions the appearance in Arabia of unorthodox believers among the Helkesaites (Mesopotamian Judeo-Christian Alkesites) who "produce a book, alleging that it fell from heaven." I am indebted to Dr. Elton Daniel for this information.

Idris, which is etymologically traceable to the Qumranic *dōrēsh ha-Torah* (interpreter of the Law) and which is mentioned once in the Qur'an in the diminutive form of 'Uzayr. The epithet *siddiq* has a Zadokite connotation, which is evident in the allusion to Enoch's heavenly ascension (Q. 19:57). The influence of the oldest section of the Book of Enoch, the Book of Watchers, is evident in the Qur'an, and the enigmatic 'Uzayr, who is said to have considered a son of God by the Jews (Q. 9:30), was quite probably an Enochic angel and a diminutive form of Ezra, another major figure of the Enochic apocalyptic lore, or both. By the time of the Fourth Ezra and in the subsequent literature, Ezra the scribe had become Ezra the prophet. Ezra was identified with Enoch and appears as the key figure in the mystical speculations of the Jewish communities of Arabia.[71]

4 Ezra circulated not only in Syriac but also in Arabic; it is the most messianic of the pseudepigrapha and the most likely influence on the Qur'an other than Manichaean scriptures.[72] In it, Ezra is clearly presented as a second Moses, and the "secret of the Most High" is revealed to Ezra in his fourth vision of a lion that destroys "the fourth kingdom [empire] which appeared in a vision to your brother Daniel." The apocalyptic Messiah of 4 Ezra is the son of God, "the Messiah whom the Most High has kept until the end of days whose joyful kingdom will last until the end comes, the Day of Judgment."[73] He will rule the world for four hundred or a thousand years before its predetermined end. Quite a few of the signs of the end of the world, including the sounding of the trumpet, correspond to the signs of the Hour in the Qur'an. Ezra is clearly presented as a second Moses (4 Ezra 14:1–6); and it is as the messianic "prophet like Moses" that he enters into Islam, with his messianism being transferred to Muhammad as in the above-mentioned poem by Abu Tālib.[74]

---

71. Casanova 1924; Newby 1988, 60–61; Erder 1990; Gill 1992; Crone 2014. An interesting refutation of his divine status is found, though, in an inscription dated to 786/170 that asserts that Muhammad, Jesus, and 'Uzayr are simply servants of God, like all other creatures. See Nevo and Koren 2003, 398.

72. For the three Arabic versions of 4 Ezra published in 1862–63 and 1877, see Widengren 1955, 227–28.

73. 4 Ezra 6:23, 7:13, 32, 73, 12;32–34, 37, 14:1–6. The word for divine secret, *raz*, is the Persian loanword and concept we found in the book of Daniel. The thousand years are, interestingly, given in one of the Arabic versions (4 Ezra 7:28, note f). This corresponds to the millennial Islamicate conception of revolution discussed in chapter 9 below.

74. Abu Tālib and Muhammad may also have heard echoes of the messianic idea of building the "House of Abraham" from the Qumran book of Jubilees. See Rubin 1990, 108.

The notion of the Messiah as the anointed son of God is prominent in the Qumran texts, and we may assume it was transmitted to the Jewish communities of Arabia. The assertion in the Qur'an (9:30) that "the Jews say 'Uzayr is the son of God as the Christians say the Messiah is the son of God" can be partly understood as referring to this heterodox Jewish belief, especially as we have Ibn Hazm's gloss that the referent is the Sadducee sect of the Yemen. To complete the explanation, however, we also need to mention that the Qur'an shares the Manichaean and Mesopotamian Gnostic view we have already discussed according to which Jesus and Ezra were messengers of God in whom the Holy Spirit manifested itself (and not his sons).[75]

The Jews of Arabia who accepted Muhammad's call to Islam were most probably nonrabbinical and Qumran-inspired heterodox Jews, being influenced by the Judaizing Christians and the biblically literate Converts (Sābi'un) of the peninsula. The Yemenite Jewish father of the famous Ka'b, presumably one of the *ahbār* like his son, expected the coming of a prophet like Moses to the Gentiles. He reportedly sealed his prediction of Muhammad's coming in a Torah, and the seal was broken by Ka'b al-ahbār to see:

> He [God] said in the Torah: "Oh Muhammad, I am sending down to you a new Torah [*tawrāh haditha*] so that you might open the eyes of the blind, the ears of the deaf and the hearts of the uncircumcised."[76]

Although Daniel is not mentioned in the Qur'an, the influence of the book of Daniel is evident. The reference to Abraham as the friend of God (Daniel 3:35), which also occurs in the Qumran Damascus Covenant, is carried over to the Qur'an (Q. 4:124).[77] Gabriel and Michael, the two archangels who are introduced to the Hebrew Bible in Daniel, are both mentioned in Qur'an 2:92. Michael, the prince and ruler of Israel at the End of Time, together with his angelic army (Daniel 7:27), reappear to aid Muhammad as the realized messiah of Medina, while Gabriel's role in hierophany and audition (Daniel 10:4–11.1) becomes central and his function as the angel of revelation (Daniel 12:4) is transmitted to the Qur'an in the late Medinan verse (Q. 66:4). In the early

---

75. Widengren 1955, 69–79, 140–42; Erder 1990, 349; van Henten 2007, 22–25.
76. Cited in Wheeler 1999–2000, 579. Wheeler considers this sentence a reasonable paraphrase of Isaiah 42:1–4, as the common prophetic source of the messianism of Jesus and Muhammad (580–83).
77. Q. 4:124: "God took Abraham as a friend (*khalil*)." See Bishop 1958, 225–26.

Islamic tradition, Gabriel appears as Muhammad's frequent counselor. Lastly, the Danielic notion of setting the seal on prophecy (Daniel 9:24) crucially influenced Muhammad's idea of final prophecy, but this time through Manichaeism, as we have seen.[78]

According to a tradition recorded by Ibn Sa'd, Muhammad asserted: "I am Muhammad, and I am the Paraclete [*ahmad*], and I am the resurrector [*hāshir*]—the people are resurrected upon my steps—and I am the final one—there is no prophet after me.".[79] An earlier variant of this tradition also includes, "and the prophet of the *malhama* [tribulations of the End of Time]." The epithet "Prophet/Messenger of the *malhama*" is attested for Muhammad in several other early traditions as well. *Malhama* is a loanword from the Hebrew *milhamah* (war), as in the Qumran *War Rule*. [80] These early hadiths clearly show traces of Muhammad's apocalyptic messianism that were developed into the later Muslim post/anti-apocalyptic doctrine of the "finality of prophecy."

No one in the small milieu of Muhammad's "informants" about the Late Antique religions of salvation needed to have the precise knowledge of the Prophet of the Last Days to the Gentiles or any of the other apocalyptic, messianic ideas outlined above. They had currency in the small literate milieus in Mecca and Medina, and any one or combination of them was sufficient to make the prophet sacred and to motivate whoever accepted Mohammad's

---

78. Casanova (1911:8, 18, 207–28) highlighted the proto-Islamic belief that "the time announced by Daniel and Jesus had come. Muhammad was the last prophet chosen by God to preside at the end of time, ... over the universal resurrection and Last Judgement." The Hebrew cognate *khotam* is the seal or signet-ring of Haggai 2:23, where Yahweh declares to Zerubbabel: "I shall take you ... and make you like a signet-ring; for I have chosen you." The notion is unmistakably messianic, or more precisely protomessianic. It is made messianic proper by Daniel, who also speaks of setting the seal on prophecy (Daniel 9:24)

79. Ibn Sa'd 1904–28, vol. 1, part 1:65. It should also be noted that the early traditions consider the seal of prophecy a physical mark of prophecy between Muhammad's shoulders, or alternatively, on his chest; it is variously described as a dark mole or a lump the size of a pigeon's egg. See *Life*, 80; Ibn Sa'd 1904–28, vol. 1, part 1:106–7, vol. 1, part 2:131–33. A later apocalyptic tradition has Muhammad saying, "I was chosen prophet together with the Hour; it almost came ahead of me" (al-Mas'udi 1970, 3:7; Widengren 1955, 12). This, together with some other similar examples, is cited in Arjomand 1998, 246.

80. Ibn Sa'd 1904–28, vol. 1, part 1:65: "I am Muhammad and Ahmad ..., I am the messenger of war [*rasul al-malhama*], ..." and one other variant. See also Tabari, 9:156n1066. Regarding the *War Rule* and Iranian influence on it, see chapter 1, XX–XX above. Rabin (1957, 118–19) also traces the Qumranic origins of the Arabic terms *hashr* and *harj* to the Hebrew *heregh* (slaughter).

gradually selected configuration of them to submit to his charismatic authority as the living Messenger of the One God in building a new world in kairotic time. The rest of Muhammad's story is well known. It is the evolution of a transcendental, universalist monotheism that presented notions of pagan Arabia and Late Antique religions of salvation in a radically new configuration and inspired the construction of the Muslim community of believers (*umma*). It is the story of realized messianism and the struggle in the path of God.

MUHAMMAD'S CALL AND THE FORMATION OF ISLAM AS REALIZED MESSIANISM

Step by step, Muhammad came to preach the absolute transcendence of Allāh al-Rahmān (Merciful God) as the One God, which was an amalgam of the Allah of the Hijāz and the Rahmān (the merciful), the universal God of South Arabia. Allah, who shared the advantage of not being the cultic god of any particular tribe with Rahmān, sublimated the latter into his foremost attributes or "most beautiful names" (*asmā' al-husnā*):

> Say: "You may call on God [*Allāh*]) or you may call on the Merciful [*Rahmān*]"; by whatever name you call Him, His are the most beautiful names. (Q. 17:110)

The enigmatic Rahim was likewise appropriated for Allah, presumably as he shared Rahmān's mercifulness.[81] Rahmān, attested as Rahmānā (in Judeo-Aramaic) in late fourth-century Himyarite inscriptions as the "Lord of heaven and earth," originated in the Judaism adopted by the Himyarite kings and was identified as the God of the Jews as well as the Judeo-Christians of South Arabia, and hence of northern Arabia, in the fifth century. The mid-sixth-century inscription recording the expedition of Abraha, the Christian Ethiopian viceroy, begins in the name of the Rahmānā (Merciful One): "with the help of His anointed [*masih*] king, Abraha."[82] The Rahmān was also known closer to Mecca in the Yamāma in central Arabia, and his angels were believed

---

81. Rahim is mentioned in the Qur'an as a name without the definite article only four times. Al-Azmeh (2014, 71–72, 311–15) traces the cumulative identity of Muhammad's "personal deity" from his Lord (*rabb*), identified at the inception as that of the Quraysh, as "The Lord of this House who . . . will give them security (*āman-hum*) from fear" through the Rahmān (Q. 106:3–4).

82. Cited in Nebes 2011, 37. The date of the inscription is 548.

to be all female (Q. 43:19). And, in an inscription further north in the Negev, he is called the "Lord of Musa and Jesus."[83]

Already in Mecca, during the so-called second Meccan period, well exemplified by sura 19 on Mary, Mary's Lord is Rahmān (Q. 19:18, 26), the universal God of the Jews and Christians of South Arabia, while baby Jesus declares from his cradle: "I am indeed the servant (*'abd*) of Allāh who has given me the Book and made me a prophet [*nabi*]" (Q. 19:30)![84] Jesus, son of Mary (Q. 19:36), then explains the immaculate conception as God's deed and reaffirms that "Allāh is indeed my Lord and your Lord, then worship Him; this is the straight path!" (Q. 19:36). The rest of the sura propounds the full identification and conjoint divine supremacy of Allah and al-Rahmān (Q. 19:44–96).[85] The Prophet's poet in Medina, Ka'b b. Mālik, confirmed God's identity with Rahmān.[86]

The identification of Rahmān with Allah encountered some resistance among the Meccans who professed "unbelief at the mention of the Rahmān" (Q. 21:36; see also Q. 13:30). According to one report, a man who had changed his name to 'Abd al-Rahmān after converting was asked by a Meccan friend to adopt a different name because "I don't know al-Rahmān!"[87] Nevertheless, the identification was successful and opened the path from pagan polytheism to pure monotheism. Other major divinities, such as the astral deities, al-'Aziz and al-Mun'im, were likewise sublimated, and lesser divinities were demoted to the rank of angels, and yet others were said to be no more than mere names and added to Allah's beautiful names: "There is no god but He [*huwa*]; for Him are the most beautiful names" (Q. 20:8). The subordination of the idols to God, already suggested by the pre-Islamic pilgrimage formulas (*talbiya*) of two tribes that addressed Allah as the "god/lord of idols" (*ilāh/rabb al-asnām*) went without offering any compensation through appropriation of their names.[88] Therefore, "Say," God orders His Messenger, "O mankind [*al-nās*]

---

83. Seidensticker 2011, 311–12, 317.
84. Replicated verbatim in Q. 3:51.
85. This conjoint divine supremacy makes plausible the assumption that Rahim (compassionate) may well have been adopted as the epithet of Rahmān, allowing the rendering of the *basmala* formula as "In the name of Allāh, the compassionate Rahmān." See Simon 1991, 133.
86. Imhof 2011, 400, line 1.5.
87. *Life*, 302.
88. Cited by Seidensticker (2011 307), citing Muqātil.

I am the Messenger of God to You all, of Him to whom belongs the kingdom of heavens and the earth. There is no god but He" (Q. 7:158).[89]

The process of universalizing the amalgamation and unification of deities culminated in the final proclamation Allah as the Lord of All Beings [*rabb al-'ālamin*]" (Q. 1:1–2, 6:70). This ecumenical "One God" or "the Lord of all" is attested in Greek funerary inscriptions in Palestine from the fourth, fifth, and sixth centuries, and we find corresponding Jewish and Christian-Palestinian liturgical terms for it.[90] This last identification thus coupled the transcendence of the amalgamated Allah with his universality. The Qur'an's opening verses (1:1–2) capture this evolution admirably: "Allāh as the Lord of All Beings [*rabb al-'ālamin*], the Merciful [*al-rahmān*], the Compassionate [*al-rahim*]." It was not Yahweh but the Lord of All Beings who sent Moses as his Messenger (Q. 7:61, 67, 104; 26:16) and who was identified, much more frequently in the later verses, with Allah as the Lord of the Ka'ba and God of Abraham, Moses, and Jesus. Muhammad's declaration, "I am the Messenger of the Lord of All Beings" is repeated three times (Q. 7:104, 26:16, 43:46). "We have not sent thee, save as a mercy to all beings (Q. 21:107). It follows that the mission of the Messenger of the God of the universe is a universal mission.

This evolution of monotheism was already completed in Mecca, even though its fuller alignment with Judeo-Christian-Manichaean religions and theological elaboration belong to the late Medinan suras. Just as Abraham had submitted or surrendered himself to the Lord of all Being (Q. 2:131), those who accepted Muhammad's new revelation of monotheism and thereby became "Muslims" were sternly required to worship the One God exclusively. Muhammad considered that anyone who rejected partners for God and declared his/her exclusive belonging to Him had submitted to the Lord of all Being (Q. 40:66) or "undergone Islam [*aslama*]" (the term *islām* soon assumed the congruent meaning of submission).[91] His message of transcendental monotheism thus struck at the heart of associationism (*shirk*)—the social or

---

89. The use of *huwa* instead of the shortened suffix pronoun *hu* in this and a number of other Qur'anic verses echoes the tetragram for Yahweh. As D. B. MacDonald suggested a century ago (Simon 1991, 134), Muhammad's rhetorical argument against his Meccan opponents over the names of God as reported in the Qur'an amounted to telling them "there is no God except the one you already call Allāh!"

90. Jefferey 1938, 209.

91. Baneth 1971, 188–89.

embedded religion of segmented Arabia, whose main beneficiary, Muhammad's own tribe of Quraysh, began to persecute him and his followers! Much later, in what is plausibly taken as the last verse of the Qur'an (Q. 5:3), which was revealed during Muhammad's farewell pilgrimage and only a few months before his death, Islam was explicitly given as the name of the new religion.

Muhammad's migration from Mecca to Medina was indeed a watershed in the formative transformation of Islam as a religion. What is particularly interesting from the viewpoint of political messianism in Medina is the transformation of catastrophism and apocalypticism into an eschatological theodicy, since the Hour did not come, and its expectation receded into an eschatological theodicy. The knowledge of the Hour (*'ilm al-sā'a*), according to the later Medinan verses of the Qur'an, was God's alone; a "day of God" was equivalent to one thousand human years and could last as long as fifty thousand years.[92] In the early Meccan scenario, the Hour had signaled the coming of Day of Judgment (*yawm al-din*) as an apocalyptic occurrence. It was now, alternatively, conceived as the Last Day (*yawm al-ākhir*) (Q. 2:4, 86 passim) and coupled with the Hereafter (*ākhira*) (Q. 2:4 passim).

The Medinan eschatological theodicy progressively detached the Day of Judgment (*yawm al-din*) from the Hour of Resurrection (Q. 22:7), when all mankind would be resurrected in order to stand before God and account for their deeds (Q. 83:5–11), and projected it to the otherworld as the distant End of Time, thus positing it as the otherworldly *eschaton* (end), when every individual was to be judged for the good and bad acts during his life on this world. The end was consequently also detached from this-worldly, immediate expectations of those struggling in the path of God and obeying God's commandments. Under realized messianism, the divine reward for the struggle in the path of God, now also called fighting for the "religion [*din*] of God" (Q. 2:193), was postponed to the Hereafter as the Messenger of God and his successors found the resources for immediate, this-worldly reward through the distribution of its spoils. After the death of the Prophet, the seal of prophecy was interpreted as the finality of the prophethood of the historical Muhammad and conceptually separated from the eschaton and the Day of Judgment.[93] Just as the "religion of Abraham" was declared the Muslim religion in Medina,

---

92. Amir-Moezzi 2016, 48 (citing seven Qur'anic verses).
93. Amir-Moezzi 2016, 50.

the apocalyptic expectation of an imminent occurrence was thus transformed into a belief in the Last Judgment in the other world and thus into a tenet of the eschatological theodicy of Islam as realized messianism. Post-Qur'anic theology accordingly conceived the Last Day as the earthly prelude to the otherworldly Last Judgment and a part of the increasingly embellished scenario for the End of Time (*akhir al-zamān*).

THE MOBILIZATION FOR HOLY STRUGGLE (*JIHĀD*) AND THE UNIFICATION OF ARABIA

When Khosraw I (531–79 CE) invaded South Arabia, much of the Hijaz, including Yathrib (the future Media), was brought under Persian suzerainty through the Arab king of Hira. The two main Jewish tribes of Nadhir and Qurayza were "kings" or fiscal agents of the Persian empire, and some time before Muhammad's arrival, Hira's appointee was 'Abdallāh b. Ubayy from the Arab tribe of Khazraj, who almost passed for a king. As the Persian-mediated authority lapsed in Yathrib, the endemic violence typical of segmented "stateless societies" was aggravated, setting Yathrib's main tribes of Aws and Khazraj in unresolved deadly conflict with each other. What was needed for the resolution of this conflict was a holy judge-arbiter (*hakam*), the only native extratribal authority known in Arabia and one similar to the judges of the Old Testament. A number of aldermen from Yathrib, mostly among the literate monotheistic elite educated by the Jews, met Muhammad at the trade fair, and reportedly gave him their pledge of allegiance. As the heavenly counterpart to the pledge, Muhammad received permission to fight (Q. 22:40–42), whereupon he ordered his companions to migrate from Mecca to the future Medina. The prophet thus chose his sacred enclave and embarked on the "migration" to it that was to mark the beginning of the Islamic era. Those who undertook the *hijra* and joined him in the sacred enclave had the special status of Migrant (*muhājir*). God's permission to fight was probably first given to the Migrants (*muhājirun*) "who have been expelled from their dwellings without any cause" (Q. 22:39), and then to all Muslims "to fight in the path of God" (Q. 2:244). The coincidence of the two orders is not accidental; it was essential to Muhammad's struggle for this-worldly translation of the apocalyptic vision that began in Medina. Migrating to the sacred enclave of Allah meant foregoing the protection of the partner-gods and the conditio sine qua non of Islam or submission to God: "To those who believed but did not make the *hijra* it is not for you [pl. to give "protection" (*wilāya*)] until they do make the *hijra*" (Q. 8:72). This is proved by the striking association between migration (*hijra*) and the struggle (*jihād*) "in the path of God" (Q. 8:71–73, 9:19–20) in the Qur'an as criteria for true faith: "those who believe and those who migrate and struggle [*āmanu wa . . . hājaru wa jāhadu*] in the path of God" (Q. 2:215).⁹⁴

Muhammad's migrants were supported by the Medinan believers and Muhammad instituted a pact of brotherhood (*mu'ākhāt*) with full ritual mixing of blood and the obligation of mutual inheritance.⁹⁵ He also organized several raids against the caravans of the Quraysh, typically by a handful of Muslims, to sustain themselves from booty. Muhammad, the prophet of the End of Time, did begin the conquest of Arabia as the prophet of the *malhama*; his apocalyptic battle was none other than the Battle of Badr in Ramadan of the year 2 AH/ March 624 CE when God, according to the Qur'an (3:123–25), sent down three thousand angels to fight alongside his army. Just as God had sent Michael to help in the great apocalyptic battle described in the book of Daniel, the Muslim tradition has Gabriel and Michael each lead a thousand angelic troops to the right and the left of Muhammad (and the archangel Isrāfīl is added at the head of another thousand to reach the number given in the Qur'an), and considers the Battle of Badr as "the day of redemption/deliverance [*furqān*], the day the two parties met" that is mentioned in Qur'an 8:41–42 as a parallel to Exodus 14:13. A more convincing parallel, I suggest, can be found between the Last Judgment and separation (*wcʾryšn*) (of the saved from the damned) in Māni.⁹⁶ With the help of the angelic host, Muhammad's three hundred or so holy warriors, who constituted almost the entire body of male Muslims at the time, defeated an army consisting of three times as many Meccans and their allies. The rich booty was distributed among the 313 or 314 holy warriors, three quarters of whom were Medinan converts.⁹⁷

The Battle of Badr, whose apocalyptic motivation is evident from the above Qur'anic account, sealed at the same time the institutionalization of holy

---

94. *Life*, 213, 79; Madelung 1986a; Lecker 1997; Lecker 2002; Crone 1994, 354–55.
95. Amir-Moezzi 2006, 39–40.
96. MacKenzie 1979, 505–6.
97. *Life*, 336; al-Wāqidi 1966, 1:23, 57–71, 113; Ibn Saʿd, 3:9; Watt and Bell 1970, 145; Rubin 2001, 456. According to al-Wāqidi, their number was 313, five of whom were not present during the distribution of booty. The angelic host returned to aid the Muslims in the Battle of Hunayn (8 AH/630 CE). See Q. 9:25–26; Rubin 2001, 456.

warfare as the distinctive Islamic path of revolutionary struggle for the religion of God (*din Allāh*): "Fight them until there is no more persecution and religion, all of it, is God's" (Q. 8:39). In fact, sura 8 of the Qur'an (*Anfāl*), believed to have been revealed as divine commentary on the Battle of Badr, or a section thereof, was often read to the Muslim armies before battle during the Muslim conquests.[98]

While winning new converts who accepted his prophetic authority, Muhammad wasted no time consolidating his authority more broadly in Medina as a judge-arbiter (*ḥakam*) according to Arabian customary law. In doing so, he needed divine succor, and the novel phrase, "obey God and His Messenger," appears some forty times in the Qur'an in verses that are mostly dated to his first three years in Medina. In a series of pacts, which were correctly executed, "Muhammad the Prophet" (*al-nabi*) secured recognition of his authority as the judge-arbiter to whom all disputes were to be referred on behalf of Allah. The context of this first historical occurrence of the term *nabi* in a pact with the Jews is highly significant in the equation of the biblical "prophet" with the Manichaean divine messengers. This equation is accordingly made in a later clause that reiterate the requirement of referring disputes to "Allāh and to Muhammad, the Messenger of Allāh."[99] This is probably the earliest equation of the Prophet and the Messenger of God. In Mecca, the term *nabi* was used mostly with reference to the descendants of Abraham but not Muhammad.

The numerous Qur'anic verses that enjoin obedience to God and his Messenger are all Medinan. Conversely, there is no verse explicitly enjoying obedience to the prophets. The potentially expansive quality of the authority of Muhammad as the Messenger of God is evident. Those subject to this authority constituted "a unified community [*umma wāḥida*] set apart from [other] people." The Qur'an (21:92) duly sanctioned the new social compact for the believers: "This community of yours is a unified community, and I am your Lord, so worship me." The unified community was religiously plural and a

---

98. Al-Wāqidī 1966, 1:131–31. Most of the Badr prisoners were ransomed to support the new Muslim community, but two anti-Muhammad pagan intellectuals were executed. Their execution signaled Muhammad's bid to be the sole master of Medina and the onset of the revolutionary power struggle with the city's Jewish tribes that has been covered elsewhere (see Arjomand 2019, ch. 8).

99. Cited in Arjomand 2009 as CM; F4.

heterogeneous political entity, comprising not only the Muslims but also non-Muslim clans. A pact of tolerance allowed the Jewish covenanters of the united community to have their religion, as the Muslims had theirs, as long as they paid the war levy (*nafaqa*) alongside the other covenanters and refrained from treason.

This last clause nevertheless points to the crucial fact that, from the moment of the constitution of the new community, Muhammad was also making constitutional provisions for the (revolutionary) struggle in the path of God. That a levy was imposed on the covenanters and their Jewish affiliates for this purpose is a minor aspect of this development. The general peace and security of God eliminated the legitimacy of the use of violence by politically autonomous segments of Arabian tribal society. The monopoly of the legitimate use of violence was in principle invested in the united community, thereby laying the foundation for a unified structure of authority—a state—devoted to the realization of the final end of the prophetic mission:

> The covenanters shall make peace only in unity. No covenanter shall make peace apart from other covenanters in fighting [*qitāl*] in the path of God—and that only as a just and equitable decision by them. And all raiding parties shall fight with us one after another. And the covenanters shall execute retaliation on behalf of one another with respect to their blood shed in the path of God.[100]

As the mobilization for holy struggle continued and the number of holy warriors increased from some three hundred in 624 (Badr) to three thousand, with thirty-six horsemen in 627, the war levy and booty from raids on the Quraysh caravans became inadequate and there was an evident need for additional fiscal prey (*tu'ma*).[101] The last remaining "kingly" Jewish clan, Banu Qurayza, became Muhammad's most lucrative fiscal prey in the final stage of the revolutionary power struggle in Medina in 627, and they were violently eliminated immediately after he repelled the besieging Quraysh army sent from Mecca in the Battle of the Trench.

Muhammad's sense of living at the End of Time and preparing for the Last Judgment had not receded despite the expansion of his political authority, and he insisted that his mosque be built, in accordance with Gabriel's instructions,

---

100. See Arjomand 2009 for this citation and all other references to the Constitution of Medina.
101. Kister 1986, 88–89.

as a "booth like the booth of Moses thy brother," and without a roof.[102] When the palm branches were replaced by bricks as the wall of the mosque about the time of the Battle of the Trench, Muhammad refused to add a roof and retained the Mosaic form appropriate for the End of Time. Success in the Battle of the Trench, however, sharpened the Prophet's political pragmatism in pursuit of the unification of Arabia. Muhammad married Umm Habiba, the widowed Muslim daughter of his distant cousin Abu Sufiyān, the leader of the pagan Quraysh who gradually ceased to take part in its military operations against him and was conspicuously absent during the negotiations for the Treaty of al-Hudaybiyya in March 628 between Muhammad and the Quraysh. Some three months later, Muhammad attacked the rich Jewish settlement of Khaybar, rewarding some 1,600 Muslims who had pledged their steadfastness in an anxious moment before the Truce of Hudaybiyya with booty and land. Muhammad was allowed to take part in a pilgrimage, which paved the way for the taking of Mecca in January 630, and to realize his dream of the believers "entering the Holy Mosque in security, God willing, with your heads shaven, not fearing" (Q. 48:27).

Within a month of the conquest of Mecca, Muhammad added some two thousand men to his army and defeated a coalition of the old opponents of the Quraysh in Hunayn. The wholesale conversion of the old Quraysh oligarchy took place rapidly, with the "winning of [their] hearts" (Q. 9:60) with a generous distribution of the booty from Hunayn. In the following year, he drew heavily on the Quraysh aristocracy for sending his first governors/fiscal agents to different tribal areas of Arabia. This policy of "winning the hearts" caused considerable resentment among old Muslims, especially the Medinan helpers who reportedly got nothing in Hunayn. Nevertheless, the wisdom of Muhammad's policy was proved by the fact that the Quraysh leaders, despite their late conversion, remained faithful to the new Islamic state and made a major military contribution to the reunification of Arabia immediately after Muhammad's death. With the conquest of Mecca and the defeat of the pagan tribal confederation in Hunayn, Muhammad appeared as the undisputed master of Arabia to the many close and distant tribes that hastened to send "delegations" to him in Medina to accept Islam and join his unified polity. One delegate stated explicitly that his tribe took the conquest of Mecca as

---

102. Kister 1962, 154.

proof of Muhammad's prophethood and hastened to declare his tribe's submission. Another from the Yemen, where Jewish messianism was strong, similarly declared:

> You are the Prophet about whom we were informed,
> And the Torah and the Prophets gave the good news of you[r coming]!

Muhammad finally had the satisfaction of seeing "men entering the religion of God in throngs" (Q. 110:2). In the last months of 630, he was able to send an army of thirty thousand men to Tabuk.[103]

The conquest of Mecca enabled Muhammad to match the doctrinal development of Islamic monotheism and prophetology with a corresponding evolution of Islamic ritual practices. Hajj as the foremost ritual of pagan prayer, and fasting as the major rituals of the Late Antique religions of salvation, were radically reinterpreted in the light of the developed transcendental monotheism.[104] The enumeration of the approved rituals and the forbidding of the pagan ones can be found in one of the latest and longest Medinan Verses, in which the completion of the new religion and its name, Islam, are announced:

> This day I have perfected your religion for you and completed my blessing to you. I have approved Islam to be your religion. (Q. 5:3)

In perfecting Islam as a world religion, Muhammad instituted the prototype of revolutionary struggle in world history as one of what the Muslim theologians was to call the "pillars of Islam."

This autonomization of a pattern of interaction endemic to Arabian stateless society into a cultural norm in the Islamicate civilization was further enhanced by the second caliph, 'Umar (644–56 CE), the true consolidator of Islam's revolution and the effective ruler of its state in Medina. He sharpened the definition of the office he had inherited by assuming the military title of Commander of the Believers (*amir al-mu'minin*), a title first given by the Prophet to the raid commanders. He consonantly transformed the struggle on the path of God into an instrument of export of revolution by means of

---

103. Arjomand 2019, ch.8.

104. The integration of two distinct pilgrimages—the *'umra* of the Meccans around the Ka'ba and the hajj of the confederate tribes allied to the Quraysh—was only achieved with Muhammad's last pilgrimage in which he delivered his farewell message announcing his most radical break with the ritual calendar of the pagan Arabs. See Q. 2:158.

integrating barely Islamicized Arab tribesmen into an army of conquest and imperial expansion. 'Umar also appointed a number of religio-ideological commissars to the forces exporting the revolution. They were called the *qurrā'* (Qur'an-readers) and recited the chapter on the spoils of war (*surat al-anfāl*), also known as the *jihād* chapter, to the troops.[105] 'Umar thus completed the Prophet's institution of the struggle on the path of God (*jihād*) as the prototype of the process of revolution in world history.[106]

THE SUCCESSION TO CHARISMATIC LEADERSHIP AND THE SUPPRESSION OF RIVAL MESSIAHS

The so-called Constitution of Medina, though a cornerstone of Muhammad's realized messianism, is a misnomer in that it did not create a state; nor, in fact, did any subsequent Qur'anic legislation.[107] The expectation of the end of the world of the coming of the Day of Judgment did not disappear at once with the adumbration of an eschatological theodicy.[108] the biggest challenge faced by the community of believers at the time of the Prophet's death, however, was not apocalyptic but realistic. It was to develop a theory of political organization and legitimate succession with almost no Qur'anic guideline.[109]

The absence of reference to the form of government and political leadership in the Qur'an is truly astonishing. It can be argued that Muhammad saw the precedent of the rulership of the families of the earlier prophets mentioned in the Qur'an as applying to his family as well, seeing a Hashemite monarchy as the obvious solution to the problem of succession after his death. This hierocratic principle of kinship to the Prophet was closest to Muhammad's intention of transforming his prophetic charisma to the charisma of his lineage by establishing a House of Muhammad on the biblical model of the House

---

105. Hinds 1971a, 358, citing Tabari.
106. See Arjomand 2019, ch.7.
107. In contrast to his lack of attention to the normative regulation of the political order, Muhammad did institute a system of religious pluralism as a part of the realistic modification of the Meccan apocalyptic vision. This accommodative pluralism was endorsed by divine revelation: "There is no compulsion in religion [*lā ikrāh fi'l-din*]" (Q. 2:256). See also Arjomand 2009.
108. Muhammad's prominent disciple and the future Commander of the Believers, 'Umar b. al-Khattab, did not believe Muhammad had died (see Madelung 1997, 38).
109. Donner 1998, 45.

of Abraham and the House of Amram/'Imrān (Moses), as in Muslim ritual prayer, or the House of David in the Qur'an.[110] Paradoxically, however, the hierocratic model found relatively little support in the revolutionary power struggle after Muhammad's death, and was only developed much later by the Shi'ite sects into the doctrine of the imamate. Three other principles were also imperfectly adumbrated in the sayings and deeds of the Prophet but had a potential for further logical development and eventual institutionalization. The most important of these was the principle of seniority or precedence (*sābiqa*) in Islam. 'Ali, the beneficiary of the hierocratic monarchical principle, in fact gave his pledge of allegiance to Abu Bakr and 'Umar, and it was this precedence in Islam that primarily assured his succession as the fourth caliph. There was also the entirely new principle of consensus (*rida wa'l-jamā'a*).[111] The weakest in terms of Qur'anic endorsement was the surviving pre-Islamic principle of nobility and leadership (*sharaf wa'l-riyāsa*). This last principle was, however, favored by the Quraysh oligarchy of late converts whose hearts Muhammad had won at the final stage in the unification of Arabia. Its beneficiary was the Banu Umayya, the rival Qurayshite clan to Banu Hāshim, who replaced the idea of the Hashemite monarchy by that of the Umayyad caliphate of the Quraysh in the second half of the seventh century.

Immediately after the death of the Prophet, Abu Bakr and 'Umar were clearly apprehensive about the hierocratic principle, which would result in the caliphate and prophethood being reunited in the same family, meaning that the Banu Hāshim would have the monopoly of both. They broke into a meeting of the Ansār led by Sa'd b. 'Ubāda, and pushed them into accepting Abu Bakr as the *khalifa* (successor) of the Messenger of God. 'Umar managed the streets of Medina and secured the allegiance of the residents, making an alliance

---

110. Neuwirth 2011. As Muhammad's male offspring had predeceased him, the Shi'a took his famous designation of his son-in-law and cousin 'Ali at Ghadir Khumm—"'Ali is the patron (*mawlā*) of whomever I am a patron of"—as his succession appointment. The oath of allegiance to 'Ali as the fourth caliph matched this formula. This hierocratic position became the principle of Hashemite legitimism when 'Ali's son briefly succeeded him as the caliph with the proclamation, "I am al-Hasan, the son of Muhammad." He was at any rate addressed thus by the leading member of the Hashemite clan, 'Abdallāh b. 'Abbās somewhat later. See Madelung 1997a, 16–17, 253, 311, 313.

111. This was also claimed by 'Ali as the basis of his legitimacy in the civil war with Mu'āwiya. See Sharon 1984, 130–32.

with an obscure Fihrite on the margin of Quraysh, Abu 'Ubayda b. al-Jarrah, who was later designated as his successor but was soon killed in battle.[112]

Abu Bakr, seconded by 'Umar and supported by the early Muslims, fought the Arab tribes that refused to accept that the Prophet had founded a state authorized to receive taxes, as well as those how followed rival Arabian prophets in what became known anachronistically as the Wars of Apostasy (*ridda*). On pragmatic grounds, Abu Bakr argued that only the tribe of Quraysh could rule a unified Arabia, and that therefore the caliphate belonged to it. Continuing Muhammad's policy of "winning the hearts," he used the leaders of the clans of Quraysh to subdue Arabia, alienating the Helpers from whose leader he had snatched the caliphate. When readmitting the defeated "apostate" tribes, meanwhile, Abu Bakr, the first caliph, and 'Umar, his successor, exacted from their members, on (re)conversion to Islam, the pledge to obey "whomever God had invested with authority [*wallā Allāhu'l-amr*]."[113] It was the third caliph, 'Uthman (644–56 CE), who subordinated the principle of precedence in Islam to that of nobility and leadership and who was accused by later generations of thus turning the caliphate into kingship (*mulk*) by establishing his own clan of Quraysh as the Umayyad dynasty.

Meanwhile, Muhammad's pragmatism in holy warfare and consequent community building did not affect the religious milieu outside Mecca and Medina, where messianism remained unrealized. Muhammad's success as the promised Gentile Prophet had engendered a rivalry among other monotheistic "false" prophets in different parts of Arabia. As the conversion of the tribes on the periphery of the Arabian Peninsula was incomplete at the time of Muhammad's death, Talha b. Khuwaylid among the Asad tribe to the northeast of Medina, Musaylima b. Habib among the Hanifa in Yamāma, and al-Aswad al-'Ansi in the Yemen put forward rival claims to prophecy.[114]

---

112. Lammens 1910, 116–17,142; Madelung 1997a, 22–46.

113. Kister 1994, 100–101.

114. A close look at "the year of the delegations" (9 AH = 630–31 CE) following the conquest of Mecca can prove this. In that year, some forty-seven tribes and three autonomous principalities sent delegations to Medina to accept Islam, to submit to Muhammad's authority, and to be included in his unified polity. Seven or eight delegations arrived in the following year (10 AH), and a last one arrived shortly before Muhammad's death (11 AH/632 CE). Six delegations consisted of a single person, one of them being the ambassador from the kings of Himyar in the Yemen; the very last delegation from the Nakha' had two hundred members. The typical

Quite a few of the tribes whose delegates had submitted to Medina were reluctant to give up their autonomy once they heard of Muhammad's death and they expelled his tax agents. The closest and most serious challenge came from tribes of Ghatafān and Tayy', who expelled the barely settled agents of Medina and allied themselves with the Asad tribe under its false prophet. Other tribes in the region around Medina offered to recognize Abu Bakr as leader but they refused to pay the tax lately imposed on them. To fight the rebellious tribes, Abu Bakr now had no option but to turn to the recent convert to Islam and the Qurayshite leader, Khālid b. al-Walid, and to draw on the loyal tribes settled in the cities of the Hijāz.[115]

After Khālid b. al-Walid won this first of the Wars of Apostasy (ridda), Abu Bakr could turn his attention to the refractory tribes and principalities in the more distant peripheries of eastern and southern Arabia. The movement of the false prophet, al-Aswad, from the tribe of 'Ans, had spread like fire in South Arabia, but it was put down by the Persian ruling elite in San'ā without any direct intervention from Medina. The Persian ruling elite in San'ā installed by Khosraw I after his conquest of the Yemen in the latter part of the sixth century, known as the abnā' (sons), was stranded during the terminal political crisis of the Sasanian empire, and their leader had accepted Islam and submitted to Muhammad's authority. The abnā' were overthrown by the "false prophet" al-Aswad, who killed their leader and married his wife. The wife, however, conspired with her compatriot, Firuz the Daylamite, as well as disgruntled Arab chiefs, and had al-Aswad murdered. Abu Bakr appointed Firuz his governor, and the latter eventually prevailed in San'ā. The result was the

---

delegation, however, had over ten members, but a few had two, three, seven, or eight (see Ibn Sa'd 1904–28, vol. 1, part 2:38–76). The delegates were lodged in a few houses owned by patricians of Medina (the Helpers), most notably Muhammad's maternal relatives (see Lecker 1995, 646). The coming of the delegates could not, however, be taken as an indication of the conversion of their entire tribes. Some of the "delegates" were self-appointed, claiming to represent their tribe. Others could not deliver their tribe subsequently, and, in at least one case, were even afraid to profess Islam openly when they returned to their tribe (see Ibn Sa'd 1904–28, vol. 1, part 2:72). Still others had been Muhammad's missionaries and were sent back to teach their tribes Islam (see Ibn Sa'd 1904–28, vol. 1, part 2:61, 68, 70). Some this category had their theophoric names changed by Muhammad; others were sent back as tax agents or governors; and quite a few of them got land grants (see Ibn Sa'd 1904–28, vol. 1, part 2:50–68)

115. Shoufani 1973, 5, 79–81; Donner 1981, 88.

integration of the first significant non-Arab social group into the new Muslim polity.[116]

The last and most serious war of apostasy was against the Hanifa tribe in the Yamāma on the northeastern periphery of the Arabian Peninsula led by Musaylima, the false prophet of the god Rahmān who was succeeded by the prophetess, Sajjāh b. Aws. The rebellion in Yamāma was eventually suppressed by Khālid b. al-Walid, who now enjoyed the title of the "Sword of Islam."[117]

With the elimination of the last rival messianic claimants—the Liar and the false prophet—the messianism of Muhammad as the Messenger of God was definitively realized beyond Medina and Mecca and, within two years of his death, throughout Arabia. Yet the realized messianic vision left untouched the twin issues of the political order of the community of believers and the succession of its charismatic leader. The caliphate was established ad hoc and entirely pragmatically by Muhammad's successors. Although the word *khalifa* occurs several times in the Qur'an, as we shall see in chapter 3, its meaning and implications were only clarified in the course of the full institutionalization of the caliphate after two devastating Muslim civil wars. As we shall see, the idea of jihad as the struggle in the path of God was fully developed in the Qur'an, and it created a pattern of revolutionary process uniquely distinctive of Muhammad's Constitutive Revolution, which made a permanent mark on the revolutionary movements in Islamicate civilization.

116. Shoufani 1973, 90–94, 137. The *abnā'* became integrated into the Muslim polity as an important military unit, and subsequently took part in the imperial expansion—notably, the conquest of Egypt.
117. Kister 2002.

CHAPTER 3

Civil Wars and the Emergence of Apocalyptic Mahdism

Muhammad's realized Messianism established the authority of the Messenger of God, but his Constitutive Revolution, beyond establishing Islam and unifying Arabia, was incomplete. The revolution remained incomplete in terms of social integration, and even more, in terms of the structure of authority. The constitutional politics of the twelve decades after Muhammad's death—that is, in the period between 632 and 750—were therefore the politics of Integrative Revolution, on the one hand, and the construction of a legitimate structure of domination, on the other. These processes can anachronistically and inadequately be thought of as nation and state building. In this century and a quarter, Muhammad's Constitutive Revolution created an epicycle of revolutions that are usually referred to as the First, Second, and Third Civil Wars (*fitnas*). The issues left unresolved by Muhammad's Constitutive Revolution thus set the parameters for the conflict and compromise in the constitutional politics that resulted in the epicycle of revolutions we must now consider.

The revolutionary epicycle began in Medina, the City of the Prophet, and the capital of the newborn Muslim empire of conquest created by 'Umar, the second caliph. It was, however, in response to serious unrest in the new garrison cities (*amsār*) or "frontier outposts" on the western and eastern peripheries of this empire. The First Civil War shifted the arena of the revolutionary epicycle eastward to Iraq, which became the main scene of the Second Civil War. The arena of revolution was to shift still farther east to Khurasan on the Iranian periphery in the third and last revolution in the epicycle.

The First Civil War began a quarter of a century after the death of the Prophet. Long gone was the apocalyptic mood that had left 'Umar totally unprepared for dealing with the problem of succession and that had caused his precipitous improvisation because he could not believe the Prophet would die before the End of Time. It was not the apocalyptic vision that moved the surviving Companions of the Prophet but their profound differences on the meaning of the new faith and its practical implication, as well as their dissatisfaction with the incomplete definition of Islam and the inadequate institutionalization of its contested fundamental premises. Each contender in the postrevolutionary constitutional politics was now forced to put forward his or her definition and institutional proposals. The narrative of the First Civil War that follows should convey the clash of principles recorded in our primary sources that determined the divergent path of development for the Sunni orthodoxy and the Shi'ite heterodoxies.

THE FIRST CIVIL WAR AND THE UMAYYAD VICTORY

The First Civil War (*fitna*) started with the murder of the third caliph, 'Uthmān, in 656, and it ended with that of the fourth caliph, 'Ali, in 661. This happened mainly because the structure of authority of the early caliphate unraveled on the issue of succession. It began, with serious division in the AH year 34 (654–55) among the Muslim ruling elite, which consisted of Muhammad's closest companions.

The conqueror and first governor of Egypt, 'Amr b. al-'Ās, who had been dismissed by Caliph 'Uthmān and who had left without a post, seems to have incited the Prophet's closest disciples to oppose the caliph and his Umayyad ruling kinsmen. 'Ali b. Abi Tālib and al-Zubayr b. 'Awwām approached Talha b. 'Ubaydallāh, who enjoyed the backing of the Prophet's widow, 'Ā'isha. In addition to these were two aristocrats of the next generation who were in Egypt: Muhammad b. Abi Bakr, the son of the first caliph and 'Ā'isha's brother and stepson of 'Ali, and 'Uthmān's own foster son, Muhammad b. Abi Hudhayfa, "the fledgling of the Quraysh."[1] The opponents of the caliph were supported by the majority of the natives of Medina, the Helpers (*ansār*). We should also count other less powerful companions slighted by the caliph—

1. Madelung 1997a, 116–17.

notably, 'Abdallāh b. Mas'ud and 'Ammār b. Yāsir. Letters were sent, especially by Talha and 'Ā'isha, to the Muslim warriors in the frontier outposts who were disgruntled with the distribution of the spoils of imperial conquests and the overcrowding of the garrison-cities, inciting them to rebellion and inviting them to come to the capital: "If you wish to begin the holy struggle (*jihād*), the place for it is now with us in Medina."[2]

Caliph 'Uthmān and 'Ali were kinsmen, and both were also Muhammad's sons-in-law; 'Ā'isha was his widow; and al-Zubayr was her brother-in-law and 'Ali's maternal cousin. It is thus tempting to see the whole affair as a family feud among the Quraysh aristocracy, but that temptation should be resisted. What is more significant in the light of subsequent events is the fact that these Companions of the Prophet, though united in their opposition to Caliph 'Uthmān and to the Umayyad clan of the Quraysh, were deeply divided on the definition of the Prophet's heritage.

Who were the provincials invited to bring their grievances to Medina by the caliph's venerable opponents? There was Mālik al-Ashtar al-Nakhaʻi, who was a veteran of the Battle of Qādisiyya, which opened up Iran, and the leader of the Qur'an readers (*qurrā'*) of Kufa. His followers were the first group of religious professionals to emerge in Islam around the nucleus of the second caliph, 'Umar's, religio-ideological commissars, who were now excluded from continuing campaigns in Khurasan. They saw the caliph's land grants on the black land of Iraq as an alienation of God's property and a threat to their stipends drawn from its proceedings. The formal accusation against Caliph 'Uthmān was formulated by another leader of the Kufan Qur'an readers, Ka'b b. 'Abdah, who told the caliph to his face that he had violated his oath of office as the Commander of the Believers (*amir al-mu'minin*): "when you swore to God you would act in accordance with the conduct (*sira*) of the Prophet." Ka'b's reference was to 'Uthmān's oath of office twelve years earlier, when both he and 'Ali were candidates for the caliphate after the murder of 'Umar. In the electoral council (*shurā*) nominated by 'Umar on his deathbed, the Prophet's disciple, 'Abd al-Rahmān b. 'Awf, had demanded that they not

---

2. Cited in Wellhausen 1902, 46.

impose their respective relatives in office on the believers, and furthermore, that they "follow the conduct of the Messenger of God."[3]

Mālik al-Ashtar and his followers repulsed the deputy governor of Kufa, who was a relative of the caliph, and forced him to appoint a man of their choice, the pious companion Abu Musā al-Ash'ari. We find a few disgruntled veterans in other garrison cities—Basra in Iraq and Fustāt in Egypt—where a tribally heterogeneous "quarter of the banner" (khitat al-rāya) proved a fertile ground for producing tribally unattached radical activists. This must have been known to one of the Kufan Qur'an readers exiled to Damascus, 'Amr b. al-Hamiq, who had gone there to spread the Kufan revolutionary sentiment.[4]

Oppositional leaders from all three garrison cities responded to the call of the Companions. The largest armed group to appear in the capital consisted of some four hundred to seven hundred Muslims from Egypt, who arrived first and began the siege of Caliph 'Uthmān's house. They were to play the main role and eventually were to murder the caliph; they were soon joined by two hundred Kufans led by Mālik al-Ashtar, who was a fervent champion of 'Ali's cause, and some one hundred to 150 Basrans under four different leaders.[5] The siege of the caliph's house lasted forty-nine days—from May 1 to June 17, 656—and both sides seemed eager to avoid bloodshed. Then, historical contingency cast its die, and the first casualty occurred on the penultimate day, when one of the besiegers was killed by a rock thrown down by a palace guard. The second casualty, on the last day, was the caliph himself.

Other than the charismatic Companions of the Prophet, the one social group that played a prominent role in the contested definition of Islam was the nascent religious elite, the Qur'an readers. This self-appointed watch guard of the Book of God was solicited by 'Ali, who, after the succession, immediately moved his capital to their stronghold—the garrison city of Kufa in Iraq. The

---

3. The variant, *sunna*, is used in some other sources for the normatively binding "conduct" of the Prophet (Schacht 1963, 364–65), but it is most likely a later interpolation. In 661, 'Ali's son al-Hasan, who briefly succeeded him, did not use the term but rather defined the ideal caliph as he "who conducts himself according to the conduct [*sira*] of the Messenger of God and acts in obedience to God." See *Ansāb*, 5:42; Bravmann 1972, 126n1, citing Bayhaq.

4. Hinds 1971a, 358–59; Hinds 1972, 452–56; Madelung 1997a, 107–118.

5. Hinds 1972, 459–61.

value-ideas of the Companions and the emerging religious elite in turn acted as competing principles in the constitutional politics of reconstructing a political order based on Islam over which the First Civil War was fought. It was behind these competing value-ideas that the social forces that were dissatisfied with the status quo because of their material and/or ideal aligned themselves, and it was from these that the caliph selected justifications for his policies. The constitutional politics of the First Civil War generated the first Islamic sect, the Khawārij (secessionists), followed by a plethora of Shi'ite sects in the following half century, and thus laid the foundation for future sectarian formations and the mutually oriented "orthodox" and "heterodox" definitions of Islam and divergent patterns of its institutionalization.

'Ali was the first to elaborate his proposal by launching a movement for theocratic monarchy. His loyal follower and partisan, Companion Abu Dharr al-Ghifāri,[6] mounted the Prophet's seat to propound, on 'Ali's behalf, the legitimist theory of theocratic monarchy as divine selection and the continuation of prophethood around which the future Shi'ite sects were to develop:

> Muhammad was selected among the offspring of Noah and the House of Abraham and descendants of Ishmael. His is the House of divine guidance/salvation ... Muhammad inherited the knowledge of Adam and the qualities of the Prophets, and 'Ali b. Abi Tālib is the legatee (wasi) of Muhammad and heir to his knowledge.

The *umma* was then accused of having erred after its Prophet in its choice of his successors, the caliphs, by not placing both "authority and inheritance in the House of its Prophet." But now, "the oppressors shall surely know by what overturning/revolution they will be overturned [*ayya inqalaba yanqalibun*]" (Q. 26:228). We thus hear for the first time, a Qur'anic term used in the sense of revolution—the meaning it was to assume a century later.[7]

'Uthmān offered his principled response to the challengers in his last public letter, which was read out in Mecca by 'Ali's cousin and political ally, 'Abdallāh b. 'Abbās. He responded to the louder criticisms of his armed attackers directly and refused their demand to abdicate, while rejecting 'Ali's conception of the caliphate indirectly by propounding his own contrasting

---

6. Abu Dharr, it should be noted, is the darling of the Marxist interpreters of Islamic history. Yet the constitutional issue he singled out to mobilize the people against 'Uthmān was the interpretation of the caliphate and not any principle of social justice.

7. al-Ya'q'ubi 1960, 2:171.

theory. Only once in the long letter did 'Uthmān repeat the Qur'an readers' "sound traditions [*sunna*] laid down by the Messenger of God and the two caliphs after him." To present himself as God's deputy (*khalifa*), he studiously avoided mentioning the Messenger of God in his prefatory salvation history:[8] It is "Almighty God, who has bestowed benefits upon you, taught you Islam, guided you away from error, delivered you from unbelief..." The emphasis is instead put entirely on God's covenant and the Commander of the Believers as his immediate deputy or caliph:

> O Believers, remember God's blessing upon you, and His compact [*mithāq*] which he made with you, when you said, "We have heard, and we obey." (Q. 5:10)

He goes on to recall another saying of the Almighty: "Those that sell God's covenant ['*ahd Allāh*] and their oaths for a little price ... for them awaits a painful chastisement" (Q. 3:71):

> As for my abdicating [the caliphate], I would rather they rage against me than to resign from the work of Almighty God and His caliphate ... I am not content— nor will God (Glory be to Him!) be content—that anyone among you should violate His covenant ['*ahd*].[9]

Thus, at the outset of Islam's first civil war, the beleaguered Caliph 'Uthmān and his foremost challenger, 'Ali, acted as history's switchmen, setting the tracks along which the major social groups that would emerge as heterodox sects and members of the orthodox mainstream were to align themselves. God's caliphate and the divinely inspired imamate emerged as the two principles (anachronistically speaking, the Sunni and the Shi'ite) under which a variety of vested and random interests were subsumed in the constitutional politics of Islam for generations to come.

The day after the murder of 'Uthmān, the Kufan occupiers moved faster than the Egyptians, among whom there was support for Talha, and Ashtar managed 'Ali's acclamation as caliph, declaring: "Whoever does not pledge

---

8. This is not to count the cited "authority verse" (Q. 4:59) and the mention of the successor of the Prophet, which seem later insertions and the doctored views of later Sunni jurists.

9. Tabari, 1:3040–45 (translation 15:239–45). To continue, "Almighty God desired for you absolute obedience and unity (*jamā'a*), and warned you against rebellion, schism and discord. If you rebel against Him, then accept the counsel of Almighty God and beware of His punishment..."

allegiance, I will strike his neck!" Talha was dragged by Ashtar's men and al-Zubayr by the Basrans, and they gave their pledge. 'Ali told Ashtar not to coerce either Sa'd b. 'Abi Waqqās, who said he would give his pledge later, or 'Abdallāh b. 'Umar, who refused to give his by reminding 'Ali of his father's attempt to institute the electoral council (*shurā*).[10] The majority of the Medinan Helpers, who had been disenfranchised since the beginning of the caliphate, needed no coercion and pledged their allegiance to 'Ali eagerly.

Talha and al-Zubayr left Medina as soon as they could and withdrew their pledge of allegiance made to 'Ali under duress. They went to Mecca to join 'Ā'isha, as did 'Abdallāh b. 'Umar. 'Ā'isha had been visiting Mecca, and she heard the news from Medina on the way back. She immediately returned to Mecca, called a meeting, and delivered a speech in the sanctuary, accusing 'Ali of complicity in the murder of the caliph, and demanding vengeance for the latter's unlawful murder[11]:

> We reproached 'Uthmān for some matters.... He recanted and asked his Lord for forgiveness.[12] The Muslims accepted his repentance, as they had no other [lawful] option.

Talha and al-Zubayr endorsed 'Ā'isha's call for revenge and secured her agreement to add the demand for an electoral council—'Umar's principle, already voiced by his son 'Abdallāh, who was in their company. Pending the convening of the council, they jointly assumed the leadership of the rebellion against 'Ali, calling themselves *amirs*. The mobilization of people and resources to fight 'Ali began in earnest, and a rich donor contributed a large sum of money, seventy riding animals for the men of Quraysh, and the famous camel for 'Ā'isha

---

10. Madelung 1997a, 143–45.

11. A supporter of 'Ali was surprised to hear 'Ā'isha's plan: "By God! You were the first to incline the blade against 'Uthmān and were saying 'Kill Na'thal' [hyena, 'Uthmān's pejorative nickname]." 'Ā'isha had in fact earlier broken with 'Uthmān when the caliph reduced the pension granted her by his predecessor, 'Umar, to the same amount as the pension of Muhammad's other widows. At that time, she had held up the Prophet's shirt in a public gathering and accused the caliph of making her husband's *Sunna* obsolete while his shirt was not yet tattered! (See al- Ya'qūbī 1960, 2:175.) 'Ā'isha's response to the pro-'Ali protestor now was coolly legalistic: "They asked him to repent, and then they killed him [meaning, after he repented]." See Tabari, 1:3112 (translation 16: 52–53).

12. Madelung 1997a, 147, citing al-Baladhuri, translation modified. 'Uthmān had in fact repented repeatedly during the crisis.

from which the coming battle took its name. As the situation of the rebels seemed precarious in Mecca, they moved to Basra with fewer than a thousand men.¹³

The arrival of 'Ā'isha, Talha, and al-Zubayr divided Basra into two camps. "The millstone of Islam is turning," 'Ali's governor told an adviser nervously, "and look at the way it will swagger on round!" The latter assented: "It will grind you long and hard."¹⁴ The governor and his troops met the venerable trio in the camel market southwest of the city. With their troops occupying the right side of the marketplace, first Talha and then al-Zubayr spoke, demanding revenge against those who had killed wrongfully and who had thereby violated the sanctity of the city of the Prophet. They were pelted by the troops on the left side of the marketplace. 'Ā'isha, the Mother of the Faithful, then interposed to deliver a moving speech. She reiterated the demand for the punishment for those who had attacked the caliph's house "and desecrated sacred blood, sacred property, and the sacred city without any blood debt or excuse." Only avenging the wrongfully slain caliph could establish the authority of "the Book of God for it to judge between them" (Q. 3:23).

'Ā'isha thus established a major argument, according to which Caliph 'Uthmān had been killed "without blood debt or [legal] excuse" by appealing to the Qur'an. To this she added in a letter she sent to the Kufans from Basra that only through revenge against the killers would "God receive His rights."¹⁵ There were no jurists and no Islamic law in existence yet, and 'Ā'isha was formulating principles of her own, not invoked by either 'Uthmān or 'Ali, on the conditions for (il)legitimate disobedience and God's right to avenge the wrongful murder of his deputy.

Meanwhile, 'Ali had left Medina with seven hundred Helpers and entered Kufa, his supporters' garrison city, where his son was able to raise another six or seven thousand men for him, and sent one of the Helpers, Qays b. Sa'd b. 'Ubāda, to Egypt as its governor with a letter that acknowledged the legitimacy

---

13. Madelung 1997a, 157. Talha and al-Zubayr approached the son of 'Umar, but he refused to accompany them.

14. Tabari, 1:3117 (translation 16:58).

15. Tabari, 1:3119, 3133 (translation 16:60–61, 75). The inviolability of the sacred city was established by Muhammad's Constitution of Medina, which, however, lacked Qur'anic status. Later jurists were to consider the Qur'anic penalties as "the rights of God" in contrast to the "rights of the people" (*huquq al-nās*).

of the first two caliphs while calling their murdered successor, 'Uthmān, a violator of the precepts of the Book of God and the tradition of his prophet. Qays read out 'Ali's letter in Egypt and accepted the oath of allegiance to him "upon the Book of God and the Tradition of His Prophet."[16]

'Ali then met his opponents at the Battle of the Camel outside Basra in December 656. Talha and al-Zubayr were killed and 'Ā'isha was captured and sent back to Mecca. 'Ā'isha had been the first in the conflict to appeal the Book of God in her speeches and had carried a Qur'an to the battlefield for her attendant to call the warriors to fight. 'Ali, for his part, had a copy of the Book of God raised to appeal to the other side in the battlefield, and he gave the order to fight after its holder was killed.[17]

'Ali soon dismissed the Helper Qays and appointed his stepson Muhammad b. Abu Bakr to Egypt in his place. This dismissal of a Medinan Helper went hand in hand with the appointment of his cousin. 'Abdallāh b. 'Abbās as the governors of Basra, and of 'Abdallāh's brother, Qahtam, to Mecca, to which Medina was soon added after the dismissal of another prominent Helper.[18] These appointments suggest a clannish appropriation of the governorships not all that different from 'Uthmān's. Be that as it may, 'Ali could not rest long after his first victory, since another opponent with fewer ideological assets but far greater material power and a better army had been preparing to face him. The governor of Syria, Mu'āwiya, took up the cause of avenging the murdered caliph, putting 'Uthmān's blood-stained shirt on prominent display, and he was joined by the former governor of Egypt, 'Amr b. al-'Ās. Mu'āwiya's line of argument was that the right of to avenge 'Uthmān belonged to his Umayyad kinsmen, who were headed by himself; this differed from 'Ā'isha's argument that the right belonged to God.

Mu'āwiya argued that 'Ali was breaking the divine law by refusing to hand over the murderers of the slain caliph, who had been wrongfully killed (*mazluman*), and that, as the latter's kinsman, he was entitled to execute the divinely ordered retaliation.[19] 'Ali countered that 'Uthmān had not been innocent and had been guilty of "innovations"—arbitrary acts that contravened the conduct

---

16. Ibn A'tham al-Kufi n.d., 1:210–11.
17. Veccia Vaglieri 1952, 25, citing Tabari; Madelung 1997, 170.
18. Madelung 1997, 182, 191–93.
19. Veccia Vaglieri 1949, 22–23.

of the Prophet and his two successors—and of refusing to carry out divine law of retaliation by a pardon issued twelve years earlier.[20] The murderers of 'Uthmān had therefore not broken any divine norm. There should be no retaliation, as killing justly is permitted by the Qur'an (Q. 6:151, 14:67, 17:35) This opinion differed more sharply from 'Ā'isha's than did Mu'āwiya's. Last but not least among the imperfectly articulated principles decisive in setting the direction of the developmental path was the Qur'an readers' invocation of the conduct of the Prophet as another normative principle that was later incorporated into the Islamic law as the Sunna.

Ideas hastily adopted in revolutionary power struggles can acquire a life of their own. 'Ali's rebuttal of the legal argument for the punishment of 'Uthmān's murderers in order to protect his stepson Muhammad b. Abi Bakr, as well as other zealous supporters landed him on very dangerous grounds. He was legitimizing and upholding the right to rebellion and regicide following one's conscience. The right of rebellion against the unjust ruler was championed by the most zealous of his followers among the Quran readers who broke away from him within a year to form their own sect, the Khawārij (secessionists). One could say that 'Ali paid for the mistake of seizing ad hoc on the idea of the right to rebellion with his life. As we shall see, he was assassinated by one of the Khawārij.

'Ali was on much safer grounds when leaving the legal argument and moving to the much more general platform of the theocratic monarchy of the House of the Prophet. In his letter to Mu'āwiya during the month of truce in which the two armies faced each other before beginning the Battle of Siffin, after affirming that power, kingship (*mulk*), and government (*sultān*) emanate from God, 'Ali reiterated the legitimist idea of theocratic monarchy that was presumably being propounded from the pulpits in his capital, Kufa:

> Know there is [God's] proof for us, the People of the House ... God's saying, "Obey God and obey the Messenger and those in authority among you" [Q. 4:59] is for us the People of the House, and not for you.... We gave the House of Abraham the Book and the Wisdom, and We gave them a mighty kingdom [*mulk*]'

---

20. At the beginning of his caliphate, 'Uthmān had pardoned a son of his predecessor, 'Ubaydallāh b. 'Umar, in a murder case. 'Ali's Iraqi supporters argued that God demands opposing a ruler who acts in variance with revealed norms, and that it is lawful to shed his blood if he does not repent. 'Ā'isha anticipated this argument and refuted it by emphasizing 'Uthmān's repentance; however, the arena of revolutionary power struggle is not a court of law, and she lost to 'Ali.

[Q. 4:54] . . . We are the House of our Prophet Muhammad. . . . Therefore, kingship is ours; woe unto you, O Muʿāwiya, we have knowledge, are indeed prior with Abraham and we are his House.[21]

Note the subtle replacement of the monarchy of Banū Hāshim that had worried Abū Bakr and ʿUmar after the death of Muhammad by its near equivalent, the "House of the Prophet." Subtle though it may have been at the time, it set the developmental path of sectarian Shiʿism in a sharply divergent direction from that of the Sunni mainstream. Furthermore, the broadening of the ideological basis of ʿAli's claim to the caliphate forced his pragmatic opponent, Muʿāwiya, into defining his position in more general terms and raised the propaganda on both sides to the level of competing creeds. During the Battle of Siffin, the legal argument and the principle of consultation (*shūrā*) fell into secondary and tertiary places, and we repeatedly hear of the "religion of ʿAli," and, by contrast, the "religion of Muʿāwiya" (or pejoratively, the "religion of the son of Harb"). Consonantly with his "religion" and legitimist contention, ʿAli wore the Prophet's turban and carried his banner. Muʿāwiya's great banner was "the banner of community" (*liwā ʾal-jamāʿa*—the term we find in ʿUthmān and are about to hear from Muʿāwiya in celebrating his final victory).[22]

There were bearers of the emergent "religion of ʿAli," the nucleus of his "party" (*shiʿa*), which later grew into the Shiʿite sects, were among Ashtar's Qurʾan readers who made Islam the basis of their solidarity and who had their own distinct battle formation.[23] There was, in addition, a somewhat distinct and more numerous group of pious activists who were likewise called *qurrāʾ* and can perhaps be considered the second generation of Qurʾan readers, who supported ʿAli zealously but did not privilege his idea of theocratic monarchy over other ideas. Thirdly, there were the Arab tribal chiefs who did not necessarily have any interest in the religion of ʿAli but who supported his caliphate.[24] Their support was clearly pragmatic and lukewarm, however, and they forced ʿAli to stop the fighting and accept arbitration. As the supra-

---

21. Ibn Aʿtham al Kufi n.d., 1:195–99. During the battle, creedal statements on ʿAli's side similarly expounded his concept of theocratic monarchy as an institution for the salvation of mankind. See Minqāri, 380–85.

22. Hinds 1971b, 9, 17–18, 25; Amir-Moezzi 2006.

23. They had followed Ashtar to Syria in exile and then to Medina.

24. Most of the tribal contingents of the garrison cities of Iraq felt constrained to support him after his victory in the Battle of the Camel.

tribal Muslim solidarity of the garrison cities had fallen apart, they reverted to their old tribal solidarity and participated in the Battle of Siffin in tribal units.

Muʿāwiya's army was organized primarily along tribal lines, with each tribe bearing its own banners and slogans. The Qurʾan readers were fewer among his supporters and did not have a separate unit in the battle.[25] The all-out Battle of Siffin began on July 26, 657, and fierce fighting raged for four days. It ceased after the famous raising of as many as five hundred copies of the Qurʾan, or sheets thereof, on the lances of Muʿāwiya's troops, who demanded to let the Book of God and not the sword judge between the two parties. This was the same appeal ʿAli himself had made a few months earlier at the Battle of the Camel, as had ʿĀʾisha, Talha, and al-Zubayr, and it was therefore an offer he could not afford to refuse. The cleverness of the stratagem became proverbial in Islamic history, but just as sociologically astute, if not more so, was the sober appeal that preceded it in the peace cry:

> O congregation of the Arabs, by God, by God, [think of] your wives and children, and of the Romans and the Turks and the Persian tomorrow when you are annihilated.[26] By God, by God, [think of] your religion. This is the Book of God between us and you.[27]

The appeal to the material interest of the Arab warriors in the security of the empire and the prevention of the appropriation of their wives and children by its subject population that would result from the decimation of the empire's Syrian and Iraqi defenders are brought out more vividly by a variant reporting: "This is the Book of God between us and you. Who will protect the frontier districts of the Syrians if they all perish, and who those of the Iraqis if they all perish?"[28]

ʿAli's lukewarm tribal supporters could remind him that the Syrians were demanding what ʿAli himself had asked for. The Qurʾan-readers who later

---

25. Hinds 1971b, 26–28.
26. The emotional power of the prospect of the loss of wives to the subject population should not be underestimated. The wife of the early Muslim conqueror and founder of Basra, ʿUtba b. Ghazwān, used to urge him onto the battlefield as follows: "If they defeat you, you will deliver us as wives to the uncircumcised!" See Ibn Aʿtham al-Kufi n.d., 2:55.
27. Minqāri 1884, 478–79.
28. Tabari, 1:3329 (translation 17:78).

became the Kharijites, too, responded to the Syrians' call: "judgment is with the Book, and it is not [legally] permissible for us to fight when they call us to the judgment of the Book." The pious Qur'an readers whose foreheads were black from prostration in prayer were not shy in asserting their right to rebellion and regicide when 'Ali showed hesitation in accepting arbitration. They walked up to him fully armed and addressed him rudely, omitting his title: "O 'Ali, accept the group who is calling to the Book of God as you are called to it, or else we will kill you as we killed the son of Affān [i.e., 'Uthmān]!" By then, 'Ali was resigned to the fact and despondent: "I was the Commander [amir] of the Faithful yesterday, today I have become the commanded [ma'mur]."[29]

'Ali signed the arbitration agreement, naming the two arbitrators who were to judge between the parties according to the Book of God and the "unifying tradition" (sunna jami'a), and returned to Kufa. Some twelve thousand of his men refused to accept the compromise with Mu'āwiya and the Syrians, whom they called infidels, and withdrew from Kufa to Harura, revoking their allegiance to 'Ali, choosing their own amir, pending the convocation of the electoral council after victory, and offering their oath of allegiance to God on the basis of "ordering what is proper and prohibiting what is reprehensible."[30] What Leon Trotsky called the typical revolutionary emergence of "dual power"—in this case the "dual power" between 'Ali and Mu'āwiya—thus became the "multiple sovereignty" considered to be typical of the early stages of all revolutions.[31]

The reasons for the secession from the community ruled by 'Ali to Harura were variously given as his having doubted his own religion (din) or of his reneging on his religion (din) and authority (sultān). These secessionists felt compelled to articulate their grievance as their own interpretation of Islam, and thus formed their own Islamic sect—the first known as the Khawārij (secessionists). Their opposition to arbitration was generalized into a basic tenet of their faith embodied in the Qur'anic verse they adopted as their battle cry: "No judgment but God's" (Q. 6:57). Adherence to the Book and the Sunna took the place of allegiance to a person, making the imam

---

29. Minqāri 1884, 484–89.
30. Madelung 1997a, 247.
31. Tilly 1978.

removable in case of deviation and making the right of rebellion another basic tenet.³²

The arbitrators met some nine months after the Battle of Siffin, but their meeting broke up in disarray and Muʿāwiyya proceeded to proclaim himself caliph in the spring of 658. In the same year, ʿAli fought the Khawārij, who were greatly outnumbered in Nahravan and massacred those who did not surrender after he had guaranteed them safe conduct. Later that summer, ʿAli lost Egypt to ʿAmr b. ʿĀs, and Muhammad b. Abi Bakr was killed in retaliation for ʿUthmān and burned inside the belly of the corpse of an ass. After Nahravan, ʿAli's army dwindled and he had to send most of what was left to suppress the tax revolts in Iran and bring back the tribute, as his cousin ʿAbdallāh b. ʿAbbās had broken with him and left with the treasury of Basra. Meanwhile, Muʿāwiya began to order a series of demoralizing raids (*ghārāt*) into the territories remaining under ʿAli's control in Iraq and Arabia. Finally, ʿAbd al-Rahmān b. Muljam al-Murādi, a Kharijite from the tribal quarter of activists in the Egyptian garrison city of Fustāt, assassinated ʿAli on January 26, 661. ʿAli's son, al-Hasan, was proclaimed caliph but saw no point in prolonging the civil war, made peace with Muʿāwiya for a pension, and abdicated.

Not counting the casualties in the "raids" of the previous two years, the minor encounters, and collateral damage, as well as the last massacre of the Khawārij, who were mostly non-Arab converts, the casualties of the First Civil War were almost entirely Arab warriors and included many members of the highest stratum of the elite.³³

Why would the stipendiary elite of a new and rapidly expanding empire, headed by the core of Muhammad's companions, tear itself so ferociously apart? Why would they murder an aged caliph who had relaxed his predecessor's austere discipline to allow them to enjoy the fabulous wealth that flew in

---

32. They also extended the binding Sunna beyond the Messenger's to include those of his two successors, as ʿAli had done in his first above-cited letter to the Egyptians and as he was to do with respect to the public land in his last years. See Madelung 1997a, 276.

33. The lowest figures for the Battle of the Camel are four hundred to five hundred for Ali's troops and 2,500 for the opposing forces; the total figure for the Battle of Siffin may be about ten thousand; the battle or massacre of the Khawārij at Nahravan claimed one thousand to fourteen hundred lives of the rebels and seven to thirteen of the attackers. When Egypt was taken from ʿAli's forces by ʿAmr b. al-ʿĀs with six thousand men, the pro-ʿAli army of two thousand men was virtually annihilated in fierce fighting,

from the imperial conquests, albeit unevenly, while the wrongs that caliph was accused of perpetrating did not include blood shedding? The explanation, I suggest, lies in the struggle for the definition of Islam when a contingent crisis arose from the accidental killing of a besieger at the caliph's residence. Some were willing to give their lives for this struggle to define the new political order in a manner that was consistent with their faith, others for defending their vested interests. The struggle turned violent because no institutional structure yet existed for adjudicating conflicting understandings of the fundamental premises of Islam.

A striking fact that emerges from the murder of 'Uthmān is the complete lack of state formation at the center of the caliphate. The defense of the caliph's palace was left to his Umayyad kin, who sought refuge in the house of the Prophet's Umayyad widow after the caliph's murder.[34] The caliph had sought additional protection from the Companions who opposed him, and the latter had sent their sons to the palace to do so. There were no regular armed forces in Medina to withstand the thousand or so occupying warriors from the garrison cities. The caliph appealed for help from his kinsman Mu'āwiya, who did have a regular army that consisted of redeployed tribal contingents in former Byzantine military districts, but he did not respond.

A second factor partly related to the first is the absence of legal institutions for nonviolent resolution of contentious disputes, which made their politicization all but inevitable. We have seen how legal issues in the absence of any institutionalized law instigated and dominated strife throughout the First Civil War. There was no judicial authority or framework for deciding on allegations of the breach of law raised by 'Ā'isha and endorsed by Talha and al-Zubayr.[35] And what was the penalty for breaching the constitutional inviolability of the city of Medina by shedding the blood of the caliph? The question was not settled either legally or politically, since Medina ceased to

---

34. Nor was the fiscal organization of the caliphate any more developed. During the crisis, Talha had simply taken the keys to the treasury'; 'Ali sent someone along to get them back and dragged him to the mosque for the forced pledge of allegiance (Madelung 1997a, 132, 140). Later, 'Ali's cousin Ibn 'Abbas just took the treasury with him when he broke with 'Ali.

35. 'Ubaydallāh b. 'Umar offered to join 'Ali in Siffin in exchange for a pardon. His addition would have been a valuable political gain but 'Ali had made it impossible by his argument against 'Uthmān that the divine law did not allow acts of clemency by the caliph. 'Ali rejected the offer of 'Umar's son, and the latter joined Mu'āwiya. See Madelung 1997a, 209.

be the capital during the civil war. And was regicide permissible under any circumstances? Most parties said it was not; 'Ali, however, siding with the Quran readers who became the secessionists, said it was and paid with his life for saying so. And was the wrongful killing of the ruler a public crime or a private crime for which the execution of punishment devolved on the kin of the victim, as Mu'āwiya claimed? There was no way to decide these issues since Islamic law as an institution had not developed yet. The Qur'an, officially collected by 'Uthmān, was the only institution—that is why we hear of the Qur'an readers as a social group but not of jurists or judges. Every side did appeal to the Book of God but the differences in its interpretation could only be settled violently.

With the abdication of al-Hasan b. 'Ali in favor of Mu'āwiya b. Abu Sufyān in 661, the idea of the theocratic monarchy of the House of the Prophet became the utopian program of the Shi'ite sects, giving way to the reality of monarchy of the Quraysh—the reality of the Muslim empire of conquest that had come into being as a consequence of Muhammad's Constitutive Revolution in Arabia, or more precisely, of his policy of winning the heart of the Quraysh military leaders. Mu'āwiya, the victor of the civil war, faithful to the slogan of his banner in the Battle of Siffin, declared the year of the undisputed Caliphate, year 41 (661–662), the Year of Unity ('ām al-jamā'a), thus opening a new developmental path for Sunni Islam.[36]

THE SECOND CIVIL WAR AND THE FAILED REVOLUTION OF THE MAWĀLI IN KUFA

The Second Civil War (680–692), like the first one, was the result of a temporary breakdown in the structure of authority caused by a crisis of succession. But unlike the First Civil War, which was entirely an Arab affair and a family feud among the Companions of Muhammad and the aristocracy of the Quraysh, the second drew in and highlighted the existence, as a growing social stratum, of Muslim subjects of the empire whose revolutionary historic mission was yet to come. This social group, sociologically an "estate" defined by its legal status or what Max Weber called status honor or social standing, consisted of Muslim subjects of the empire who had had to become "clients"

36. Al-Azmeh 2014, 401.

(*mawāli*) of an Arab individual or clan when converting to Islam. The Second Civil War was a failed Integrative Revolution of this estate (which would have to wait for another half century to be integrated). The most interesting feature of the Second Civil War, however, was that it marked the birth of a distinctive form of messianic millennialism in Islam.

The caliphate of the Quraysh thus moved to Syria and was appropriated by the Umayyad clan, or more narrowly by the House of Abu Sufyān. Like his father Abu Sufyān, Muʿāwiya (r. 660–680) was a master of old Arabian tribal domination, and a skillful maker and manager of tribal coalitions among the Arab tribes settled in Syria; he made Damascus his capital. Muʿāwiya's governors, however, with one exception, were not from his own clan or even from the Quraysh but were new men serving the master of the empire. He succeeded in making the caliphate hereditary for the benefit of his son, Yazid, whose sudden death in November 683 encouraged the sons of the losers of the First Civil War, ʿAli and al-Zubayr, to make a bid for the caliphate.

The new Sufyanid caliphate of the Quraysh rested on Muʿāwiya's alliance with the tribe of Kalb.[37] The tribes opposed to the Kalb favored the caliphate of ʿAbdallāh b. al-Zubayr, who took refuge in the sanctuary in Mecca. The Kalb and their allies made a complicated deal with the elder of the Umayyad clan, the old secretary of ʿUthmān and Muʿāwiya's relative, Marwān b. al-Hakam, and defeated the opposing tribal coalition in the Battle of Marj Rāhit in 684. The caliphate of the Quraysh then shifted to Marwān b. al-Hakam (d. 685), and remained hereditary among his offspring, the Marwanid branch of the Umayyad dynasty. The rump Kalbite military support was sufficient for Marwān to regain Egypt, but it was left to his son, ʿAbd al-Malik (r. 685–705), to rebuild the shattered authority structure of the empire in the east, and to revamp the military tribal support for it.[38] That task took much

---

37. The Kalb was already in the Syrian desert at the time of the Muslim conquest and brought a cluster of immigrant Arab tribes into a tribal confederation it dominated—the Qudāʿa. This pitted the Kalb-dominated Qudāʿa against the southern tribes, the Yaman, and the Qays tribal confederation that dominated the army (*jund*) of the district of Qinnasrin in the Jazira (northern Mesopotamia).

38. The tribal alignment that sustained the Marwanid caliphate, however, was altered by the inclusion of the defeated southern (Yemenite) tribes as part of the Qudāʿa confederacy, which dominated the armies of the four districts of Syria and Palestine, as opposed to the Qays in the army of Qinnasrin and the Jazira. See Crone 1994b, 44–49.

longer because the challenge to Umayyad rule outside Syria was far more serious.

The sons of the former caliphs and companions who now formed the pensioned aristocracy of Medina refused to accept Yazid as the new caliph. Husayn b. 'Ali, Muhammad's grandson through his daughter Fāṭima, was invited to Kufa to lead a revolt but was abandoned by the Kufan notables and killed with his family in Karbala in October 680. 'Abdallāh b. al-Zubayr, 'Ā'isha's favorite nephew and probably the richest man in Arabia, took refuge in the sanctuary and proclaimed his caliphate in Mecca, which he held for over a decade until 692.

Husayn b. 'Ali was mistaken in his perception that the death of Mu'āwiya in 680 had opened an opportunity for him. In fact, what the sociologists of social and political movements call the "opportunity structure" for opposition and protest movements had not changed because the tribal military structure sustaining it solidly held for Yazid b. Mu'āwiya, whose mother was a Kalb. Husayn paid for his misperception with his life, while Ibn al-Zubayr took refuge in the holy sanctuary in Mecca, now in the Arabian periphery of the Umayyad empire, biding his time; he was very lucky that Yazid died suddenly. Shortly before his death, Yazid's forces had in fact suppressed the rebellion in nearby Medina and had obliterated the Helpers as a nontribal component of the Muslim polity completely. It was Yazid's death in 683 that created a major rift among the tribes that sustained the Umayyad regime, shattered the structure of its political and military domination, and thus created a new opportunity structure that gave Ibn al-Zubayr and his brother, Mus'ab, the chance to make the countercaliphate a reality in a situation of dual power that lasted some eight years. The opportunity opened by this fragmentation of power between the Umayyads and the Zubayrids was in turn seized by the growing Kharijite movement, and by a proto-Shi'ite movement that emerged in 'Ali's last stronghold, Kufa, to avenge his son Husayn, thereby creating a situation of what the American sociologist Charles Tilly calls "multiple sovereignty."

Two groups of the Khawārij acted immediately. The first group, called the Najadāt after their leader, Najada b. 'Āmir, seized large parts of the Arabian Peninsula and held it during Ibn al-Zubayr's countercaliphate in Mecca. A more missionary group, known as the Azāriqa after their leader, Nāfi' b. Azraq, seized Ahvaz in the hinterland of Basra after losing control of the city itself in 684, proselytized among non-Arabs that boasting about race and giving preference to one over the other is unbelief (*kufr*), and they spread their intensified proselytization into the Iranian territories to the east—notably, to Fars and Kerman—under the leadership of Qatari b. Fujā'a (d. ca. 698), expanding their mission into Sistan. In 687, the Azāriqa invaded Iraq and occupied the Madā'in and the area near Kufa. Coins bearing the name of Qatari b. Fujā'a are proof that the Khawārij held Fars for at least three years after the end of the Second Civil War. Qatari b. Fujā'a altered the Sasanian coins by adding the profession of God's unity and "Muhammad is the Messenger of God" to the sovereign (obverse) side around the image of Shāhanshāh; finally, he added the slogan of the Kharijite theocracy, "*La hukm illā li'llāh*" (command is but God's), and a less-known legend to the same effect: "*Bi'smillāh wali al-amr*" (in the name of God, the sovereign).[39]

At the beginning of the unrest, Ibn al-Zubayr had accepted the principle of *shurā*, election of the caliphate through a council, and he even appears to have developed a significant formula in connection with that principle—namely, the choice of *al-ridā* (the acceptable one) by an electoral council. But the senior surviving sons of 'Umar and 'Ali who were in Mecca refused to pledge their allegiance to him; the latter, known after his mother as Muhammad b. al-Hanafiyya (d. 700), in fact put himself forward as an alternative candidate. To gain support of the Kharijites, Ibn al-Zubayr adopted their Qur'anic slogan, "command is but God's" (*lā hukm illā l'illāh*), by 686. He then proclaimed his own caliphate and took the oath of allegiance "on the Book of God, and the Sunna of His Prophet and the [exemplary] conduct (*sira*) of the pious Caliphs."[40]

Without the support of the secessionist insurgents in Arabia, Ibn al-Zubayr's control of Mecca was so tenuous that in 688, the Umayyads had their own pilgrimage procession in addition to that of the Kharijites and the followers of Ibn al-Zubayr and Ibn al-Hanafiyya. Nevertheless, the countercaliph held on to power until 692 when, after being abandoned by his men in exchange for pardon by the Syrians, he chose death while fighting in front of the Mecca sanctuary at the age of seventy-three. The Second Civil War thus ended with a whimper; however, one episode in it was of great significance for the integra-

---

39. Madelung 1988, 54–57; Heidemann 2011, 168–69.
40. Ibn Sa'd 1904–28, 5:119; *Ansāb*, 2:655–57, vol. 4, part 2:105.

tive dimension of revolution and especially for the reemergence of apocalyptic messianism: the rebellion of Mukhtār in Kufa.[41]

The uprising of al-Muhktār b. Abi 'Ubayd al-Thaqafi, the son of one of the early Muslim conquerors of Iran and the brother-in-law of 'Abdallāh b. 'Umar, reawakened the apocalyptic mood of the early years of Islam among new converts as well as the Yemenite tribesmen settled in the garrison city of Kufa. The uprising began in October 685 and ended with the death of Mukhtār on April 3, 687.

Revolution was already afoot when Mukhtār began his uprising in October 685. The nucleus of the party (shi'a) of 'Ali survived his assassination in Kufa but was severely persecuted under Mu'āwiya. Mālik al-Ashtar's successor as the leader of the Qur'an readers, Hujr b. 'Ali al-Kindi, was judicially murdered and succeeded by another old Qur'an reader, Sulaymān b. Surad al-Khuzā'i. Sulaymān had been one of the signatories of the letter inviting Husayn to come to Kufa and began a clandestine movement of repentance as the failure to defend Husayn was a sin and required repentance (tauba). His followers were accordingly called the Penitents (tawwābun). When the news of Yazid's death reached Kufa, the Penitents urged their leader to begin an uprising, saying, "This tyrant is dead, and the authorities are weak!"[42] Mukhtār had refused to testify against Hujr and had been preventively imprisoned at the time of the killing of Husayn in Karbala. When he was released from prison, he went to Ibn al-Zubayr in Mecca and fought against the Umayyad army that had invaded Mecca just before the death of Yazid. He offered Ibn al-Zubayr his allegiance in exchange for the governorship of Kufa, but his offer was refused and he at any rate rushed back to Kufa empty-handed in May 684, finding the movement of the Penitents (tawwābun) in full swing.[43] Mukhtār began to compete with the leadership of the movement with Sulaymān b. Surad but did

---

41. The uprising was, however, not the first to take place after the opening of opportunity for rebellion with the death of Yazid in November 683. There was a popular rebellion in Basra for nine days during which the prisons were opened, and the garrison city was without a government until the people agreed to accept the Hashemite 'Abdallāh b. al-Hārith "and invested him with authority because of his probity and being a relative of the Messenger of God." Yazid's governor, 'Ubaydallāh b. Ziyād fled to Syria. See Akhbār T, 283.

42. Tabari, 2:596 (translation 20:90); Kohlberg 1997, 826. The harm they inflicted on themselves as penance during their processions in Kufa is the origin of Shi'ite self-flagellation to mourn the martyrdom of al-Husayn in Karbala.

43. Tabari, 2:509 (translation 20:92).

not have much success until the latter's death. In the meantime, he began to recruit for his own movement by turning the Penitents' punitive introversion and self-flagellation into an extropunitive call for vengeance against Husayn's killers. In addition to recruiting among the Penitents, he also recruited heavily among the southern Arabian tribesmen who were disgruntled with the 'Umayyads' rule and who expected its millennial end. Mukhtār produced a letter of endorsement from Muhammad b. al-Hanafiyya al-Mahdī calling Mukhtār his "trustee" (amīn) and "helper" or vizier (wazīr), and he assumed the leadership of the rebellion. His brightest success was winning over Ibrāhīm, the son of Mālik al-Ashtar, who had serious doubts about the authenticity of the endorsement letter and Mukhtār's millennial inspiration but who joined him pragmatically and in fact proved his ablest general.[44]

As an Arab political entrepreneur deprived of office, Mukhtār was clearly aware of the fragmentation of authority and resented the ruling elite he considered to be his equals.[45] This dispossessed member of the ruling class was also quick to learn the lesson on political mobilization from the revolutionary, puritanical Khawārij. He recruited among the new social stratum—the non-Arab clients converted to Islam—most notably the chief of the *mawālī* of Kufa, the Persian client of the Bajila, Kaysān b. Abī 'Amra, who had a religious following of his own, the Kaysāniyya, and who had already recruited heavily among the client population of Kufa, the Hamrā' (the fair-skinned—literally, the reds). Their number is put at twenty thousand; of special military value among them were the Asāwira (horsemen), the cavalry contingent that had defected from the Sasanians and was quartered in Kufa. After seizing power, Mukhtār appointed Kaysān his chief of police, presumably putting him in charge of organizing revolutionary gangs in the streets of Kufa. These gangs were recruited from the *mawālī* and were equipped with clubs (*khashab*), which they called *kafirkubāt* (infidel-smashers) in Persian. They were alternately called Mukhtāriyya or Khashabiyya. Mukhtār chose for them the Penitents' battle cry: "Revenge for Husayn" (*ya la-tha'rāt al-Husayn*).[46]

---

44. Wellhausen 1975b, 128–29.

45. In a very probably apocryphal but nevertheless intelligent report, Mukhtār confesses that his motive in the uprising was not religion but worldly ambition, since his colleagues were in power while he was left out in the cold, with the cry for vengeance of Husayn being his only political asset. See Akhbār T, 307.

46. Tabari, 2:538, 694 (translation 20:124–25, 21, 61); Moscati 1950b, 257; van Arendonk, 1086.

The rebellion began in mid-October 685. A number of Arab notables of Kufa were incited into fighting Mukhtār and his Persian clients by being told by their commander, "Curses upon you! Do you want to flee before your slaves?" They were, however, captured one by one and slain. After seizing power in Kufa, Mukhtār carried out his program of revenge against the nobility of Kufa responsible for the death of Husayn, confiscated their property, and gave it to the Persians who had supported Kaysān. From Kufa as his base, Mukhtār soon dominated the imperial hinterland to the north and northeast, appointing governors to Mawsil, Azerbaijan, Isfahan, and Rayy.[47]

He sent those club-wielders that were no longer needed in the streets of the garrison city to march on Mecca in order to release Muhammad b. al-Hanafiyya, who had been imprisoned by Ibn al-Zubayr, and he organized others into infantry units sent to Jazira with Ibrāhim b. al-Ashtar.[48] An Umayyad general who secretly visited Ibrāhim's camp told him, "My sadness intensified as I entered your army camp, as I did not hear a word of Arabic spoken until I reached you."[49]

The inclusiveness of Mukhtār's army is remarkable, and it contrasts sharply with Ibn al-Zubayr's murderous purges of the non-Arab clients from his army. Increasing Arabism doomed Ibn al-Zubayr's caliphate to eventual collapse while the integrative rebellion of Mukhtār spread through Mesopotamia and southwestern Iran in 686. But Mukhtār's reliance on the clients backfired, and the Kufan Arab Shi'a, including the prominent Qur'an readers, defected. Mukhtār was abandoned in the citadel by August 686. At this point, his support seemed limited to the extremist southern Arabian Shi'a, who carried in a procession a purportedly holy chair of 'Ali.[50]

Meanwhile, those Kufan tribal chiefs who had escaped from Kufa and had gone to Basra sought the help of Mus'ab b. al-Zubayr, telling him "how their own slaves and *mawāli* has risen against them" and how Mukhtār had given their property to the Persians. Mus'ab felt too weak to act on his own and sent

---

47. Akhbār T, 292; Wellhausen 1975b, 129–30; Hawting 1993, 522.

48. Tabari, 2:693–95 (translation 21:59–62).

49. Akhbār T, 294. According to another eyewitness report, the Syrian general, Rabi'a b. al-Mukhāriq, told his troops: "People of Syria, you are fighting only runaway slaves and men who have abandoned Islam and ... do not speak Arabic!" See Tabari, 2:647 (translation 21:8); see also Wellhausen 1975b, 129.

50. According to one report in Tabari, Mukhtār had bought it at a junk shop.

the leading Kufan notable, Muhammad b. al-Ash'ath b. Qays, to bring back al-Muhallab b. Abi Sufra, the general who was fighting the Khawārij in Fars. Muhammad b. al-Ash'ath told al-Muhallab that "our slaves and *mawāli* have taken our wives, children, and families from us by force!" When Muhallab came, Mus'āb and the Kufan exiles marched toward Kufa in his company. In the army that Mukhtār sent out to meet them, the *mawāli* had their own division under the command of Kaysān Abu 'Amra. This caused considerable resentment, and one of Mukhtār's Arab commanders told his superior, "*Mawāli* and slaves are weaklings … Although you are walking, they have many men on horseback with them [presumably the Asāwira]. Order them to dismount with you so that they can have an example in you to follow." The Zubayrid army defeated Mukhtār's army and marched on to Kufa, where the latter took refuge in the government palace. He lasted a few months longer in the citadel but made a sortie with nineteen men on April 3, 687; he was killed at the age of sixty-seven. The number of armed men in the government palace and the castle who finally surrendered after the death of Mukhtār is put variously at one thousand Arabs and one thousand *mawāli*.[51] His troops who remained were scattered throughout Mesopotamia for months after his death; they included many runaway slaves.

The integrative dimension of Mukhtār's rebellion makes it the first revolution of the *mawāli*, even if it is a failed one. The fragmentation of authority during the revolutionary situation of multiple sovereignty gave not only the Muslim clients but also the slaves the opportunity to mutiny. Two instances of slave mutiny are reported, the first at the very beginning of the civil war in Medina, the second in in Mesopotamia in the summer of 687 that was reported in the eyewitness Syriac account of John bar Penkaye. The leadership of Mukhtār's failed rebellion was entirely Arab, however. The Persian clients needed six more decades to gather force, and, as we shall see, their successful revolution would begin not in metropolitan Kufa but in Khurasan on the periphery of the Umayyad Empire. More to the point is that two revolutionary leaders in Khurasan and Kufa would be themselves clients and not Arabs.

---

51. Akhbār T, 304; Tabari, 2:718, 721 (translation 21:85–88). Much higher figures of two thousand Arabs and six thousand Persians are given by Akhbār T, 309.

THE REEMERGENCE OF APOCALYPTIC MESSIANISM
IN THE FIGURE OF THE QAʾIM-MAHDI

The twin social bases of Mukhtār's rebellion contributed apocalyptic and millennial religious notions of their own around which the "extremist" Shiʿite groups (*ghulāt*) became organized. These notions were amalgamated and Islamicized after the suppression of the revolt into distinctive beliefs of the emergent Shiʿite sects. The term *Mahdi* in the messianic sense appears with the Yemenite/southern Arabian supporters of Mukhtār, and it is used by Mukhtār himself for Ibn al-Hanafiyya, in whose name he led the rebellion. The key idea of the savior of the End of Time, the Mahdi, was also absorbed into mainstream orthodoxy, even though some Sunni traditionists Mujahid (d. 106?) and Hasan al-Basri (d.728) insisted there was no Mahdi other than the returning Jesus. Others, however, made the Mahdi Muhammad redivivus by insisting, on the authority of the Companion ʿAbdallāh b. Masʿud, that his name would be that of the Prophet, and his father's name, the latter's. The Sunni Mahdi was in effect believed to be the returning Muhammad b. ʿAbdallāh, the Messenger of God.

The messianic figure of the Shiʿa, by contrast, was originally not the Mahdi but the Qaʾim. The Kaysāniyya, who actively supported Mukhtār, spread the two fundamental ideas to which the conception of the Mahdi was assimilated somewhat later. The first was the messianic riser (*qāʾim*) of the End of Time. The second was the idea of *ghayba* (occultation) of the messianic Qaʾim, which developed out of the more general belief in *rajʿa* (return of the dead). When Muhammad b. al-Hanafiyya died in the year 700, the Kaysāniyya maintained that he was in concealment or occultation (*ghayba*) in the Radwa Mountains and would return as the Qāʾim and the Mahdi. The Kaysāni poet, Kuthayyar (d. 723), hailed him as "He is the Mahdi Kaʿb, the brother/fellow of the Ahbār, had told us about," and affirmed that "he is vanished in the Radwa, not to be seen for a while, and with him is honey and water."[52] When Muhammad b. al-Hanafiyya's son, Abu Hāshim, who had succeeded him, died childless in 717–18, some of his followers maintained that he was, like his father, the Mahdi and was alive in concealment in the Radwa mountains. The Kaysāniyya also spread the idea of *rajʿa*, the return of the dead, especially of the dead imams,

---

52. Muruj, 3:277.

with the help of such Qur'anic precedents as the resuscitation of the Companions of the Cave and the owner of the ass, whether Jeremiah or Ezra, who became the apocalyptic figure expected at the centennium of the Islamic era. The expectation of the return of this Mahdi from occultation grew so widespread that the term *al-qā'im* (the Standing One, the Riser, the Redresser) became a major ingredient of the Shi'ite apocalyptic tradition. The notion of occultation acquired chiliastic connotations through its association with the manifestation or parousia (*zuhur*) of the apocalyptic Qā'im. The forceful poetry of the Kaysāni al-Sayyid al-Himyari (d. after 787), who later joined the Imamiyya, helped spread the idea:

> That the one in authority [walī al-amr] and the Qā'im ...
> For him [is decreed] an occultation [ghayba]; inevitably will he vanish
> And may God bless him who endures the occultation
> He will pause a while, then manifest his cause
> And fill all the East and West with justice.[53]

Considerable light on the origins of the idea of the Qā'im (Standing One, Riser, Redresser) is cast by a valuable Syriac text, which predates Islam and is suggestive of the influence of Kaysāni Persian clients on the development of the notion. According to this text, the Liar (*daggāla*) will beguile the Magi by telling them that Pishyōtan, one of the Zoroastrian immortals, has awakened from his sleep, "and he is the Standing One (*qā'im*) before the Hurmizd, your God, who has appeared on earth." Two very interesting terms in this short passage were destined for prominence in Islamic apocalyptic lore. The first is the Liar (*daggāla*), the Liar of Qumran whom we met in chapter 1. By this time, the figure had been fully apocalypticized in the Syriac literature,[54] having become the Dajjāl of the Islamic apocalyptics—the "Antichrist," to be killed by the Anointed Jesus upon his Second Coming.

More importantly, this text gives us the word for a new apocalyptic messianic figure, *qā'im*. The term *qāi'm* from the Aramaic Samaritan *qa'em* ("the living one," or "the one standing permanently") and the Syriac *qa'em* both of which are used to translate the Greek ὁ ἑστώς (the Standing One) in the Gnostic Samaritan literature. On etymological grounds, this derivation is supported by a Shi'ite tradition according to which the sixth Imam allegedly

---

53. Cited in Arjomand 2016, 46.
54. See Reynolds 2001, 63–64n29 for the reference to the Syriac texts on the *daggāla*.

explains the term *qā'im* as "because he rises after he has died."⁵⁵ According to the explanation in the Syriac Gnostic texts from Mesopotamia, the Holy Spirit stands before the face of God the Father, as do the angels according to what is said in the Gospel: "in heaven their angels do always behold the face of my Father which is in heaven."⁵⁶

Meanwhile, the southern Arabian tribes who supported Mukhtār were another major source of the apocalyptic ideas that spread through Kufa during the Second Civil War. Although it comes from the Qur'anic root, *h-d-y*, the term *Mahdi*, meaning "the rightly-guided one," does not occur in the Qur'an. In all likelihood, it came into Islam as an apocalyptic term from the southern Arabian tribes who settled in Syria under Mu'āwiya as its governor during the caliphate of 'Uthmān and expected "the Mahdi who will lead the rising of the people of the Yemen back to their country" to restore the glory of their lost Himyarite kingdom. This Mahdi, it was believed, would conquer Constantinople or was, alternatively, separated from a second Mahdi who would conquer Constantinople in other traditions. He would be followed by the Qahtāni (also called the Yamāni), who was supposed to lead the Yemenite tribes in fierce warfare against the Quraysh and destroy them.⁵⁷

In short, *qā'im*, the Arabic cognate of the Syriac term for the Standing One as the savior of the End of Time must have been in use in Mesopotamia for some time before the term *Mahdi* was taken from the Sunni apocalyptic lore of southern Arabian origins and was adopted as a late synonym for it. The pristine apocalyptic messianism of Paleo-Islam was thus resuscitated and found embodiment in the Qa'im-Mahdi as the savior of the End of Time.

The important role of the Yemenite tribes in the formation of the Islamic apocalyptic tradition was, however, by no means confined to this instance.⁵⁸ Quite apart from the transmission of much of the Judeo-Christian apocalyptic lore through the southern Jewish kingdom of Dhu Nuwās in the early sixth century and the learned southern Arabs under Islam, Ka'b al-Ahbār and

---

55. Arjomand 2000.
56. Cited in Van Reeth 2012a, 447.
57. Nu'aym b. Hammād 1991, 236–39, 242–49.
58. The Ash'arites and Himyarites of Kufa settled in Qumm in central Iran after the suppression of Mukhtār's rebellion (687) and, in another wave after the failure of the rebellion of 'Abd al-Rahman b. al-Ash'ath (d. 700), acted as an important channel for the transmission of the apocalyptic lore to Shi'ism.

Wahb b. Munabbih (d. 728 or 732), the southern Arab tribes settled in Syria and introduced a major nonbiblical tribal trend into classical Islamic apocalypticism. The leading role in this trend was played by Ka'b's Himyarite tribe, whose apocalyptic imagination was kindled by the sense of dispossession resulting from the loss of their kingdom to the Quraysh: "This matter (= the reign) was among the Himyar, then God took it away from them and placed it among the Quraysh. But it will return to them." The agent of this restoration would be the above-mentioned Qahtāni (the descendant of the tribal ancestor of the southern Arabs). The Qahtāni is the oldest nonbiblical figure in the Islamic apocalyptic tradition and was already recognized as such at the time the term *Mahdi* acquired its definitive messianic connotation. The Qahtāni was to rule after the final demise of the Quraysh and to the End of Time, and then his reign would witness the apocalyptic battles (*malāhim*) that culminate in the conquest of Constantinople: "Under the reign of this Yemenite Caliph who will conquer Constantinople and the Roman domain, the Dajjāl shall come forth, Jesus will descend in his time. . . . " A tradition asserting that the Qahtāni was a Yemenite Qurayshite required that the legendary hero be killed at the Greatest Tribulation (*al-malhama al-uzma/al-kubra*). Alternatively, he was to be killed in arms before the appearance of a man from the House of Ahmad who would in turn be followed by the Dajjāl and Jesus.[59]

In addition, apocalyptic traditionists introduced the southern Arabian deliverer, al-Mansur, whose name was frequently invoked on the battlefield with the cries of *"yā Mansur, yā Mansur!"* According to his great-great-grandson, Zayd b. 'Ali (d. 740), Muhammad himself had adopted the slogan *"yā Mansur amit* (O Mansur, kill)!" in the apocalyptic Battle of Badr. In due course, the Manur, too, was appropriated by the ruling Quraysh. The tradition, "Mansur is the Mansur of the Himyar," was accordingly modified to "the Mansur is the Mansur of the Banu Hāshim [the clan of the Prophet]." Another apocalyptic figure contributed by the southern Arabs was the Saffāh, which means both the shedder of blood and the generous spender (of gold and silver). The southern Arabian traditionists claimed that the Saffāh's name was men-

---

59. See Madelung 1986a for all citations. The southern Arabian tribes settled in Syria were split and fought on opposite sides in the decisive Battle of Marj Rāhit in 684. According to Madelung, the apocalyptic output occasioned by Marj Rāhit introduced the figure of the Qahtāni, together with details from the early Umayyad history.

tioned in the Old Testament: "The Saffāh will live for forty years; his name in the Torah is the flier of the sky."[60]

One other minor apocalyptic figure that emerged during the Second Civil War is the Sufyāni. The Sufyāni was made possible once the Sufyanid branch of the Umayyads lost the caliphate after the Battle of Marj Rāhit. This makes Yazid, who died at the beginning of the Second Civil War, a very likely first prototype.[61] The probable provenance of the Sufyāni legend from Shi'ite circles tends to confirm the hypothesis that he was originally a "Yazid redivivus" held responsible for the martyrdom of Husayn and elevated to the rank of the second evil personality of the Islamic apocalypse—second only to the Dajjāl.

In all these waves of generation of political apocalypticism between the rebellion of Mukhtār and the Hashemite Revolution, many historical details, *ex eventu*, enter the apocalyptic traditions. Many of the main actors of early Islamic history are thinly disguised as apocalyptic figures: Mu'āwiya becomes "the head of kings" (*ra's al-muluk*); Marwān b. al-Hakam becomes "the son of the blue-eyed woman" (*ibn al-zarqā'*). To anticipate our next revolution for the sake of completing the argument, the last Umayyad caliph, Marwān II (744–750) was made into "the red [-haired]" (*ashab*), and the "Ass of the Jazira," while others, such as the Lord of the West (*sahib al-maghrib*) are generated by forgotten historical figures, such as 'Abd al-Rahmān al-Fihri, who had led the great Berber Revolt of 739–43 in North Africa.[62] Al-Fihri's's apocalyptic

---

60. See Arjomand 1998 for references. Some events during the Second Civil War also gave rise to millennial notions that spread widely and were absorbed into the Muslim apocalyptic tradition—notably, the dispersal in the desert in 683 of an army sent by the Umayyad caliph Yazid against Ibn al-Zubayr, which, on hearing the news of Yazid's death, generated what may be the first *ex eventu* prophecy about the unnamed restorer of faith who was later taken to be the Mahdi (see Madelung 1981a). A few years later, Musā, the son of Ṭalḥa (one of the losers of the First Civil War), was proposed by his circle as the Mahdi after he fled from Kufa during Mukhtār's rebellion to Basra. See Ibn Sa'd 1904–28, 5:120–21.

61. In the Kufan Shi'ite apocalyptic traditions, the Sufyāni becomes the sender of the army that will be swallowed in the desert; he is made to appear simultaneously with the Mahdi at the End of Time. The leader of the first Syrian rebellion against the Abbasids in 751, Abu Muhammad al- Sufyāni, would claim to be this known apocalyptic figure, "the Sufyāni who had been mentioned" (Madelung 1986b, 14). The historical Sufyāni in turn supplied some details of the Sufyāni apocalyptic legend. One apocalyptic tradition considers 'Umar II one of three Mahdis, and places him *after* the Sufyāni. See Nu'aym b. Hammād 1991, 222.

62. Nu'aym b. Hammād 1991, 150.

disguise is especially complimentary: the commander of his vanguard is "a man whose name is the name of Satan."

In an interesting parallel to the immediate failure and millennially long-term success of the Essene revolutionary coalition partner in the Maccabean revolt discussed in chapter 1, the failed Mahdist rebellion of the *mawālī* in Kufa resulted in the growth of millennial beliefs that periodically ignited fires in the minds of Shi'ite revolutionaries through subsequent centuries. A new pattern of motivation was thus born in this second civil war of Muslims that now included a considerable number of non-Arab subjects of the empire of conquest. Apocalyptic messianism reemerged and was added to the mobilizational repertoire alongside jihad, the constitutive struggle in the path of God.

THE MARWANID COUNTERREVOLUTION AND THE DEVELOPMENT OF SUNNI ORTHODOXY

The paradox of counterrevolution was highlighted by the German historian of Rome, Theodor Mommsen, who asserted that restoration is always revolution.[63] Counterrevolution seeks to appropriate the successful ideas of the preceding revolution in its restoration of the status quo ante. No establishment could afford to absorb the apocalyptic messianism of the Kaysāniyya and the other extremist followers of Mukhtār, as well as the Marwanid establishment under the winners of the Second Civil War, 'Abd al-Malik b. Marwān (685–705) and his governor in the east, al-Ḥajjāj b. Yusuf al-Thaqafī (d. 714), fiercely suppressing as they did all other expressions of pro-'Alid partisanship and Shi'ism.

Nevertheless, the competitive countermobilization necessary for winning the civil war in Mesopotamia and Arabia had far-reaching consequences. The Kharajite rebels, too, had converted a large number of people in Iran and recruited them into their revolutionary movement. In Mesopotamia, too, they appear to have been successful in their competitive mobilization against Mukhtār, and they won over the runaway slaves from the army of Ibrāhim al-Ashtar who had joined the Khawārij.[64] The Umayyad winner of the Second

---

63. Cited in Arjomand 2019.

64. Around the time of Mukhtār's death, the slaves had mutinied and killed Ibrāhim's lieutenant, even joining the Kharijite movement, at least nominally. In his eyewitness account in Syriac, John bar Penkaye records that they called them *shurṭe*, taking the term as an indication of "their zeal for righteousness" (see Hoyland 1997, 198). Hoyland, however, mistakes the

Civil War, Caliph 'Abd al-Malik, too, engaged in competitive countermobilization, recruiting slaves into his army in Mesopotamia with the promise of freedom and taking some of them back to Syria to form the Syrian Khashabiyya that later became a presence among the groupings of young men (*fityān*) in Syrian cities.

Seven years of intensive counterrevolutionary mobilization left Caliph 'Abd al-Malik with an Arab tribal army that was much more powerful and better organized than that of Yazid b. Mu'āwiya and had ancillary *mawāli* contingents. This army produced the unprecedented concentration of power that made possible state building and bureaucratic administration in Syria and Iraq. A centralized imperial state, whose absence in Caliph 'Uthmān's Medina we found so striking, was thus created at the end of the Second Civil War. The export of revolution, used metaphorically for 'Umar's imperial conquests in chapter 2, now became full reality. Al-Hajjāj b. Yusuf recovered the areas ruled by the Kawārij in Mesopotamia and Iran (Fars and Sistan), while Qutayba b. Muslim al-Bāhili (d. 715) embarked on the reconquest of Khurasan and the conquest of Transoxiana. Qutayba's conquests were indeed the export of the Islamic revolution; they expanded the Umayyad Empire considerably and created a vast and prosperous periphery where the conversion to Islam gathered great momentum, making it the site of the next and socially most profound Islamic revolution, which we shall consider in the next three chapters.

'Abd al-Malik b. Marwān, however, chose not to make any inclusive concessions to the *mawāli* who served his imperial state building, and he decided not to compromise the Arabism of its restoration. The Arabism of his regime was best reflected in the change of the language of the imperial bureaucracy from Persian and Greek to Arabic. This went hand in hand with the appropriation of the Islamic platforms of the Zubayrid anticaliph and of the Kharijite rebels.

'Abd al-Malik assumed the title of God's deputy (*khalifat Allāh*), whose conception we have traced to the last letters of the third caliph, 'Uthmān, and who minted it on his new coinage. Although the Marwanid governors in the

---

term *shurte* for its Arabic cognate, *shurta*, rather than the intended *shurāt* (Khawārij). The Kharijites called themselves *shurāt* (those who sell themselves to God/purchase paradise). See Rotter 1982, 215–16.

east, al-Hajjāj b. Yusuf and Khālid al-Qasri, affirmed that the caliph of God was equal or even superior to his prophet, the idea was only theoretically articulated on the basis of the Qur'an by the last universally recognized Umayyad caliph, al-Walid II.[65] It came too late to help the self-destruction of the Umayyad caliphate (which we shall analyze in chapter 4), but it helped the Abbasids of the next revolution to consolidate postrevolutionary caliphal absolutism, as we shall see in chapter 6. Last but not least, Hajjāj set up a commission to edit Caliph 'Uthmān's codex of the Qur'an, using the improved Arabic alphabet and the evolving grammar of classical Arabic, which had been given advanced publicity through the inscription of certain selected verses in the Dome of the Rock built by 'Abd al-Malik on the site of the Jewish Second Temple in Jerusalem around 692.[66]

The coinage of the restoration, too, sought to appropriate the Islamic symbolism of the rebels of the Second Civil War. After a series of unhappy experimentation with jarringly inappropriate Roman and Persian iconography between 692 and 697, 'Abd al-Malik found a proper mode for his numismatic celebration of the triumph of the Marwanid counterrevolution against the pious anticaliph, Ibn al-Zubayr, as well as the Kharijite rebel, Qatari b. Fujā'a, by issuing coins that included their key Islamic legends while eliminating all images and replacing them by pure words of God: the profession of monotheism in Qur'an 112, and the proclamation of the messengership of Muhammad (the *shahāda*). The teleology of the progressive realization of messianism finally unfolded itself through the Arabist counterrevolution. Coins issued after the completion of the currency reform avoided images of human sovereigns altogether and consisted of divine words only. The word of God was indeed the supreme one (Q. 9:40)!

The triumphalism of the construction of the Dome of the Rock to celebrate the end of the Second Civil War is reflected in the Qur'anic inscriptions marking the victory of Islam over Christianity (and Judaism). Mu'āwiya had been tolerant, indeed kind, to his Christian subjects in the conquered territories of the Byzantine Empire, Syria and Egypt; he had prayed at Golgotha and Mary's grave when proclaiming himself caliph in Jerusalem; and he employed a Christian, Sarjun b. Mansur, for taking over Byzantine administration and

---

65. Heidemann 2011; Crone and Hinds 1986, 26–29, 116–26.
66. Gilliot 2006; Al-Azmeh 2014, 463–64.

in the creation of his government bureaucracy. Under the Marwanids, too, the system of religious pluralism prevailed and the process of conversion to Islam was gradual and relatively smooth. It was in the outlying eastern periphery of Khurasan that the development of the system of religious pluralism was rocky, and the process of orderly conversion broke down in the second quarter of the eighth century. This breakdown was a major cause of Islam's social revolution, the Abbasid Revolution in 750, which is the subject of our next three chapters.

The winner and the losers of the Second Civil War alike made their lasting contribution to the elaboration of Islam into a fully developed world religion of the Book and the core of Islamicate civilization. Islam now had an orthodoxy and heterodoxies that were mutually oriented with reference to the fundamental premises of the Islamic religion contained in a standardized Qur'an. The orthodoxy established the political order of the caliphate on the faith, while the Shi'ite heterodox sects perpetuated the utopia of the theocratic monarchy of the House of the Prophet that was elaborated into a distinctively Islamic form of apocalyptic messianism and remained a major component of Islamicate civilization.

CHAPTER 4

The Self-Destruction of the Umayyad Empire

After the death of 'Abd al-Malik in 705, the Marwanid imperial state he had established was inherited by his four sons who ruled it for nearly four decades down to the death of the last of them, Hishām in 743. The transition to the next Marwanid generation in that year was the beginning of their end. As predicted by the Tocquevillian ideal type of revolution briefly presented in the Introduction, the breakdown of the authority structure of the state is a major cause of revolution. This is well illustrated by the very serious breakdown of the Marwanid imperial state that is here characterized as the self-destruction of the Umayyad Empire, which set in motion what Muslim historians call the third *fitna* (sedition or civil war)—the prelude to what we shall call the Hashemite Revolution.

The end of the Umayyads' turn in power (*dawla*) and the beginning of the revolution were a coup d'état that was completed with the murder on April 15, 744 of the Umayyad caliph al-Walid II, a grandson of 'Abd al-Malik, the consolidator of the Marwanid imperial state.[1] The caliph al-Walid b. Yazid b. 'Abd al-Malik was a dissolute poet and a harpist, brilliant in his poetry but ostentatious in his drinking and other vices.[2] By the time he became caliph, he was probably in his late thirties, having long lived under his uncle Hishām (720–743), who was trying to remove his from the line of succession. While

---

1. See chapter 9 below for the meaning of this term.
2. Just like the Roman emperor, Nero! For the parallel, see Arjomand 2019, ch. 4.

anxiously awaiting his turn and seeking to justify his claim to succession, he developed the Marwanid theory of God's caliphate.

This enterprise was not merely self-serving. It was also intended to save the Umayyad caliphate as divinely sanctioned not long after the Shiʻite uprising of Zayd b. ʻAli b. al-Husayn b. ʻAli in Kufa, which Hishām had suppressed in 740. To do so, he sought to appropriate the Shiʻite rebel's theory of the imamate as a continuation of prophecy representing the transposition of the idea of the Hashemite monarchy espoused by ʻAli during his caliphate a century earlier. Walid accordingly divided the sacred history into the era of the prophets and the era of the caliphs (counterposed to that of the divinely inspired imams of the Shiʻa). He also invoked God's decree (*qadar Allāh*) to justify his entitlement to his caliphate in order to take the wind out of the sails of the Qadariyya, another opposition group persecuted by Hishām. Caliph al-Walid II was evidently inept when it came to reading God's decree, which was interpreted otherwise by God himself, who brought about al-Walid II's destruction by putting his cousin, Yazid b. al-Walid b. ʻAbd al-Malik in power in Damascus while the caliph was in his desert palace.

As the army sent by his cousin from Damascus reached Walid's desert palace in Transjordan, the caliph heard someone shout, "Kill the enemy of God in the way Lot's family was killed!" He ran into the citadel and, as the assailants struck him, he reportedly grabbed a copy of the Qur'an so as to be martyred while reading it like the third "rightly guided" caliph ʻUthmān had been in the first *fitna*, exclaiming, "This is a day like the day ʻUthmān was killed." His allusion to his Umayyad kinsman ʻUthmān, who had adumbrated the claim to be God's caliph, was very apt. Some sources indeed begin the Umayyad caliphate with ʻUthmān and end it with al-Walid II.[3]

THE STRUCTURE OF THE UMAYYAD IMPERIAL STATE AND THE CALIPHATE OF AL-WALID II

The efficient cause of Caliph al-Walid's downfall, however, was his ineptitude in backing the wrong faction in Umayyad tribal politics.[4] The political and military structure of the Marwanid state was prone to endemic violent change.

---

3. Tabari, 2:1799–1800 (translation 26:153); Judd 2008, 456.
4. Hinds 1986, 116–26; Judd 2008, 440–42.

With the consolidation of the Marwanid imperial state, its military organization underwent considerable change. The tribal contingents of the armies of conquest settled in "quarters" and "fifths" in the garrison cities and were reorganized into a few regional armies; each army (*jund*) was known by its geographical location and consisted of regiments under different commanders. Each regiment was identified with the tribes it comprised, and its commander (*qā'id*) was assimilated to a tribal chief. The fifths system of the garrison city of Basra was replicated in Marw in Khurasan by Qutayba b. Muslim as he was embarking on the conquest of Transoxiana. There was thus a broad coincidence of military and tribal membership combining regimental and tribal composition. As we have seen, this was made up of two extensive, mutually antagonistic alliances among the "northern" and "southern" Arabian tribes. The tribal realignment at the end of the Second Civil War was accompanied by a major revision of tribal genealogies; a redrawing of the division between the southern and northern Arabs remained stable thereafter.[5] The regiments of the regional armies identified in this tribal nomenclature tended to coalesce into factions that were increasingly polarized into a southern and a northern Arabian faction conceived in terms of two great tribal confederations: the *Yamān* and the *Qays* (*Mudar* in Khurasan and parts of Iran). A further major cause of tension was the extension of military recruitment to non-Arab clients whose number also increased in the command structure and who demanded equal treatment and honor with the Arabs. This was especially the case in Khurasan, where the *mawāli* were registered in the *diwān* (fiscal bureau) by the end of the seventh century, though with lower pay or none, and natives were recruited into contingencies under the command of clients from local nobility and royal families. It is no wonder, then, that the *mawāli* played a much more significant military role in the destruction of the Marwanid regime than in the Second Civil War.[6]

As the governors combined military and administrative functions, military factionalism pervaded government. The appointment and the dismissal of the major governors, especially those of Iraq and Khurasan, meant the turnover of the subgovernors and officials identified with their respective tribal faction. When Nasr b. Sayyār became governor of Khurasan in 738 and replaced all

---

5. Hawting 1987, 53.
6. Kister 1972, 92; Crone 1994b; Hawting 1987, 51–52; Zakeri 1995, 233–42.

the subgovernors with northerners, he was told that such complete factional bias was unprecedented, but he denied that he was doing anything unusual.[7] In the late Umayyad period with its polarized factionalism, the dismissal of governors was thus a major cause of endemic instability and, as we shall see, contributed to the final crisis of government in the third *fitna*. The last point to note about the late Umayyad power structure is its lack of centralization or rather, the reversal of the earlier centralization associated with the father of Caliph Hishām b. ʿAbd al-Malik by his son, who moved his residence from Damascus to Rusāfa. His successor, al-Walīd II, resided in desert palaces and never set foot in Damascus during his short caliphate, while the later caliph, Marwān II's, capital was at Harran in Mesopotamia. The late Umayyad Empire thus had no capital but three metropolitan zones—namely Syria, Mesopotamia (the Jazira), and Iraq. This made the revolutionary process more drawn out, since there was no single center of power to be seized by the revolutionaries.

Early in the century, it seemed possible for a statesman belonging to a minor tribe, such as Qutayba b. Muslim al-Bāhili, who governed Khurasan from 705 to 715 and who conquered Transoxiana, to act as an agent of centralization by reducing the endemic conflict between the military tribal factions and by maintaining the balance of power. In later decades, however, this remedy seemed to be of no avail. Khālid b. ʿAbdallāh al-Qasri and his brother Asad were also from a small tribe, the Bajila, and his bent for state building was early demonstrated by his siding with his fiscal agents against tribal leaders and by his dislocating resistant tribes. Nevertheless, the force of growing tribal factionalism was such that, by the end of his time in office, he had made himself into the leader of the Yaman, thus intensifying factional polarization.

The decade and a half of peaceful rule by the Marwanid governor of the east, Khālid al-Qasri, from 724 to 738 is an important and neglected chapter in early Islamic history. It was a period of prosperity and continuous administration before the storm broke out. The state bureaucracy expanded during this period.[8] Khālid, a man of cosmopolitan culture whose favorable disposition toward the non-Muslims earned him accusations of Manichaeism

---

7. Tabari, 2: 1664 (translation 26:192).
8. The large number of officials arrested after the dismissal of Khalid in 738 proves this. See also Gabrieli 1935b, 120–28.

(*zandaqa*) and the pejorative appellation, Ibn al-Naṣrāniyya (son of the Christian woman), employed non-Muslim Persians as his tax officials on a large scale.[9] The same was true of his brother Asad, whom Khālid twice appointed governor of Khurasan. As governor of Khurasan from 724 to 727–8, and from 735 to his sudden death in 738, Asad developed a cordial relationship with the Iranian nobility—notably, Barmak and Sāmān in Balkh—and he is reported to have brought back a large retinue of landlords (*dehqāns*) to Iraq after his first tenure. Khālid al-Qasrī's policy (we may call its selective integration of native clients and dispossessed Arab elites) was effective in keeping the Hashemite aristocratic opposition under control. Although he ruthlessly suppressed small groups of Shi'ite extremist sectarians, Khālid appears to have maintained good relations with the Abbasid patriarch, Muhammad b. 'Ali, and he put the latter's brothers, Dāwud and 'Isā, on his payroll as market officials in Iraq. Dāwud b. 'Ali especially enjoyed his favor, as did the 'Alid Zayd b. 'Ali, who did not rebel until two years after Khālid's fall.[10] The wisdom of this policy of selectively integrating the dispossessed aristocracy is proved by the fact that its reversal, which began with the Qaysite takeover of the east from Khālid and his Yemenite followers and continued under Walid II, precipitated the revolutionary crisis.

At a turning point that can be said to mark the prelude to revolution, the caliph, Hishām, abruptly dismissed Khālid in 738 and appointed the Qaysite Yusuf b. 'Umar al-Thaqafi as his successor.[11] The dismissal was kept secret

---

9. *Aghānī*, 22:24, 261. The reference to Khalid's mother and lowly status could be much more scurrilous. When he lost his nerve during the uprising of (only) seven or eight Shi'ite extremists under al-Mughira b. Sa'id in 737, the poet Ibn Nawfal al-Himyari wrote:

O Khālid, may God not reward you with good,
And a penis in your mother's vagina as an *amir*!

. . . .

Your mother is a servile non-Arab and your father a scoundrel,
Lowly followers are not equal to the chiefs. (Tabari, 2:1621 [translation 25:155])

10. Tabari, 2:1501, 1635–38, 168 (translation 25:38, 167–170, 26:4–5, 168); *Ansāb*, 3:81, 87; *Ansāb*, 6B:28, 187, 202, 237, 247. Khālid was indeed accused of instigating his rebellion on account of his good relations with Zayd.

11. Hishām was reportedly infuriated by Khālid's haughtily referring to him as "son of the retarded women," and had no difficulty in retaliating by calling Khālid "son of a stinking woman" of humble origin "from the small, contemptible [tribe of] Bajila." (Tabari, 2:1646 [translation 25:177]).

and was carried out as a coup d'état. Three hundred and five of his fiscal officials were arrested with Khālid and tortured for the purpose of extortion. Caliph Hishām not only stopped the subsidies sent to the Abbasid Muhammad b. 'Ali but revoked the latter's tax exemption and imprisoned and tortured him to pay back the rebated taxes. State building thus proved reversible so long as the military structure of the Marwanid Empire remained prone to endemic tribal factionalism.

It is interesting to note that the young Persian servant or slave, who was to be renamed Abu Muslim and become the Master of the Revolution *sāhib al-dawla*), was first sent to Muhammad b. 'Ali by his master, Abu Musā al-Sarrāj (the saddle maker), an Abbasid partisan who stood as guarantor for the payment of taxes demanded by the caliph to secure the release of his imam. More critically, elite defection at the highest level can be said to have begun under Hishām with Khālid al-Qasri himself. After being tortured and seeing the mistreatment of the women in his household, Khālid indicated that he could support the claim of the Abbasid Muhammad b. 'Ali to the caliphate against Hishām. In an exchange that reveals Khālid's insight into the fragility of the late-Umayyad regime, he counted on mobilizing support in Syria, Arabia (the Hijaz), and Iraq and is reliably reported to have said: "By God, if the lord of Rusāfa—meaning Hishām—does wrong . . . and if he snorts a snort, Rusāfa [Hishām's capital] will collapse on all sides." Not wanting to admit Khālid's insight that the edifice of the state had hollowed from within and could collapse at a slight push, the caliph again mocked the pettiness of Khālid's own tribe: "You are talking raving nonsense! Are you threatening me with the insignificant, vile tribe of Bajila?"[12]

Despite their growing salience, the secretaries of the state bureaucracy had little power and institutional security. The Persian Zoroastrian, Dadhoyeh, the father of 'Abdallāh b. al-Muqaffa', whom we shall soon meet in chapter 5, was among the fiscal officials of Khālid dismissed with him. He is known as al-Muqaffa' because he "was tortured for the return of [collected] funds, and was deformed [*taqaffa'a*]." Sālim b. 'Abd al-Rahmān (or 'Abdallāh, another typical, though less obviously generic, name for a convert or *mawlā*), who was a friend of Khālid al-Qasri's, survived him as the head of the caliph's secretariat and was assisted by his Persian son-in-law, 'Abd al-Hamid b. Yahya

12. Tabari, 2:1816; *Ansāb*, 3:84–85.

al-Kātib, the most famous of all Umayyad secretaries.[13] There was to be yet another turnover of officials when Walid II succeeded Hishām in February 743 and dismissed all the Yemeni officials and governors. However, Marwān II (744–750), who picked up and promoted Hishām's most brilliant and energetic secretary, 'Abd al-Hamid, made an impressive effort to repair the interruption in the administrative development. 'Abd al-Hamid vigorously expounded and further developed the doctrine of autocracy as the rule of God's caliph, but the effort came to naught. By this time, it was too late to repair the endemic cycle of violence and changeover, and so long as it remained uncorrected, the reversal of the centralization of power and state building could not be stopped.[14]

As long as the cyclical rotation of governors and generals between the two major military-tribal factions, the Yaman and the Qays, was insulated from any crisis of succession at the level of the caliphate, the regime could take it in stride and survive. This had been the case for four decades, while the four sons of 'Abd al-Malik, the victor of the Second Civil War, had taken turns to succeed him and one another with only a brief interruption by a cousin, 'Umar II b. 'Abd al-'Aziz (719–20). But with the death of Hishām, the caliphate had passed to the generation of 'Abd al-Malik's grandsons. Quite a few of Caliph al-Walid II's royal cousins felt they had equal title to the caliphate, and when he turned the Yaman out of power, the cycle of rotation of the governors and chiefs of armies caused an intensive dynastic feud that resulted in the self-destruction of the Umayyad state. The reckless Walid II thus bears the burden of responsibility for initiating the self-destruction of the Umayyad regime. This collapse—or more precisely, this self-destruction—of the military base of the Umayyad Empire in the wars of succession among Umayyad princes who were supported by the opposing northern and southern Arabians tribal contingents began in 744.[15] Al-Walid II's responsibility should be mitigated in view of the desperate situation of military weakness he inherited from his predecessor, however. In the last three years of Hishām's reign, the overextension of the Umayyad Empire resulted in a series of military disasters, most

13. 'Abbās 1988, 25–29. 'Abd al-Hamid was most probably from the Sasanian city of Anbār in Mesopotamia, though Istakhri (140) claims him for Fars.
14. *Ansāb*, 6B:233–34; 'Atwān 1980, 251–53; Qāḍi 1994.
15. Wellhausen 1902; Dennett 1939; Blankinship 1988; Blankinship 1994; Crone 1994b; Sakhnini 1998.

notably the Berber rebellion of 738, which decimated most of the 175,000-strong Syrian army that had been the mainstay of the Arab imperial regime, and scattered the remainder across the periphery of the empire, further sapping its strength.

After his succession, Caliph al-Walid II sold Khālid al-Qasri, now the chief of the Yemenite tribal faction, to his next in line as governor of Iraq, Yusuf b. 'Umar al-Thaqafi from the Qays; the latter matched his kinsman al-Hajjāj in cruelty. Khālid was tortured to death in November 743 by al-Thaqafi in order that his vast fortune might be extracted.[16] Walid's murderers were Yemenites who were thus avenging Khālid while installing as caliph their own Umayyad prince, Yazid b. al-Walid b. 'Abd al-Malik, who became Caliph Yazid III.[17] Probably more widespread beyond the Yaman was the sentiment that God defeated al-Walid b. Yazid so as not to leave the caliphate between the wine cup and the harp.[18]

As soon as Walid II was killed, the late caliph, Hishām's, son, Sulaymān, who was imprisoned in Amman, was set free, took the Jordanian treasury, and set out for Damascus, where he consolidated his alliance with Yazid III by giving him his sister in marriage. Yazid III was the first Umayyad caliph with a Persian mother, a princess (Shāh-Āfarid) captured in Soghdia, and he boasted of his mother's royal descent:

16. In a poem circulated by the opposition, the Yaman was viciously taunted by Walid:
We are kings who rule men by force,
inflicting on them humiliation and punishment.
...
Behold Khālid a prisoner in our midst!
Had they been true men they would have protected him,
their lord and master in days of yore.
We have made shame dog him like a shadow.
And here is their murderers' retort:
In avenging Khālid, we have left the Commander of the Believers [al-Walid]
prostrate upon his nose, though not in an act of worship! (Tabari, 2:1781, 1823 [translation 26:133,178])

Walid also sold Nasr b. Sayyār to Yusuf b. 'Umar al-Thaqafi, who matched his kinsman Hajjaj in brutality, but Yusuf was never able to lay his hands on the latter. See Tabari, 2:1764 (translation 26:115).

17. Tabari, 2:1823 (translation 26:178).
18. Ibn 'Abdun as cited in Gabrieli 1935a, 24.

I am the son of Kisrā [Persian king of kings]; my father is Marwān.
One grandfather is a Caesar; the other a Khāqān.[19]

He had risen against his cousin as the leader of a coalition of humiliated Yemenite military tribal factions and the *mawāli* belonging to the Qadarite movement, a movement reemerging after its suppression by Hishām. Qadarism was one of the incipient rationalist trends that was absorbed by the Mu'tazilite movement, which was then emerging in Basra, and by the rational jurisprudence that Abu Hanifa, the Murji'ite leader and founder of the Hanafi school of law, had developed in Iraq. Meanwhile, Jahm b. Safwān, was developing a kindred Murji'ite rational theology in Khurasan in close connection with the Mu'tazilite Amr b. 'Ubayd, and with Abu Hanifa and his followers. The historian Mas'udi highlights the connection between Yazid III and emergent Mu'tazilite rationalism, pointing out that the Mu'tazila considered Yazid III superior to the pious 'Umar II.[20] As we shall see in chapter 5 below, Yazid also pardoned al-Hārith b. Surayj, the leader of the Murji'ite rebellion of 737 in Khurasan and Transoxania who had taken refuge with the Turks.

YAZID III AND THE FAILED REVOLUTION FROM ABOVE

In March 744, Yazid rode to Damascus on a black ass with twelve disciples—just as the Anointed One was expected to do.[21] Yazid is also almost certainly the Syrian caliph hailed as the Mahdi in an apocalyptic tradition.[22] He proceeded with careful calculation, however, and carried out a well-planned coup on which he spent lavishly. Yazid III, backed by the southern tribal contingents, also announced the revolution from above with a program of mass mobilization among the sedentary, nontribal populations in the region around Damascus, based on a Qadarite contractarian ideology. His agents had mobilized people in the villages and small towns around Damascus, and he gathered

---

19. Tabari 2:1874 (translation 26:243n1185).
20. Muruj, 4:58, 63. Although this is probably anachronistic, Yazid III is said to have believed in the five principles of Mu'tazilite rational theology. See Madelung 1965, 24; Van Ess 1991–97, 2:1.
21. Tabari, 2:1789–90 (translation 26:142–43). Tabari's date is curiously imprecise; *Aghāni* (6:138) gives the wrong year (127) but very probably the correct month, Jumada II.
22. Nu'aym b. Hammād 1991, 220; Madelung 1986, 148–49.

his thirteen brothers and urged them to disperse among the people to mobilize support for his regime. This mobilization was not all that successful, however, and fewer than one thousand men gathered to Yazid. He then sought to recruit men for an expedition by giving them two thousand dirhams each, but of the two thousand men who enlisted, eight hundred deserted, and only 1,200 reached the destination.[23]

The people of the region seemed to have had their own ideas and plans as the period of multiple sovereignty was evidently at hand. The people of Hims refused to accept Yazid III and rose against him, killing his governor and electing in his place Muhammad al-Sufyani, an agitator seasoned in the Berber Revolt, who persuaded them he would be acceptable as caliph in Damascus. Yazid had to send Sulaymān b. Hishām and his disciplined private army, the Dhakwāniyya, as well as the less effective army that had returned from Jordan after killing Walid. Over three hundred citizens of Hims and over fifty of Sulaymān's men were killed in the confrontation before Khālid al-Qasri's son, Yazid, arranged the peaceful submission of the city. A Sufyāni was imprisoned but another rebel leader was appointed governor of Hims. Meanwhile, the people of Palestine and Jordan also rebelled and chose as ruler their own Umayyad prince; he accepted their call. Yazid III again sent Sulaymān and his army to intimidate and negotiate the submission of Palestine and Jordan in exchange for the appointment of one of the rebel leaders as governor of Palestine.[24] Again, the rebels won despite submitting to the (nominal) caliph.

Yazid III had less trouble in Iraq, since Yusuf b. 'Umar, who was the head of the northern Arabian faction, fled on hearing of the appointment of Mansur b. Jumhur al-Kalbi, a Yemenite fired up as much by the desire to avenge the death of Khālid al-Qasri as he was by the Qadarite ideology.[25] Mansur b. Jumhur, however, had no control over Khurasan, which was in theory under his authority but to which Nasr b. Sayyār had in fact summoned the people to take the oath of allegiance to himself. Mansur had to be content with sending his brother to Rayy as its governor and leaving Khurasan to

---

23. Tabari, 2:1792–97 (translation 26:141–50); Wellhausen 1902, 362.
24. Tabari, 2:1827–34 (translation 26:185–93).
25. Yazid's first choice for governor of Iraq declined because he had no base in either southern or northern Arabian *jund* (army of tribal contingents). See Tabari, 2:1836 (translation 26:196).

Nasr.[26] Mansur b. Jumhur was at any rate soon dismissed as "a rough Bedouin," and Yazid replaced him with a pious member of the royal house, 'Abdallāh, son of the late caliph, 'Umar II b. 'Abd al-'Aziz, who was still revered in Iraq.

Yazid III had joined the Qadari movement whose leaders in Damascus belonged to his inner circle during his short caliphate, and they imprinted their ideology on the uprising and gave it revolutionary potential. Ghaylān al-Dimashqi, who had launched the Qadari movement and grafted it on the culture of the scribes, the Umayyad bureaucratic class, preached a theology of justice that allowed for the imamate of non-Arabs on the basis of merit and knowledge of the Qur'an and the Sunna. He was pronounced a heretic by the jurist Awzā'i (d. 774) and was executed by Hishām. Like Ghaylān, Yazid III's Qadari advisors were all clients belonging to the secretarial class serving in the Umayyad bureaucracy. The client Abu'l-Walid 'Umayr b. Hāni', an official in the tax bureau, was an active leader of Yazid's revolt and was appointed to his government, and five other clients who constituted an ideological team working under him were the followers of the Qadarite Makhul b. Abi Muslim (d. 737), himself a client descending from a war captive in Kabul (just like Abu Hanifa). Yazid III's reformist caliphate had its strongest nonmilitary base among the Qadarites of Syria and the Mu'tazilites of Basra. The founder of Mu'tazilism in Basra, Wāsil b. 'Atā (d. 748 or 749), was part of a Basran delegation to Yazid's governor of Iraq, the Umayyad 'Abdallāh b. 'Umar, and he became one of his advisors. The reformist caliphate was continued briefly after Yazid III's death by his brother, Ibrāhim. The latter, however, was defeated by Marwān II, who executed 'Umayr b. Hāni' and had his head paraded on a spear. Quite a few of the Qadarite ideologues managed to escape to Basra and take refuge with the Mu'tazilites, who were being mobilized against the Umayyad regime.[27]

Yazid III's advisors selectively appropriated the oppositional Kharijite and Shi'ite programs within a Qadarite frame for a revolution from above in a manner that foreshadowed the Mu'tazilite doctrine of the imamate by elec-

---

26. Tabari, 2:1837, 1845–47, 1854 (translation 26:197, 207–10, 219). The long and elaborate oath of allegiance to Nasr included these words: "I declare to Nasr, having pledged allegiance to him . . . . You have safeguarded Khurasan for the Muslims when the earth was about to convulse."

27. Van Ess 1970, 277–82; Van Ess 1978, 101–2; Van Ess 1991–97, 2:18.

tion.[28] The crushed rebellion of Zayd b. 'Ali in Kufa four years earlier must have been fresh both in their minds and in Walid's when the latter formulated his theory of the caliphate as the deputyship of God. In considering the concatenation of revolutionary ideologies in the late Umayyad period, it is worth noting that Zayd had in turn appropriated the platform of Khurasanian "people of equality," which we shall consider in chapter 5, while replacing its principle of consultation or elective council (*shurā*) with the legitimist Hashemite principle of the excellence of the House of Prophet.[29] In April 744, soon after gaining control of Damascus, Yazid attached placards with these words to the spears of the soldiers he dispatched to the Jordanian desert: "We summon you to the Book of God and the Sunna of His Prophet; and let the matter [of the caliphate] be decided through consultation [*shurā*]." When the people of Hims refused to swear allegiance to him, Yazid sent envoys telling them "that he was summoning them to the *shurā*." But it was only after the murder of his cousin that Yazid III delivered a major policy speech that set forth the main principles of the Qadarite political theory. These were later elaborated and modified in an authoritarian direction in a proclamation sent to his first governor of Iraq, Mansur b. Jumhur, who was, incidentally, a follower of Ghaylān al-Dimashqi. In the speech, he justified the murder of Walid in terms of the latter's deviation from Islam,[30] but he tried to appeal to his non-Muslim subjects as well by promising fiscal lenience.[31] Above all, he abandoned the Marwanid theory of God's caliphate that had only just been

---

28. Muruj, 4: 60, para. 2257.

29. This can be clearly seen in the pledge of allegiance Zayd had given to his followers: "We summon you to the Book of God and the Sunna of His Prophet, and to wage war against those who act tyrannically, to defend the disinherited [*mustad'afin* (Q. 28:4–5)] . . . to distribute this booty [*fay'*] [as pensions] equally among those entitled to it . . . to bring home those who have been kept on the frontiers, and to help the House of the Prophet [*ahl al-bayt*] against those who have opposed us and disregarded our just cause" (Tabari, 2:1687).

30. "I have rebelled out of righteous anger for God's cause, His Prophet, and His religion, and I came to summon people to God, the Sunna of His Prophet when . . . there had appeared that stiff-necked tyrant who declared licit every forbidden thing. . . . Nor did he confirm the truth of the Book or believe in the Day of Reckoning. . . ." See Tabari, 2:1834 (translation 26:193).

31. *Fragmenta* 1871, 142; Tabari, 2:1804, 1826–27. In 2:1835 (translation 26:194), we read: "I will not close my door against you so that the strong among you will devour the weak, nor will I place on those of you who pay the poll tax [burdens] which will drive you from your lands and decimate your progeny . . ."

elaborated by his murdered predecessor, and he offered the novel Qadarite theory of the caliphate based on popular consent:

> If I do not keep faith with you, depose me, with the proviso that you should [first] ask me to repent and if I do so accept my repentance. If you know of anyone of proven probity ... and you want to give him the oath of allegiance, then I would be the first to give him my allegiance and submit to him ...
>
> Obedience consists solely in obedience to God. So obey him [the caliph] as long as he obeys [God].[32]

Yazid III's revolution from above extended to Egypt, where trouble had been brewing during Hishām's caliphate, trouble that included a rebellion of the Qur'an readers. Yazid III confirmed the governor of Egypt, Hafs b. al-Walid al-Hadrami (d. 746), who was visiting Syria, and ordered him to return to Egypt and recruit thirty thousand men into the army. Hafs promised anyone who would convert to Islam exemption from the poll tax, and thus managed to convert 24,000 people, some of whom joined his army of volunteers. His levies were committed to the revolution from above, and agitprops from the clients and Christian clerics (*muqāmisa*) called the Disciples of Lamentation (*ashāb al-nudba*) were appointed to every twenty or twenty-five men. These commissars of the army pressured Hafs to accept the office from Marwān II after Yazid's death, which he did reluctantly, but he was deposed by Marwān before long anyway. Hafs b. al-Walid regained power at the head of a popular rebellion but perished in the revolutionary turmoil in the summer of 746.[33]

In the proclamation sent to his governor of Iraq, Yazid reiterated his outrage over his predecessor's violation of the ordinances of God and his pledge to observe them, and he stated that the leaders of the army he had sent "called upon al-Walid to agree that the matter [of the caliphate] should be referred to an electoral council in which the Muslims should decide for themselves whom they would agree to appoint to rule." He also reinstated the Marwanid theory of the caliph as God's deputy (*khalīfa*) and tended to modify the idea of consultation over election of the ruler, changing it into implied consent. God was pleased with his deputies, Yazid averred, until Hishām died and "the command passed to the enemy of God, al-Walid; God's Caliphs succeeded

---

32. Tabari, 2:1835 (translation 26:194–95).
33. Severus 1947, 116; Lapidus 1972, 252.

each other as guardians of His religion, passing judgment therein by His ordinance and following therein His Book." The implication of this theory was then spelled out:

> So heed and obey me and those whom I appoint to succeed me and on whom the community has agreed. I have a similar duty toward you. I shall certainly deal with you according to the ordinance of God and the Sunna of His Prophet.[34]

The caliph was not the only one to move toward an authoritarian position. The Qadarite ideologues themselves were not at all sure about the impact of their contractarian ideology and urged Yazid III to appoint as his successor his half-brother, Ibrāhim, and have the oath of allegiance sworn to him quickly.[35] In any event, the abortive attempt at revolution from above came to an end when Yazid III died, probably as a result of poisoning, in October 744.[36] The caliphate of his brother, Ibrāhim, remained shaky indeed, requiring a repeated but futile retaking of the oath of allegiance.[37] Ibrāhim, furthermore, was not generally recognized as caliph. Sulaymān b. Hishām recognized him but Marwān b. Muhammad, who held Mesopotamia (the Jazira), Azerbaijan, and Armenia, instead pledged allegiance to the two young sons of Walid II. Marwān must have recruited heavily in his provinces to form an army of 120,000 men, but Sulaymān's mustering of 80,000 men a few months after leading the much smaller armed forces of Yazid III seemed equally impressive. Marwān defeated Sulaymān, however, and put his army to flight, and the people of Hims avenged themselves by reportedly massacring as many as 17,000 of the latter's men. Sulaymān himself returned to Damascus with what was left of his army, appointed Yazid b. Khālid al-Qasri governor, and authorized him to kill Walid II's two sons, together with the murderer of his own father, Yusuf b. 'Umar, who was in the same prison.[38]

When subduing Damascus, Marwān, who was still called *amir*, had the imprisoned rebel, Abu Muhammad al-Sufyāni, brought to him in chains. Sufyāni quickly seized the opportunity to hail him as caliph, asserting that he had been so designated by the sons of the murdered caliph al-Walid II.

---

34. Tabari, 2:1843–45 (translation 26:205–7).
35. Tabari, 2:1870 (translation 26:238).
36. Tabari, 2:1873–74 (translation 26:243).
37. Al-Azdi 1967, 60.
38. Tabari, 2: 1876–79 (translation 26:249–53).

Marwān allowed the Syrian army to choose governors of their own military districts for Damascus, Hims, Jordan, and Palestine, and he felt compelled to confirm a man who had betrayed him in Armenia for the last position.

In the year 744, as Tabari magisterially puts it, "the unity of the House of Marwān was disturbed and discord prevailed." Mas'udi's spin is more analytical. The days of Yazid III were strange for "the multiplicity of chaos and confusion, discord of opinion and collapse of the awe [of government] [hayba]."[39] The feuding members of the ruling dynasty indeed destroyed each other and the legitimacy of their dynasty. The fact that the ruling house of the Arab empire's last three caliphs had non-Arab mothers was without doubt also damaging to its legitimacy.[40] Walid II had been decried as a sinner, but Yazid III was blamed for sowing disunity and Marwān was the first to call him "the deficient" (nāqis) and spread the contemptuous term:[41] Yazid III had displayed the severed head of Walid II despite the sensible advice of a client that it would result in the loss of legitimacy for the ruling dynasty. Yazid's own body was exhumed after Marwān's entry to Damascus and hung on one of its gates.[42] Shakiest of all was Marwān II's legitimacy. Not only was he the murderer of his royal cousins; he was also a red-haired and blue-eyed son of a Kurdish concubine whom his father had acquired, so the rumor went, when she was already pregnant with him and on whose account he was contemptuously called "son of the slave-girl of the Nakha'."[43] Marwān II was also called "the Ass of the Jazira" and "Marwān the Ja'di," on account of rumors that he was the nephew of the Qadari heretic, Ja'd b. Dirham, who had "corrupted his religion."

Another important sign of the disintegration of Umayyad authority was the choice of their own governments by the garrison cities of Syria under Yazid III and Marwān II. This indicated a serious erosion of Umayyad central power as well as legitimacy. The lack of legitimacy of the caliphate of Marwān II

---

39. Tabari, 2:1825; Muruj, 4:58.

40. The mothers of Ibrāhim, who had succeeded Yazid III for a brief period, and of Marwān II were also concubines.

41. *Ansāb*, vol. 4, part 2:356. The term can also be translated as "inadequate"; it can mean "reducer" and it is explained by Yazid's later reduction of the army's pay, but the pejorative intent cannot be doubted. "The deficient Qadari [heretic] has lorded it over us/ and incited war among the sons of our fathers" (Tabari, 2:1891 [translation 27:3]).

42. Tabari, 2:1807, 1891–92 (translation 26:161, 27:1–3).

43. Nakha' was the tribe of Ibrāhim al-Ashtar, the original owner of Marwān's mother.

facilitated the disintegration of Umayyad authority, creating a situation of multiple sovereignty in which rival revolutionary states came into being—two Kharijite states in Iraq and the Yemen and a Hashemite one in central and western Iran under 'Abdallāh b. Mu'āwiya. It was in this situation, then, that Abu Muslim's rebellion broke out in Khurasan in 747. The revolutionaries in Khurasan were hissing and kicking donkeys in parades and calling them Marwān, and henceforth the last Umayyad caliph was widely called *Marwān al-ḥimār* (Marwān the ass).[44]

THE REBELLION OF 'ABDALLĀH B. MU'ĀWIYA AND THE FIRST HASHEMITE STATE

When news of Marwān's challenge to Ibrāhim following the death of Yazid III reached Kufa in the last months of 744, the Shi'a who had survived the 740 uprising of Zayd b. 'Ali incited the urbane Hashemite, 'Abdallāh b. Mu'āwyia, who was Zayd's son-in-law, to rebel against the Umayyads. He was, during his time in Kufa, the guest of the Umayyad governor, 'Abdallāh b. 'Umar.[45]

By that time, tribal factionalism had infected Kufa and seriously undermined Umayyad authority and Ibn 'Umar was vacillating in view of the uncertain outcome of the civil strife in Syria and looked both weak and like he was in favor of the unpopular Qays contingents. The leaders of the Yemenite faction, Mansur b. Jumhur and Ismā'il al-Qasri, defected to Ibn Mu'āwiya forthwith. This was followed by the defection of the police chief of Kufa who belonged to the Rabi'a tribe and who was wooed by both tribal factions. Ibn 'Umar acted with determination, however, and whittled down Ibn Mu'āwiya's huge following by offering five hundred dirhams for each of their heads; he then won back his police chief, who negotiated the departure of the rebels from Kufa.[46]

---

44. *Akhbār T*, 361; Tabari, 2:1826–34 1892, (translation 26:184–93, 27:3); *Ansāb*, 3:159; *Fragmenta*, 154; Sakhnini 1998, 28–32.

45. *Aghāni*, 22:238. He was named after his grandfather and the head of the Tālibid clan of Banu Hāshim, 'Abdallāh b. Ja'far (al-Tayyār). See also *Aghāni*, 22:217–18, 225. It should be noted that the leader of the Shi'a in Kufa was a client (*mawlā*) of the notorious clan of 'Ijl (Tabari, 2:1886–87 [translation 26:262]), notorious for its tendency to "extremist" Shi'ism, including the teaching of Abu Mansur al-'Ijli who had just died. See Tucker 1977, 66–67.

46. Tabari, 2:1879–88 (translation 26:254–63).

But the revolution was afoot and Ibn 'Umar's authority did not extend beyond Kufa. He appointed Sufyān b. Mu'āwiya al-Muhallabi to the town of Shapur in Fars, but the incumbent governor, Masih b. al-Hawāri (Messiah, son of the disciple!) refused to hand over power to the new governor and brought in the Kurds to keep him in office. Sufyān was driven back to the village of Dawraq in the Ahvaz province and did not prevail on the dismissed governor until 746–47, by which this time Ibn 'Umar himself had defected to the Kharijite rebels! Sufyān's cousin, Sulaymān b. Habib al-Muhallabi, governor of Ahvaz, had also defected to Ibn Mu'āwiya. Central Iran and Fars were taken over by Ibn Mu'āwiya and his Hashemite revolutionaries.[47]

The special status of the clan of Hashim (Banu Hāshim) as the family (*ahl al-bayt*) of the Prophet and his kin (*dhawu'l-qurba*) (Q. 44:23) as the basis of the project of Hashemite monarchy was well established already in Muhammad's time.[48] The six decades between the second and third civil wars witnessed the formation of the Hashemite ideology around it, which extolled the virtues of the family of the Prophet—that is, the politically dispossessed aristocracy of Medina belonging to the Banu Hāshim, especially but not exclusively the descendants of Muhammad's uncle, Abu Tālib and the latter's son, 'Ali. The Hashemite ideology was developed by Shi'ite poets and intellectuals such as Kuthayyar 'Uzza, Sa'id b. Jubayr, and al-Kumait b. Zayd, who based the legitimist claim of the Banu Hāshim to rule as divinely sanctioned on Qur'an 44:23: "Say, 'I ask you no recompense for this other than the love of my kin.'" This made loyalty to Muhammad's kin against the Umayyads, who had usurped their right to the caliphate, a religious duty.

Ibn Mu'āwiya was the patron of the literary side of the incipient Hashemite movement. He promoted the *Hāshimiyyāt* of the poet Kumait b. Zayd and commissioned him to write new poems to whip up tribal factionalism ('*asabiyya*). Kumait died in 743, shortly before Ibn Mu'āwiya's uprising in Kufa, but his propaganda popularized the principle of Hashemite legitimacy that made his patron charismatically popular and helped him come to power and establish the first Hashemite state in Iran. According to Mas'udi, the campaign to aggravate the rift in the military base of the Umayyad regime by setting the

---

47. Tabari, 2:1977–78 (translation 27:87); Sourdel 1954, 309–10. An Umayyad army under Ibn Dubāra reconquered Ahvaz later; Suleymān al-Muhallabi fled to Ibn Mu'āwiya.

48. Madelung 1989, 10.

southern and the northern Arabian tribes, the Yemen and the Nizār, against each other in an honor contest was highly successful: "People became divided into parties, and tribal factionalism spread in the desert and the cities . . ., and the matter slipped into the transfer of the [divinely sanctioned] turn in power [dawla] from the Umayyads to the Hashemites." The conflict endemic in the late Umayyad military and political organization thus became epidemic and produced a great revolution that swept away Ibn Muʿāwiya and the memory of his Hashemite state.[49]

We must, however, retrieve the historical memory of the first Hashemite state to avoid the anachronism entailed by naming that great revolution *Abbasid* after its eventual winners. After his departure from Kufa toward the end of 744, Ibn Muʿāwiya proceeded to the former Sasanian capital, al-Madāʾin, where his movement quickly gathered momentum, the people gave him the oath of allegiance, and a further group of Kufans joined him. He organized his followers and took advantage of the military vacuum created by the collapse of Marwanid authority to take possession of Hulwan and the Jibal region and the vast area in western and central Iran from Hamadan and Rayy to Isfahan. The Kufan slaves fled to join him in Iran.[50]

Sometime in the following year 128 (745–46), Muḥārib b. Musā, a client who was a local strongman, "came walking in his sandals to the government house of Estakhr [Persepolis] and expelled the governor," telling one of his men: "Have the people swear allegiance!" When he was asked on what, he replied, "On what you love and hate!"[51] When a new governor appointed by Ibn ʿUmar arrived, Muḥārib killed him, and only then went to Isfahan to invite Ibn Muʿāwiya to come to Fars, which the latter did. He then set up a state there and began collecting taxes. ʿAbdallāh b. Muʿāwiya moved to Estakhr, appointed his brothers governors of other provinces, and Iran was lost to the Umayyad Empire.[52]

Ibn Muʿāwiya did not adopt the formula of "the acceptable one" (*al-rida*) of the Hashemite movement in Khurasan but claimed the caliphate in his own

---

49. *Muruj*, 4:70, no. 2272. The idea of transfer of turn in power/empire, *translatio imerii*, goes back to the book of Daniel. See chapter 9 below.
50. Tabari, 2:1880–81 (translation 26:255).
51. *Aghāni*, 22:229.
52. Tabari, 2:1977 (translation 27:86). It was recaptured only during its last gasp two years later in 748, but at that point the whole empire was collapsing.

right. His major innovation was numismatic: he propagated Hashemite legitimism through his currency.[53] Ibn Muʻāwiya's coins in Iran from 746 to 748 bear the above-mentioned Qurʾanic verse (42:23) on which Hashemite legitimism was founded:

> Say: "I ask you no recompense for this other than the love of my kin."[54]

Meanwhile in Syria, by contrast, Muhammad al-Sufyānī's glib opportunism may have been enough to gain the scoundrel his freedom from prison, but it was evidently not sufficient to assure Marwān II's legitimacy. The latter must have known this because he gathered the remaining members of the Umayyad clan to unify them behind him. He married two sisters of Sulaymān b. Hishām to his own two sons whom he designated as his successors one after the other. But as soon as Marwān left Syria for his capital Harran in Mesopotamia, some ten thousand of his men went over to Sulaymān and persuaded him to foreswear his allegiance, and in 745 all of Syria revolted against Caliph Marwān II. The latter returned in the summer and killed the Yemenite governor of Damascus, Yazid b. Khālid al-Qasri. Meanwhile. Sulaymān proclaimed himself caliph in Hishām's palace in Rusāfa and took the Qinnasrin garrison city. Other Syrian troops joined his army, increasing its size to seventy thousand. Marwān II stroke back and, in the summer of 746, "he had finished with Syria; it lay in fragments at his feet."[55]

By this time, the former governor of Iraq, the Yemenite Mansur b. Jumhur al-Kalbi, having fought the Kharijites and cut off the hand of a Kharijite woman who had seized the bridle of his horse and called him a sinner, was affected by the rebels' zeal and joined them, declaring "I have become a Muslim!" The next governor, Ibn ʻUmar, after being defeated by the Kharijites on the battlefield, followed his example more pragmatically and defected to the Kharijite rebels, taking the oath of allegiance to their commander of the

---

53. *Aghānī*, 22:229; *Ansāb*, 2:73–74.

54. Van Vloten 1892, 443; Miles 1938, 16–18; Wurtzel 1978, 165–69; Bernheimer 2006. These were minted in Ibn Muʻāwiya's name as well as in that of his brother, al-Hasan, who was his governor in Rayy and Hamadan and. This unprecedented legend also appears on the coins of Ibn Muʻāwiya's other governors and was first introduced experimentally in one issue with the fuller version of Qurʾan 42:23 (Bernheimer 2006, 383), which was unsuitably long since the legend was added to the standard Qurʾanic citations of the late Umayyad coin type.

55. Wellhausen 1963, 381.

believers, al-Dahhak b. Qays, in the spring of 745. Central and southern Iran was also outside Umayyad control and ruled by Ibn Mu'āwiya's Hashemite revolutionary coalition dominated by his brothers and clients. Sulaymān b. Hishām and the remnants of the Syrian uprising, notably his four thousand-strong Dhakwaniyya regiment, joined the revolutionaries—first the Kharijites in Iraq through the mediation of Ibn 'Umar, and then the more secure state of Ibn Mu'āwiya in Iran.[56]

A handsome freethinker and poet, even if rumored to be sadistically inclined, 'Abdallāh b. Mu'āwiya was a suitable figurehead and coalition leader but not a charismatic leader for fiery zealots. As a convenient figurehead enjoying Hashemite legitimism, he was picked by the instigators of rebellion in Kufa and Fars but managed to attract a huge following anyway. This was in no small measure owing to the fact that he clearly tolerated a diversity of religious beliefs, as most historical reports accuse him and his inner circle of *zandaqa* (Manichaean or neo-Mazdakite heresy).[57]

Whatever ties they may have had to the clandestine Hashemite movement in Khurasan that later brought them to power, the leading members of the Abbasid family, 'Abdallāh and 'Isā b. 'Ali, who were Ibn Mu'āwiya's first cousins through his mother, also joined him in Fars; they were accompanied by their nephew, Abu Ja'far—the future caliph, al-Mansur. This is a remarkable fact in retrospect as it proves that the Abbasids had no control over Abu Muslim, who declared his revolution on behalf of "the acceptable one (*al-rida*) from the House of the Prophet" and established a rival Hashemite state in Khurasan that overlapped Ibn Mu'āwiya's state in Iran for a period of more than a year. The Abbasid 'Abdallāh b. 'Ali was captured by 'Āmir b. Dubāra,

---

56. Tabari 2, 1906–13 (translation 27:17–23).

57. *Aghāni*, 22:225, 231–33. Notable among the members of his circle was his secretary, 'Amāra b. Hamza. Ibn Mu'āwiya was particularly close to their cousin, al-Husayn b. 'Abdallāh, who was, like himself, a freethinker suspected of *zandaqa*. Abu Ja'far even became a district official of the Hashemite state near Ahvaz when was seized and flogged by the Umayyad governor, Sulaymān al-Muhallabi, before his defection. Heresiographical accounts of Ibn Mu'āwiya and his followers, who later became organized into the sects variously called Harbiyya and Janāhiyya, prove that his followers fell roughly into two groups: the extremist Shi'ite groups marked by their adulation for the family of the Prophet in Iraq and who considered him the legatee of Abu Hāshim, Muhammad b. al-Hanafiyya's son; and the much more numerous neo-Mazdakite Khorramiyya in western and central Iran. See Moscati 1950, 259; Tucker 1980, 47; Madelung 1988, 7.

the Umayyad general who retook Estakhr in 748, and ratted on his master and cousin, who had fled, by accusing Ibn Muʿāwiya of sodomy, leading his captors to more than a hundred colorfully dressed boys.[58]

Ibn Muʿāwiya was apprehended by Abu Muslim's agents in Herat and imprisoned. He tried to win over his jailers to his cause by telling them the Khurasanians were the most foolish people in the world for believing a masterless scoundrel (Abu Muslim), whereas he himself was the true Hashemite caliph of God. Judging by the imperious letter he wrote to Abu Muslim from jail, he himself foolishly put his hope in Abu Muslim claiming to be the trustee (*amīn*) of the House of Muhammad. Ibn Muʿāwiya thus told the latter, "God has favored you by entrusting you with our cause [*amranā*]," complaining that "while people bask in prosperity owing to our turn in power [*dawlatanā*], we ourselves are in affliction because of it." He appealed to Abu Muslim to restore his collapsed revolutionary state: "you are the restoring trustee [*amīn mustawdiʿ*] *and* the chosen leader!" But Abu Muslim had much more use for a martyred Hashemite, Yahyā b. Zayd, whose body he brought down and buried with great publicity for the Hashemite cause, than for a living one. Ibn Muʿāwiya was secretly murdered in jail but he was also given the posthumous satisfaction of having his grave opened to visits as the shrine of a martyr.[59]

Meanwhile, Marwān II had been somewhat compensated for his lack of legitimacy by channeling his considerable talent at innovative military reorganization, and he soon created a strong reformed army. He also had the army and the treasury of Yazid III taken from Damascus but controlled little territory besides his capital and the shattered Syria. Much of Mesopotamia, the Jazira, the backyard to his capital Harran, was in the hands of Kharijite rebels whose number increased from an original two hundred to one thousand and then to four thousand under the leadership of al-Zahhāk b. Qay al-Shaybani. The Kharijite insurgent state expanded by capturing Kufa and holding it through 745, and Zahhāk had the satisfaction of the dismissed Umayyad governors Ibn ʿUmar and Mansur b. Jumhur, as well as the Umayyad Prince, Sulaymān b. Hishām, taking the oath of allegiance to him as their

---

58. Tabari, 2:1980 (translation 27:89); *Ansāb*, 2:74; *Aghāni*, 22:233.
59. Al-Jāhiz 1932/1851, 2:75–76; *Ansāb*, 2:77; Wellhausen 1963, 500; Moscati 1949–50, 485.

imam![60] In Kufa, Zahhāk celebrated his victory by minting coins bearing the Qur'anic verse (12:40) that served as the Kharijite revolutionary slogan: "there is no command but God's" (la hukm illā l'illāh)![61]

THE INTERNAL COLLAPSE OF THE MARWANID REGIME

Marwān's military genius and efficient administration began to pay, however. the two generals of his reformed army, 'Āmir b. Dubāra and Yazid b. 'Umar b. Hubayra, began the counteroffensive against the sundry rebels.[62] Ibn Hubayra, a Bedouin raised to the rank of commander by Marwān II, defeated the Kharijites in Iraq. 'Āmir b. Dubāra crushed the Hashemite revolutionary state in central Iran and took back Ibn Mu'āwiya's realm. His success was ephemeral, however, as a rival branch of the Hashemite revolutionary movement now controlled Khurasan. The Khurasanian revolutionary army, marching eastward under Qahtaba b. Shabib, decisively defeated Ibn Dubāra, annihilating his army and capturing its equipment near Isfahan in 749.

Defections of high officials of the old regime are a clear sign of the advance of revolution. The defections of the Umayyad prince, Sulaymān b. Hishām, to the Kharijites and then to Ibn Mu'āwiya have already been mentioned. The defection of the last governors of the garrison cities of Iraq, Kufa and Basra, to the Hashemite revolutionaries also critically contributed to the success of the revolution and set the stage for the Abbasid coup.

On August 28, 749,[63] the eve of Husayn's martyrdom, a date appropriately chosen for a Kufan uprising and for the final act of vengeance for his father against the Syrian Qaysite forces, Khālid al-Qasri's son Muhammad, who was the Umayyad governor and leader of the Yemenite faction of its army, defected to the Hashemite revolutionaries just ahead of their advancing Khurasanian revolutionary army. "Muhammad b. Khālid b. 'Abdallāh al-Qasri put on black in Kufa, rising at the head of eleven thousand and calling the people to the acceptable one from the House of Muhammad, and captured

---

60. Tabari, 2:1897–1909 (translation 27:9–19); Dennett 1939, 252–59.
61. Van Vloten 1892, 443; Miles 1938, 17; Husayni 1969, 32.
62. Dennett 1939; Bligh-Abramski 1988, 228.
63. August 28, 749/Muharram 132.

Kufa."⁶⁴ The Khurasanian revolutionary army marched into Kufa some four days later but without its commander, Qaḥṭaba b. Shabīb, who had drowned after being stricken down while crossing the Euphrates. His son al-Ḥasan had taken over the command of his army and brought it to Kufa.⁶⁵

The last Umayyad governor of Ahvaz, Sufyān b. Muʿāwiya al-Muhallabī, approached the Hashemite revolutionaries and was co-opted and appointed governor of Basra with the instruction "to proclaim the claims of the House of ʿAbbās in the city, to common people to their Qāʾim [riser], and to drive out Salm b. Qutayba."⁶⁶ Salm b. Qutayla b. Muslim al-Bāhili, the last Umayyad governor of Basra then sent his own emissary to the Abbasid headquarters to obtain a guarantee of safe conduct and withdrew from Basra, leaving it in charge of a certain Talibid Muhammad b. Jaʿfar, who raised the black banners of revolution. Salm was fully co-opted by the Abbasids before long, and he critically helped Abu Jaʿfar survive the greatest challenge to Abbasid rule by crushing the ʿAlid uprising in Basra in 763.⁶⁷

64. *Ansāb*, 3:138. Al-Yaʿqūbī (1960, 2:345) similarly states that Muhammad "took Kufa for the Banu Hashim and proclaimed their mission, driving away the Umayyads and their supporters, and put on black." According to Tabari (3:19 [translation 27:141]), "some of the common sort" split from him when they thought the Umayyad forces were returning, but he carried the day with the Yemenite cavalry defecting from Marwān and with his own clients. Hearing that Syrian horsemen were coming, "he sent a detachment of his clients" to confront them, but the horsemen said they were from Qasri's own tribe of Bajila and wanted "to enter the service of the Amir!" *Akhbār D* (367) does not mention the Yemenite troops, presumably in order to magnify the role of Abu Salama and the clandestine missionaries.

65. By this time, according to the pro-Abbasid *Akhbār al-dawla*, the leader of the clandestine Hashemite mission, Abu Salama, encouraged other Arab notables of Kufa and his followers to join Muhammad al-Qasri as revolutionary partner. See *Akhbār D*, 367–68. It is more likely, however, that Abu Salama "was [still] in hiding in Kufa and al-Ḥasan b. Qaḥṭaba [b. Shabib] surrendered the leadership [*riʾāsa*] to him" (al-Azdi 1967, 119).

66. Tabari, 3:21–22 (translation 27:143–44 [modified]). Sufyān al-Muhallabī used force but tried to persuade Salm to step down; however, negotiations between the two had broken down. He then used force again and was defeated by Salm. Sufyān had first been promised the governorship of Basra, the homeland of the Muhallabi family, by Qaḥṭaba b. Shabīb, while the latter was advancing southward at the head of the Khurasanian revolutionary army. See *Ansāb*, 3:174; *Akhbār D*, 355–56. According to al-Yaʿqubi (1960, 2:345), however, it was Sufyan himself who "captured power in Basra and put on black [*sawwada*]."

67. *Ansāb*, 3:174–76; Tabari, 3:22 (translation 27:144); Madelung 1989, 23; Arjomand 2019, 235–37.

The last important defection that sealed the fall of the Umayyad Empire was that of another Umayyad Prince, the nephew and son-in-law of Marwān II, Abān b. Yazid b. Muhammad b. Marwān, who had been left in charge of the capital, Harran, after the caliph was defeated at Zāb, and who had fled at the end of January 750. He wore black and surrendered the capital to the advancing 'Abdallāh b. 'Ali to whom he gave his oath of allegiance.[68]

Co-optation of Umayyad officials continued after the Abbasid seizure of power in Kufa. An important factor facilitating the co-optation of members of the former Umayyad ruling elite was the influence of two domineering women on the new caliph, Abu'l-'Abbās, whose Arab aristocratic pedigree stood out in the upstart revolutionary circle of clients and Khurasanians. Abu'l-'Abbās's mother Raita, and his powerful wife, Umm Salama, belonged to the Hārithi and Makhzumi noble lineages, respectively, and they had both been married to Umayyad princes.[69] The new caliph's brother, Abu Ja'far, also systematically embarked on the co-optation of Ibn Hubayra's generals and agents in Iraq. He held Wasit after the defeat of Marwān II for a year. Abu Ja'far, as the second command in the collective Abbasid family rule, was impressed by the imperious Bedouin and would move into his magnificent palace after his accession to the caliphate and rename it the Hashemiyya. Abu Ja'far gave Ibn Hubayra and his family a guarantee of safety (amān) as a condition of his surrender but was forced to break his word by the Khurasanian revolutionary commander Abu'l-Jahm, Abu Muslim's "eye" on the new caliph, and he murdered Ibn Hubayra and his sons. Abu Ja'far, however, received with open arms the Umayyad general who surrendered in Jazira, Ishāq b. Muslim al-'Uqayli, and his co-optation of Umayyad generals and secretary/administrators continued after his own accession to the caliphate.[70]

---

68. Tabari, 3:45 (translation 27:169). His example was followed by governors of lesser cities facing the black revolutionary army advancing toward Syria.

69. *Akhbār D*, 201, 234; *Ansāb*, 3:161. Women of the Abbasid family, too, were conspicuous in the aristocracy under the old regime. Two of Muhammad b. 'Ali's sisters, Umm 'Isā and Lubāba, had vowed to "fight in the path of God," and took part in the campaign against the Byzantines in 756–57/139. See Tabari, 3:125 (translation 27:54).

70. *Akhbār T*, 371; Tabari, 3:67–69 (translation 27:190–92); Bligh-Abramski 1988, 230–34. Abu Ja'far's guarantee of safety to one of Ibn Hubayra's generals, Khalid b. Salama al-Makhzumi, was similarly broken by the new caliph who had him killed.

I have examined a major aspect of the Hashemite Revolution as an Integrative Revolution from the periphery of the Umayyad Empire elsewhere.[71] The next two chapters discuss, respectively, the process and the consequences of the Hashemite or Abbasid Revolution, which is considered, by common consent, *the* social revolution of Islam. This extensive treatment is justified by the significance of Islam's social revolution in the translation of its universalism as a world religion into a political order based on the theoretical equality of all Muslims and the enlargement of the political community beyond the Arabs to include the non-Arab clients as the subjects of the Muslim empire of conquest.

71. Arjomand 2009, ch. 9.

CHAPTER 5

The Process of the Hashemite Revolution

'Ali's capital, Kufa, remained the center of 'Alid opposition after the suppression of Mukhtār's rebellion, but it was an Arab-dominated garrison city in the heartland of the Umayyad Empire that offered little opportunity for successful revolution. The rebellion of Zayd b. 'Ali in 740 was a complete failure and the uprising of the Hashemite 'Abdallāh b. Mu'āwiya similarly failed in Kufa itself, despite the virtual breakdown of Umayyad government authority. Moreover, as we have seen, it was only after Ibn Mu'āwiya was expelled from Kufa and had gone to Iran that he succeeded in establishing the first Hashemite state. His success in Iran pointed to the coming revolution as the revolution of the Iranian *mawāli*, indicating that a revolutionary movement that grew in a distant periphery of the empire had a much better chance of toppling the Umayyad imperial state than any in the heartlands of the Arab empire: Syria, the Jazira, or Iraq.

THE OUTBREAK AND PROCESS OF REVOLUTION IN KHURASAN

No periphery of the empire was more suitable for a revolution than Khurasan and the recently conquered Transoxania—the stage for the great Murji'ite rebellion that had been quelled shortly before the disintegration of the authority structure of the Umayyad imperial state a decade earlier in 737.[1] Indeed,

---

1. Arjomand 2019, ch. 8.

it was in the village of Sefidhanj in rural Khurasan that revolution broke out on the night of June 9, 747. Abu Muslim, the freed slave serving Ibrāhim b. Muhammad, the head of the Abbasid family of the Prophet's uncle, and the imam (leader) of a branch of the Hashemite revolutionary opposition which had its own clandestine mission, started the uprising. On that day, the man known by the typical convert's name of 'Abd al-Rahmān b. Muslim, who adopted Abu Muslim as his patronymic and nom de guerre, "unfurled the banner sent to him by the imam," together with the flag upon which was written the Qur'anic verse (22:30): "Permission is given to those who fight because they have been oppressed; surely God has the power to aid them [to victory]!" Thus began the revolutionary struggle in the path of God on behalf of the Banu Hāshim in Khurasan led by Abu Muslim al-Khurāsāni, who became known the Master of the Revolution/Mission (*sāhib al-dawla/da'wa*).[2]

The path for the revolution that thus broke out on the eastern periphery of the Umayyad Empire had been paved by earlier integrative movements, the above-mentioned movement of the above-mentioned Murji'a who had themselves arisen in the course of their missionary activity, which had resulted in the conversion of the inhabitants of Khurasan and Transoxania in the early decades of the eighth century. The Murji'a became known as the "people of equality and justice," and their key ideas were reflected in the teachings of their leader, Abu Hanifa (d.767)—namely, the doctrine of *irjā'*, which meant leaving the judgment on the worth of the Muslims to God while accepting their profession of Islam at face value. Just as notable was the acceptance of the recitation of the Qur'an in Persian, which was even more clearly meant to establish the equality of Arab and non-Arab Muslims. The first major political manifestation of unrest among the new converts to Islam who demanded equality and justice was the great Murji'ite revolt, led by al-Hārith b. Surayj, which began in 734.[3]

The major innovation of al-Hārith was the grafting of millennialism onto the egalitarian Islam of the Murji'a. This combination is pithily demonstrated on an unpublished coin that was minted in 734–35 (116 AH) during the rebellion of Hārith and that bears the legend *li-* (or *al?-*) *mansur* and *al-'adl* (justice) on its margin. The legend captures the messianism of the movement in al-Mansur (presumably his title) and its demand for social justice as commanded

---

2. Tabari, 2:1954; Arjomand 2019, 220.
3. Van Ess 1991–97, 1:183, 2:491; Arjomand 2019, 217–18.

by God.[4] (See figure 1.) The political formula crafted by Hārith was original. First, he combined the typical call to the Qur'an and the Sunna of the Prophet with the novel idea of the caliphate by consent that was on later occasions spelled out as the advocacy of an electoral council (*shurā*), to choose a candidate for the caliphate, the "acceptable one (*al-rida*)."[5] He then added the millennial element symbolized by the raising of the messianic black banner and assumed the title of al-Mansur (the [divinely] aided, the victorious). Hārith was "He of the Black Banners," who was to tear down the walls of the Umayyad capital, Damascus. The battle cry of his followers, correspondingly, was *"ya mansur!"* Although his own tribe of Tamim was northern Arabian, this battle cry had a particularly strong appeal to southern Arabian tribes (Yaman), as did the millennial title, *mansur*, on his unpublished coin, which refers to the messianic figure "who would restore the kingdom to Himyar with justice" and is variously called Mansur Himyar, Mansur al-Yaman, and the Qahtāni.[6]

Hārith fled to the Turks after the suppression of his rebellion in 737, but he returned to Marw during the turmoil of the Third Civil War in 745. During Yazid III's Qadarite revolution from above, Hārith secured a pardon from the caliph through the intercession of Abu Hanifa. When issuing his pardon, Yazid III assured Hārith and his followers that he was "angry on God's behalf that His commandments have been neglected" and would uphold "the Book of God and the Sunna of the Prophet."[7]

---

4. The Murji'ite profession of monotheism and Muhammad's mission to bring the religion of truth (Q. 112 and Q. 9:33) are on the reverse side of the coin.

5. It was modeled on that appointed by 'Umar, as we saw in chapter 3 above.

6. Lewis 1968, 17. As we saw in chapter 2, Muhammad's battle cry in the Battle of Badr was reported as *"ya mansūr amit!"* The title had been assumed by several scions of the old Himyarite kingdom as would-be restorers of its lost glory—lastly by 'Abd al-Rahmān b. Muhammad b. al-Ash'ath who rebelled against the Umayyads in 701 (see *Ansāb*). The battle cry of the rebellion of Ibn al-Ash'ath, as in the uprisings in Kufa of Mukhtar and of Zayd, was the same *"yā mansūr amit!"* See Tabari, 2:1701, 1703 (translation 26:39, 41).

7. Tabari, 2:1867–68 (translation 26:236). It was not at all difficult for the emissaries sent by Harith from Tirmidh to Damascus to find common ground between the Murji'ite principle of equality of all Muslims and the principles of the revolutionary caliph's kindred Qadari movement. They told Yazid III, "O Commander of the Faithful, you killed your cousin in order to establish the Book of God ... So appoint as governors people from [local] noble families and attach to every governor men ... knowledgeable in Islamic law to make them adhere to the terms of your covenant." Yazid replied, "I will do so," but he did not have the time to carry out this promise. See Tabari, translation 26:236.

FIGURE 1. A *dirham* minted in Balkh in 116AH (734–35) during the Murji'ite rebellion of al-Hārith b. Surayj in the Tübingen University coin collection, inventory no. 94-33-1.

Center: There is no God but God, etc.

Margin: God commands justice, [a?]l-Mansur

امر الله بالعدل لمنصور

On the reverse side (not shown), we have:

Center: God is One, God is everlasting; He does not beget and is not begotten, and equal to Him is no one (Q. 112:1–4).

Margin: Muhammad is the Messenger of God. [It is He who] sent him with the guidance and the religion of truth to manifest it above every religion though the unbelievers be averse (Q. 9:33).

After the collapse of Yazid III's Qadari revolution, Hārith engaged in a dialogue with the last Umayyad governor of Khurasan, Nasr b. Sayyār; this ended in failure. By this time, the Murji'ite chief theologian, the client Jahm b. Safwān, had joined Hārith and was acting as his secretary and chief ideologue. Jahm's followers, the Jahmiyya, were particularly strong in Tirmidh. Hārith had his program, presumably incorporating some additional contractarian principles of the Qadari revolution, read in public first by Jahm b. Safwān and then in the streets and mosques of Marw. Hārith predictably refused Nasr's summons to swear allegiance to Marwān II and urged the governor to accept the electoral council. Jahm represented Hārith in a formal arbitration, which Nasr had been forced to agree to, and ruled that he should abdicate in favor of an electoral council. Nasr refused to accept the ruling, however. Jahm b. Safwān was killed during the unrest and clashes that followed in the spring of 746, and Hārith now made an opportunistic alliance with the tribal leader of the Yaman, Juday' al-Kirmāni, who refused to accept an electoral council after ousting Nasr from Marw and instead fought, killed, and crucified Hārith in May 746![8]

The death of al-Hārith left his movement in disarray.[9] Although the Abbasid missionary, Qahtaba b. Shabib, had refused to support him against Kirmāni in the last months of the crisis, his agents wooed some of the Murji'ites in the years after the death of Hārith.[10] The Murji'ite Ibrāhim b. Maymun al-Sā'igh, a disciple of Abu Hanifa, joined the Abbasid mission with his followers in Balkh, and some of these "people of insight" came to Abu Muslim's camp at the outbreak of the revolution in 747. Others unfurled the alternative Murji'ite black banners but Abu Muslim put down the uprising and executed Ibrāhim b. Maymun al-Sā'igh together with another Murji'ite leader who was likewise a disciple of Abu Hanifa.[11] There can be little doubt that the Murji'ite revolt inspired the

---

8. Madelung 1965, 241; van Ess 1991–97, 2:493–507. The clash of principles made this outcome inevitable. Bishr b. Jurmuz, a Murji'ite preacher who had been with Harith since at least 737 in Tirmidh and who now led four or five thousand of his followers in protest against the alliance with Kirmāni, told Hārith, "I only fought beside you seeking justice, but [your new allies] are fighting out of tribal factionalism, so I am not fighting on your side." See Tabari, 2:1931 (translation 27:41).

9. Tabari, 2:1918–33 (translation 27:29–43); Madelung 1982, 35–36.

10. Van Ess 1991–97, 2:492.

11. Arjomand 2019, 218.

rival Hashemite revolutionary movement. Abu Muslim not only adopted Harith's black banner and modified his battle cry *"yā mansūr!"* (victorious!) to *"yā Muhammad, ya mansūr!"* He also modified the demand for "the acceptable one" to the Hashemite "acceptable one from the House of Muhammad."[12]

The Hashemite revolutionary movement under Abu Muslim created a revolutionary coalition in which the Arab tribesmen who had long been settled in and culturally and linguistically acclimatized to Khurasan were prominent. The army he recruited and put under the commander of Arab Khurasanians, however, was recruited on a completely new and revolutionary principle that made it overwhelmingly non-Arab. Moreover, if there were any settled Arabs and clients among them, their tribal affiliation was not recorded in the army registry (*diwān al-jund*), since they were identified only by their native villages. Abu Muslim ordered the commissioners appointed for the registration of the volunteers who had joined the revolutionary camps "to enter them in a register with their names, their fathers' names and their villages."[13] It is likely that most of the men thus recruited to the revolutionary army had no tribal affiliation of any sort, and it is certain that the vast majority of them fought on foot and with axes and especially clubs known as *kāfirkūbāt* (infidel-smashers). Last but not least, he systematically recruited slaves who were eventually sent to the revolutionary army of Abivard and Nesa under the command of the Arab missionary, Musā b. Ka'b. By 750, Abu Muslim had set up a revolutionary state in Khurasan and had exported the Hashemite Revolution to Transoxania, and he could now comfortably turn westward to the metropolitan core of the Umayyad imperial state that was rapidly disintegrating. He sent his revolutionary armies to fight and defeat, first the Umayyad general 'Āmir b. Dubāra, who had reconquered central Iran for Marwān II, and then the last Umayyad caliph himself on the banks of the River Zāb in Mesopotamia.[14]

Khurasan's revolutionary power struggle remained entangled with the export of revolution into Transoxiana. After executing al-Hārith b. Surayj, Kirmāni defected from Nasr b. Sayyar and made an opportunistic alliance with Abu Muslim. Abu Muslim appointed two tribal aldermen connected with Kirmāni as his governors in Balkh and Samarqand in order to distance

---

12. Tabari, 2:1921, 1972 (translation 27:31, 82).
13. Tabari, 2:1957 (translation 27:68).
14. *Akhbār D*, 81; Arjomand 2019, ch. 9.

them from Kirmāni's sons, 'Ali and 'Uthmān, and to eliminate them all as soon as it was convenient to do so! After subduing the Murji'ite uprising, Abu Muslim's governor, Abu Dāwud, ceded his governorship of Balkh to 'Uthmān al-Kirmāni, to trick and kill him, while Abu Muslim himself was doing the same with 'Uthmān's brother, 'Ali, who was killed in Abiward by another Hashemite agent, Bassām b. Ibrāhim.

The tension between imperial expansion and the religious and social goals of the Hashemite Revolution had in the meantime become explosive. In the spring or summer of 750, the Arabs of Bukhara rose under the leadership of a Hashemite revolutionary, Sharik b. Shaykh al-Mahri, who preferred as "the acceptable one" an 'Alid in place of the Abbasid now proclaimed as the new caliph in Iraq. Sharik rebelled with the declaration: "Not for this have we followed the House of Muhammad, for the shedding of the blood and acting unjustly." This is the first instance of an uprising where the ethnic factor is pronounced, and in it we find the Khurasanian Arabs rising against Abu Muslim while the native nobility and population of Bukhara sided with him.[15]

Abu Muslim sent the client Ziyād b. Sālih al-Khuzā'i with an army of ten thousand to suppress the uprising, and he succeeded in doing so with great cruelty after burning the city. Nasr b. Sayyār had cultivated good relations with the Soghdian nobility on the edge of the empire, especially his father-in-law Qutayba b. Ghurak, the king of Bukhara (*Bokhārāt khodā*), with whom he had signed a treaty giving amnesty to those who had accepted Islam but who had subsequently become apostates from the faith. Abu Muslim appears to have been the beneficiary of Nasr's good relations. The king of Bukhara was foolish enough to trust him and to help Ziyād's army by rousing the local inhabitants of seven hundred castles of the *dehqān*s around the city against the Arabs inside. Sharik al-Mahri was killed in August 750 and the city of Bukhara was burnt. In the following year, Abu Muslim then mercilessly ordered the execution of the king of Bukhara on the charge of apostasy and incorporated his dominion into the revolutionary empire, appointing Ziyād b. Sālih governor of Bukhara and Soghdia.[16]

Meanwhile, as we saw in chapter 4, the Khurasanian army had marched through Iran and achieved major victories in Iraq. After winning his last major

---

15. Tabari, 3:74; Moscati 1949–50, 487–88.
16. Tabari, 3:80 (translation 27:203); Narshaji, 86–89; Barthold:195; Karev 2002.

victory in the Battle of Nahavand in western Iran, the Khurasaian Arab commander of Abu Muslim's revolutionary army, Qahtaba b. Shabib, sent part of his army under the command of the client Abu 'Awn ('Abd al-Malik b. Yazid) westward to Shahrazur in Mesopotamia to face Marwān II, and to advance toward Kufa. While crossing the Euphrates, Qahtaba was struck down and drowned but the Khurasanian revolutionary army proceeded to Kufa. His son, al-Hasan, assumed command of the advancing revolutionary army with the client Abu'l-Jahm b. 'Atiyya, who represented Abu Muslim, the Master of the Revolution in Khurasan as his "eye" and reported to him. The subjects of his reports were first his commander, Qahtaba, and later the new Abbasid caliph.[17]

Kufa, it will be recalled, had been declared for the black, Hashemite Revolution by Muhammad b. Khālid al-Qasri. It had had its own clandestine Hashemite movement under an obscure vinegar merchant, Abu Salama al-Khallāl, whose activities during or following the rebellions of Zayd b. 'Ali and Ibn Mu'āwiya in the 740s are totally unknown. The Khurasanian revolutionary army found Abu Salama and paid allegiance to him. Qahtaba had remained faithful to Abu Muslim to the end and had sent him the heads of the fallen enemies from Nahavand. His army was evidently distraught at the death of its commander. With Abu Muslim far away, Abu Salama, whose clandestine organization had had far fewer members than Abu Muslim's, swiftly responded to the revolutionary soldiers' despondent need for replacement of their charismatic leader. He was greeted emotionally by the Khurasanians who asked each other in Persian while weeping with excitement, "Did you actually see Abu Salama?" Abu Salama set up his provisional government as the "vizier [*wazīr*, helper] of the House of Muhammad" with its headquarters in the Khurasanian army camp outside the city, and he left Muhammad al-Qasri in charge of the city as its new governor.[18]

The acceptable Hashemite caliph (*al-rida*) proclaimed by Muhammad b. Khālid al-Qasri in Kufa was not identified by him or by Abu Salama, any more than he had been identified by Abu Muslim as head of the revolutionary

---

17. *Ansāb*, 3:156; Tabari, 3:67 (translation 27:190).
18. *Akhbār D*, 374–75; Tabari, 3:21 (translation 27:143).

state in Khurasan in the preceding two years.[19] The leader of the clandestine Abbasid mission, Ibrāhīm al-Imām, together with the former governor of Iraq, 'Abdallāh b. 'Umar, had been killed by Marwān II's order in the same jail, very probably in 748, and his brothers and uncles had secretly made their way to Kufa.[20] For at least forty days after formally taking charge of the Khurasanian army, Abu Salama had kept the news of Ibrāhīm al-Imām's death a secret while hiding the Abbasid family practically under house arrest and sending letters to the heads of the two main branched of 'Ali's descendants, the Hasanid 'Abdallāh b. al-Hasan and the Husaynid Ja'far b. Muhammad al-Sadiq. Knowing the division of the Khurasanians in the revolutionary army between those favoring an 'Alid and an Abbasid, Abu Salama thus appears to have combined the principles of Hashemite legitimism and *shurā* or choice of the caliph by an electoral council, and is said to have intended to "make it [the caliphate] a *shurā* between the sons of 'Ali and al-'Abbas." Abu'l-Jahm's mission, however, appears to have been to forestall any choice by Abu Salama and to force him to accept a new caliph of Abu Muslim's preference from the house of his former owner, the Abbasid Ibrāhīm al-Imām.[21]

According to one of the many apocalyptic prophecies circulating in the late Umayyad era, a woman from the Hashemite clan of Hārith would give birth to the destroyer of the Umayyad house. Abu Muslim's man Abu'l-Jahm managed to find out where the Abbasid family was being kept by Abu Salama; he went to them, asking, "Which of you is 'Abdallāh b. Muhammad, the son of the Hārithi woman?!" Abu'l-'Abbās, the brother of the deceased Ibrāhim, was pointed out to him.[22] Abu'l-Jahm took him to his army camp and forced Abu Salama to greet him as the new caliph. Abu'l-'Abbās was put on a caparisoned horse, probably on November 28, 749,[23] and thence proceeded to the mosque of Kufa, with Abu Salama being insulted and forced to accompany him in the procession. Although some accounts attribute a perfunctory short speech to

---

19. See chapter 4, XX above.
20. Muruj, 4:84–85, para. 2294; Blankinship 1988.
21. Omar 1969, 139–45; *Fragmenta*, as cited in Crone 1989, 100.
22. Al-Ya'q'ubi, 2:345; *Akhbār D*, 201n3, 207. The only other brother from an Arab mother, Yahyā, would also have qualified as his mother belonged to the clan of the Tālibid al-Hārith b. Nawfal. See *Ansāb*, 3:281.
23. Corresponding to Rabi' II 12, 132 AH. This is Tabari's date. See Tabari 3:37 (translation 27:161).

him, Abu'l-'Abbās was nervous and speechless at the pulpit; his uncle, Dāwud b. 'Ali, mounted it and stood three steps below him to deliver the speech that proclaimed the reign of the House of the Prophet:

> Ye people, verily—and I swear by God—this position has not been occupied after the Messenger of God by anyone more entitled to it than by 'Ali, son of Abi Tālib, and this Qā'im [Riser] behind me.[24]

The Qā'im in this oration was not just a figure of speech and we have incontrovertible epigraphic evidence that Abu'l-'Abbās indeed claimed to be the Qā'im, the apocalyptic Riser and Redresser of the rights of the House of the Prophet. We know from Mas'udi that Abu'l-'Abbās also soon assumed the title of Mahdi, the Sunni equivalent of Qā'im.[25]

Dāwud b. 'Ali went on to demonizing the still-surviving Umayyad house, referring to Marwān II as the "enemy of the Merciful and ally of Satan," but his main point was to secure for his nephew and the Abbasid dynasty the right of legitimate succession to Muhammad on the principle of hereditary legitimism of the Hashemite monarchy. In the fuller version of the speech, he also mentioned the cause of his wronged 'Alid cousins, probably as a conciliatory gesture to Abu Salama who favored them, and he expressed his special gratitude to the Khurasanians who had put his nephew in power:

> People of Kufa, by God we were wronged and bereft of our right until God ordained for us our party [shī'a], the people of Khurasan, and by them revived our right... and through them He made our revolution prevail.

While pointing to his nephew, Dāwud b. 'Ali ended his speech in a proper apocalyptic tone with these words: "So know that this authority is with us and shall not depart from us until we surrender it to Jesus, son of Mary [at his Second Coming]!"[26]

---

24. Al-Ya'qubi, 2:350. As a good Sunni, Tabari (3:33) substitutes the "Commander of the Faithful" for the Qā'im, with which the Shi'ite historians, al-Ya'qubi and Mas'udi (see Muruj, 4:76, para. 2279), had no difficulty. Tabari does, however, retain Dāwud's apocalyptic tone by recording his end the speech.

25. Tanbih, 338; al-Duri 1981. Four years later, in 754, Abu'l-'Abbās reportedly predicted his own approaching death as the Qā'im from the House of Muhammad. See *Ansāb*, 3:178.

26. Tabari, 3:32–33.

Of the Abbasid Muhammad b. 'Ali's sons, Abu Muslim and his Khurasanian agents had picked a suitable figurehead in Abu'l-'Abbās 'Abdallāh, a younger brother of their deceased imam. He was chosen mainly because of his personal insignificance, the sonorous titles of Qā'im and Mahdi notwithstanding. His having a mother of noble Arab stock from a family singled out in the above-mentioned prophecies about the Umayyad doom was, however, an additional asset of his as compared to his older half-brother with the same name, 'Abdallāh, who was the son of a Berber concubine. Abu Muslim's man had passed over the more competent and therefore threatening members of the Abbasid family: the elder 'Abdallāh b. Muhammad, and three of his uncles—'Abdallāh, Dāwud, and 'Isā. The elder brother of the new caliph, disadvantaged by having a Berber slave instead of a noble Arab for a mother, was the future Caliph al-Mansur and the consolidator of the Abbasid Revolution. A determined revolutionary intellectual, "tall, dark and slender,"[27] he was also called 'Abdallāh b. Muhammad, which enabled him to continue using the same seal and the same formula and nomenclature on the coins after the early demise of the younger brother: "God's Servant 'Abdallāh, Commander of the Faithful" (*'Abdallāh 'Abdallāh amīr al-mu'minīn*).[28] The two brothers could only be distinguished by their patronymics, Abu'l-'Abbās and Abu Ja'far, respectively. Abu Ja'far was not only lean but also mean and stingy, as indicated by his later nickname, Abu'l-Dawānīq (father of farthings).

One of the new caliph's numerous uncles, Dāwud, who had delivered the inaugural speech for his hapless nephew, took over Kufa from Muhammad b. Khālid al-Qasri for a short time and was then appointed governor of Arabia and the Yemen. He only had some three months to live, and he died in October 750 after massacring the Umayyads residing in Medina. The career of another uncle, 'Isā, started with the governorship of Fars but it was cut short at the beginning by Abu Muslim's appointee to the same province, and 'Isā became an advisor to his nephew at his court.[29]

---

27. Tanbīh: 343.
28. Tanbih, 340, 342–43. The same name appears on the copper coins minted in Estakhr for Abu'l-'Abbās in 133/750–51 and for Abu Ja'far in 140/757–58, and in Rayy. See Miles 1959, 57–58; see also Miles 1938, 23.
29. Tabari, 3:81204 (translation 27:204, 28:161). After the death of Dāwud, Abu'l-'Abbās gave the governorship of Arabia and the Yemen separately to two of his maternal uncles, Ziyād and 'Ali, brothers of Raita b. 'Ubaydallāh al-Hārithi.

The most ambitious of the uncles was 'Abdallāh b. 'Ali, "a man of sallow complexion, with a handsome face and slender forearms" who had served under Ibn Mu'āwiya in Fars but who had "heaped abuse upon 'Abdallāh b. Mu'āwiya when he was put to flight" later. He now secured a critical appointment as the commander of the army facing the last Umayyad caliph, Marwān II. In addition, 'Isā, son of the uncles' deceased brother, Musā, became the governor of Kufa, and the new caliph's full-brother, Yahyā, was sent to share the government of Mosul with the Khurasanian client, Muhammad b. Sul.

Meanwhile, Abu Muslim had been quick to take over Ibn Mu'āwiya's domains in Iran after the defeat of the resurgent Umayyad armies of Marwān II under Ibn Dubāra. He continued Ibn Mu'āwiya's coinage in Rayy with this Hashemite legend: "Say: 'I ask you no recompense for this other than the love of my kin' [Q. 42:23]," which was consistent with the oath of allegiance he had administered on behalf of the acceptable one (*al-ridā*) from the House of God's Messenger. Abu Muslim installed one of his agents in the government of Fars before the new Abbasid caliph had a chance to send a governor. When Abu'l-'Abbās appointed his uncle, 'Isā b. 'Ali, as governor of Fars (and Kerman) and sent him there, Abu Muslim's appointee to the same governorship, Muhammad b. al-Ash'ath, who had orders to cut off the hands of anyone appointed by the rival revolutionary faction in Kufa, not only refused to hand over the government but also disarmed the Abbasid 'Isā and made him take a public oath never to wear a sword.[30] Having thus been barred from serving in the prosperous provinces he had known earlier as a Hashemite revolutionary under Ibn Mu'āwiya, 'Isā b. 'Ali drew closer to his nephew, and became an influential advisor to the new caliph.[31] Although he did not give an inch in Khurasan or Fars, Abu Muslim was prepared to come to terms with the Abbasids in Iraq over the head of his distant rival, Abu Salama.

Abu'l-'Abbās remained in the army camp for months with Abu'l-Jahm, thanks to whom Abu Salama's appointee, Muhammad b. Khālid al-Qasri, gave up his post to the new caliph's uncle, Dāwud, b. 'Ali. More significant was the new caliph's success in securing the command of the Khurasanian army amassed against Marwān II for his other uncle. Abu Salama had con-

---

30. *Ansāb*, 3:89; Tabari, 3:73 (translation 27:194).

31. As we shall see, 'Isa emerged as the king maker after the latter's unexpected death in 754/136.

firmed Abu 'Awn as commander of three thousand men and added two more contingents of three thousand men each to his army facing Marwān in Mesopotamia. Abu'l-'Abbās managed to dispatch three contingents totaling 4,500 men, or half of Abu Salama's army under the command of his uncle, 'Abdallāh b. 'Ali, to the front; he later reinforced them by merely thirty men. Abu 'Awn felt obliged to defer to the uncle of the new caliph, and he vacated his commanding pavilion to him. Marwān's army, startled by the number of non-Arabs (Persians) in the Khurasanian army, was routed on the banks of the River Zāb by the Abbasid army on January 25, 750.[32]

The first short phase of the revolutionary power struggle in Iraq ended with the assassination of Abu Salama, the Vizier of the House of Muhammad in February 750, only three months after the Abbasid seizure of power. The murder of Abu Salama had been advised by Abu Ja'far and opposed by Dāwud, but it gave Abu'l-'Abbās the chance to exercise his nominal authority as the new caliph and it enabled him to appoint his brother, Abu Ja'far, as the governor of Mesopotamia, Armenia, and Azerbaijan. It also consolidated the power of the Khurasanians, since Abu Salama's vizierate was given to none other than Abu Muslim's eye, the client Abu'l-Jahm, while another client, Khālid b. Barmak, a *dehqān* of Balkh and the founder of the most famous dynasty of Abbasid viziers, was appointed head of the fiscal bureau. The Arab Khurasanian missionary, 'Abd al-Jabbār b. 'Abd al-Rahmān al-Azdi, took over as the police chief.[33]

Meanwhile, 'Abdallāh b. 'Ali had swept through Syria, taking the oath of allegiance to the revolutionary regime, while Marwān was making a last effort to replenish the remnants of his army, first in Palestine and finally in Egypt. 'Abdallāh b. 'Ali sent his brother Sālih at the head of a Khurasanian army, with the Khurasanian client-general Abu 'Awn and the Arab Khurasanian general 'Āmir b. Ismā'il in his vanguard, to confront Marwān in the summer of 750. 'Abdallāh b. 'Ali al-Saffāh kept the military districts of Syria for himself, leaving the district of Palestine to his brother Sālih. Marwān fled to Egypt where he was pursued by the Khurasanians who found him in a church in Busir. According to a well-known report that is revealing about the assimilation of the Arab Khurasanians and their fluency in Persian, 'Āmir b. Ismā'il,

---

32. Corresponding to Jumādā II 11, 132 AH. Tabari, 3:38–39 (translation 27:162–63).
33. Al-Azdi 1967, 140–145; al-Jahshiyārī 1938, 93–94.

who belonged to the Musliya clan, of which the former chief missionary, the client Bukayr b. Māhān,, shouted his fateful order to his men to kill the last Umayyad caliph: *Daḥid yā javānakashān!* (Young men, strike them!)[34]

The sources do not specify the formula required by ʿAbdallāh b. ʿAlī when taking oaths of allegiance. It may not have been the same as Abu Muslim's (to the acceptable Hashemite), but the assumption that it was taken in his nephew's name is anachronistic. That he took the oath of allegiance in his own name can by no means be ruled out.[35] What we know for certain is that after the massacre of the members of the Umayyad dynasty in Syria, he assumed the messianic title of *al-saffāḥ* (the blood-shedder, also the generous). The Syriac *Chronicle of 819* mentions ʿAbdallāh b. ʿAlī as the king succeeding Marwān II, bypassing his nephew of the same name—that is, Abu'l-ʿAbbās.[36] It is interesting to note that he gave the Khurasanians the fatal order in Persian, which he evidently remembered from his time in Fars with Ibn Muʿāwiya: Strike (*daḥid*)!

After the final defeat of Marwān II on the banks of the Nile, Ṣāliḥ b. ʿAlī returned to Palestine and Abu ʿAwn took over the government of Egypt. Abu'l-ʿAbbās confirmed Abu ʿAwn's appointment and the latter served as the governor of Egypt throughout his caliphate. The revolutionary process in the last year of Marwān II's reign and the Khurasanian domination in Egypt in the subsequent years extended Islam's Integrative Revolution to that country. It is interesting to note that the important integrative step that incorporated Egypt into the Abbasid Empire definitively followed the revolutionary precedent of the Qadarite Yazid III. Marwān II stepped up fiscal exaction from the Coptic peasants in Egypt to refurnish his battered army and thus provoked the rebellion of the Bashmur. This rebellion was not quelled when the Khurasanian revolutionary army arrived and was hailed as the liberator with divine support. In desperation, Marwān II adopted the Qadarite promise of

---

34. Tabari, 3: 50–51 (translation 27:174–75). Tabari's Persian appears somewhat jumbled. The actual phrase was probably either *daḥid yā javānakān* or *daḥideshān yā javānakān*.

35. Conrad 1991. It is also clear that ʿAbdallāh, the king (*al-malik*) of Severus's *History of the Patriarchs of the Coptic Church of Alexandria*, is ʿAbdallāh b. ʿAlī and not his nephew, Abu'l-ʿAbbās.

36. Ibn Qutayba 1983, 2:208. *Maqātil* uses this title to refer to ʿAbdallāh b. ʿAlī as one of the Abbasids who had joined Ibn Muʿāwiya (cited in Bernheimer 2006, 392). The fact that Ibn Qutayba attributes this to al-Mansur suggests that ʿAbdallāh b. ʿAlī may well have adopted this messianic title in addition to al-Saffāḥ.

tax exemption and registration in the *diwān* for a stipend of ten dinars after converting to Islam, and he managed to recruit a thousand converts to his army in this way. Abu 'Awn rewarded the Copts for their help in defeating Marwān by exempting them from the poll tax for two years, and he is said to have restrained two agents of the central government sent to reimpose it. On the third year, however, he doubled the poll tax and "'Abdallāh, the king, wrote to all of his empire to declare that everyone who adopted his religion . . . should be exempted from the poll-tax. . . . Many of the rich and poor denied the Christian religion and followed him." Abu 'Awn, who was still the governor, carried out 'Abdallāh b. 'Ali al-Saffāh's order and produced a wave of conversion to Islam in Egypt similar to that witnessed in Iran.[37]

Meanwhile, the insecure new caliph, Abu'l-'Abbās, had sent his brother Abu Ja'far to Khurasan to solicit Abu Muslim's help with eliminating Abu Salama. According to his own account, Abu Ja'far went to Khurasan with great trepidation, and Abu Muslim met him and sent an assassin to kill Abu Salama. Abu Salama, as we have seen, was ambushed and killed by the assassin sent by Abu Muslim three months after the Abbasid coup. As is typical in the power struggle among revolutionaries, Abu'l-'Abbās hypocritically praised Abu Salama and had one of his brothers lead the funeral prayer while blaming the Kharijites for the assassination of the vizier of the House of Muhammad.[38]

According to the report by a man who claimed to accompany Abu Ja'far from Rayy to Khurasan, Abu Muslim did not merely receive the future caliph, Abu Ja'far, with disrespect, as most accounts agree, but actually carried out his most important purge in the revolutionary power struggle by killing Sulaymān b. Kathir, the previous head of the Abbasid clandestine mission in Khurasan, on suspicion of conspiring with Abu Ja'far.[39] No wonder Abu Ja'far

---

37. Severus 1947, 152, 156–59, 173, 187–90. Although Coptic peasant rebellions occurred periodically, beginning in 753/135 and extending to the following century, Egypt also joined the major 'Alid rebellion of 762/145 against Abu Ja'far (see Lapidus 1972, 256–57), the integrative revolution encompassing that country as it became definitively incorporated into the Abbasid Empire.

38. Tabari, 3:58–59 (translation 27:182–83).

39. Omar 1969, 155–57. Sulaymān's son, Muhammad was also accused of being a follower of the heretical (Khorrami) Khidāsh, and he was executed. Less probably, Abu'l-'Abbās is said to have arranged for the murder of Abu Salama by correspondence and then sent his brother, Abu Ja'far, to obtain Abu Muslim's oath of allegiance.

ran back to his brother shaken and told him that his caliphate was insecure while Abu Muslim lived as there was room only for one of them. As we shall see presently, Abu'l-'Abbās never felt powerful enough to eliminate Abu Muslim, and it was left to Abu Ja'far himself to trap and murder Abu Muslim after reminding him of the murder of Sulaymān b. Kathīr.[40] Abu Ja'far's apprehension about Abu Muslim was fully justified on objective grounds as well; the latter was acting with assertive independence and building his own empire. His Hashemite coinage with the Qur'an 42:23 legend soon ceased, and he minted in Khurasan and Transoxania in his own name thereafter, first as *Abu Muslim* and then as *al-amir 'Abd al-Rahmān b. Muslim*.[41]

When Abu Ja'far returned from his nerve-wracking mission to Khurasan, Abu'l-'Abbās tried to secure him a military position, as he had done for his uncle 'Abdallāh b. 'Ali. Evidently from a position of great weakness, he sent the following request to the Khurasanian commander Hasan b. Qahtaba during the siege of Wasit: "The army is your army, and the officers are your officers. Still, I should like for my brother to be present, so listen to him and obey him and help him as best you can!"[42] Abu Ja'far thus inserted himself into a commanding position in the Khurasaian revolutionary army. Meanwhile, the news of rebellions against 'Abdallāh b. 'Ali in Syria stimulated an uprising in Mesopotamia under the leadership of an Umayyad general from the frontier of Armenia who was joined by the Kharijites belonging to the Rabi'a tribe. Abu Ja'far took some of the troops from the siege of Wasit, and, reinforced by his uncle from Syria, defeated the rebels. Abu'l-'Abbās then appointed Abu Ja'far governor of Mesopotamia (the Jazira), Armenia and Azerbaijan.[43]

Abu Ja'far's defeat of the Kharijites in this first year of Abbasid rule did not end the resistance of the Kharijiites, who remained faithful to their own stringent principles of theocracy, puritanical rigor, and equality, and who did not join the revolutionary coalition that acknowledged the Abbasid

---

40. Tabari, 3:59–61 (translation 27:183–85); *Ansāb*, 3:168; Yusofi 1989/1368, 126–27.
41. Arjomand 2019, ch. 9; Bernheimer 2006, 391.
42. Tabari, 3:71 (translation 27:194).
43. Tabari, 3:56–58 (translation 27:180–81). See also map 2. Abu Ja'far accepted the rebel Umayyad general, Ishāq b. Muslim, into his service.

caliphate.⁴⁴ Their rebellions subsequently became endemic after the consolidation of Abbasid caliphal autocracy. Kharijite rebellion against the Abbasids broke out in nearby Mesopotamia as well as in the distant Oman and North Africa in the 750s. Independent Kharijite imamates were established in Oman and in Ifriqiyya, where an Iranian convert, 'Abd al-Rahmān b. Rustam, founded the city of Tahart and the Rustamid dynasty in 761.⁴⁵

Meanwhile, the Khurasanian revolutionary army became the mainstay of the Abbasid regime, since the revolutionary power struggle was in process. It continued to be called *abnā' al-dawla* (sons of the revolution), but as the revolution was consolidated and they assumed police and administrative dues, the meaning of the term subtly changed to "sons of the state." The regime established by the Hashemite Revolution in its first five years, 750–54, however, should sociologically be described as a regime of dual power: Abu Muslim, as the charismatic leader of a unitary state in Khurasan, and Iran formed one power; the three 'Abdallāhs presiding over collective rule by the Abbasid family formed the other.

The Umayyad Arabist political and military elite frequently described the armed Hashemite revolutionaries as *'ajam* (dumb, Persian), *hajin* (half-breed), *'uluj* (infidel hulks) and other derogatory terms for non-Arabs and the offspring of mixed races. But, apart from the failed pro-Umayyad counterrevolutionary risings of the "whites" in Syria and Mesopotamia, we only have one major recorded rebellion that demonstrates a broader popular spread of the ethnic Arabist sentiment. The Khurasanian revolutionary army, though perhaps not as enthusiastically received as in Iran, encountered only one major revolt of an exclusively Arab ethnic character. The revolt of Mosul in 750–51 was triggered by an Arab woman throwing water on a Khurasanian soldier. The Rabi'a tribal chiefs of Mosul resented the appointment as their governor of the Khurasanian *dehqān* Muhammad b. Sul, protesting, "Are we to be ruled by a client of the Khath'am!" The new caliph, Abu'l-'Abbās, appointed his blue-blooded but incompetent brother Yahyā their governor and send him to Mosul, with perhaps as many as twelve thousand troops, including four thousand more Khurasanians and four thousand black slaves (*zunuj*).

---

44. One exception to this involves Shaybān b. Salama in Khurasan, who joined the revolutionary coalition with the Abbasid missionary Lāhiz b. Qurayz and alongside 'Ali and 'Uthmān al-Kirmāni, both of whom had succeeded their father as Yemenite leaders. They were all eliminated by Abu Muslim before long in the revolutionary power struggle. See Blankinship 1988, 595.

45. Veccia Vaglieri 1949, 33–35.

The Integrative Revolution had clearly expanded from the Khurasanian periphery to Metropolitan Iraq, which had black plantation slavery that was tapped for revolutionary recruitment. The real power remained with the Persian client Muhammad b. Sul, however, and in the terrible massacre of the people of Mosul that ensued, "twelve thousand persons of the purest Arab stock other than clients and slaves were killed." Abu'l-'Abbās then sent Muhammad b. Sul to Armenia, and appointed his uncle Ismā'il b. 'Ali governor of Mosul. Ismā'il held the governorship of Mosul for eight years, but when he departed in 759, the real power in the city was probably still with the commander of the Khurasaian garrison, the client Ibn Moshkān.[46]

A fanatical Hashemite partisan, Sudayf b. Maymun, rode from Mecca to Hira to greet the new revolutionary caliph, Abu'l-'Abbās, thus:

> The kingdom with the firm foundation has dawned
> Through the mighty ones from the Banu 'Abbās ...
> You are the Mahdi of the [Banu] Hāshim and its guide
> How many people have hoped for you after despairing!

Sudayf then incited Abu'l-'Abbās to order the killing of Sulaymān b. Hishām, the Umayyad prince who had first defected to the Hashemite cause under 'Abdallāh b. Mu'āwiya and who had later joined the court of Abu'l-'Abbās. Sulaymān and his sons were seized and killed by the Khurasanians with the infidel-smashers (*kāfirkūbāt*)![47]

In the same year as the Mosul rebellion or a year later, Bassām b. Ibrāhim, the Hashemite missionary for Abiward, rebelled in Tadmur.[48] He called for an 'Alid caliphate, and his rebellion spread to Iraq. It was near the Madā'in that he was defeated by the Arab Khurasanian general, Khāzim b. Khuzayma al-Tamimi, and he fled to hide in Kufa. The 'Alid on whose behalf Bassām had risen is not identified in the sources. But, since Bassām was given away in Kufa by Ismā'il b. Ja'far, the 'Alid in question was probably Ja'far b. Muhammad al-Sādiq, who had also been approached by Abu Salama. Ja'far al-Sādiq,

---

46. Al-Ya'qubi, 2:357; al-Azdi 1967, 146; Omar 1969, 312–14.

47. *Aghāni*, 4:345–46.

48. Al-Azdi 1967, 140. He was one of the very few Khurasanian cavalrymen to join the revolution under Abu Muslim before coming with the Khurasanian army to take Ahvaz for the Hashemites; he was then attached to 'Abdallah b. 'Ali in Syria. Tabari (3:75–76) puts the event in the year 134/751–52; al-Azdi puts it in 133.

however, came to terms with the first two Abbasid caliphs instead. However that may be, Khāzim b. Khuzayma showed little regard for the new caliph, Abu'l-'Abbās, and killed his maternal uncles for allowing Bassām to spread his rebellion. This outraged Abu'l-'Abbās (and presumably his mother), who wanted to have Khāzim killed, but Abu'l-Jahm and the other Khurasanian generals prevented that from happening, suggesting that Khāzim be shipped to Oman on a mission impossible against the Kharijites. The latter, however, returned triumphant and remained a major pillar of the Abbasid regime.[49]

A revolutionary power struggle was continuing, however, and by 753, the new caliph, Abu'l-'Abbās, and his brother, Abu Ja'far, were feeling strong enough to instigate Ziyād b. Sālih and another Transoxianan governor to rise against Abu Muslim, who was in Samarqand, seemingly distracted by his imperialist venture, which had been in full swing since his victory over the Chinese at the Battle of Talas in 751. Ziyād rebelled against Abu Muslim, declaring, "We have taken the oath of allegiance to establish justice and revive the [prophetic] traditions [sunnan], and this tyrant and oppressor has taken the way of tyrants, which is the opposite of that and has thus corrupted the people of Khurasan."[50] Ziyād b. Sālih did have considerable support among the Abbasid revolutionary cadre. Abu Muslim's first chief of guards, Abu Ishāq Khālid b. 'Uthmān, rose in sympathy at the head of a group of extremists called the Rāwandiyya in Taleqan and was joined by another prominent Abbasid missionary, 'Isā b. Māhān, who was a friend of Ziyād b. Sālih. The latter and his supporters, however, underestimated the loyalty of the revolutionary army to their charismatic leader, Abu Muslim. Ziyād was dropped by his men and killed by a *dehqān* he had taken refuge with, and his head was sent to Abu Muslim in Samarqand.[51]

---

49. *Ansāb*, 3:131–32, 138; Tabari, 3:76–78 (translation 27:199–201). Within two years, however, the Ibadi Kharijites were again in control of Oman, and they established their imamate there. See Veccia-Vaglieri 1949, 34.

50. *Ansāb*, 3:168–69.

51. Tabari, 3:82–84 (translation 27:205–8); Barthold (1928) 1968, 195–96; Karev 2002, 25. 'Isā b. Māhān was, however, acting as a double or triple agent among the Rāwandiyya under Abu Muslim's governor of Balkh, Abu Dāwud Khālid b. Ibrāhim, and was in liaison with the pro-'Alid rebel Bassām b. Ibrāhim, in Syria or Iraq. Abu Dāwud was informed of 'Isā b. Māhān's double-dealings by Abu Muslim and gave him to a few Rāwandis to be beaten to death in a sack with clubs and battle-axes.

REVOLUTIONARY POWER STRUGGLE FROM MULTIPLE SOVEREIGNTY TO DUAL POWER

In Iraq, meanwhile, after the assassination of Abu Salama in February 750, Sufyān b. Mu'āwiya, who had been appointed governor of Basra by him, was immediately dismissed, and Abu'l-'Abbās appointed his uncle Sulaymān b. 'Ali in his place. Sulaymān pursued the policy of receiving the former Umayyad officials into the new administration. Defections from members of the Umayyad bureaucracy had followed those of the governors during the revolution, and their co-optation continued. Notable among the secretaries who followed the governors in defecting to the new regime was 'Abdallāh b. al-Muqaffa', secretary to Dāwud, son of Yazid b. Hubayra, the last Umayyad governor of Iraq. Sulaymān's policy of co-optation worked well in the long run, though co-optation was not always easy in the short run. Ibn al-Muqaffa' tells us that many of his colleagues in a party of noblemen from Basra who had gone to see Abu'l-'Abbas balked at mixing with the lowly revolutionaries in his entourage. But in the long run, the old regime turncoats and the new revolutionary elite did mingle with each other.

The second stage of the revolutionary process was the power struggle over the succession to Abu'l-'Abbās, who died in his thirties in June 754. The triangular struggle for power that followed his unexpected death is distorted by its presentation in the official historiography as a rebellion by his uncle and it is in serious need of reconstruction.[52] Shortly before his death, Abu'l-'Abbās met Abu Muslim in Anbar, the old Sasanian city he had chosen as the seat of his government. Abu Muslim was in effect ruling the east independently. As we have seen, he had treated the caliph's brother, Abu Ja'far, with contempt in Khurasan, and had done very little since then by way of acknowledging the authority of the new Abbasid caliph. Abu Muslim now requested the caliph's permission for Hajj and continued his journey toward Mecca in an unmistakably regal fashion, accompanied by his Persian counselor, the nobleman Nayzak, and other Khurasanian generals, distributing largesse, receiving petitions, and even assessing the military potential of the tribesmen he was passing by. The caliph thought it prudent to send his older brother, Abu Ja'far, to lead the Hajj instead of Abu Muslim.[53]

---

52. Kennedy 1981a, 57–65.
53. Tabari, 3:99–100 (translation 28:19–20).

Abu Ja'far had been arguing for the elimination of Abu Muslim from the beginning but had not yet convinced the caliph that the time for acting was ripe. Abu Muslim and Abu Ja'far were traveling separately in the Hijaz when they received the news of the caliph's unexpected death. Abu Ja'far may suddenly have seen Abu Muslim as his possible ally against his uncle, 'Abdallāh b. 'Ali al-Saffāh. All the same, he was afraid of Abu Muslim, who had not greeted him as a caliph when the news of his brother's death reached Arabia. Abu Ja'far was in a very weak position: "there were only six coats of mail in his whole camp"; an aid told him that the people are Abu Muslim's "men, completely obedient to him, and hold him in the highest awe, while you have no one with you."[54] Abu Muslim and Abu Ja'far headed separately for Anbar, the seat of the caliphate in Iraq. Abu Muslim reached it first. Abu Ja'far went to Kufa instead, reaching it in July 754, only to find that the governor of Kufa, his nephew 'Isā b Musā, who was close to the uncles' faction, had left for Anbar, the seat of the vacant caliphate. Abu Ja'far decided to stay in Kufa and he made his installation in the nearby Hira.

Meanwhile, the deceased caliph's uncle, 'Isā b. 'Ali, led the funeral prayer for his nephew in Anbar.[55] 'Isā was reportedly given Abu'l-'Abbās's last will and testament on the latter's deathbed, and he took charge of the government and public treasury.[56] 'Isā took the oath of allegiance for himself as the new caliph, but when Abu Muslim arrived, people abandoned him.[57] As we have seen, Abu Muslim had humiliated 'Isā b. 'Ali at the outset of Abbasid rule four years earlier, just as he had humiliated Abu Ja'far, and he now turned to the other 'Isā, the nephew—that is, to 'Isā b. Musā, It was natural for Abu

---

54. Tabari, 3:100.

55. Except for al-Ya'qubi, all authorities agree on this. See Tabari, 3:88 (translation 27:212; Ansāb, 3:178; al-Azdi 1967, 160. In al-Ya'qubi (2:362) Ismā'il b. 'Ali is mentioned before 'Isa b. 'Ali as the uncle who led the funeral prayer, but this account, too, clearly shows 'Isā as the uncle in charge of Anbar; indeed, it suggests the caliph asked his uncle to lead the prayer on the model of Abu Bakr (as successor designate to the Prophet after the latter's death).

56. Some accounts attribute this last feat to 'Isa b. Musa (see Tabari, 3:92 [translation 28:8]). The arrival of 'Isā b. Musā in Anbar, which was under the control of his uncle, 'Isā b. 'Ali, has caused confusion in the historical record about the relation between the two 'Isās. Conversely, the person who declined to accompany Abu Muslim to the caliph's tent but arrived on the scene of his murder later was 'Isā b. Musā (Tabari, 3:116 [translation 28:40]), though some reports misidentify him as 'Isā b. 'Ali (Akhbār T, 382). The emendation in al-Azdi 1967, 161 is equally misleading.

57. Akhbār T, 378.

Muslim to choose 'Isā b. Musā as his would-be stooge, as the latter had no army of his own and had just left his seat of government in Kufa for the scene of caliph-making. Abu Muslim "invited ['Isā b. Musā] to a meeting so that he might render his oath of allegiance to him, but 'Isā refused."[58] 'Isā b. Musā refused, probably because he knew he would be entirely dependent on Abu Muslim. Instead, he made a deal with his uncle Abu Ja'far on the condition that he himself would be next in the line of succession to the caliphate after Abu Ja'far. This left only one other Abbasid candidate for succession to Abu'l-'Abbās: 'Abdallāh b. 'Ali, who had a large army of Syrians and Khurasanians and was already called king in his dominion.

'Abdallāh b. 'Ali al-Saffāh, the winner of the decisive Battle of Zāb and the destroyer of Marwān II and the Umayyads, was by far the more powerful contender for the Abbasid caliphate than his brother, 'Isā, who had been forced by Abu Muslim's man to foreswear wearing a sword.[59] 'Abdallāh, by contrast, had conquered Syria for the revolution, massacred the members of the Umayyad family in Syria, and integrated what was left of the Umayyad army districts of Syrian, Jordan, and Palestine into his the Abbasid army.[60] He was the original bearer of the title *al-Saffāh*, and was generally presumed to be the next in line for succession to the caliphate.[61] Therefore, "'Isā b. 'Ali and those present from the Abbasid revolutionary partisans (*al-abnā'*) in the army were reluctant to write to 'Abdallāh b. 'Ali," but they wrote to his brother Sālih, who was the governor of Palestine and Egypt, to break the news of Abu Ja'far's succession to him personally.[62] 'Abdallāh b. 'Ali al-Saffāh, needless to say, did not wait for their communication and proclaimed himself caliph and the Commander of the Believers in Syria. One of the Syrian generals who took the oath of allegiance to him warned 'Abdallāh b. 'Ali, however, not to repeat the Umayyads' mistake and to avoid dissension within the ruling family: "If

---

58. Tabari, 3:100 (translation 28:20–21). Abu Ja'far used Abu Muslim's trust in 'Isā b. Musā to lure him to the fatal meeting in his tent a few months later. See al-Ya'qubi, 2:366–67; Tabari, 3:105, 116 (translation 28:27, 40).

59. See XX, above.

60. He also had the Umayyad Hishām's body exhumed seven years after its burial and administered 120 lashes even after it had disintegrated.

61. *Akhbār D*, 148; al-Ya'qubi, 2:322; Lewis 1968, 16. Abu'l-'Abbas himself is reported to have said on his deathbed that he had promised succession to his uncle. See *Ansāb*, 3:79.

62. Al-Ya'qubi, 2:364.

your affair (*amr*) and that of the man in Anbar can be composed, you will remain supreme, and if you disagree, there will be civil war [*fitna*]."⁶³ 'Abdallāh heeded this advice, and wrote to the man in Anbar—that is, his brother, 'Isā: "he wrote to 'Isā b. 'Ali and others and informed them that the generals of the army and the people had taken the oath of allegiance to him on the basis of the validity of his designation as successor by Abu'l-'Abbās."⁶⁴ In August 754, he moved to Harran and appointed his brother 'Abd al-Samad heir apparent and governor of the Jazira.⁶⁵

At this point, Abu Ja'far's anxiety about his uncle 'Abdallāh clearly outweighed his fear of Abu Muslim, and we hear of him coming from Kufa to Anbar to plead with Abu Muslim to fight his uncle.⁶⁶ Having failed to set up 'Isā b. Musā as his hand-picked caliph, Abu Muslim was persuaded. He may have regarded the powerless Abu Ja'far as a lesser evil than the powerful 'Abdallāh al-Saffāh. At any rate, Abu Muslim's army met Abdallāh's at Nisibin. The skirmishes continued for some five or six months, but there was no major confrontation. Abu Muslim's strategy was to scatter 'Abdallāh's Syrian troops while 'Abdallāh was afraid of the loyalty of his Khurasanian troops to Abu Muslim and massacred some seventeen thousand of them, causing the defection of Humayd b. Qahtaba, whose brother Hasan was in Abu Ja'far's camp. 'Abdallāh b. 'Ali was eventually routed at the end of November 754 and fled to Basra to take refuge with its governor—his brother Sulaymān. He remained there for some months, while his brother and successor designate, Sālih, took refuge with 'Isā b. Musā, who was the governor of Kufa. Abu Muslim took control of 'Abdallāh b. 'Ali's camp and "granted a general amnesty to the Syrian army without killing anyone."⁶⁷

After this victory, Abu Muslim cursed Abu Ja'far as he dismissed an agent sent by the new caliph to supervise the division of spoils. Abu Ja'far reacted by persuading the Khurasanian Arab Abu Dāwud Khālid b. Ibrāhim to accept the governorship of Khurasan with an order to kill Abu Muslim. This move may have been intended to put pressure on Abu Muslim to see him and reach some accommodation. Abu Ja'far at any rate used all his wits and contacts to

---

63. *Ansāb*, 3:105.
64. Al-Ya'qubi, 2:365.
65. *Ansāb*, 3:106.
66. *Ansāb*, 3:107; al-Azdi 1967, 164.
67. Tabari, 3:98 (translation 28:14–17).

persuade Abu Muslim to visit him before returning to Khurasan. The latter reportedly wrote the caliph an insolent letter, stating he had been mistaken in accepting his late brother, Ibrāhim, as his imam before the revolution, accusing the latter of distorting the meaning of the Qur'an, and implying his own superior authority in understanding it. This was fully consistent with reports in Muslim heresiography that Abu Muslim's followers considered him their charismatic imam, and the divinely ordained reincarnation of earlier prophets and of 'Ali. Abu Ja'far used the service of his recently established chancery, headed by the defecting Umayyad secretaries headed by Abu Ayyub al-Muriyāni al-Khuzi, who became his vizier, to write to Abu Muslim persuasively. The Khurasanian general, Abu Humayd al-Marwarrudhi, was also persuaded to use his influence to direct Abu Muslim to the caliph. Most important of all, Abu Ja'far prevailed on his nephew, 'Isā b. Musā, to invite Abu Muslim and guarantee his safety.[68] Abu Muslim was eventually persuaded and foolishly agreed to meet the new Abbasid caliph, Abu Ja'far.

The key players at this fateful stage of the revolutionary power struggle were all Khurasanian sons of the revolution (*abnā' al-dawla*) whom Abu Ja'far's agents had won over for the conspiracy to ambush Abu Muslim. They agreed to come out of hiding and strike when the caliph would give them the signal, and "kill the slave."[69] Abu Muslim's council of Khurasanian advisors, Nayzak, the prince of Tokharestan, the *dehqāns* of Khwarazm, and the Khurasanian Arab Mālik b. Haytham al-Khuzā'i, the commander of his guards, told him not to walk into the trap and to return to Khurasan immediately. But Abu Muslim, reportedly relying on a prophecy of his death (misunderstood by him), insisted that he would see Abu Ja'far, at which point Nayzak told him to kill the caliph as soon as he was in his presence. In the event, Abu Muslim was disarmed before he entered Abu Ja'far's tent. The caliph hurled a series of accusations at his trusting guest, including his insolence in claiming descent

---

68. Tabari, 3:105 (translation 28:27,263); Crone 1980, 175; van Ess 1991–97, 2:16. When 'Isa protested this treachery and abuse of Abu Muslim's trust in him, Au Ja'far retorted, "Would there have been any sovereignty or authority or command of prohibition for you [i.e., the 'Abbasid dynasty] with Abu Muslim [alive]?" See Tabari, 3: 116.

69. The traitors were the Khurasanian client, 'Uthmān b. Nahik, who was made his police chief, together with his brother, and Shabib b. Wāj, the Khurasanian agent Abu Muslim had sent to destroy the neo-Zoroastrian prophet, Beh-Āfarid, some five years earlier. See al-Ya'q'ubi, 2:367; Sadighi 1938, 127–28n3.

from a member of the Abbasid family, in asking for the hand of one of the caliph's aunts in marriage, and In murdering the Abbasid chief of mission, Sulaymān b. Kathīr. He then gave the fateful signal he knew the Khurasanians understood so well: *dahid* (strike)! Abu Muslim was ambushed and fell to the assassins' swords in the caliph's tent. His head was thrown, together with a quantity of coins, to his troops awaiting outside the tent in the encampment. This was on February 12. Ja'far b. Hanzala, the Umayyad defector who became one of Abu Ja'far's companions, hailed his new patron: "From this day, Commander of the Faithful, will your caliphate be reckoned."[70]

Abu Muslim's officers were bought with more ample remuneration after consulting the registry, and Abu Ja'far even co-opted Nayzak in the fullness of time. 'Isa b. Musā and others, who had been used to trap Abu Muslim, were informed of the deed; their stupor demonstrates that they were not party to the conspiracy. The caliph then sent Abu Muslim's head to Abu Dāwud to parade throughout Khurasan.[71]

The murder of Abu Muslim immediately revealed the heterogeneity of the social forces that had backed the revolution in a series of rebellions against Abbasid rule in Iran and Khurasan. There was also an attempt to assassinate Abu Ja'far by an Abu Muslimite fifth column in his palace in Hāshimiyya—the city and palace of the treacherously murdered last Umayyad governor of Iraq, Yazid b. 'Umar b. Hubayra al-Fazāri.[72] These events preoccupied Abu Ja'far in the first five years of his insecure rule, and he postponed dealing with the unresolved issue of the legitimacy of the Abbasid caliphate in terms of the promise of the Hashemite Revolution. It was not until 762 that he finally faced this issue, and, despite his limited military power and resources, he daringly provoked the rebellion of his 'Alid cousins, who claimed better title to the

---

70. Tabari, 3:108, 114–16 (translation 28:30, 38–40); Bal'ami, 2:1084–86, 1091.

71. Bal'ami, 2:1091–92; Gardizi 1984/1363, 272–73; Moscati 1950a, 103.

72. When he was second-in-command to his uncle, 'Abdallāh b. 'Ali, in the collective revolutionary Abbasid rule, Abu Ja'far had been impressed by the imperious Bedouin, Ibn Hubayra, and gave him and his family a guarantee of safety (*amān*) as a condition of his surrender, but Abu Muslim, through his "eye" on the new caliph Abu'l-Jahm, forced Abu Ja'far to break his word and murder Ibn Hubayra and his sons. Abu Ja'far's guarantee of safety to one of Ibn Hubayra's generals, Khalid b. Salama al-Makhzumi, was similarly broken by the new caliph who had him killed. Abu Ja'far moved into Ibn Hubayra's magnificent palace after his accession to the caliphate. See Tabari, 3: 67–69 (translation, 27:190, 192).

promised Hashemite caliphate.[73] After suppressing this 'Alid rebellion, he succeeded in appropriating the Hashemite Revolution and thus in bringing it to an end. He then moved on unchallenged to consolidate the Abbasid caliphal autocracy.

More immediately, his power struggle against his uncles continued. During the second half of 754, 'Abdallāh b. 'Ali al-Saffāh had been recognized as the new ruler in Syria, the Jazira, and beyond, and his caliphate has been recorded in the Byzantine lists and by many apocalyptic traditions. Among the latter, two traditions attributed to Ja'far al-Sādiq in Medina are worth citing. The first reflects the seriousness of the crisis of succession:

> The days of 'Abdallāh b. 'Ali will be numbered; they [i.e., the Abbasids] will disagree among themselves... The decay of their cause comes from the same direction as began their prospering.

The second reveals the millennial expectation of an 'Alid victory associated with it:

> Disagreement among the Banu 'Abbās is certain; and the call [from the sky] is certain; and the rising of the Qa'im is certain.[74]

With Abu Muslim out of the way, Abu Ja'far turned his attention to this more delicate and still unsettled affair in the following months. Having dispatched an army to the vicinity of Basra, Abu Ja'far dismissed his uncle Sulaymān and appointed Sufyān b. Mu'āwiya al-Muhallabi governor of Basra, with yet another "dense army" under his command, to remove the uncles' faction from the power structure. 'Abdallāh al-Saffāh still had his generals and followers with him, and Basra was swarming with "twelve thousand Khurasanians," who obviously knew what had happened to Abu Muslim. At one point, people came to 'Abdallāh b. 'Ali to pay him an oath of allegiance, but Sulaymān cautiously dissuaded them. Sulaymān then went to see Abu Ja'far to resolve the crisis, and asked his brother 'Isā b. 'Ali, who had offered protection to their brother, to mediate. 'Abdallāh remained in Basra when his brothers Sulaymān and 'Isā negotiated with his nephew Abu Ja'far. 'Abdallāh b. al-Muqaffa' was the uncles' chief secretary in their negotiations with Abu

---

73. Arjomand 2019, 232–38.
74. Al-Kulayni 1957–60/1377–79, 8:212, 310.

Ja'far, and he drew up the crucial document of the settlement, for which he paid with his life. Knowing the uncles were negotiating from a position of relative strength, he drew up an agreement (*amān*) that did not respect the dignity of Abu Ja'far and made his caliphate revocable in case of violation. Having obtained the *amān* that guaranteed the safety of 'Abdallāh b. 'Ali and his followers, Sulaymān and 'Isā, had 'Abdallāh swear allegiance to Abu Ja'far, and they took him and his retinue to the new caliph in Hira, where he resided in 'Isā b. 'Ali's house. Abu Ja'far reportedly bought the agreement of his uncles with a gift of one million dirhams to each of them.[75]

The role of 'Isā b. 'Ali in the power struggle within the Abbasid camp was pivotal. He negotiated with all parties and kept his options open. When Abu Ja'far arrived at Anbar, sometime between August and November 754, and came to terms with Abu Muslim and 'Isā b. Musā, whom he made his heir apparent, he called 'Isā b. 'Ali and other members of his family and asked them why they had failed to write the dream he had had in Iraq "upon golden tablets and hang it upon the necks of the youth."[76] 'Isā asked God's forgiveness for this remission, and he asked Abu Ja'far what the dream was; Abu Ja'far told him. 'Isā must then have assented in propagating a dream in which the Prophet had invested his nephew, Abu Ja'far, in the Ka'ba.[77] 'Isā also kept on good terms with his brother, 'Abdallāh b. 'Ali, and negotiated on his behalf with their nephew after Abu Muslim defeated him. 'Isā b. 'Ali was, however, willing to sacrifice his secretary Ibn a-Muqaffa' to remain in the good graces of a nephew who was lean and mean.[78]

During the year of power struggle over the succession to the first Abbasid caliph, Abu Ja'far eventually incarcerated his contending uncle, 'Abdallāh b.

---

75. *Ansāb*, 3:107, 111; al-Murtadā 1907/1325, 1:94; Eqbāl (1927/1306) 2003/1382, 33–35. Al-Ya'qūbi (2:368) gives the precise date of Thursday, Dhi'l-Hijja 17, 137/June 3, 755, as the day 'Abdallah b. 'Ali was brought to Abu Ja'far.

76. All this was in retrospect put in the eleventh-hour testament Abu'l-'Abbās allegedly left with 'Isā b. Musā (conveniently substituted for 'Isā b. 'Ali) (see Tabari, 3:87 [translation 27: 212]); and this after overcoming his reservations about breaking his promise to 'Abdallāh b. 'Ali, as well as after giving up the intention he expressed to designate his minor son, Muhammad. See *Ansāb*, 3:178–79.

77. Al-Azdi 1967, 162.

78. We do not know what Sulaymān might have done after the cruel execution of his Persian protégé, Ibn a-Muqaffa', to save his honor, since he died later in the same year. See Eqbāl (1927/1306) 2003/1382, 35.

'Ali.⁷⁹ It was a perilous time for the children of the revolution, who had to make a choice among Abbasid contenders as well as between Abu Muslim and the Abbasid dynasty. They had to make their choices fast and often more than once, and the ones who were slow or made the wrong choice perished. Abu Ja'far turned many of the children of the revolution into secret and double agents in the process. Muhammad b. Sul, the *dehqān* of Gorgan and first Abbasid governor of Mosul, was one such agent.⁸⁰ The sons of Qahtaba found themselves in two opposite camps, and one of them, Humayd, had to jump ship to save his neck after the nervous 'Abdallāh b. 'Ali slaughtered his Khurasanian troops to prevent their defection to Abu Muslim. Those who had already defected from the Umayyad regime, by contrast, appeared more skillful in weathering the storm of the revolutionary process.⁸¹ The one major exception, however, was Ibn al-Muqaffa'.

IBN AL MUQAFFA' AND HIS MANIFESTO FOR THE CALIPHATE OF THE HOUSE OF 'ABBĀS

Among those who perished in the Hashemite revolutionary power struggle, the uncles' secretary deserves special attention. Al-Baladhuri's valuable account of 'Abdallāh Ibn al-Muqaffa' opens with the confirmation that he joined the faction of the sons of 'Ali, the uncles of the first Caliph, at the beginning of the Abbasid revolution:

> When the revolution [*al-dawla*] came, he became an associate of the Banu 'Ali b. 'Abdallāh and wrote their letters. He was most inclined toward 'Isā b. 'Ali at whose hand he converted to Islam.⁸²

---

79. Abu Ja'far kept his uncle, 'Abdallāh b. 'Ali, under house arrest for nine years. After failing to trick his nephew and successor-designate, 'Isā b. Musā, into killing him and thereby falling prey to judicial murder, he finally had the uncle killed while in the embrace of a concubine by ordering the destruction of the house over his head. See *Ansāb*, 3:112.

80. *Ansāb*, 3:106–7.

81. Hishām b. 'Amr al-Taghlibi, the last Umayyad governor of Mosul who had refused to admit the defeated Marwan II and who had donned the 'Abbasid black and defected to 'Abdallāh b. 'Ali in January 750, to give one example, was in Abu Muslim's camp in November 754 and fought 'Abdallāh alongside him; he survived both 'Abdallāh and Abu Muslim to enter Abu Ja'far's service, together with his brother. See Tabari, 3:96 (translation 28:15n78); Crone 1980, 167–68.

82. *Ansāb*, 3:218.

Ibn al-Muqaffa' was a second-generation Persian Umayyad official who last served as the secretary to Ibn Hubayra's son before switching sides and joining the Hashemite revolutionaries. Ibn al-Muqaffa' became secretary to 'Isā b. 'Ali and converted to Islam "at his hand," and then became tutor to his nephews—Sulaymān's sons. The uncles' faction whose service Ibn al-Muqaffa' entered did very well in the first stage of the revolution under Abu'l-'Abbās, the first Abbasid caliph (750–54), and Ibn al-Muqaffa' prospered. He recovered his estate in Fars, and the horses raised on it were famed in the high society of Basra. But Ibn al-Muqaffa''s life then came to a tragic early end in 755 because he backed what turned out to be the losing side in the revolutionary power struggle in the crisis of succession to Abu'l-'Abbās.[83]

Ibn al-Muqaffa''s famous original political work, the *Risāla fī'l-saḥāba* (Essay on the companionship) belongs to this obscure but critical stage of the Abbasid Revolution. Elsewhere, I have argued that this tract was written as a revolutionary program, not for Abu Ja'far, later Caliph al-Mansur, as is generally assumed, but for the uncles' faction.[84] My hypothesis is that it was written during the critical months after the death of Abu'l-'Abbās when Ibn al-Muqaffa''s patron, 'Isā b. 'Ali, was indisputably the master of the situation at Anbar, and 'Isā's brother, 'Abdallāh b. 'Ali al-Saffāh, had proclaimed himself the designated heir to Abu'l-'Abbās and the Commander of the Believers in Syria. The tract may later have been presented to Abu Ja'far by the author in a desperate attempt to save his neck during the tense negotiations in 755—that is, after the murder of Abu Muslim and alongside the *amān* for 'Abdallāh b. 'Ali.

The *Risāla* was substantially written either as a common program of action for the uncles' faction, while his patron 'Isā was "the man in Anbar" in order to be presented to 'Abdallāh al-Saffāh during their negotiations over succession to the caliphate, or possibly for the latter directly. It is interesting

---

83. *Ansāb*, 3:91, 176–77, 219–20; Muqaffa', 50–51; Eqbāl (1927/1306) 2003/1382, 33; Goitein 1968, 161.

84. There is no evidence for this assumption other than a reference to Abu'l-'Abbās as the deceased caliph. Pellat (1976, 2) comes quite close to my hypothesis (Arjomand 1994) when he surmises that the tract was written at the instigation of the caliph's uncles, 'Isā and Sulaymān, "who probably did not dare address their nephew, al-Mansur, directly." The common presumption that this program of action was written for Abu Ja'far, the rival of his patrons during the revolutionary power struggle of 754–55, whom Pellat anachronistically calls al-Mansur, is too improbable to accept.

to note that in the *Risāla,* the term *amān* is used not in the sense of a guarantee of safety, but much more generally as "regulation," and at least one source speaks of not just one but seventy *amāns* (regulations), all written by Ibn al-Muqaffaʿ in connection with the settlement of the affair of ʿAbdallāh b. ʿAlī.[85] In other words, either there was a series of agreement between the uncles and Abu Jaʿfar penned by Ibn al-Muqaffaʿ, or there were different drafts of regulations outlining his program for postrevolutionary state building. The phrase in the preface, "God has effected the most delicate benefaction for the Commander of the Faithful by uprooting those who were partners in his power but contrary to his way and opinion," suggests the victory of Abu Jaʿfar over his uncles and Abu Muslim and could well have been added for the purpose of presenting an edited version to the new caliph to save the author's own life.[86] If so, it was in vain, and Ibn al-Muqaffaʿ was in fact hacked into bits and thrown into an oven piece by piece by Abu Jaʿfar's governor of Basra.

The *Risāla* should at any rate be read as the product of revolutionary power struggle during the first Abbasid crisis of succession. The unceremonious manner in which the Commander of the Believers is referred to in the third person, interspersed with the occasional "May God increase your honor" (*akramak allāh*),[87] the frequently imperative tone, the fact that the caliph is never named, and the repeated reference to previous discussions (the phrase, "the Commander of the Believers is reminded that, etc.," occurs seven times), all attest to the revolutionary and somewhat impertinent tone of the document. No proof that we are dealing with a document of the revolution is better, however, than the insight into the violence and insecurity of the revolutionary process in Ibn al-Muqaffaʿ's memorable description of a revolutionary leader: "He is like the rider of a lion. Whoever sees him is terrified, but the rider's terror is even greater."[88]

---

85. Muqaffaʿ, 25; al-Ashʿarī al-Qummī 1963, 67. Shaked (1987) has demonstrated the point philologically, arguing that the term was Ibn al-Muqaffaʿ's Arabic rendering of the Sasanian *zinhar.*

86. Muqaffaʿ:25; Arjomand 1994.

87. The term is particularly appropriate for figures catapulted to high office by the revolution and it occurs in other documents from the period. At one point, the imperative tone is so impertinent, that Pellat decides to render the verb in the passive (I suspect wrongly). See Muqaffaʿ, 44–45, para. 37. In the first section (Muqaffaʿ, 22–23, para. 8), Ibn al-Muqaffaʿ makes clear that the proposals are in earnest, and that no flattery is intended.

88. Muqaffaʿ, 25. The image is used with different wording in Ibn al-Muqaffaʿ's so-called *Adab al-kabīr.* See Kurd ʿAli 1913, 65.

In short, 'Isā's secretary, Ibn al-Muqaffaʻ, presented a comprehensive program of reconstruction to end the revolutionary power struggle that foreshadowed both the integrative and the centralizing long-term consequences of the Abbasid Revolution. As one would expect from a Persian client, Ibn al-Muqaffaʻ advocated a policy of vigorous integration—of "the mixing of one people with another, the Arabs with the Persians (*ʻajam*) and the people of Khurasan with those of Basra and Kufa (*al-misrayn*)." The social basis of the Abbasid regime consisted of the peoples of Khurasan and Iraq (Basra and Kufa), who were already mingled. Their integration was to be consolidated by the broadening of the new political elite by recruitment from the people of merit in Iraq.[89] Ibn al-Muqaffaʻ also entered a plea for the integration of the people of Syria ('Abdallāh al-Saffah's power base), who had by then been sufficiently punished, and he recommended that their fiscal deprivation should be ended and their leaders be selectively co-opted. He also recommended lenient treatment and fiscal rebates for the old, dispossessed aristocracy of Medina and Mecca.[90]

As regards the reorganization of the revolutionary state to increase efficiency and centralization, Ibn al-Muqaffaʻ drew on his expertise in Persian statecraft to propose a reform of the administration and a far-reaching military, fiscal, and judiciary reorganization. He proposed an end to the haphazard recruitment of the revolutionary elite, and the opening of careers to talent. Here, it is amusing to see the Persian aristocrat argue for a meritocracy of office, now that the caste-based Sasanian social system had collapsed for good and fiscal and administrative expertise was the sole remaining asset of the Persian bureaucratic class. What Ibn al-Muqaffaʻ envisioned in the place of the old social system was a learned elite, in charge of the education of the masses, under the ruler as the head of the body politic: "The need of the elite for an imam, through whom God assures its welfare, is like the need of the masses for an elite, and even greater."[91]

Military reorganization received much space and attention in the tract. Ibn al-Muqaffaʻ proposed the separation of fiscal and military functions, the promotion of officers on the basis of merit, and regular pay for the army,

---

89. Muqaffaʻ, 36–39, paras. 30–31. Here Ibn al-Muqaffaʻ is clearly promoting the interest of his own class, the Basran administrative elite protected by Sulaymān b. ʻAli, as well as their Kufan counterpart.
90. Muqaffaʻ, 46–49, 60–61.
91. Muqaffaʻ, 38–41, 65. As Pellat points out (11), the term *nasab* (noble birth) is only used once, whereas *hasab* (merit) occurs five times.

making the provision that salaries should be adjusted in case of a shortfall in the revenue. Ibn al-Muqaffa''s discussion of the revolutionary guards confirmed the prevalence of millennial expectations and an extremist (*ghāl*) attitude among the Khurasanian revolutionary troops, which, in his opinion, had to be overcome by the imposition of discipline. To this end, he recommended the ideological control of the Khurasanian army by commissars on the basis of a code of rules (*amān*). Ibn al-Muqaffa' also proposed fiscal reform and the institution of an intelligence service along pre-Islamic Persian lines.[92]

More fundamental than the specific suggestions made by Ibn al-Muqaffa' regarding revolutionary contingencies and the proposals for reconstruction was his original theory of government. He rejected the political theories of the Kharijites and the Shi'ites, the erstwhile partners in the anti-Umayyad revolutionary coalition, and affirmed his loyalty to the household of the Commander of the Believers. He then proposed his own theory of imamate, which envisions a separation of the religious and political spheres of authority. The caliph has no authority over religious or religiolegal norms with clear scriptural basis (*athar*). In all other political, administrative, and judicial matters, he should act according to tradition (*sunna*) and his own judgment (*ra'y*).[93] Ibn al-Muqaffa' does not define the term *sunna* in this tract, but it clearly means tradition in a broad sense, and it includes the precedent (*sira*) of the earlier caliphs as well as the ancient kings, and the approved custom (*al-ma'ruf al-mustahsan*). Here, as in Ibn al-Muqaffa''s translations of the Persian works on political ethics, we find *sunna* used in the broad sense of the tradition of the ancients—prophets and kings. The central concept of *sunna*, which is equated with *sira* in this proposal, is not the prophetic Sunna of later Islamic jurisprudence, but the tradition and custom as the approved precedent and manner of the ancient kings and prophets. The ancient Persian theory of government was thus transformed into the idea of the caliphate nearly a decade before the Abbasids built their new capital, which they did as close as they possibly could to the ruins of the palaces of the Sasanian Empire.[94]

---

92. Muqaffa', 22–25, 32–37, 58–61.
93. Muqaffa', 24–33.
94. Muqaffa', 42–43, 46–47; Arjomand 2010. All this supports my argument that the document under consideration is a program to be agreed on by a party during a political crisis or, to be precise, the triangular crisis of succession to the first ineffectual 'Abbasid ruler in the fifth year of the revolution.

To conclude, the analysis of the stages of revolutionary power struggle in this chapter has informed our periodization of the Abbasid Revolution. The installation of the first Abbasid caliph as the Qa'im in Kufa in the last days of November 749 occurred in the typical revolutionary situation of multiple sovereignty. Marwān was still the Umayyad caliph and Abu Muslim was the independent Master of the Revolution (*sāhib al-dawla*) in Khurasan. The period of multiple sovereignty ended with the defeat and killing of Marwān II in Egypt nine months later—in August 750. The next four years, ending with the premature death of the first Abbasid caliph, saw the consolidation of a system of dual power, opposing the Abbasid family's collective rule in the west to Abu Muslim's autocracy in the east. The period of dual power ended in February 755 with the murder of Abu Muslim by Abu Ja'far, the second Abbasid caliph and the true consolidator of the Abbasid Revolution, who proceeded to put an end to the collective rule of the House of 'Abbās. As we shall see in chapter 6, the revolution continued on the ideological plain, however, until Abu Ja'far brought it under his full control in 763, appropriating the Hashemite Revolution and making it Abbasid.

CHAPTER 6

The Integrative and Centralizing Consequences of the Abbasid Realized Mahdism

An event so momentous as to be conceived as *the* social revolution of Islam would, by that conception, have far-reaching, indeed, open-ended consequences; the analysis of this event, therefore, would have to be selective. My selection of the consequences of the Abbasid Revolution has two criteria. First, is the specific feature highlighted by this study—namely, the suppression of an alternative millennialism and the containment of the Hashemite apocalyptic messianism through its transformation into the realized Mahdism of the Abbasid autocracy. This could be considered the short-term consequence of the revolution and it explains how the process of revolution comes to an end with the termination of the revolutionary power struggle. Secondly, the general consequences of the Abbasid Revolution as predicted by my integrative and centralizing ideal-types of revolution. These would be the consequences of our revolution in the long run.

THE REACTIVATION OF MILLENNIALISM IN THE REBELLIONS OF ABU MUSLIM'S FOLLOWERS IN IRAN

Unlike the first two Abbasid caliphs, Abu Muslim was a truly charismatic leader. If not explicitly so in his lifetime, he became a fully messianic figure after his death. As soon as the news of Abu Muslim's murder reached Iran, Mas'udi tells us, "the Khurramiyya (neo-Mazdakis) became agitated. They constituted what later heresiographers consider a sect named after him as the Muslimiyya or Abu Muslimiyya, believing in the apocalyptic imamate of Abu

Muslim. Some of them maintained that he was not dead and would not die before becoming manifest again to fill the earth with justice."[1] Others held kindred millennial beliefs concerning him, and yet others believed that his daughter, Fatima, inherited his charismatic imamate. The evidence of heresiography thus demonstrates that Abu Muslim, the Master of the Revolution in Khurasan and Transoxiana from 747 to 755, had retained his charisma as a messianic leader to the end, and that his followers converted his memory into a reservoir for their millennial aspirations. *Abu Muslimiyya*, as an umbrella term, should not, however, obscure the fact that Abu Muslim's followers organized themselves into various sectarian groups locally and rebelled in a number of different locations. "Abu Muslimiyya," affirms our heresiographers, "are called by different names in different locations: They are called the Khurramiyya in the region of Isfahan, Mazdakiyya and Sunbadiyya in Qazvin and Rayy, the Reds [*muhammira*] in Mahin, Quliyya in Azerbaijan and the Whites [*mubayyida*] [variant, the Magians (*moghān*)] in Transoxiana."[2]

The first of Abu Muslim's officials and disciples who rose to avenge his blood was a Zoroastrian called Sonpādh.[3] He may have been at Nishapur or Hulwan and reportedly had been entrusted with Abu Muslim's treasury as the latter was leaving Iran for his pilgrimage to Mecca. Sonpādh's rebellion spread quickly; he defeated the governor of Rayy and captured that city. The millennial beliefs that motivated his followers were predominantly neo-Mazdakite; these followers expected the imminent manifestation of Abu Muslim—according to one account, they expected his return from the apocalyptic copper castle in the company of Mazdak and the Mahdi. According to the same source, Sonpādh/Sunbādh also produced a letter from Abu Muslim predicting the end of the Arab empire according to the Persianate theory of revolution outline in chapter 9 below.[4] Furthermore, the report of

---

1. *Muruj*, 4:144.
2. Shahrastani as cited in Browne 1902, 1:311. The variant, *moghān*, for *mubayyida* is given in *Tabsirat a-'awāmm* as cited in Mashkur 1948, 32.
3. His name is variously recorded as Sonbād/Sunbād, Sonbādh/Sunbādh, and Sunfādh. It can be taken as a theophoric name and *pāt* means "protected by" in Pahlavi. See Sadighi 1938, 135n2.
4. Nezām al-Molk 1962, 261; Sadighi 1938, 137–39, 149. This account is consistent with what we know about neo-Mazdakite apocalyptic beliefs. The terms *Mazdaki* and *Sunbādi* (Mazdakite and Sonpadhite) are used interchangeably for the survivors of this movement in Qazvin and Rayy by Shahrestāni and *Tabsirat al-'Awāmm*.

the possession of Abu Muslim's treasury also indicates a further millennial motive for the revolt—namely, the Mazdakite belief in a hidden treasure for the benefit of the king of Tabaristan.[5]

According to Balādhuri, Sonpādh restored Zoroastrianism in Rayy, began killing the Arabs with wooden clubs and sticks (*bi'l-khashab*), "and wrote to the king of Daylam that the empire of the Arabs has ended" (Abu Muslim's alleged prediction). Sonpādh assumed the title of the Victorious General (*piruz ispahbadh*), and, during the seventy days of his rebellion, reportedly amassed an army of some eighty thousand for marching on Iraq. He wrote to the local king of the nearby Daylam that he had sent at least a part of Abu Muslim's treasury to the king of Tabaristan, Ispahbadh Khurshid, whom he must have considered the instrument of the prophesied overthrow of the empire of the Arabs. Abu Ja'far dispatched Jahwar b. al-Marrar al-'Ijli, a "partisan of the revolution [*ahl al-dawla*]," to put down the rebellion. After a fierce battle, some sixty thousand of Sonpādh's followers were killed, and he fled to the king of Tabaristan whose brother killed him.[6] Ispahbadh Khurshid sent Sonpādh's head to the Abbasid caliph Abu Ja'far! But he refused to return Abu Muslim's treasure or to give his own son as a court hostage.

Another missionary of Abu Muslim's in Khurasan who moved to Transoxiana and rose to avenge him was Ishāq the Turk, so nicknamed because his mission was in Turkistan. He organized his supporters on the basis of a variant admixture of Neo-Mazdakite ideas and the cult of Abu Muslim and tore down the Abbasid black banners and replaced them with white ones. Ishaq's followers also dressed in white and became known as the Whites (*Mubayyida* or *Sepid-jāmagān*), and their beliefs were in line with the Abu Muslimiyya millenarian movement initiated by Sonpādh. Ishāq, too, considered Abu Muslim in occultation (*ghayba*) in the mountains of Rayy and expected his manifestation, this time in the company of Zoroaster, whose prophet he was said to be. To reinforce his own authority and gain support of the 'Alid partisans, he also claimed descent from Zayd b. 'Ali.[7]

---

5. Anthony 2012, 475–76.

6. *Ansāb*, 3:246; Sadighi 1938, 132–35, 148. Judging the caliph too insecurely established, Jahwar in turn rebelled against him but was defeated by another one of the *abnā' al-dawla*, Muhammad b. al-Ash'ath al-Khuzā'i. See Arjomand 2019, 228.

7. Browne 1902, 1:314–15, citing Ibn al-Nadim; Mélikoff 1962, 56.

In July 757, a group of Whites (*Sepid-jāmagān*) killed the governor of Khurasan, Abu Dāwud Khālid b. Ibrāhim, doubtless because he had betrayed Abu Muslim to the Abbasid caliph three years earlier. There were also strong indications of the clandestine spread of the 'Alid mission on behalf of the fugitive 'Alid Mahdi, Muhammad b. 'Abdallāh b. al-Hasan, as well as his brother Ibrāhim, whom we shall consider presently. Abu Ja'far sent 'Abd al-Jabbār al-Azdi, a former Hashemite missionary and the first Abbasid revolutionary police chief in Kufa, back to Khurasan to deal with the situation. He was ethnically an Arab-Khurasanian and could have been chosen because he knew the native Khurasanians well despite, or perhaps because of, his known 'Alid inclination.[8]

On arrival, 'Abd al-Jabbār must have judged the Abbasid cause a lost one against the combined forces of the Abu Muslimite and 'Alid Mahdist movements, and he rebelled against the Abbasid caliph when a Persian hulk (*'ilj*) who became his court astrologer told him a great kingdom was writ in the stars for him in Khurasan. 'Abd al-Jabbār foreswore his allegiance to Abu Ja'far and raised the white banner of the rebellious Mubayyida and made an alliance with a *dehqān* called Barāz-banda, who claimed to be Ibrāhim, the brother of the above-mentioned 'Alid Mahdi. At this point, the Khālidiyya, named after their leader, Abu Khālid, who had continued under Abu Muslim to uphold the tradition of the Persian arch-heretic Khidāsh, resurfaced, arguing that the testamentary designation of Abu Hāshim reverts to the 'Alids after the death of the Abbasid Ibrāhim al-Imam. Abu Khālid, who had been in hiding for a long time, rose with five hundred of his followers during the rebellion of 'Abd al-Jabbār, presumably siding with the Whites and Barāz-banda, but was killed. The rebellion of 'Abd al-Jabbār and the millenarian Mubayyida lasted almost exactly two years. The Abbasid forces defeated the pretender Barāz-banda and captured 'Abd al-Jabbār after most of his troops deserted him in July 759. He was sent to Abu Ja'far, and in vain sought to plead first for mercy and then for a merciful death because of his contribution to "this revolution and mission." Abu Ja'far called him a son of a whore, and ordered his hands and feet to be cut before killing him and displaying his corpse on the cross.

---

8. *Ansāb*, 3:229–30; Akhbār D: 403–4; al-Tabari 1879–1901/1985–2000, 3:146 (translation, 27:89–90); Bal'ami, 2:1102; Gardizi 1984/1363, 275; Moscati 1947; Arjomand 2019, 219–20, 233–37.

Yet another disciple of Abu Muslim who became a messianic leader on his own count and the most successful and famous rebel against the Abbasids, was a Khurasani villager, Hāshim b. Hakim, who had joined the Rizāmi branch of the extremist Rāwandiyya, which tried to assassinate the Abbasid caliph, and who then became secretary to 'Abd al-Jabbār when the latter arrived in Khurasan as the governor in 757. He became the legendary veiled prophet of Khurasan, al-Muqanna', elaborating the millenarian beliefs of Abu Muslimiyya, with an enlarged role for himself as the successor and reincarnation of Abu Muslim. He once again unfurled the white banner, thus taking over the leadership of the Mubayyida, and openly rebelled in 775. According to Biruni, "he made obligatory for them all the laws and institutions that Mazdak had established."[9] Abu 'Awn, who had served for years as the governor of Egypt, was reappointed governor of Khurasan in December 776 but was unable to cope with the new anti-Abbasid movement in Khurasan and was dismissed after a year.

Although, according to Muslim heresiographers, Muqanna' claimed prophecy and divine incarnation, the coins he struck in Bukhara, Samarqand, and Nasaf during his rule between 776 and 780 put forth a more modest claim, and one that also strikingly attests to the continuity of his movement with the rebellions to avenge Abu Muslim. His copper coins were issued "by the order of Hāshim, friend [*wali*] of Abu Muslim" and carry the revolutionary slogan: "God commands loyalty and justice" (*amara Allah bi'l-wafā' wa'l-'adl*). Muqanna' finally died in his besieged castle in December 782 or January 783, but he had ordered his wives to burn his body, and many of his surviving followers claimed he had ascended to heaven. In short, he certainly became an apocalyptic messianic figure after his death even if he had not been fully one as a living charismatic leader. The rebellion of Muqanna' began after the consolidation of the Abbasid regime, and was thus forced to assume a local and autonomist character, even though it spread over much of Soghdia. In an interesting attempt to indigenize the Hashemite Revolution of his youth, Muqanna' substituted the Persian battle cry of "*Hāshim, yāri!*" (Help, O Hashim!) for the Arabic "*yā Mansur amit*" of old.[10]

---

9. Biruni 1879, 194.

10. Gardizi 1984/1363, 280–83; Kochnev 2001, 143. Gardizi states that his sect survived to his time (the eleventh century)

The anti-Abbasid millennial movements we have considered have been described as Neo-Mazdakite and, with less discernment, as Zoroastrian (standing for pre-Islamic Iranian); they can be considered "nativistic" in view of their localism and seclusion that made for their autonomy.[11] This localism was more by necessity than by choice, however, as their millennialism harked back to the same Manichaean-Mazdakite apocalypticism that had impressed Muhammad by its universalist scope. The Mubayyida, to take the most striking example, were designated *Sepid-jāmagān* (white-wearers), because they revived and generalized the wearing of white clothes by the Manichaean elect and a host of sects following the Manichaeans in antiquity.[12]

Just as Muhammad's prophetic revolution was not complete until the suppression of rival prophetic claims in Arabia, so the completion of the Abbasid integrative revolution required the political suppression of counter-millennialism into undergrown heterodox movements.[13] Their neo-Mazdakite/Manichaean character notwithstanding, the Abu Muslimite and Mubayyida uprisings had the long-term effect of integrating the Khurasanian and Transoxanian periphery into the Abbasid Empire created by Abu Muslim that was rapidly undergoing conversion to Islam, especially to its heterodox Shi'ite variety, whose beliefs were gradually absorbed through borrowing and assimilation.

THE DEFEAT OF THE 'ALID MAHDI AND THE CLOSURE OF THE HASHEMITE APOCALYPTIC MESSIANISM

The apocalyptic dimension of the Hashemite Revolution (744–63) clearly emerges from our analysis in the last two chapters without anachronistically focusing on later Shi'ism. The 'Alid and the Abbasid branches of the House of the Prophet vied for the leadership of the revolutionary movement that overthrew the Umayyad caliphate. The clandestine revolutionary movement that eventually chose the House of 'Abbās for its leadership was, however, named the Hāshimiyya, and we accordingly called their revolution Hashemite and derived it from the Banu Hāshim on account of the first revolutionary

---

11. Crone 2012.
12. Van Reeth 2016, 252–67.
13. See chapter 1, above.

anti-Umayyad state—that of Ibn Mu'āwiya from 744 onward.[14] The Abbasids broke their early affiliation with the 'Alid Shi'a under the second caliph, al-Mansur. As we shall see in chapter 7, the trend in political messianism/Mahdism resurfaced in Shi'ite sects under the leadership of the House of 'Ali from the end of the eighth century onward.

At some time after the murder of Walid II and onset of *fitna* in 744, the politically dispossessed aristocratic families of Medina, the city of the Prophet, gathered in Abwā' to prepare for the fall of the Umayyads. The head of the Hasanid branch of the Hashemites, 'Abdallāh b. al-Hasan, proposed as countercaliph his son and the Prophet's namesake, Muhammad b. 'Abdallāh, who was later to be called the Pure Soul (*al-nafs al-zakiyya*); despite the opposition of his cousin Ja'far b. Muhammad, who was the head of the Husaynid branch, he obtained the pledge of allegiance from many of those present to his son Muhammad as the Mahdi of Banu Hāshim. Among those present who swore allegiance to Muhammad b. 'Abdallāh as the Mahdi of Banu Hāshim was the future Abbasid caliph, Abu Ja'far al-Mansur, representing the Abbasid family.[15]

The 'Alids had to accept the Abbasid coup of 749 as a *fait accompli*. The head of the Husaynid branch of the family, Ja'far b. Muhammad, did not trust the Khurasanians and did not respond to their overtures, concentrating his efforts on organizing his following into a sect with its distinct religious discipline and law, and developing a corresponding theory of the imamate. Abu Ja'far al-Mansur, as the second Abbasid caliph, developed good relations with him, consulted him on some legal matters, and called him al-Sadiq (the truthful), the epithet retained by his followers who were later called the Imāmi Shi'a. The Hasanid branch, headed by 'Abdallāh b. al-Hasan, was more reluctant to give up the claim to the Hashemite caliphate it had gained in Abwā', and it appeared more responsive to the Khurasanians who wanted an 'Alid caliph. Nevertheless, 'Abdallāh b. al-Hasan came to terms with the first Abbasid caliph, Abu'l-'Abbās, though without revealing the whereabouts of his sons, Muhammad and Ibrāhim, and without explicitly giving up the latter's

---

14. According to another old interpretation we have mentioned, the Hāshimiyya was so named after Abu Hāshim, son of Muhammad b. al-Hanafiyya, and was the bearer of the messianic or Mahdist tradition of the Kaysanniyya, the earliest recorded messianic grouping.

15. Maqātil, 253–57; Nagel 1970, 256–59. He was reminded of this years later in the letter the designated Mahdi wrote to him during his uprising in 762. According to one report, he had given him his pledge of allegiance not once but twice. See Maqatil, 295.

claim to the caliphate. According to one report, Abu'l-'Abbās bought 'Abdallāh b. al-Hasan with one million dirhams.[16] His successor Abu Ja'far, however, did not think the legitimacy of the Abbasid caliphate was secure while the Hasanid challenge remained.

In 761, having settled the affair of 'Abd al-Jabbār in Khurasan, Abu Ja'far dismissed Muhammad b. Khālid al-Qasri as governor of Medina and replaced him with Riyāh b. 'Uthmān al-Murri, a nobody who was perfect for playing the role of his henchman. Riyāh rounded up the Hasanids, including thirteen prominent ones in addition to 'Abdallāh b. al-Hasan himself, and paraded them in a most humiliating fashion in chains before transporting them to Iraq. The sons of 'Abdallāh b. al-Hasan were thus provoked to expedite their long-planned uprising to repossess, for the House of 'Ali, the Hashemite Revolution highjacked by their Abbasid cousin in 762.

In September 762, Muhammad b. 'Abdallāh b. al-Hasan rose as the Hashemite Mahdi with 250 men in the city of the Prophet, Medina, and proceeded with cries of 'God is Great!" to storm the prison and release the prisoners, including the former governor, Muhammad b. Khālid al-Qasri. Like Yazid III, he rode on a donkey, but this time he did so in a white shirt and with a white turban, and his men availed themselves of the two loads of swords smuggled in by the agents of his brother, Ibrāhim. Like the Khurasanian rebels after the murder of Abu Muslim, the Hashemite rebels in Medina and Mecca donned white, as they were to do in Basra, when Ibrāhim began his ill-timed uprising shortly before the death of his brother. It is worth noting that Hasan b. Mu'āwiya, 'Abdallāh b. Mu'āwiya's brother, had also been at the gathering at Abwā'. He joined the Hashemite rebel Mahdi. Hasan was given the highest position in the new rebel state of the Mahdi Muhammad b. 'Abdallāh as the governor of Mecca, and his sister, Hammādah bt. Mu'āwiya, was prominent in the 'Alid revolutionary leadership.[17] The uprising of Muhammad b. 'Abdallāh's brother Ibrāhim in Iraq, too, looked like the resumption of the former Hashemite revolutionary government of Ibn Mu'āwiya.

Muhammad b. 'Abdallāh had no personal charisma and no political skills and was killed by the forces sent by Abu Ja'far on December 12, 762, his rebellion in Arabia having lasted two and a half months. Just two weeks before its

16. *Fragmenta*, 214; Ya'qubi, 2: 369; Maqātil, 256.
17. Tabari, 3:3:200, 202 (translation, 28:156, 158).

MAP 2. The Abbasid Empire (750–800) and independent states on its periphery.

collapse and Muhammad's death, his brother Ibrāhim began his uprising in Basra. Ibrāhim assumed the title of al-Hādi (righteous guidance), termed his brother's rising in Medina as a manifestation (*zuhur*), and the coins he struck in Basra correspondingly bore the Qur'anic verse, "Truth has come, and falsehood is perishing!" (Q. 17:83). Ahvaz, Fars, and Wasit fell to the rebels one after the other. In fact, the area captured by Ibrāhim's missionaries beyond

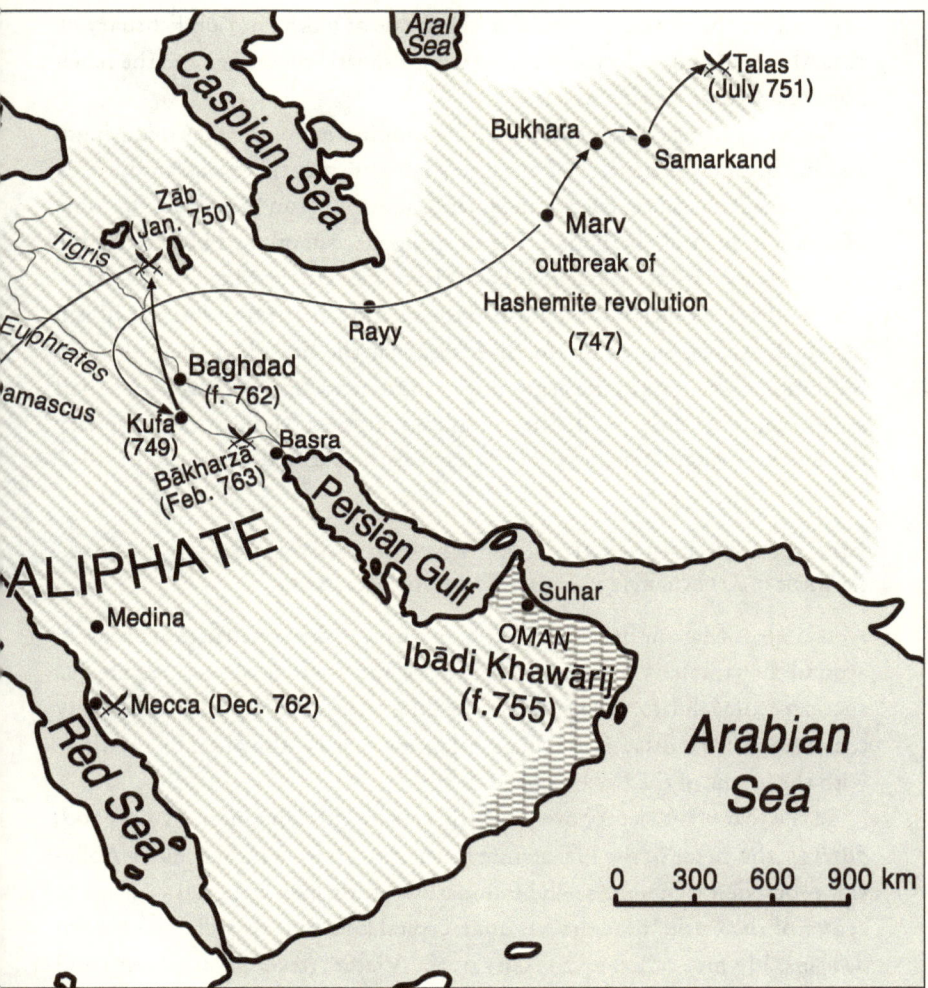

the center of the rebellion, Basra, amounted to much of the prosperous area formerly ruled by 'Abdallāh b. Mu'āwiya during the first Hashemite state, and it enabled Ibrāhīm to put together a far more numerous army than his brothers. Caliph Abu Ja'far knew Ibrāhīm's military superiority and spent the most anxious time of his reign waiting for the troops he had asked for from Rayy in Iran and those he had recalled from Medina. Nevertheless, Abu Ja'far defeated Ibrāhim, who was killed in the Battle of Bākhamrā' on February 18, 763. Ahvaz was taken by the Abbasid troops shortly thereafter and the rebellion collapsed in Wasit and Fars.[18]

Shi'ite uprisings did not stop with the elimination of the Hasanid Mahdi and his brother. A quarter of a century later, in 786, there was an uprising against the Abbasids in Mecca under the leadership of an 'Alid from the same Hasanid branch of the house. The uprising was suppressed but one of the leaders escaped from the Battle at Fakhkh and went to the Maghreb. Muhammad b. Idris (788–91) thus established the Idrisid dynasty and spread Shi'ism in North Africa. It was in North Africa that the Shi'a had their ultimate revolutionary success in the beginning of the tenth century. There, as we shall see in chapter 7, the Ismā'ili Shi'a produced our next Mahdist revolutionary movement—what later came to be known as the Fatimid Revolution.

THE END OF THE HASHEMITE REVOLUTION AND THE ABBASID AUTOCRACY AS REALIZED MAHDISM

Abu Ja'far al-Mansur began his caliphate with a major construction program around the sanctuary in Mecca between 754 and 758 that was resumed by his successor al-Mahdi (775–85) that marked the transfer of imperial sovereignty to the Abbasids in Islamic architectural terms, just as 'Abd al-malik had done with the Dome of the Rock in Jerusalem.[19]

In the year of his victory over his 'Alid cousin and claimant to Mahdihood, 762/145, the victor of the Hashemite Revolution, now definitely made Abbasid, proceeded to complete the foundation of his own imperial city at the center of the world, near the Sasanian capital and on land still belonging to *dehqāns*. He first called it the "City of the Victor" (*madinat al-mansur*) and then the "City of Peace" (*madinat al-salām*).[20] And with that victory, the Hashemite Revolution was thus irreversibly appropriated by the Abbasid

---

18. For a full account of the Hasanid rebellion and its strong support by the *mawāli*, see Arjomand 2019, 232–38.

19. Already in the first year of Abbasid rule, Dāwud b. 'Ali, in his capacity as the governor of Mecca and Medina, had put a dome over the assembly area near the Zamam well for which their ancestor, 'Abbās, had been the custodian in pre-Islamic times. Al-Mansur and al-Mahdi sent carpenters from Iraq for further work around the well. See Grabar 2005, 63–67.

20. The old Persian name of the city, Baghdād (given by god), survived, however.

House. This accomplishment was sealed by the appropriation of contested charismatic titles of Qa'im and Mahdi. As Bal'ami put it in his concise rendition of Tabari's sprawling reports, Abu Ja'far, having killed the original 'Alid charismatic claimant to Mahdihood, to whom he himself had pledged allegiance during the late Umayyad period of multiple sovereignty, appropriated it for his own son: "Abu Ja'far gave him the title of Mahdi and said: 'Muhammad b. 'Abdallāh, the Mahdi of the House of Muhammad is this my son, not that Muhammad b. 'Abdallāh b. al-Hasan.'"[21] On the same occasion, he himself assumed the messianic title of *al-Mansur*, which had first been assumed by the Murji'ite rebellion three decades earlier.[22] This left the title assumed by the last messianic rebel, Ibrāhim, the brother of the 'Alid Mahdi, who had just been slain—namely, *al-Hādi* (the righteous guide). It would in due course be appropriated by Caliph al-Mansur for his grandson as the successor of his son, *al-Mahdi*. This conversion of messianic figures into the regnal titles of the caliphs of the Abbasid dynasty meant their drastic routinization—what I take to be the hallmark of realized Mahdism. With the Abbasids' realization of Mahdihood by their victory over all their partners and rivals in the revolutionary coalition against the Umayyads, the charisma of the apocalyptic Qa'im mentioned by the Abbasid Dāwud in his inaugural oration in November 749 was transformed into an honorific attribute of the institution of the imperial caliphate of the House of 'Abbās. The age of caliphal absolutism had begun and the apocalyptic messianism that had motivated the Hashemite Revolution dissolved into the charisma of the lineage of the Abbasid House, the ruling dynasty of a Muslim empire newly reintegrated on the basis not of Arabism but of Islam.

Abu Ja'far al-Mansur's descendant, Abu Mansur Muhammad b. Ahmad, who assumed the title of al-Qāhir according to the routinized charisma of the caliphal office in 932, asked his companion Muhammad b. 'Ali al-Misri al-Khurāsāni al-Akhbāri, who was an expert in historical traditions, to tell him about his ancestor al-Mansur. This is what he heard:

---

21. Bal'ami 1987/1366, 2:1102. An influential tradition attributed to 'Abdallah b. Mas'ud made the Mahdi Muhammad revidivus of the End of Time: "His name will be my name and his father's name my father's." Abu'l-'Abbas and Abu Ja'far did not fit the bill, both their names being the reverse of the required one—namely, 'Abdallah b. Muhammad. And although they had both laid claim to be the Mahdi (Lewis 1968, 16, 21n11), they could not make it stick.

22. Tanbih, 41; chapter 5, above (fig. 1).

He was by God the first to create a split between the descendants of al-'Abbās b. 'Abd al-Muttalib and the House of Abu Tālib [b. 'Abd al-Muttalib]; until then their cause was a single cause. And he was the first caliph to surround himself with astronomers and act according to astronomical ordinances; the Zoroastrian astronomer Nawbakht, ancestor of the Nawbakhtis, was with him, and accepted Islam from his hand... And he was the first caliph for whom books were translated from the Persian language into Arabic, including the *Book of Kalila wa Dimna* and the *Book of Sind-Hind* [astronomical tables][23]... In his days, Muhammad b. Ishāq published books on the warring expeditions and manners [*al-maghāzī wa'l-siyar*] [of the Prophet] and the traditions on the beginnings; and before that there was no collection, known source or composition on the subject. And he was the first caliph to employ his clients and slaves in his government, appoint them to important functions and give them precedence over Arabs. The caliphs who succeeded him among his descendants followed this example until the Arabs' domination collapsed, their leadership vanished, and their status lapsed.[24]

One cannot ask for a more concise summary of the consequences of the Abbasid Revolution than what its consolidator, Abu Ja'far al-Mansur, is here given the credit for being the first to institute. He put the new caliphal absolutism on solid normative foundations. The turncoat poet, Ibn Harmah, did not fall short of invoking divine sanction for the new autocracy in a panegyric on Abu Ja'far's victory over the Hashemite Mahdi as countercaliph.[25] Discarding the Hashemite revolutionary principle of the caliphate of the Qa'im as the "acceptable one [*al-ridā*] from the House of Muhammad" for a new version of the caliphate as the absolute rule of God's Deputy, Ibn Harmah wrote the following verses:

> It was not the people who gave you the caliphate but
>   the King, the Exalted One [i.e., God] gave you that.
> The legacy of Muhammad is yours, and you are
>   the source of legitimacy when [other] principles are discarded.[26]

In the final oration of his reign, modeled on the so-called farewell speech of the Prophet, delivered on the day of the 'Arafat in 775, Caliph al-Mansur

---

23. The list continues with the books of Aristotle in logic and other subjects, the *Almagest* of Ptolemy, the *Book of Euclid*, the *Book of Arithmetic*. and other ancient books from Greek, Latin, Pahlavi, Persian, and Syriac.

24. *Muruj*, 5:211.

25. "You have wrested the caliphate from one who carved it" (Tabari, 3:202).

26. Tabari, 3:203. In the original, *usūl* is used for what I translate here as "sources" as well as "principles."

asserted his claim to divinely ordained autocracy: "I am the authority [*sultān*] of God upon His earth, and I govern you through His guidance and His direction to what is right."²⁷ Paradoxical as it seems, as compared to the attempt at the Arabist doctrine of caliphal absolutism elaborated by the late Umayyad caliphs, Hishām, Walid II, and Marwān II, which was based exclusively on Islam, the Abbasid doctrine of the autocracy of God's caliph reflected the integrative dimension of the Abbasid Revolution, systematically incorporating the ancient Persian theory of kingship.²⁸

THE INTEGRATIVE CONSEQUENCES OF THE ABBASID REVOLUTION

A remarkable exchange of letters between the Abbasid caliph, Abu Ja'far (al-Mansur), and the Hashemite Mahdi who had risen against him lays out the contrast between the original revolutionary legitimism of Qa'im as the acceptable one from the House of the Prophet and the modified principles of legitimacy of the Abbasid incipient caliphal autocracy. The exchange appears to have been initiated by the caliph who opened his letter, "from the servant of God [*'abd allāh*], 'Abdallāh, the Commander of the Believers, to Muhammad b. 'Abdallāh," with the Qur'anic Verses (Q. 5:33–34) specifying death and crucifixion as punishment for those waging war against God and his Messenger; however, the letter offered its recipient a grant of immunity if he would repent. The response, "from the servant of God [*'abd allāh*], the Mahdi, Muhammad b. 'Abdallāh to 'Abdallāh b. Muhammad," began with different Qur'anic Verses (Q. 28:1–6) on Moses and Pharaoh and ended with the assertion that Abu Ja'far's grant of immunity was worthless, as proved by those he had given to Ibn Hubayra, his uncle 'Abdallāh, and Abu Muslim:

> To you I extend a grant of immunity like the one you extended to me, because the right to do so belongs to us . . . Our paternal ancestor, 'Ali, was the legatee and the imam, so how could you have inherited his authority when his own descendants are still alive? . . . I am at the very center of the Banu Hashim's kinship lines. My

---

27. Tabari, 3:426 (translation, 29:131, modified slightly); Arjomand 2010.
28. I have argued in chapter 5, above, that the manifesto of Ibn al-Muqaffa' significantly contributed to this incorporation.

paternity is purest among them, undiluted with non-Arab blood, and no concubines dispute for me [in precedence].[29]

This contemptuous reference to the caliph's concubine mother was reinforced by the one to the Mahdi's descent from Fatima through women of the noblest Arab blood. The final word in Tabari's report was the caliph's, however, and with it he berated his 'Alid cousin for priding himself on "kinship through women" and articulated the new Abbasid principle of superiority of uncles over daughters, asserting generally that "God gave the uncles status equal to fathers," and more specifically that "not one of 'Abd al-Muttalib's sons outlived the Prophet but al-'Abbās, who ... was his heir." "We, not you," concludes Abu Ja'far, "are heirs to the Seal of the Prophets."[30]

With greater sociological subtlety, Abu Ja'far propounded the social and religious egalitarianism of the new Muslim society that underlay the centralization of power under caliphal absolutism. Son of a Berber concubine who upheld the honor of fellow half-breeds against the blue-blooded 'Alid challenger of his rule:

> God's way is to choose for His religion whomever He wills, as when He said: "You do not guide whom you like, rather God guides whom He wills. He best knows those who are rightly guided" [Q. 28:56]. .... The best of your forefather's sons and the most excellent people among them are nothing but concubines' sons ...; there is no one the equal of Muhammad b. 'Ali's son, Ja'far [al-Sadiq], yet his grandmother was a concubine.[31]

Far from being a disadvantage, having a Berber concubine mother made Abu Ja'far al-Mansur the perfect autocrat for emerging from Islam's social revolution—the revolution of the non-Arab clients (*mawāli*). The Abbasid autocracy resulting from the consolidation of power that ended the revolutionary process fostered the growth of the secretarial class and integrated them into the new caliphal autocracy. The new or rather greatly expanded class exercised administrative and political power insecurely, depending on the will and whim of the caliph, but it independently enjoyed enormous cultural dominance. 'Abdallāh b. al-Muqaffa', as we have seen, perished during the

---

29. Tabari, 3:208–10, 3:208–09 (translation, 28:166–68, slightly modified).
30. Tabari, 3:211, 215 (translation, 28:169–70, 175–76).
31. Tabari, 3: 12–13 (translation, 28:171–72).

revolutionary power struggle among the contenders for succession to the first Abbasid caliph, but it was otherwise with the political culture he propagated. Some important elements of the outlook of the Persian secretarial class (*kuttāb*) became permanently embedded in the new Islamic society ushered in by the Abbasid Revolution and shaped its literary culture (*adab*).

The incorporation of the Persian client secretaries into an expanded caliphal bureaucracy was accelerated by the son and grandsons of Khālid b. Barmak, a Persian aristocrat from Balkh who had joined the Hashemite revolutionary movement.[32] During the period referred to as "the rule of the House of Barmak" (*sultān al-Barmak*) under Caliph Hārun al-Rashid (786–803), the growth of the bureaucracy went hand in hand with the dominance of the scribal culture.[33] A Basran Manichaean and protégé of the Barmakis rendered Ibn al-Muqaffa''s prose translations of *Kalila wa Dimna* and the *Book of Mazdak* in Arabic verse for the pleasure of the caliph Harun al-Rashid. Even the great 'Abd al-Hamid al-Kātib, the staunchest supporter of the last Umayyad caliph, Marwān II, was rehabilitated, and his administrative epistles became the object of emulation for the subsequent generation of secretaries. The reason for this rehabilitation, which is also the key to the continuity between the pre- and the postrevolutionary regimes, was revealed to 'Abd al-Hamid's son, Ismā'il, by no less a person that the great vizier Yahyā b. Khālid al-Barmaki: "We never seek an argument in support of sovereignty [*mulk*] without finding that your father had preceded us in adducing it."[34]

Some decades later, in the ninth century, Jāhiz gives us this portrait of a secretary:

> [He] has learnt the maxims of Bozorgmehr, the Covenant of Ardashir, the Epistles of 'Abd al-Hamid and the Adab of Ibn al-Muqaffa', and has taken the *Book of Mazdak* as the fountainhead of his learning and the *Kalila wa Dimna* collection as the secret treasury of his wisdom . . . His first task is to attack the composition of the Koran and denounce its inconsistencies. . . . Then he straight away interrupts the conversation to speak of the policies of Ardashir

---

32. We met him in chapter 5 above as one of the first appointees of the Hashemite revolutionary government in Iraq. Khālid's father, Barmak, however, was the guardian of the Buddhist temple of Naw Behār (*nava vihāra*) in Balkh who joined the court of the late Umayyad caliph Hishām (d. 743) with a retinue of five hundred and converted to Islam at his hand.

33. Sourdel 1959, 1179.

34. Cited in al-Qādi 1993b, 237.

Papakan, the administration of Anushirvan, and the admirable way the country was run under the Sasanians.[35]

Abu Ja'far al-Mansur put the Abbasid caliphal absolutism on a solid sociological foundation, reaching beyond the secretarial bureaucracy to an Islamic society that was rapidly expanding among the subjects of its empire and was soon to compromise the great majority of them. He was the perfect first consolidator and centralizer of power after the revolution of the non-Arab clients whose call to Islam in the Hashemite mission swept aside the Arabism of the Umayyad Empire and established the equality of all Muslim subjects of the Abbasid Empire as a matter of principle. Indeed, the progress of the Integrative Revolution under his autocracy benefitted the non-Muslims as well. To give one important example, Abu Ja'far allotted a huge estate by the Jawhar canal, connecting the Tigris and the Euphrates below the former Sasanian capital, al-Madā'in, to Nawbakht, the Zoroastrian astrologer who had predicted the fall of Ibrahim and cast the horoscope for the foundation of the city of the victor as the City of Peace (*madinat al-salām*). Nawbakht's descendants converted to Islam and constituted one of the celebrated Abbasid vizieral dynasties while acting as the patrons of the Imami Shi'a.[36]

The passive democratization of Islam's Integrative Revolution in the mideighth century had far-reaching sociocultural consequences that are generally acknowledged. In Iraq, the garrison city of Basra was soon outdone by Baghdad itself as a melting pot of the clients (*mawāli*) and even newer converts. From Basra, Abu 'Amr b. al-'Alā' (d. 770), added the promotion of Arabic grammar to the study of the Qur'an by dispatching his students to tribal informants to gather information on "the speech of the nomadic Arabs [*kalām al-'Arab*]," and the information was fed by the Persian client Sibawayh (d. 796) into the construction of the first grammar of classical Arabic. Another Persian client, Muqātil b. Sulaymān (d. 767), wrote the oldest surviving commentary on the Qur'an. Yet another client at the court of Abu Ja'far's brother in Mesopotamia and of his son in Rayy who finally moved to and died in Mansur's City of Peace, Ibn Ishāq, was the great-grandson of a certain Yasār (a

---

35. Cited in translation in Pellat 1976, 274; I have changed the word "Testament" to "Covenant" (of Ardashir).

36. Tabari, 3:318 (translation, 28:291); Eqbāl 1933/1312; Khoury 1983; Noth 1994, 157–67; Zaryāb-Kho'i 1989/1368, 1–94; Hoyland 2001, 245–46.

typical name for the earliest converts) who had been captured in one of the early battles against the Sasanian Empire. Ibn Isḥāq produced the definitive life (*sira*) of the Prophet as a part of his world history of salvation, and thus completed the ad hoc reconstruction of the history of Islam by preceding generations of the *mawāli* as a universalist, world religion rather than an Arab one.

The typological centralizing and integrative consequences of Islam's social revolution combined to make the Abbasid caliphate the autocracy of a new Muslim empire integrated on the basis of Islam as a world religion, replacing Arabism, the basis of the caliphate of the Quraysh in the Umayyad Empire of conquest. This in turn affected the development of a universalistic Islamicate civilization. The development of the Islamicate civilization, to conclude, can be considered the longest-term effect of the integrative revolution of the *mawāli* motivated by reactivated apocalyptic messianism.

CHAPTER 7

Apocalyptic Messianism in the Fatimid Revolution

In chapter 3, we traced the emergence of the messianic figure of the Qā'im, conceived as the savior and imam in occultation among the apocalyptic beliefs of the Kaysāniyya at the end of the seventh century. The term *qā'im* (riser/redresser) was rich in connotation and surplus of meaning as the riser by the sword (*al-qā'im bi'l-sayf*), and as the redresser of truth (*al-qā'im bi'l-ḥaqq*) and of the [rights of] the House of Muhammad (*qā'im āl Muḥammad*). By the ninth century, quite a few of the Shi'ite sects that populated the millennial landscape expected the Qā'im to end his occultation.[1] Revolutionary messianism for the 'Alids, who lost the Hashemite Revolution to the Abbasids and became organized as the Zaydi sect under the descendants of al-Hasan b. 'Ali, had peaked in the 762 uprising of Muhammad b. 'Abdallāh, *al-nafs al-zakiyya* (the Pure Soul), the namesake of the Prophet foretold in Mahdist traditions, which were examined in chapter 6. 'Abdallāh, the father of that Mahdi and the head of the Hasanid descendants of 'Ali, claimed to be in possession of the sword and the armor of the Prophet, which would evidently be put at the disposal of his son as the Lord of the Sword, and the wide following of the Hasanid Mahdi included an "extremist" group, the Mughiriyya, who considered him the Qā'im-Mahdi while he had been in hiding in the mountains of

---

1. All these terms will appear a century later in the Kitāb al-kashf (Book of revelation) by Ja'far b. Mansur al-Yaman, the son of one of the Ismā'ili messianic revolutionaries, Ibn Hawshab, who led the first successful revolution they inspired in the Yemen at the turn of the tenth century.

Tamiyya before his uprising and later claimed that he was alive and immortal, residing in the same mountains. *Ex eventu*, the rebellion of the Pure Soul contributed richly to the Shi'ite apocalyptic tradition. Indeed, "the killing of the Pure Soul" became one of the signs of the Hour: "There are only fifteen nights between the killing of the Pure Soul and the rising of the Qa'im."[2]

Although Ja'far al-Sādiq, the head of the Husaynid branch of the 'Alids and the sixth imam of the Imamiyya, denied his Hasanid cousins' claim, and reportedly asserted that he himself had inherited the sword and the armor of the Prophet from his grandfather and was holding them in his house, he was apparently not able to prevent his own sons from joining the uprising of the Pure Soul. Ja'far's son, Musā al-Kāzim (d. 799), is reported among the participants, and in fact learned to harness the persisting political messianism of his cousins' followers to longer term designs of his own, albeit more subtly. Musā competed in clandestine political activism with the surviving "Zaydi" followers of his cousin, the Pure Soul. There is ample evidence in the early Shi'ite books on sects to prove that he followed the example of the latter in claiming to be the Qa'im-Mahdi. According to an apocalyptic report: "He is the divinely guided redresser [*al-qā'im al-mahdi*]; if [you see] his head rolling toward you from the mountain, do not believe it, for he is your lord [*sāhib*], the Qa'im." After the "Zaydi" rebellions of Musā's other Hasanid cousins in al-Fakhkh, the Maghreb, and Daylam, Hārun al-Rashid imprisoned Musā in 793 and the latter died in prison. His corpse was prominently displayed on a bridge in Baghdad but his followers suspended judgement on his death "because of numerous undeniable traditions proving that he was the Qa'im-Mahdi!"[3]

After Musa's death, the followers who considered him alive and in occultation as the Qa'im-Mahdi became known as the Wāqifiyya (cessationists) and were far more significant for the general dissemination of chiliastic ideas among the Shi'a than the Kaysaniyya.[4] Their books on the occultation (*ghayba*) are especially important for introducing many apocalyptic traditions

---

2. Cook 2002, 214–21. Further, "Five [are the signs] before the rising of the Qa'im: the Yamāni [presumably the Qahtāni], the Sufyāni, the caller who calls from the sky [sometimes identified as Gabriel], the swallowing in the desert, and the killing of the Pure Soul" (cited in Arjomand 2002, 116).

3. Arjomand 2002, 117.

4. Because they believed the imamate had ceased with him.

about the return of the Qa'im-Mahdi. Musā b. Ja'far's Sevener Shi'a constituted a direct historic link with the early Ismā'ili revolutionaries, as did other Sevener groups upholding the imamate of other sons of Ja'far.[5]

The civil strife that followed the collapse of Hārun al-Rashid's division of the empire between his two sons, al-Amin (d. 813) and al-Ma'mun (d. 833), include the last 'Alid rebellions in which many Imami Shi'ites participated alongside the Zaydis. In the summer of 814, within a year of the killing of al-Amin, Hasan al-Harsh, a condottiere formerly in command of the east bank in Baghdad, led sundry discharged soldiers and tribesmen in a rebellion that revived the formula of the clandestine Hashemite revolutionary coalition against the Umayyads by appealing to "the one agreed upon [al-riḍā] from the House of Muhammad." In January of 815, the same call to al-riḍā by another discharged condottiere, Abu'l-Sarāyā, set off the great rebellion under the nominal leadership of the Hasanid Muhammad b. Ibrāhim, also known as Ibn Tabātabā. It is interesting to note that the first positive appeal to the Prophet's daughter, Fātima, is found in Abu'l-Sarāyā's battle cry: "Yā Fātima, yā Mansur [i.e., Ibn Tabātabā]."[6] The nominal supreme leadership of Abu'l-Sarāyā's rebellion soon passed to another Hasanid, Muhammad b. Muhammad, but two of Musā al-Kāzim's sons occupied key positions in the rebellion: Ibrāhim b. Musā took possession of the Yemen, and his brother Zayd b. Musā, who led the movement in Basra, setting ablaze the houses of the Abbasid partisans and burning them alive, thus earning the nickname, "Zayd of the Fire" (zayd al-nār). Zayd escaped after the suppression of Abu'l-Sarāyā and rose in Basra in his own name in the following year. In 815, the Hijaz joined the 'Alid revolts of Iraq at the instigation of other 'Alids who had chosen as their caliph Ja'far al-Sadiq's last son, Muhammad b. Ja'far al-Dibāj. It was to this reclusive full brother of Musā al-Kāzim that the chiliastic expectations of the rebellion were explicitly attached. He assumed the title of amir al-mu'minin and is reported to have said that he hoped he was al-mahdi al-qā'im. The widespread great rebellion of 815 clearly demonstrates the tenuousness of the sectarian boundary that separated the Imami Shi'a from the Zaydiyya in the early ninth century.[7]

---

5. Arjomand 2016, 47–48. As we shall see in our next chapter (8) below, Musā Seveners in the Maghreb can similarly be linked to the Almohad revolutionaries two centuries later.

6. Fierro 1996, 137–38.

7. Arjomand 2016, 49–52.

In March 817, Caliph al-Ma'mun dashingly appropriated the defeated rebels' formula in a move to bring about a historic reunification of the Abbasid and 'Alid branches of the House of the Prophet, by making 'Ali b. Musā al-Ridā his successor-designate. This venture he called "the Second Mission" (da'wa thāniya). Al-Ma'mun undertook his bold initiative to unify the 'Alid and Abbasid houses amid the widespread expectation that he would be the last member of the Abbasid dynasty to rule "before the lifting of the veil" and "the advent of the Qa'im-Mahdi."[8] 'Ali b. Musā al-Ridā died suddenly in September 818, however, but the three later imams who were his descendants were called Ibn al-Ridā in evocation of al-Ma'mun's historic move.[9] Their agents refrained from armed opposition to the Abbasid caliphs and instead organized the Imamiyya into the fastest growing Shi'ite sect. The death in 874 of the childless eleventh imam of the Imamiyya, Hasan al-'Askari, however, resulted in a devastating crisis. The Imami Shi'a split into fourteen groups, and the ideas of the Wāqifiyya on the occultation of the Qa'im-Mahdi gained currency once more. Meanwhile, the great slave rebellion of the Zanj (869–83) had broken out in southern Iraq under the leadership of the 'Alid (Zaydi) 'Ali b. Muhammad, who proclaimed himself the Mahdi in his capital, Mukhtariyya (the chosen city). It is precisely in this time and milieu that the origins of the Ismā'ili sect of the heresiographers as well as that of the Fatimid Revolution to be examined is to be sought. Indeed, Hamdān Qarmat, the eponymous founder of the Qarmati Ismā'ili movement, met the Zanj leader but rejected his claim to the 'Alid imamate as the Mahdi and proceeded to organize his own Shi'ite revolutionary movement.[10]

---

8. As a letter of his brought to light by Madelung shows, Ma'mun himself shared this expectation, as he had been told by his father, "on the authority of his ancestors and what was found in the Book of Revolution (Kitāb al-dawla) and elsewhere that, after the seventh of the descendants of al-'Abbās, no pillar will remain standing for the Banu al-'Abbās" (Madelung 1981b, 343, translation slightly modified).

9. The Second Mission was an implicit reference to the Hashemite Revolution as the first calling to the one agreed on (al-ridā) from the House of Muhammad. He conferred the very title of al-Ridā on 'Ali b. Musā, the quietist brother of the recently defeated rebels who was in his fifties, and he made him his successor to the caliphal throne in preference to the members of the Abbasid dynasty.

10. Brett 2001, 8; Brett 2017.

NOMADS AND INTELLECTUALS IN THE PROCESS OF THE FATIMID REVOLUTION

Apocalyptic messianism is the distinctive mark of the Ismāʻili movement that emerges out of the blue in the last quarter of the ninth century after the death of the last Ibn al-Rida, the great grandson of ʻAli b. Musā al-Ridā and the eleventh imam of the Imamiyya, Hasan al-ʻAskari. The apocryphal belief that a grandson of Jaʻfar al-Sādiq, Muhammad b. Ismāʻil, had not died and was the Qāʼim-Mahdi, can be presumed to have gained circulation during the severest crisis of the Shiʻite imamate caused by the childless Hasan al-ʻAskari's death in 874. Within a few years of his death, Ismāʻili activists made their first appearance in Iraq and the Yemen and engaged in propaganda on behalf of the expected Qāʼim-Mahdi. These missionaries considered this hidden imam the proof (*hujja*) of God and the seventh and last imam of the Islamic era. He was soon to remove the veil of external reality by abolishing the Law and to reveal the True Religion.

The literate urban individuals belonging to various Shiʻite faction in this era of "perplexity" (*hayra*) who formed the Ismāʻili missionary sect were craftsmen and traders by profession—a social background Max Weber considered typical for urban petty intellectuals in the formative periods of congregational world religions. Thus, a certain ʻAbdallāh the Elder from a presumably Sevener Shiʻite family in Daylam in northern Iran, left his native mission to a brother in Taleqan, and moved south the city of Ahvaz. Daylam had been the center of missionary activity and later the unsuccessful Zaydi Shiʻite rebellion of Yahyā b. ʻAbdallāh in 792, which rebellion had given circulation to an apocalyptic myth that there were treasures in Taleqan hidden for the helpers of the Mahdi at the End of Time.[11] In Ahvaz, ʻAbdallāh the Elder opened a branch for the surrounding region that was entrusted to a carpenter, Husayn al-Ahwāzi, in 875 or 878. It was in Ahvaz that Husayn recruited two Persian natives, Hamdān, nicknamed Qarmat (short-legged), who was a carter, and the latter's brother-in-law, Abu Muhammad ʻAbdān. When ʻAbdallāh the Elder was later forced to move to Basra, Hamdān Qarmat also moved to Iraq but further north into the vicinity of Baghdad, and, assisted by ʻAbdān, he established an Ismāʻili mission and began sending out missionaries. Notable

---

11. Anthony 2012, 462.

among his missionaries were Abu Saʻid b. Bahrām al-Jannābi, a pelt dealer native to Ganāva on Iran's coast of the Persian Gulf who was sent to the Bahrain on its opposite coast, Hamdān's brother Maʻmun, who was sent to Fars, and a weaver from the Sawād (black land) of Kufa, Hasan b. Farah b. Hawshab b. Zādān, who was sent to the Yemen and became known there as Ibn Hawshab.[12] In Iraq, meanwhile, Hamdān's followers became known as the Qarmatis (Carmatians). It is quite possible that his nickname was already in use by an earlier leader of the movement in Khurasan, where Sevener Shiʻa, who believed in ʻAbdallāh b. Jaʻfar al-Sādiq as the seventh imam, were numerous.[13] In the meantime, ʻAbdallāh the Elder had been dislodged from Basra and moved to Salamiyya near Hamāʼ in Syria. In the late 890s, we find his grandson Muhammad, with the unflattering nickname of Abuʼl-Shalaghlagh in Salamiyya at the head a network of his missionaries.

Ismāʻili missionaries were sent away from the heartland of Abbasid government, in Iraq, to the inaccessible peripheries of the empire to proselytize, and they carried books of instruction with them. The three books surviving from this period are all attributed to Ibn Hawshab. They contain instructions on the esoteric meaning of the Qurʼan through the allegorical interpretation (*taʼwil*) that became the hallmark of Ismāʻilism.[14] They reveal the intense apocalyptic expectations of the mission in this period. Preaching the apocalypse meant preparing for the imminent manifestation (*zuhur*) of the Qaʼim-Mahdi, the Qaʼim of the Resurrection (*qiyāma*). The revolution to be led by him was indeed the revelation, as suggested by the title of one of these books—*Kitāb al-kashf* (The book of revelation).

As a former Imami versed in the Shiʻite apocalyptic tradition, Ibn Hawshab cited the chiliastic apocalypse of Jābir al-Juʻfi, according to whom ʻAli himself spoke of the Second Christ (*al-masih al-thāni*) as "the one rising in truth" (*al-qāʼim biʼl-haqq*) and who is the king of this and the other world, while affirming "I am he and he is me." Ibn Hawshab also reported other early Shiʻite materials in its commentaries on the apocalyptic verses of the Qurʼan in which the expected redeemer rises as al-Qāʼim bi-amr Allāh (riser by God's command)—the title,

---

12. Halm 1996, 26–31; Madelung 1978, 661; Madelung 1997b, 116.
13. Madelung 1978, 661.
14. Much later, after the eventual political failure of Ismāʻilism, this feature paved the way for its eventual transformation into Sufi mysticism.

as we shall see, to be appropriated by the second Fatimid caliph—and the riser by the sword (*al-qā'im bi'l-sayf*), wearing the armor of the Prophet and wielding his sword, the *dhu'l-fiqār*. His expected savior, the Mahdi of the End of Time and the Greatest Proof (*al-hujja al-kubrā*) of God is indeed the Qa'im of the Resurrection.¹⁵ He is clearly connected with the Last Judgment and the Resurrection of the dead. The Day of Judgment in Qur'an 78:17 is an appointed time of sorting, and "the day of sorting is the Mahdi through whom God sorts between truth and falsehood, believer and denier." Even more apocalyptic are Ibn Hawshab's s glosses on Qur'an 80:33, 88, 104, and especially 89.21–22: "And your Lord Nay! When the earth has been levelled, pounded and crushed; and your Lord has come and the angels, rank upon rank": "And your Lord has come" means the Qa'im, . . . the Master of the Age [*sāhib al-zamān*]!"¹⁶ The identification of the Qa'im with the Day of Judgement does not preclude the typically cyclical Ismā'ili conception of eternal return: "The religion of God does not end with the uprising of the Messengers and Imams in the world but reaches to Qa'im after Qa'im by God's command and election [*bi-amr Allāh wa ikhtiyārihi*]." Finally, the notion of *raj'a* (return) is linked to the coming revolution of the Qa'im in a somewhat novel way as "return of the right to those entitled to it after the domination of the tyrants and the concealment of the Proofs and the Imams."¹⁷

We know from the second instruction book, *Kitāb al-rushd wa'l-hidāya* (Book of righteousness and guidance) that the covenant, alternately called the '*ahd* or *mithāq*, was sworn as an oath by the neophyte, who pledged to adhere to the exoteric (*zāhir*) as well as the esoteric (*bātin*) teachings of the sect, but especially to observe the secrecy of the inner meaning (*bātin*). The covenant was "a covenant with God, insistent on His rights" ('*ahd li'lllāh al mu'akkad bi-huquqihi*). God also bound himself to whoever pledges the oath. In return for its observance, the novice (*ghulām*) is not just to be admitted to the broth-

---

15. Daftary 1990, 118. The origins of the idea are obscure; the parallel that comes to my mind is Dan. 12:1–2, where "Michael will arise" at the time of the end, and his rise is immediately followed by the resurrection "of those who are sleeping in the Land of Dust." The verb עדמ ('*md*) used in the verse is the postexilic synonym for םוק (*qwm*, to rise) whose active participle is *qā 'im* (riser). (See Collins 1993, 390.) Closer in time, there is resonance with the Syriac text on the Pishyōtan rising from his sleep quoted in chapter 3, above.

16. Cited in Velji 2016, 47, 53–54, 65; Daftary 1990, 118.

17. Ja'far b. Mansur al-Yaman, 1952, 8, 23, 34, 62, 72–73, 78, 85–89.

erhood of the Friends of God (*auliyā' Allāh*) but is also guaranteed salvation and paradise. The gloss on Qur'an 74:42–47 further links the covenant to the apocalypse and the Day of Judgment: "'We used to deny the Day of Judgment until certainty came upon us' means that we denied the Mahdi!" The believers, by contrast, affirm that "we did not deny the Mahdi; rather, we continuously gave him our loyalty, and we are of the people of his oath/covenant [*'ahd*] and of his protection [*dhimma*]."[18]

According to these prerevolution books of instruction attributed to Ibn Hawshab, each of the seven messengers of God ("speakers," in Ismā'ili terminology) sent for the salvation of humankind speak out or institute their law, which is in need of a completer (*mutimm*) who is his imam, aided by his twelve proofs (*hujjas*) who learn the esoteric inner knowledge, as compared to the exoteric knowledge of the laws of the messenger of God. These proofs are the last links of the chain in the rope of salvation (*al-urwa al-wuthqā*) that reaches down from God to the believer through his messengers, and the latter's legatees to the imams.[19]

The chain of salvation frames the relation between the teacher and the pupil in the third instruction book, *Kitāb al-'ālim wa'l-ghulām* (Book of the scholar and the pupil). The teacher is evidently himself one of the Friends of God and "missionaries [calling] to the Good" (*du'āt al-khayr*), who provides guidance to salvation through exoteric and esoteric knowledge and thus prepares for the millennial revolution of the "People of the Good." They are likened to brilliant stars revolving around the imam as the great sun whose light of guidance is reflected by his proof (*hujja*) and gate (*bāb*) as the shining moon. The saving knowledge thus imparted to the pupil results in righteous action (*'amal*) and purity on his part in accordance with obedience to "those in authority" (Q. 4:59). It thus prepares the neophyte to become a missionary (*dā'i*) calling for the Mahdist revolution, or more strictly speaking, for the manifestation of the Riser with the Sword, the Qa'im of the Resurrection.[20]

We have no historical record of Hamdān Qarmat, though Madelung speculates that he may have rejoined 'Abdallāh the Elder's faction under the name of Abu 'Ali through his future father-in-law, Firuz, who was a member

---

18. Ivanow 1948, 91 (as cited in Velji 2016, 33–34); Halm 1996b, 91–93.
19. Ivanow 1948, 70–77.
20. Ivanow 1948, 94.

of the latter's household in Salamiyya. Abu 'Ali would then have been sent to Egypt as an agent, and at any rate had a successful second career there. In Egypt, where he also used his Persian name, Shahryār, Abu 'Ali attained the highest rank of *bāb al-abwāb* (the highest gate) during the Fatimid caliphate. However that may be, Abu 'Ali had recruited two Shi'ite brothers in Kufa before going to Egypt: Husyan b. Ahmad b. Zakariyā', who became known as Abu 'Abdallāh *al-Shi'i* (the Shi'ite), and his brother, Abu'l-'Abbās Muhammad b. Ahmad.[21] He took both brothers with him to Egypt in 892, reportedly after obtaining, through Firuz, the assent of the Salamiyya master, Abu'l-Shalaghlagh Muhammad.[22]

The Kufan weaver, Ibn Hawshab, had been an Imami Shi'ite who became disillusioned about "the fraud which the followers of Muhammad b. al-Hasan al-'Askari were perpetrating, namely that the Imam was supposed to be alive, and that he would emerge in the end, without ever tasting death."[23] Ibn Hawshab arrived in the Yemen in the company of a Yemenite native, 'Ali b. al-Fadl, in August 881. Both were converts from Imami Shi'ism during the critical decade following the death of the eleventh imam.[24] The process of the Mahdist revolution in the Yemen consisted in the power struggle between the top two missionaries competing with each other in apocalyptic claims.

The mission to the Yemen was highly successful and Ibn Hawshab's followers took up arms within a few years and secured his rule in that country and he was accorded the apocalyptic title of *Mansur al-Yaman* (victor of the Yemen), as the apocalyptic helper of the Mahdi at the End of Time.[25] In 892, Abu 'Abdallāh al-Shi'i was sent to him for training and spent a year in the Yemen. After 900, however, the second missionary, 'Ali b. al-Fadl, defected from the new Salamiyya master who was calling himself the Mahdi and claimed Mahdihood for himself. Firuz, who had originally converted him, also defected and fled Salamiyya to him in the Yemen. According to an eleventh-century Yemenite polemicist, 'Ali b. al-Fadl's model in claiming Mahdihood was none other than his former fellow missionary, whom we shall

---

21. If this were the case, Hamdān could not have sent 'Abdān to Salamiyya in 899, as is reported below, and 'Abdān must have met the imam and broken with him on his own.
22. Ja'far 1952, 291, 306; Madelung 1997b, 119.
23. Cited in Halm 1996, 32.
24. Daftary 2018, 16.
25. Iftitāh, 33.

discuss presently—Abu Saʻid al-Jannābi. Ibn Hawshab had Firuz killed before long and remained faithful to the new Mahdi of Salamiyya until his death in his *dār al-hijra* (abode of migration) in December 914. ʻAli b. al-Fadl, meanwhile, abolished the Islamic *shariʻa* and declared war on Ibn Hawshab in 911 and ruled the southern highlands of the Yemen until his death in October 915.[26] ʻAli b. al-Fadl's son was then killed by the Yaʻfurid local ruler in the following year and Ibn Hawshab's constituency suffered from a terminal crisis of succession. The Ismāʻili Revolution in the Yemen thus collapsed in the second decade of the tenth century and the country reverted to the local dynasties and to Zaydi Shiʻism.[27]

In Salamiyya, meanwhile, just before his death, Abu'l-Shalaghlagh designated his nephew and adopted son Saʻid the Mahdi. When "the man in Salamiyya" died in 899, Hamdān reportedly sent ʻAbdān to meet his successor. The latter returned to Iraq to report that Abu'l-Shalaghlagh's successor in Salamiyya was denying the existence of Muhammad b. Ismāʻil and was himself claiming to be the Mahdi. ʻAbdān, as the leader of the Ismāʻili intellectuals in Iraq, opposed Salamiyya and the heretical claim emanating therefrom. He was murdered by Zakarōye b. Mehrōye, another Persian missionary who at the time sided with the Salamiyya faction. ʻAbdān's nephew, however, continued to write books in his name and thus to perpetuate his intellectual heritage.[28]

Before his death, ʻAbdān had introduced an entirely new element into the nascent Ismāʻili movement in Iraq and Iran, veering it in a philosophical direction. He embarked on a prolific career of writing books and pamphlets, in which he was assisted by his nephew, Abu'l-Qāsim ʻIsā b. Musā. His only extant book, *Kitāb al-Rusum waʻl-izdiwāj waʻl-tartib* (Book of norms, pairing, and order) offers a concise Ismāʻili theology, replete with citations from the Qur'an. It is cast in a Pythagorean philosophical framework that highlights the essential duality or "pairedness" (*izdiwāj*) of all created being. Although the admission of the existence of God is innate, as what cannot be seen can only be proved through its products, "the knowledge of God can be obtained through the [inspired] teaching [*taʻlim*] of the Prophets and Messengers." This

---

26. Canard 1952, 293; de Blois 1986, 17.
27. Brett 2001, 77.
28. Canard 1952, 284; Halm 1996, 62–63, 193–95.

"salvific knowledge" (al-*ma'rifa al-nājiya*) through inspired instruction constitutes the divine guidance of humankind.

Within his dualistic Pythagorean framework and citing Qur'an 23:17 ("We created you seven pathways; We were not neglectful of creation"), 'Abdān formulated a novel and distinctively Ismā'ili sacred history consisting of the guidance of humankind through a cycle of seven speaker-prophets—Adam, Noah, Abraham, Moses, Jesus, Muhammad, and the coming Qa'im. Each speaker-prophet had a foundation (*asās*), who is his legatee (*wasiy*), and seven imams who assure the continuation of divine guidance by the protection of their speaker-prophet's law (*shari'a*), and "each Imam among them had a Proof [*hujja*] for the people of his time." Muhammad has 'Ali as his foundation, followed by a cycle of seven imams from the latter's offspring. The cycle of Muhammadan Imams will be closed by the same expected Qa'im. Of these seven imams, six were concealed, upholding the law as laid down by Muhammad, permitting what he permitted and forbidding what he forbade. They called attention to the appearance of the Qa'im with truth, the avenger of injustice, the slayer of the accursed Satan. Lastly, this treatise writes the Ismā'ili mission into the salvation history of the humankind.

The seven pathways to God mentioned in Qur'an (23:12–14, 17) are the Friends of God, the appellation the Ismā'ilis had chosen for themselves. The Prophet had twelve helpers to spread his mission and called them "repositories of my secret." All the ranks of the Ismā'ili mission on behalf of the Qa'im are inserted into the picture: The helpers are the aldermen (singular, *naqib*) and their sons are the missionaries (singular, *dā'i*), the sons of sons are the licentiates (singular, *ma'dhun*), and the lay members of their congregations, the believers (singular, *mu'min*). As for the highest rank of the Ismā'ili hierarchy, every legatee has twelve adjutants (singular, *lāhiq*), each of whom is a gate (*bāb*) that sends missionaries to provinces (singular, *jazira*). At the end of the treatise, 'Abdān expands on the significance of the sacred number seven, enumerating the seven pillars of Islam as the profession of faith (*shah'āda*), the prayer, almsgiving (*zakat*), fasting, the Hajj, Jihad, and "obedience to the Imam in each age and time."[29]

The famous Ismā'ili encyclopedia, *Rasā'il ikhwān al-safā' wa khillān al-wafā'* (Epistles of the brethren of purity and friends of fidelity), has been variously

---

29. Madelung and Walker 2011, 140, 144–47, 150, 159 (translation, 117, 126, 129–32).

dated to the mid-tenth century or later.[30] However, it has been shown convincingly that the oldest epistles should be dated to the period of "concealed imamate" (*satr*)—that is, after the death of Hasan al-'Askari in 874 and before the establishment of the Fatimid caliphate in 909—when "the proof of God on his earth is hidden and concealed." The Epistles accordingly speak of the "Mahdi [rightly guided] imams" (*a'immat al-mahdiyyun*) in the plural rather than a Mahdi/Qa'im in the singular. The period of "concealed imamate" (*satr*) must be that of the composition of Epistles, where, using the vocative, "Know O Brother," it speaks of "the exalted person, the composer [*munshi'*] of the Epistles." The author of this epistle could have been someone like the son of Ibn Hawshab who affirmed the forged genealogy of the first Fatimid caliphs during the concealed imamate by identifying their putative ancestor as 'Abdallāh b. Muhammad b. Ismā'il, stating that he went into concealment and his followers and missionaries lost contact with him.[31] This early dating of the Epistles, established by Hamdani and endorsed by Madelung, is indirectly supported by the philosophical bend of the Epistles of the brethren of purity and the veneration for the number seven, while distancing the encyclopedia from other Sevener Shi'a, the Waqifiyya, and the Imamiyya.[32]

It can therefore be argued that after the death of their eleventh Imam, Hasan al-'Askari, the Brethren working for the exalted composer of the Epistles sought to recruit among the Imamiyya, as Ibn Hawshab must have done. In refuting the Imami contention that their "expected Imam is in hiding from the fear of his opponents," the Epistles (4:199) contend that "on the contrary, he is present among them and they know him but refuse to recognize him." This is remarkably close to Ibn Hawshab's own account of his encounter,

---

30. Madelung 1978, 663. This late dating is on the basis of the implied date of 983/373 in a misleading letter from Abu Hayyān al-Tawhidi.

31. Hamdani 1979, 68–74. It is true that the son of Ibn Hawshab was writing much later and after he had joined the service of the Fatimid caliphs, but this merely proves that the Fatimid caliphs sought to appropriate the Epistles by attributing their composition to their ancestor.

32. Epistles, 4:199–200; Hamdani 1979, 74. During the annual convention of the Middle East Studies Association in Washington, DC in November 2017, Professor Hamdani confirmed to this author that his early dating was based on the evidence from Epistles 45–48 and one other epistle. He remains confident that these were written by the original editor. The revolutionary program I attribute below to the intellectuals' constitution, the Brethren of Purity, is taken from these Epistles.

during training, with a "very learned Shaykh" who knew his father to be a Twelver. "When I was administered the oath of allegiance," he records, "I was made to know that he was the Imam of the Age."[33]

Finally, the publicist intent of the Epistles makes ʿAbdān at the very least one of the Brethren of Purity and a contributor to their encyclopedia, if not its editor. In any event, the encyclopedia (Epistles) can be taken as the ideological spearhead of the clandestine movement of the circle of intellectuals recruited to the movement by ʿAbdān and Hamdān Qarmat. Therefore, reading the Epistles as the propaganda organ of the Ismāʿili revolutionary intellectuals in the heartland of the Abbasid caliphate makes good sense.

If we may be allowed to infer what the constituency the Brethren of Purity were seeking to mobilize for their apocalyptic revolution was, an important clue can be found in the ranking of the seven (!) social classes in the chapters on society/sociology, where the "artisans and craftsmen" are put in the first place, followed by "businessmen and traders" in the second place, and "construction engineers and worker" in the third place. "Kings, rulers, and statesmen" are placed after these urban strata, which can be taken as the core targeted constituency of the Brethren; they are followed by domestic servants and petty workers, and then the unemployed and the idle. Men of religion, most notably the jurists, whom the heretical Brethren had no hope of converting, are put at the bottom of the list and subjected to scathing criticism. On their side, the rich—wealthy merchants and rural landlords (singular, *dehghān*)—and high-ranking bureaucrats are severely criticized while the poor are highly praised. Needless to say, the Abbasid caliphs against whom the Brethren were mobilizing the three praised classes praised above were tyrants: usurpers of the rights of the House of ʿAli and murderers of the Friends of God. This inference about those who joined the Mahdist revolution would be consistent with the above-mentioned social background of the craftsmen and traders who led the earliest Ismāʿili missions—such as Hamdān, ʿAbdān, Ibn Hawshab, and Jannābi.

The Epistles contain a revolutionary program for government and a theory of revolution, both of which are couched in the latest available sciences. The state of the art in political science and statecraft—what Ibn Muskuya in the eleventh century would call the Persian and the Greek wisdom (*hikma*)—are

---

33. Iftitāh, 38.

thus drawn on for framing the Ismāʻili mission's divinely inspired program for government. In this frame, elaborated in the substantive epistles/chapters devoted to the "political sciences," the functions shared by prophecy and kingship in the Persianate wisdom are underlined, while philosophy is considered "the loftiest of all preoccupations after prophecy," and the influence of Greek political philosophy, monumentalized by Fārābi (d. 950), a possible contributor, is unmistakable. "Prophetic politics" and "kingly politics" are accordingly placed above the three other types of politics in the enumeration of the "political sciences."[34]

The program for government itself is outlined as follows:

> Our remaining goal, O Brother, after our consensus on its precondition of purity of the Brethren, is to cooperate and aggregate our bodily power and to put that amassed power into unified management of our souls, and to build a spiritual virtuous city rectified in the kingdom of the Lord of the Greater Law [i.e., God] who owns bodies and souls.[35]

As the first step to the erection of this virtuous city of God, the Brethren also sanctioned a transitional program for government. "Reason" (*ʻaql*), through empowerment by the lawgiver, "can establish the position of a Head and Leader [*al-raʼis waʼl-imām*], and in this, O Brother, we follow the Tradition of the Law [*sunna al-shariʻ*]." In this view, as the maintenance of order in the affairs of religion and the world requires a head (*raʼis*), "we consent to a Head for society of our Brethren, and the arbiter among us is Reason, which God Most High has appointed Head to those who excel among his creatures!"

The time for setting up this government of the Brethren of Purity, who alternately called themselves the People of Justice (*ahl al-ʻadl*), was at hand. God had said (Q. 3:134): "Such days We turn out in turn among peoples!" It was the millennial moment of the turn in power among nations, the transfer of the divinely ordained world domination from one people to another. "Thus is cast the verdict of our time for the turn in power/state [*dawla*] of the People of the Good [*ahl al-khayr*]":

> Know, O brother of mine, that the state of the People of the Good will begin first with a group of the learned, the wise and the best and most excellent concurring

---

34. Enayat 1977, 30–38, 45.
35. Epistles, 4:220.

on a single opinion and agreeing on a single rite and single religion and concluding a covenant ['ahd] and a contract [mithāq]![36]

The oldest techniques for the fabrication of predetermined futures are numerology and astrology. The Epistles recast the ancient art in the light of the latest findings of the science of astronomy, thus developing their political astrology in a way that amounted to an astrally determined cyclical theory of history. The revolution of the stars determines major changes in world history. In the chapter on "revolutions and cycles," we read that inauspicious conjunctions of stars result in "corruption of the time, departure of people from moderation, cessation of Revelation, dearth of the learned, tyranny of kings, corruption of people's morals ... and destruction of cities and provinces." Changes in the sovereignty of the dynastic houses (ahl bayt) and civil wars occur at the conjunctions of Saturn and Jupiter every twenty years, changes in world domination from one nation to another at the shifts from one triplicity to another every 240 years, and the greatest revolutions of all, changes in religion by the great prophet-lawgivers, occur every 960 (solar) years or every (lunar) millennium at the great conjunction of Saturn and Jupiter at the shift back to the initial triplicity of the signs of fire.[37] The Brethren of Purity reconciled this duodecimal system of the Zodiac with the heptads of Judeo-Christian sacred history. The Prophet is made to say: "The life of this world is seven thousand years; I have been sent in the last of these millennia."[38] Each millennium (= 960 solar years) is divided into two complete cycles, each consisting of four 120-year quarters of ascension, apogee, decline, and clandestinity. The term *Qa'im* is given a new meaning in this astrological theory of history. Each 120-year quarter cycle is inaugurated by a Qa'im, who is followed by six imams. The seventh imam who completes the heptad is the Qa'im of the next quarter-cycle. The Qa'im of the Resurrection would be expected at the end of the millennium of Muhammad, which is the final millennium.[39]

The cogent program for a revolution of the intellectuals thus assured by a predetermined future sadly foundered on the weakness of the urban strata in the heartland of the Abbasid caliphate, and it fell on the deaf ears of the

36. Epistles, 1:131, also 1:19–22, 4:181, 189.
37. Epistles, 3:256–59; Marquet 1972, 53–56.
38. Cited in Marquet 1972, 51.
39. Epistles, 1:98–99, 3:256–59, 4:259.

Bedouin in the surrounding desert. Debilitated though it was by internal dissension and the ascendancy of the slave palace guards, the caliphal state nevertheless managed to suppress the revolutionary movement of the Ismāʿilis and push it underground in the cities. Ideational embers whose sparks were to ignite the fire of millennial revolts, were, however, prepared underground.

In Salamiyya, in Syria, meanwhile, each missionary (*dāʿī*) under Abuʾl-Shalaghlagh was called the proof (*hujja*) of the hidden imam and was said to be in charge of an "island" (*jazira*), where he would establish a communistically organized "abode of migration" (*dār al-hijra*) on the model of the Prophet, and would raise contributions ostensibly on behalf of the expected Qaʾim-Mahdi. In the late 890s, shortly before his death, the proof in Salamiyya reportedly decided to split the mythical Mahdi-Qaʾim-Imam into its three component parts, claiming the imamate for himself and designating his nephew (he had no son) the Mahdi, and the latter's young son the Qaʾim. As we shall see, this assertion is anachronistic and the separation of the Qaʾim and the Mahdi only took place after the Fatimid Revolution. Nevertheless, the nephew, Saʿid b. al-Husayn, at some later point renamed himself Abu Muhammad ʿAbdallāh, assuming the title of al-Mahdi biʾllāh (rightly guided by God), and styled Abuʾl-Qāsim Muhammad, his infant son, al-Qāʾim bi-amr Allāh (riser by God's command). Thus, not only was the new Qaʾim called Muhammad b. ʿAbdallāh; he was also given the *kunya*, Abuʾl-Qāsim, to become the Prophet's exact clone. As we have seen, this or a similar move was firmly rejected by ʿAbdān as the leader of Ismāʿili intellectuals, but it was accepted for dubious reasons by the clandestine missionaries active among the Bedouin in Iraq.

The extent of Salamiyya's control over the latter, if any, is far from clear. Indeed, two "missionaries" active among the nomads nearby availed themselves of secondary apocalyptic titles that suggest premeditated independence. These were the two sons of the Persian missionary who murdered ʿAbdān—namely, Zakarōye b. Mehrōye. They established an ephemeral state based on their own apocalyptic claims among the nomads of Iraq and the Jazira in 902–3. The older son mobilized the clans of Banu al-ʿUllays and Banu al-Asbagh of the Kalb for his cause, naming himself Yahyā b. Zacharia (presumably John the Baptist), whom the Qurʾan mentions as one of the prophets and blesses "on the day he is born and the day he dies and the day he is raised alive" (Q. 19:15). He also claimed to be a descendant of Muhammad b. Ismāʿil and maintained that his crippled arm was a miraculous sign. He was named the Shaykh by his nomadic followers who called themselves the Fatimids (*al-fātimiyun, al-fawātim*) after the daughter of the Prophet, Fātima, from whom the 'Alid imams, including Muhammad b. Ismā'il, descended.[40] They are the first group on historical record to designate themselves as such. Yahyā was also known as the Man of the She-Camel (*sāhib al-nāqa*), as he claimed the camel mare he rode on the battlefield was divinely guided, evoking the She-Camel of God (*nāqat Allāh*) (Q. 11:64), whose killing by the nation of the prophet Sālih had brought about its destruction.

When the Shaykh fell in battle during an unsuccessful siege of Damascus in July 903, his brother, al-Husayn, saw to the disappearance of his body, and took over the leadership of the Fatimids. He claimed his birthmark was his sign, and he accordingly became known as the Man of the Birthmark (*sāhib al-shāma*), and his aide and cousin assumed the obscurely apocalyptic Qur'anic epithet of al-Muddathir ("the one who covers himself"). In the fall of 903, the Man of the Birthmark had the Friday sermon read in the name of "the Lord of the Age [*sāhib al-zamān*], the Commander of the Believers, the Mahdi." He evidently had a different Mahdi in mind than Abu'l-Shalaghlagh's nephew Sa'id, as he attacked the latter who fled Salamiyya just in time. The Fatimids destroyed Sa'id's house and killed all the members of his household left behind. The uprising of the Man of the Birthmark was suppressed by Abbasid forces, and he was killed in January 904.[41]

The father of the two, Zakarōye, went into hiding after the fall of his sons. Two years later, in 906, Zakarōye sent a missionary who led the Fatimid Bedouin in raids into southern Syria and Jordan but who was then killed by the band he was leading. Another of Zakarōye's missionaries was preaching about the time of the appearance (*zuhur*) of the hidden imam while attacking Kufa with the battle cry, "Vengeance for Husyan!" Finally, Zakarōye himself appeared after seven years of occultation in his village near Qadisiyya slightly to the south of Kufa. He was confronted by the forces of the Abbasid caliph's government, which lost 1,500 men in October and November of 906, but he finally fell in battle in January 907. Some of Zakarōye's followers, however, denied his death and expected his return.[42]

---

40. Fierro 1996, 138–39.
41. Tabari, 3:2218–20; Madelung 1978, 660; Halm, 1966a, 70–82.
42. Madelung 1978, 661; Halm 1996a, 183–90.

The other Persian impostor, Abu Saʻid b. Bahrām of Ganāva, known as al-Jannābi, in the meantime, had found his nomadic tribes on the Bahrain coast of the Persian Gulf, securely out of reach of the caliphal armed forces. He had been sent there by ʻAbdān, probably in 886 or 887, and converted many nomads. After his master ʻAbdān was murdered in 899, Jannābi in turn murdered his fellow Ismāʻili missionary Abu Zakariā, captured Hajar, and massacred its population, probably in 900, thus becoming the sole ruler of Bahrain until he was murdered by one of his slaves in 913. Al-Jannābi thus established the Qarmati state in Bahrain and ruled it in complete independence. He also probably claimed the imamate and Mahdihood for himself, as his son, Abu Tāher was certainly to do. At the very least, Abu Saʻid al-Jannābi claimed to be "the messenger of the Mahdi," and he was murdered, along with several of his missionaries, in the year 300 AH, the year he had predicted for the appearance of the Mahdi. The Qarmati state, according to tenth-century geographers, had a "treasury [khazina] of the Mahdi" where one fifth of the revenues was kept for the Lord of the Time (sāhib al-zamān). According to Nāser Khosraw, who visited the Qarmati state in Bahrain in the mid-eleventh century, Jannābi was still expected to return from the dead.[43]

Meanwhile, the second-generation Daylamite, Saʻid b. al-Husayn, a.k.a. Ahu Muhammad ʻAbdallāh, could not remain in Salamiyya after it was attacked by the Bedouin of the Man of the Birthmark, and so, taking along his son, who was to pose as the Qaʾim to back his own bogus claim to Mahdihood, he began his decade-long peregrination that took him through Egypt and Ifriqiyya to Sijilmasa in the remote southwestern corner of the Maghreb. On one of the legs of this long journey, he was robbed by the bandits who took his books on astrological oracles and esoteric writings. This anecdote notwithstanding, political astrology played an important role in the history of the Ismāʻili revolutionaries. The conjunction of Saturn and Jupiter in the year 296 AH (908–9 CE) must have stimulated the Ismāʻili missionary Abu ʻAbdallāh al-Shiʻi, who set up the Fatimid state for the Mahdi in North Africa in 909.[44] A year later, in 910, when Saʻid b. al-Husayn, the man whom Abu

---

43. De Blois 1986, 14–17; Madelung 1996, 40; Halm 1996a, 250.

44. The books on political astrology were later recovered in Egypt by his son; they presumably contained the prediction of the passing of world domination from the Arabs at the conjunction of Saturn and Jupiter in the year 296 (908–9). See de Goeje 1886, 121–22.

'Abdallāh had proclaimed the Mahdi, was setting out from Sijilmasa for Qairawan to claim his empire, he rejected his astrologer's horoscope, and instead took a meteor shower as one of the auspicious signs for his mission and reinterpreted the horoscope centered on Mercury himself, shouting, "Mercury is our turn in power [*dawla*]!" Whether or not the books of astrology were taken from him by the bandits in Egypt, this was fully in line with the political astrology of the Epistles, where the "appearance of turn in power among some peoples and nations" was said to result from the influence of Mercury.[45]

Nor was political astrology any less conspicuous farther afield in the Qarmati state in Bahrain. Biruni mentions a prediction, based on erroneous astronomical calculations, of the appearance of the Qā'im at the eighteenth conjunction after the birth of Muhammad, which is made to coincide with "the tenth millennium, which is presided over by Saturn and Sagittarius." At that time, according to the prediction, the era of Islam and the rule of the Arabs will come to an end. The Qa'im will rise and "will restore the rule of Magians." In Rayy, a city in central Iran, Abu Hātim al-Rāzi had been spreading the same astrological prediction about the coming of the Qa'im.[46]

We can read in Biruni that the Qarmatis in Bahrain "promised each other the arrival of the Expected One [*al-muntazar*] in the seventh conjunction of the Fiery Triplicity." This was far from an isolated incident, as the heresiographer al-Baghdadi, writing in Nishapur later in the century, reports extensive millennial activism in Khurasan. In 927, in anticipation of the conjunction in the following year (928), Abu Tāhir Suleymān al-Jannābi, Abu Sa'id's son who had just turned twenty, invaded Iraq. The Qarmatis in the Sawad of Iraq publicly advocated the cause of the Mahdi, and occupied Kufa under the leadership of 'Abdān's nephew, 'Isā b. Musā, who proclaimed the rise of the Mahdi and the end of the era of the *shari'a*. Although he was a leader of the clandestine movement of the urban intellectuals, 'Isā b. Musā had evidently thrown in his lot with the Bedouin fellow millenarians. Abu Tāhir himself reached the neighborhood of Baghdad in January 928 as the forerunner of the Mahdi, and he divided its palaces among his followers. He was pushed back by the Abbasid forces at the last minute, however.

---

45. Stern 1983, 105; Epistles, 3:256.
46. Biruni 1879, 196–97; Madelung 1988, 96.

The Qarmati nomads also attacked the *hajj* caravan under Abu Ṭāhir. On January 11, 930, they suddenly turned up in Mecca and massacred the pilgrims around the Kaʿba while one of Abu Ṭāhir's missionaries mockingly recited Qurʾan 106: 3–4: "Let them worship the Lord of this House who ... shielded them from fear!" To celebrate the coming of the millennium and the new religion, the Qarmatis carried off some relics allegedly connected to Abraham, Moses, and Mary. Most spectacularly, the Black Stone was removed from the corner of the Kaʿba and taken to the Bahrain![47]

The *dénouement* came in the following year, 931. A young man from Isfahan or Khurasan, who had been enslaved by the Qarmatis in their raids on Iraq in 928 and taken to Bahrain, was proclaimed their expected Qaʾim. They had presumably kept up their millennial expectation, which seemed on the verge of realization with the arrival of the Black Stone from Mecca to mark the end of the era of Islam.[48] Meanwhile, the young man from Isfahan, who claimed to be the descendant of the ancient Persian kings, soon found his way to the inner circle of the Qarmati elite and was told by one insider to approach Abu Ṭāhir al-Jannābi: "Go to Abu Ṭāhir and tell him that you are the man to whose allegiance his father and he himself had summoned the people. If he then asks you for signs and proofs, reveal these secrets to him."[49] Abu Ṭāhir, whose poetry proclaims that he would live until the coming of Jesus, son of Mary, recognized the signs and publicly surrendered sovereignty to the Qaʾim from Isfahan in 931. According to the eyewitness account of the physician Ibn Hamdān, Abu Ṭāhir declared:

> Know then, community of men, that the [true] religion has henceforth appeared. It is the religion of our father Adam, and all the belief we had was false. All the things missionaries made you hear, their talk about Moses, Jesus, and Muhammad, was falsehood and deceit. The [true] religion is in fact the religion of Adam, and those are all wily Dajjāls [Antichrists]; so curse them!"[50]

---

47. Halm 1996a, 254–57.
48. Halm 1996a, 64, 258–59. A few years earlier, in January 925, a man claiming to be Muhammad b. Ismāʿil had appeared and gathered a large band of Bedouin around him between Kufa and Baghdad. Later that year, the caliphal police discovered a group of Qarmatians, called the Baqliyya, whose members carried clay seals stamped with the inscription, "Muhammad b. Ismāʿil, the Mahdi-Imam, the Friend of God!" What appears like spontaneous Mahdistic agitation among the Baqliyya was suppressed, and some of the survivors drifted to Bahrain and became known there as the "thicket dwellers." See Madelung 1996.
49. Cited in de Goeje 1886, 132. See also Madelung 1996, 46, 50.
50. Madelung, 1996, 46–47 (translation slightly modified).

The Mahdi of Isfahan ruled for eighty days; this ended in disaster. The Ismāʿili millenarians from Iran had sought to put Islam in the perspective of the history of religions, identified Zoroaster with Abraham, and at least one of their theorists, Nasafi, had presented the religion of Adam as the natural religion, religion without the law. The Isfahani Qāʾim, who evidently took the astral sign to indicate the end of the era of world domination by the Arabs and the beginning of domination by the Persians, ordered the worship of fire, established links with the Zoroastrian clergy in Iran, and had the biblical prophets, as well as the imams, including ʿAli, cursed in public. All this must have proved too much for Abu Ṭāhir and his missionary, Abu Sanbar, who had owned the young Isfahani as a war captive. They changed their minds and had the latter seized and killed.[51] Abu Ṭāhir then claimed Mahdihood for himself. In a letter to the Abbasid caliph, he called himself al-Qāʾim bi-amr Allāh (riser by God's command), as the Fatimid crown prince was doing in North Africa, and further exclaimed, with reference to himself, "The Expected [*muntazar*] Imam has manifested himself to you like a raging lion!"[52]

The Ismāʿili Revolution failed to spread from Bahrain into the heartland of the caliphate. The Qarmati state, however, survived as a small independent state on the periphery of the Muslim world, but it played no role in the unfolding of the Fatimid Revolution.

It was otherwise with the Ismāʿili mission in Ifriqiyya. Constructing the pattern that inspired Ibn Khaldun's theory of revolution, the Kufan intellectual Abu ʿAbdallāh, who was sent by Ibn Hawshab from the Yemen via Mecca on a mission to North Africa around the year 892, established a *dār al-hijra* (abode of migration) and called its Berber tribesmen to God, as Muhammad had done in Arabia three centuries earlier. His abode was in a remote nomadic periphery in Ifriqiyya and out of reach of the Abbasid caliphal state. Abu ʿAbdallāh had introduced himself in Mecca as a Yemenite (*al-sanʿāni*) to a group of Kutāma pilgrims and went back to Ifriqiyya with them. There he broadened his identity into "the Easterner" (*al-mashriqi*), and those he converted to the Ismāʿili cause were called "the Easterners"! In converting the Shiʿite-leaning Kutāma Berbers into an Ismāʿili community of faith, Abu ʿAbdallāh called himself the Shiʿite (*al-shiʿi*) while setting up a militant theo-

---

51. Madelung 1988, 99.
52. Cited in de Blois 1986, 17.

cratic state in the North African desert by reconstituting the Kutāma tribal confederation:

> He divided up the Kutāma into seven parts, and raised an army out of each seventh, and assigned a commander for each one of these.... He called the commanders and the missionaries "The Elders" [*mashāyikh*] ... He left in the hands of the Elders both the believers' administration and the share of the booty God has given to the ruler of the Muslims.[53]

The insurgent missionary state mustered an infantry of seven hundred and a cavalry of two thousand for its army and collected the war booty it gained for its concealed imam, just as the Qarmatis were doing in the Bahrain, the opposite nomadic periphery of the debilitated Abbasid Empire. The tribal constitutional reforms of Abu ʿAbdallāh aimed at the construction of a new community of believers out of the stateless tribal polity of the Kutāma, and as such invite comparison with Muhammad's so-called Constitution of Medina. Abu ʿAbdallāh was a strict disciplinarian, and during nearly a decade of missionary work, he enforced the Qurʾanic penalties (*hudud*), although he did not go quite as far as Muhammad had done in transferring revenge bloodshed from the victim's clan to the community.[54] Instead, he ordered that *hudud* executions be carried out by the culprit's own clan to avoid blood feud. Despite his severity, he also failed to correct "abhorrent" tribal customs that were at variance with Qurʾanic commandments.

Abu ʿAbdallāh carried out this building of a nomadic confederate state alongside his main missionary work among the Kutāma, work that consisted in extolling the virtues of the family of the Prophet or the Five, which consisted of Muhammad, ʿAli, Fatima, Hasan and, Husayn.[55] From the beginning, when he settled in the Saktān clan's village of Ikjān, "he held sessions preaching ... the excellence of ʿAli b. Abi Tālib ... and those of the imams among his offspring, peace be upon them." All this must have earned him the nickname of *al-Shiʿi* (the Shiʿite). He had to move from Ikjān to Tawazur, where, we are told by Qadi al-Nuʿmān, he also held sessions on the esoteric teachings of the Ismāʿili sect called wisdom (*hikma*) for the initiates. On the evidence of the

---

53. Iftitāh, 127.
54. See chapter 2 above.
55. Alternatively, the Companions of the Cloak (*ashāb al-kisāʾ*), as the Fatimid caliph al-Mansur was to call them (cited in Walker 2014, 425).

books of instructions for clandestine missionary activism, we can tell that Ismā'ili esoteric doctrine had been learned individually in the heartland of the Abbasid Empire. Out of reach of the caliphal police in Kutāma, Abu 'Abdallāh introduced collective teaching of esoteric doctrine in his wisdom sessions. These sessions were attended by Kutāma women, young and old, who went to hear about "*belles lettres* and politics" even more eagerly than the men did.[56]

As his fame spread and the Kutāma men and women flocked to his preaching sessions, Abu 'Abdallāh al-Shi'i called his followers "brethren," and, when calling each one of them "O, our brother!" so they called themselves as such. He was thus cultivating them as the Brethren of Purity and the People of the Good, enjoining on them "good work [*'amal khayr*] as the means for getting close to God . . ., and so whoever joined the calling in their tribe became like stars in good deeds!" There was, by contrast, little or no discussion of the current clandestine 'Alid leadership, or imamate, of the movement: Abu 'Abdallāh's followers told each other that "he was calling them to a secret matter [*amr maktum*] which they did not know."[57] Even in 909, when he had overthrown the Aghlabids, Abu 'Abdallāh al-Shi'i had not yet made up his mind about the "agreed upon [*al-ridā*] from the Household of the Prophet" championed by the early ninth-century 'Alid/Shi'ite rebellions against the Abbasids. Indeed, as he divulged reluctantly to an inquisitive disciple during one of his teaching sessions in Qayrawan, he was upholding the imamate in occultation of Muhammad b. Ismā'il b. Ja'far, taking *Ismā'il* interpretively/allegorically to refer generically to the ancestor of all the Arabs (rather than specifically to the predeceased son of the sixth imam, Ja'far al-Sādiq), and he understood the long occultation to serve as a cover for any 'Alid (presumably the one to be "the agreed on").[58]

Like the leaders of the more numerous Imamiyya ("Twelvers") in the period of perplexity following the death of the eleventh imam, Abu'l-Shalaghlagh had adopted the notion of occultation (*ghayba*) from the Waqifiyya Seveners, and modified it into the doctrine of "Imamate of concealment [*satr*]" to justify his clandestine leadership of his small following as their imam. After Abu'l-Shalaghlagh's death, the Qa'im-Mahdi whose advent was to end the concealed

---

56. Iftitāh, 73, 133–34; Halm 1996b, 98–99.
57. Iftitāh, 76; Brett 2001, 88.
58. Madelung and Walker 2000, 55–56 (translation, 107).

imamate was split and projected onto his nephew and the latter's son for the uprising at the apocalyptic dawn—the outbreak of the coming revolution. Abu 'Abdallāh did not acknowledge this theory until late in 909, when he decided to accept Abu Shalaghlagh's nephew, whom he had never met before, as the Mahdi.

After nearly a decade of missionary work and confederative state building in the Kutāma hinterland, the citadel of Mila fell to Abu 'Abdallāh in 902, shortly after the departure for Jihad in Sicily of the Aghlabid amir, Ibrāhim II—the last effective Aghlabid ruler of Ifriqiyya on behalf of the Abbasid caliphate. Abu 'Abdallāh also recaptured Ikjān, his original *dār al-hijra*, where he now built a castle and began biding time for the crumbling of the Aghlabid state, which in fact began the following year. Amir Ibrāhim II died in Sicily in October 902, and his successor, 'Abdallāh II, was murdered by his own son, Ziyādat Allāh III, in July 903. Qadi al-Nu'mān reports that apocalyptic prophecies about the rise of the Mahdi circulated among the Shi'a in that year (290 AH), when the sun of God would rise in the west (*maghrib*) according to astrological calculations! At that time, there would be "revolution in the state" (*tanqalibu'l-dawla*) as "the awaited command of God" and "the state of the Qa'im-Mahdi [*dawlatu'l-qā'im al-mahdi*] draws near." Abu 'Abdallāh, the Shi'ite, and his Easterners began their final onslaught in 906, capturing Tubna and finally taking Raqqada and Qayrawan in the last week of March 909. Abu 'Abdallāh entered Raqqada on March 25, with the Kutāma tribesmen around him "like a plague of locusts," and he received defecting delegations from Qayrawan, which was granted a general amnesty in response. Ziyādat Allah fled Qayrawan, and the Aghlabid rule in Ifriqiyya came to an end.[59]

Abu 'Abdallāh's older brother, Abu'l-'Abbās, joined him in Qayrawan as a partner in government and was left in charge as coregent of the republic of the People of the Good when Abu 'Abdallāh decided to leave for the southwestern Maghreb in June 909 to rescue the man he had finally chosen to recognize and present as the Mahdi. Abu'l-'Abbās, whom we traced to Cairo around 890, had probably joined the fugitive Abu Muhammad Sa'id there, and had accompanied him to North Africa as far as Tripoli.[60] From Tripoli, Abu'l-'Abbās, in the company of a group of Kutāma converts, went to

---

59. Iftitāh, 85–89, 214; Brett 2001, 92.
60. Madelung and Walker 2000, 156–66.

Qayrawan, where he was imprisoned by the Aghlabids on account of his clandestine mission and remained in their prison until he was released in March 906 by his brother's forces. Abu'l-'Abbās was, by all account, an intellectual and a man of great learning, and he took over the teaching sessions in Qayrawan, as that capital city provided an ideal urban setting for these doctrinal and philosophical sessions and debates.

Once in possession of Raqqada and Qayrawan, the missionary brothers began to implement the Brethren of Purity's revolutionary blueprint for the state of the People of the Good. Abu 'Abdallāh's first proclamation in Qayrawan on March 31, 909, which was also sent out to be read from every pulpit in Ifriqiyya, can indeed be taken as the constitution of this revolutionary state:

> Bismillah ... Verily God, praise be upon him, has ennobled the status of justice ... and set it up as a scale among his creatures.... And he has made incumbent the profession of the way of truth and the abolition of the traditions of oppression and tyranny upon whomever God has enabled [to carry it out] in his lands and among his servants ... The best of the people is he whom God makes understand, as he has made me understand from the knowledge of his book, that he is responsible for his subjects ['mas'ul 'an ra'iyyatihi][61] and committed to justice and kindness among them. "God enjoins justice and kindness, and charity to the kin" [Q. 16:90], and forbids indecent behavior, reprehensible conduct, and oppression ... "[62]

The proclamation then cites the famous saying of the Prophet that "the book of God and my offspring, the People of the Household, are the two weightiest in my heritage," and enjoins adherence to the tradition of the Messenger of God and the "exemplar of the People of his Household [sira ahli baytihi]" as the firm rope of salvation, only to add that the Messenger of God's good news on the coming of the "People of Justice and Truth at the End of Time" was the basis of his determination in the erection of justice for the subjects.[63] The proclamation ends thus:

> I hope from God to make me reach the profession of justice and revival of the right. And so I have ordered ... befriending of the subjects and kindness to them, mak-

---

61. The phrase refers to a famous maxim of statecraft and political ethic expressed as a hadith of the Prophet.
62. Iftitāh, 233.
63. Iftitāh, 233–34.

ing them beneficiaries of justice and knowledge thereof, the cutting off the hand of oppression and abolition of tyranny upon them, and the enforcement of this writ upon all state officials in all districts of Ifriqiyya.[64]

This constitutional document of the short-lived state of the People of Justice/the Good is issued on the authority of Abu 'Abdallāh al-Shi'i himself, and its emphasis is on justice as the cornerstone of legitimate rule, with only a politically inconsequential reference to the family of the Messenger of God. Consonantly with this proclamation, Abu 'Abdallāh's first coin did not have on it "the name of anyone, but in place of the names he put, on the one side 'The Proof of God [*hujjat Allāh*] has arrived', and on the other, 'And the enemies of God have dispersed!'"[65] A few months later, however, for reasons we shall never know, he decided to deliver the state to Abu Shalaghlagh's nephew as the Mahdi, and left Qayrawan to Sijilmasa to meet him for the first time and to rescue him. Abu 'Abdallāh then wrote to the Brethren in Ifriqiyya that God had kept his promise and "made a proof among His proofs appear on his earth, and [he] rescued the son of the Messenger of God!"[66]

At this point, the Daylamite mountebank on the edge of the western Sahara, Abu Muhammad Sa'id b. al-Husayn, when he revealed himself and converted his concealed imamate into a public one, proclaimed himself "guided by God" (*mahdi bi'llāh*).[67] The Fatimid Mahdi, as we will henceforth call him, emerged as such from the concealed imamate inherited from his uncle, Abu Shalaghlagh, and, drawing his lesson from the Zakarōye brothers who had mobilized the Bedouin and sacked his headquarters in Salamiyya seven years earlier, he immediately made for the Kutāma nomads as his natural allies against the urban Epistles intellectuals led by Abu'l-'Abbās and Abu 'Abdallāh al-Shi'i. He thus began the process of appropriating the revolution of the intellectuals and their state of the People of the Good.

In January 910, having first visited the mission's *dār al-hijra* in Ikjān of the Kutāma to take the dues collected on his behalf as the Mahdi over the years, he entered Raqqada ceremoniously, surrounded by Abu 'Abdallāh as the head of the shaykhs and the Friends of God, with his sixteen-year-old son behind him.

---

64. Iftitāh, 235.
65. The Shi'ite term for the holy imams, including the one in occultation.
66. Iftitāh, 217, 242.
67. Alias 'Ali, among others!

On the next day, Friday, January 5, 910, he issued a decree ordering the preachers of Raqqada and Qayrawan to a prayer for him: "O God, bless your servant and thy Deputy [*khalifa*], the Redresser [*qā'im*] of the cause of thy servants in your lands, 'Abdallāh Abi Muhammad, the *Imam al-Mahdi billāh* [rightly guided by God], the Commander of the Believers, as thou bless his fathers, thy righteous and rightly guided caliphs [*kulafā'ika al-rāshidin al-mahdiyyin*]."[68]

It is important to note that the title initially assumed by the Fatimid Mahdi is in fact God's deputy, readily understandable to the Sunni majority of his new subjects, while the Qa'im expected by the partisans converted by Abu 'Abdallāh the Shi'ite is equated with the imams described as "rightly guided"— that is, as the Imam-Mahdis! This ambiguous locution displays and unpacks the Imam-Qa'im-Mahdi complex in a novel fashion, reflecting the division attributed to the Fatimid Mahdi's uncle and determines the succession of the Fatimid caliphs in reverse order.

The Fatimid Mahdi then took a leaf from the Epistles of the Brethren of Purity intellectuals in this, his first proclamations in Qayrawan, which was copied and read from pulpits throughout Ifriqiyya, celebrating the revolution of the disinherited of the earth with God's words: "We willed to be gracious to those that were abased in the land and made them leaders [*a'imma*], and to make them the inheritors, and to establish them in the land" (Q. 28:5–6). And further: "We wrote in the Psalms after the Torah was revealed: 'The righteous among my servants shall inherit the earth'" (Q. 21:105).[69]

The main point of the proclamation was, however, to reaffirm the legitimacy to rule of the lineage of Muhammad, the rope of salvation linking humankind to God:

> There is indeed no matter linking God and His servants except the love of the Family of Muhammad the Messenger of God, God's blessing and peace be upon him. As said God, may his mention be glorified: "Say, for this I ask for no recompense, except the love of kin" [Q. 42:23];[70] and as said the Messenger of God, God's blessing and peace be upon him: "The case of my family among you is like the case of Noah's ark."[71]

---

68. Iftitāh, 249; Halm 1996a, 147; Brett 2017, 35.

69. Iftitāh, 250–51.

70. As we have seen in chapters 4 and 5 above, this verse had been inscribed on the coins of the Hashemite state of Ibn Mu'āwiya as well as those of Abu Muslim and the early Abbasids.

71. Iftitāh, 253–53.

To back his legitimacy as a descendant of Muhammad and ʿAli, the Fatimid Mahdi turned to the Kutāma tribesmen for a strong power base, and he distributed the provinces among the seven Kutāma divisions as armies and set up Kutāma garrisons in major cities. He also revived the Aghlabid state and fiscal administration, manning it with pardoned defectors, and took over its armed forces, including a contingent of military slaves, among them blacks, Slavs, and Byzantines.[72] With this power base created in the months after the revolution, he was ready to engage in a power struggle against his revolutionary partners by striking against the urban intellectuals under Abu ʿAbdallāh.

The clash of principles in the two recorded inaugural proclamations of the chief missionary for the People of the Good and the claimant to Mahdihood suggests the inevitability of the power struggle between them as partners in the revolution. A clear signal for the onset of the revolutionary power struggle was the resentment of Abuʾl-ʿAbbās and his followers at the appropriation of the booty stored in Ikjān by the Fatimid Mahdi. But it is entirely possible that the inevitable power struggle was triggered by the discovery of the Fatimid Mahdi's bogus genealogical claim. In an account of the alleged confrontation between representatives of the two factions he is referred to by his real first name as Saʿid. However that may be, the Fatimid Mahdi did indeed strike once, with the Kutāma support behind him, he felt strong enough. In the second year of the revolution, on February 18, 911, he invited Abu ʿAbdallāh and Abuʾl-ʿAbbās to mid-day dinner and had them murdered by his guards.[73] After the liquidation of the urban Brethren of Purity, and feeling secure with his alternative tribal support base, the Fatimid Mahdi denied their millennial theory of the imminent return from occultation of Muhammad b. Ismāʿil as the eponymous imam of the revolutionary movement, and changed his genealogy, now claiming descent not from Ismāʿil b. Jaʿfar but from his older brother, ʿAbdallāh. This genealogical claim was stated years later in a letter to the Yemenites, and presumably also to Sevener Shiʿa in the East to win them over, since they considered ʿAbdallāh b. Jaʿfar their last imam.[74]

As required by his grand design, which was wrongly attributed to his uncle Abu Shalaghlagh, the Fatimid Mahdi was soon to relinquish the title of

---

72. Halm 1996a, 149, 152.
73. Halm 1996a, 159–68; Brett 2017, 37.
74. Hamdani and de Blois, 1983.

al-Qā'im to his son, already cloned as the Prophet, Abu'l-Qāsem Muhammad, calling himself "the Mahdi [rightly guided] by God." The Fatimid Mahdi further forced his son to live up to his role as the Qā'im by trying to conquer Egypt, but the latter failed.

THE ROUTINIZATION OF REVOLUTIONARY CHARISMA AND ITS RESACRALIZATION INTO AUTOCRACY IN THE FATIMID EMPIRE

The intense charisma of the apocalyptic Qa'im-Mahdi was, like all forms of charisma, subject to what Max Weber called routinization; and as Weber pointed out further, the routinization of political charisma in traditional societies takes the form of the legitimation of patrimonial, dynastic kingship.[75] Just as with the early Abbasids, the early Fatimid caliphs appropriated the mythical protagonists of the Islamic apocalypse for their regnal titles, thus presenting the reign of their dynasty as what we have called realized messianism. Caliph al-Mahdi bi'llāh (910–34) was succeeded by al-Qā'im bi-Amr Allāh (934–46), with whom the Fatimid rule all but collapsed, and the latter was himself succeeded by al-Mansur bi'llāh (946–53). Caliph al-Mansur's successor, Caliph al-Mu'izz bi'llāh (953–75) could dispense with an apocalyptic regnal title but he replaced them with his claim to be the omniscient imam as he inaugurated the new postapocalyptic phase of exporting revolution and imperial expansion.

The first step in the transformation of charismatic revolutionary leadership after the success of revolution was already taken by the Fatimid Mahdi himself after becoming the ruler of the Aghlabid realm and reviving its government and fiscal bureaucracy. This consisted in the patrimonialist routinization of the charisma of the apocalyptic Imam-Mahdi-Qā'im of the revolutionary struggle in the path of God for the benefit of the Fatimid dynasty established by him. It was transformed into the charisma of lineage of the son of the Messenger of God through "our father, 'Ali" and "Fatima, the radiant" (*al-zahrā'*). This went hand in hand with the demotion of apocalyptic Mahdihood and its replacement by the imamate. In his first proclamation, using an expression equally intelligible to his new Sunni subjects, who were referred to as the

---

75. Weber 1978, 2:1141–43.

Muslims, and to his Shi'a, who were referred to as the believers (mu'minin), the Fatimid Mahdi highlighted his charisma of lineage as the legitimate successors to the Messenger of God as God's righteous (rashidun, for the Sunnis) and rightly guided (mahdiyyin, for the Ismā'ilis). In the letter he wrote to the Ismā'ili followers of Ibn Hawshab in the Yemen, in which he used 'Ali instead of Sa'id as his given name and, as we have pointed out, claimed descent from the sixth 'Alid imam, Ja'far al-Sādiq, through a son other than Ismā'il, he quoted his father, who, significantly, is called "son of the Messenger of God." He further predicted the appearance of many Mahdis or divinely guided leaders until the coming of the Hour. Apocalyptic and specifically Shi'ite Mahdihood is thus played down in favor of descent from the Messenger of God as a principle of legitimacy acceptable to his Sunni subjects as well as his Ismā'ili revolutionary adepts who constituted the ideological elite of his new patrimonial kingdom, alongside the Kutāma political elite of the Fatimid dynastic state.[76]

The Fatimid Mahdi's son became Caliph al-Qāim bi-amr Allāh in 934. He was, however, totally unbefitting the apocalyptic title he bore, and hid himself from public view for some ten years within the Mahdiyya, the palace fortress built by his father. In 944, ten years into his reign, the revolt of the Kharijite Abu Yazid broke out and spread quickly through his realm. Caliph al-Qā'im did not reemerge from his palace complex in the Mahdiyya and died there under mysterious circumstances, but his son, the crown prince Ismā'il did, and he eventually managed to suppress the revolt that all but destroyed the Fatimid dynasty a third of a century after its beginning.

Ismā'il restored Fatimid rule after its near collapse and ascended the throne, assuming the apocalyptic title of Caliph al-Mansur bi'llāh (victorious/ aided by God) on account of his victory over Abu Yazid, who was subsequently called the Dajjāl (Antichrist) in the *ex eventu* apocalyptic reconstruction of Fatimid historical memory that thereby sought to framed the near disaster as a God-ordained victory of the Fatimids and to integrate it into the salvation history of mankind. Caliph al-Mansur died four years after this victory at the age of forty, leaving his son, who assumed the title of al-Mu'izz bi'llāh, to reap the benefit of his victory. Mansur had, however, overseen the reconstruction of the Kharijite rebellion of Abu Yazid as a minor apocalypse in the official

76. Hamdani and de Blois 1983, 177; Brett 1994, 31–35.

historical memory, and harnessed it to imperial expansion. Under his son, Caliph al-Muʿizz, the Fatimids conquered Egypt in 969, and their empire, which extended from Ifriqiyya to Egypt and Syria, lasted two more centuries until it was overthrown by Saladin (Salāh al-Din al-Ayyubi) in 1171.

In preparation for the imperially realized Mahdism of Caliph al-Muʿizz bi'llāh, the two main ideologues of the caliphate, Qadi al-Nuʿmān (d. 974) and Jaʿfar b. Mansur al-Yaman (d. 990), forged the collective memory of the rise of the Fatimids as the final chapter in the history of salvation, and elaborated the doctrine of the Fatimid caliphate as the infallible imamate of the descendants of ʿAli and Fātima. This official theory of realized messianism was implicit in the regnal titles of their imperial master's predecessors, the Mahdi, the Qa'im, and the Mansur. Jaʿfar b. Mansur al-Yaman had Jaʿfar al-Sadiq prophesy the realization of God's design for humankind through the descendants of his grandson, Muhammad b. Ismāʿil, whose missionaries followed Muhammad's in establishing a *dār al-hijra* in the land of their enemies in the West (*maghrib*) and brought about his prophecy that the sun would rise in the West, signaling the renewal of Muhammad's Islam as Muhammad had renewed the pure Islam of Abraham.[77] This, incidentally, restored the long-liquidated Abu ʿAbdallāh al-Shiʿi's eponymous genealogy over that of the Fatimid Mahdi. Be that as it may, this reconstruction of the historical memory made the most bitter episode in Fatimid history into its final stage of the realization of the apocalypse, and it now ended with the addition of al-Mansur, the victorious killer of the Dajjāl, to the Qa'im-Mahdi pair to complete the apocalyptic trinity according to the script starring the Mahdi, the Qa'im, and the Mansur, as the Abbasids had done.[78] Routine history could now resume its course in the Fatimid Empire.

As we shall see in the following section, Qadi al-Nuʿman took on the weightier challenge of reworking the doctrine of the imamate into the caliphate of God as sacred authority (*wilāya*) in this world, appropriately incorporating it into his monumental book of Ismāʿili law, *Daʿāʾim al-islām* (The pillars of Islam) in its first chapter on *wilāya* (authority).

The Fatimid Mahdi had also taken the first step toward the Sunnitization of the imamate as the caliphate of God by his pledge to maintain the Sunna of the Prophet, with no mention of the inner meaning of religion or the final

77. Jaʿfar 1952, 254–63.
78. See chapter 6, above.

cycle of sacred history ushered in by the clandestine Imam-Mahdi-Qa'im as the Qa'im of Resurrection. His son, Caliph al-Qā'im, asserted in a Friday sermon that he had no right to reduce those of his flock (ra'iyya—i.e., subjects), just as the flock could not diminish the rights of the imam. "Among the rights of the flock against the Imam," he continued, "is the maintaining of the Book of God and the Sunna of His Prophet, may God bless him and his family."[79] Al-Qā'im's son, Caliph al-Mansur, felt the need for an official statement on the doctrine of the imamate after his victory, and wrote a treatise on confirming the imamate (Tathbit al-imāma). In it he amplified the imamate as the charisma of the Fatimid dynasty by proving the legitimacy of their succession to the Messenger of God against the Sunni arguments in favor of the succession of the first two caliphs, Abu Bakr and 'Umar, using the earlier apologetics of the Imami Shi'a and thus bringing the Fatimid doctrine of the imamate into line with the mainstream, Imami Shi'ite position in rational theology (kalām) that derived it as a so-called "principle [asl] of religion" from reason. Significantly, there is no mention of the imam as a divinely inspired esoteric teacher, and all his knowledge, as well as his authority, is derived from the Prophet Muhammad.[80]

The subsequent postrevolutionary institutional implications of the routinization of Mahdist apocalyptic charisma into the Fatimid imamate-caliphate of the imperial era were far-reaching. Under Caliph al-Mahdi, millennial revolutionary activism became differentiated into the dynastic state/turn in power (dawla) and the mission (da'wa). The alignment of the imamate with the general Shi'ite theological position and apologetic 'Alid legitimism by al-Mansur bi'llāh made possible the differentiation of the missionary and the judiciary authority and the Sunnitization of the former and the bureaucratization of the latter. Caliph al-Mansur wrote an Ismā'ili legal compendium for "the believers"—that is, the Ismā'ili Shi'a—as the infallible imam, and, much more consequentially, appointed the first Sunni judge of the capital, Qayrawan, where the Maliki community leaders had supported the rebellion of the Kharijite Dajjāl. The mission (da'wa) had been directed by the bāb al-abwāb, the gate of gates (to the originally concealed charismatic imam). Al-Nu'mān b. Muhammad was already the head missionary (dā'i) and was holding his

79. Cited in Walker 2014, 426–27.
80. Madelung 2003, 77.

sessions of wisdom devoted to esoteric interpretation by 953 when Caliph al-Muʿizz, the son of the victorious Mansur and the consolidator of his restoration, authorized him to hold public sessions on the exoteric science of Ismāʿili jurisprudence on Fridays. In 954, he was appointed judge of highest court of the Fatimid realm, the *mazālim* or ruler's court of grievances. With indefatigable energy, Qadi al-Nuʿmān developed the Fatimid institution of *majālis al-hikma* at several levels beyond those for the initiates. Almost two decades later, the elderly Qadi al-Nuʿmān accompanied Caliph al-Muʿizz in moving from Ifriqiyya to Egypt as the army judge in 973 and remained in that position until his death in the following year. After his death, the supervision of the judiciary as well as the mission in Egypt passed on to his two sons. His grandson, al-Husayn b. ʿAli b. al-Nuʿmān (d. 999), however, inherited only the judiciary and was the first Fatimid official to be invested with the title and rank of the *qāḍi al-quḍāt* (chief justice). By that time, a different official headed the mission with the parallel title of *dāʿi al-duʿāt* (chief missionary) and was in charge of the export of the Ismāʿili Revolution to the fragmenting Abbasid Empire to the east.[81]

There is no way to document the relation between Caliph al-Muʿizz's modification of the Fatimid legitimist patrimonial ideology and his imperial project. All we can know is that the one preceded the other. Al-Muʿizz biʾllāh rejected the Fatimid Mahdi's account of the imamate based on his manipulations of ad hoc justifications of its clandestine leadership of the Ismāʿili movement before the revolution. Nor was he happy with his father's compromise with Sunnism and Imami Shiʿism in *Tathbit al-imāma*. We may say, then, that instead of these modest efforts to Sunnitize the Shiʿite idea, he wanted to Shiʿitize the Sunni idea of God's caliphate as earthly rule. He bid Qadi al-Nuʿmān to do so by bringing Sunni caliphate into line with the Shiʿite doctrine of the divinely inspired imamate as the instrument for the salvation of humankind. The Qadi carried out his infallible imam's order. In the *kitāb al-wilāya* (Book on authority), which opens *Daʿāʾim al-islām* (The pillars of Islam), Qadi al-Nuʿmān refuted any notion of dependence of the imam on the people to prove his divine appointment. Any intimation of the choice of the head of the state of "the People of the Good," intimated in the *Epistles of the Brethren of Purity*, is firmly rejected:

81. Halm 1996b, 101–4; Walker 2006, 77–81.

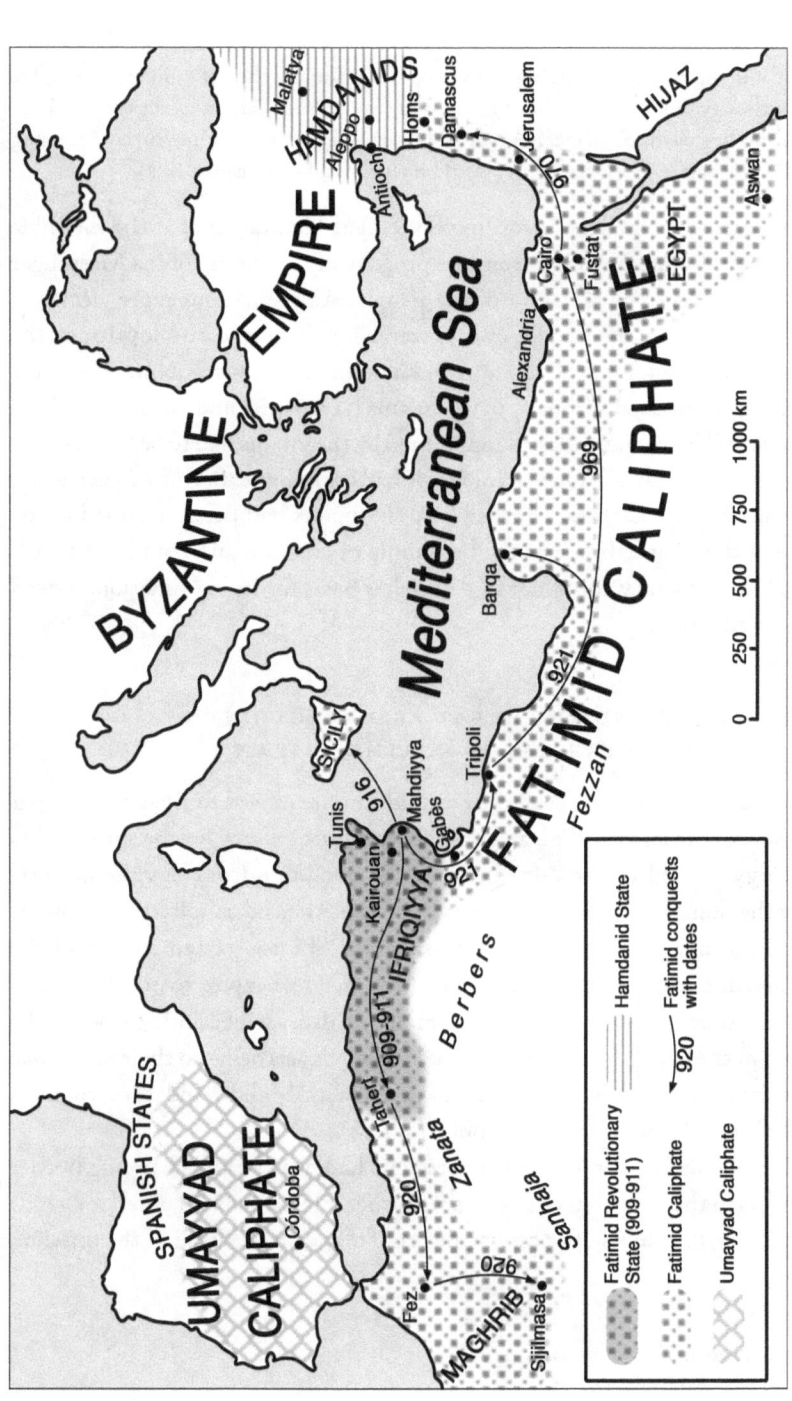

MAP 3. The Fatimid Empire (909–70).

If it is the people themselves who appoint the Imam, then the Imam derives his authority from their authority .... The people, then, are in effect the "Imams" according to the plain meaning of this [assertion], while he [the imam] is one among their officials. They, therefore, would have the right to dismiss him![82]

The truth of the matter, according to Qadi al-Nuʿmān, is that the infallible imam is appointed by God from the progeny of the House of his Messenger for the guidance or salvation of the people. As spelled out more clearly in another treatise, the people owe unwavering allegiance and loyalty to the imams whose infallibility they must acknowledge and must submit all matters to them. The sacred authority of the imams is transitive and extends to all the officials of their state. All those appointed by the imams had to be held in high esteem and loved! The Qadi accordingly had his imam-caliph al-Muʿiz declare that his name and those of other Fatimid imams had been inscribed at the base of the divine throne at the beginning of creation and read by Adam.[83] Imperial autocracy could not find a higher basis for its legitimation, indeed its sacralization.

APOCALYPSE AND THE GREAT RESURRECTION IN MOUNTAIN FORTRESSES OF NORTHERN IRAN

A century after the center of the Fatimid Empire moved to Egypt, making it the seat of the imam-caliph and an elaborate bureaucracy for the spread of its ideology beyond North Africa. Export of revolution from Egypt and Syria into the domains under the suzerainty of the Abbasid caliphate want on for a full century. Then a branch of the Ismāʿili Shiʿism gained control of the clandestine organization operation in the Seljuq Empire to the East. The Nizāri Ismāʿilis who upheld the imamate of a deceased Fatimid prince broke off from the Fatimid mission in Cairo. Some Nizāris believed their imam was in occultation and would return as the Qaʾim-Mahdi, and they found a redoubtable leader in Hasan Sabbāh (d. 1124).

Unlike his Daylamite compatriots, who had been stranded among Berber nomads in the Maghreb two centuries earlier, Hasan Sabbāh opted for a hidden imam with himself as his visible proof (*hujja*) at the head of the mission.

---

82. Cited in Walker 2014, 421.
83. Al-Azmeh 1997, 193.

Drawing on the notion of the inspired teaching (*ta'lim*) of 'Abdān in pristine intellectualist Ismā'ilism, Hasan as the proof of the hidden imam claimed supreme authority in teaching the adepts gathered in inaccessible fortresses, since the cities were under the effective rule of the Seljuqs. Hasan seized the fortress of Alamut in 1090 and proceeded to create an Ismā'ili state consisting of fortresses in the mountains of northern and northeastern Iran while propounding "the new mission" (*da'wat-e jadid*) in contradistinction to the old Fatimid mission. The Nizāris, who called each other "comrade" (*rafiq*), used a number of impregnable fortresses in the mountains of Iran and Syria for training the zealous devotees (*fidā'i*) and for developing the technique of political assassination in the revolutionary struggle against the Seljuq Empire.[84]

The fortified periphery of the Muslim world he chose as the theater of operation was located and peopled very differently from the North African Berber hinterland. Crucial to his mission was the fact that he proselytized among settled Persians recruited in the cities of northern and central Iran. Hasan Sabbāh accordingly took the unprecedented step of replacing Arabic with Persian as the language of the Ismā'ili mission. Like Abu 'Abdallāh al-Shi'i, he was a strict enforcer of *shari'a* in his state. He considered this appropriate for his age as its Qa'im had not yet appeared and would only do so at the end of the seventh cycle of ages. Hasan designated Kiā Bozorg-Omid his lieutenant in the fortress of Lammsar, and made him his successor before his death in Alamut in June 1124.[85]

Forty years after his death, on August 8, 1164, the ruler of the Nizāri Ismā'ili fortresses, Bozorg-Omid's grandson, Hasan II b. Mohammad b. Bozorg-Omid, proclaimed the Resurrection as the deputy (*khalifa*) and proof of the imam, the Qa'im of the Resurrection (*qiyāma*). He was evidently impatient with the calculations of the Brethren of Purity and, refusing to wait until their appointed time, which was the end of the Islamic millennium, he used a different horoscope.[86] The Resurrection meant that the era (*dawr*) of the law and external reality had come to an end and the era of inner reality had begun.

---

84. Hodgson 1955b; Lewis 1985, 48–49.
85. Ivanow 1933, 21–22; Daftary 2003.
86. Lewis1985, 72; Jambet 1990, 35–43. Hasan II later hinted that he himself was the imam and the Qa'im of the Resurrection.

All believers could know God and the cosmic mysteries through the imam, and God would constantly be in their hearts.

Hasan II was fatally stabbed in January 1166, but his son Mohammad II confirmed the continuation of the Resurrection which lasted for a total of forty-six years to 1210. The mission was now "the call to [or, preaching of] Resurrection [da'wat-e qiyāmat], and the Nizāris considered themselves "the saved community of the Qa'imites [qā'imiyun]."[87] As time went on, the doctrine of the Resurrection as developed by Mohammad II, who claimed the imamate for himself and his father as putative descendants of Nizār, made the imam the manifestation of the word and command of God through whose vision the believers could find themselves in paradise. He added the Sufi level of truth (haqiqa) to the Ismāʿili levels of external and inner reality and identified it with the Resurrection. This paved the way for the transformation of the Nazāri Ismāʿili state into a Sufi order after the conquest of its mountain fortresses by the Mongol Hülegü in 1256.

Hasan II, "upon whose mention be peace," was now considered the Qa'im as well as the imam, but the meaning of the term changed radically because of the declaration of the Resurrection. A treatise written some forty years into the Resurrection, *Haft Bāb-e Sayyiduna* (The seven gates of our Lord), reaffirmed the old Ismāʿili idea that "the Prophet designated our Lord, 'Ali b. Abi Tālib as the Qa'im of the Resurrection," but also asserted that "all the Imams are 'Ali (bless him) himself, and will be." It is true that the Qa'im of the Resurrection, "in this period of ours, . . . in the clime of the sun, . . . in the land of Babylon among the lands of the 'Ajam [non-Arabs], . . . in the midst of the Jabal, that is, the mountains of Daylamān at the castle of Alamut, he was Our Lord [Hasan II]." But the Qa'im is no longer restricted to that particular incarnation. He is the eternal imam and the primordial Adam who completes the cycle of revelation (kashf). With the Resurrection, the Qa'im as the new Adam is and will ever be in the heart of the people of truth, imparting to them the authoritative teaching (taʿlim) that transcends the duality of external and internal reality and makes possible the full pantheistic plenitude of existence.[88]

In the same treatise, we find fascinating evidence of the persistence of apocalyptic notions. The figure of Melkizedek, which, as we have seen, had

---

87. Juvayni, 3:240; Ivanow 1933, 5, 7, 41; Daftary 1990, 388–95.
88. Ivanow 1933, 14, 18, 41; Hodgson 1955b; Buckley 1984, 144, Jambet 1990.

been built into Mānī's notion of the Paraclete, resurfaces over a millennium later in *Haft Bāb* as Malik Yazdāq. He is the theophanic prototype, "the Greater Name of God," which manifested itself in Adam and Abraham and which will be present at the Resurrection. He last manifested himself in our Lord (*mawlānā*), and his authority derives from (is the *vali* of) the eternal imam.[89]

By completing the cycle of revelation, the Great Resurrection is the apocalyptic appropriation of the world through the universal integration of saving knowledge into the daily lives of the people of truth. With this ultimate kenosis of the apocalyptic into Sufi mystical pantheism, the realized apocalypticism of Ismāʿilism took the form, not of the patrimonial rule of the Fatimid dynasty or the sacral authority of the imam-caliphs of Cairo, but of the mystical life of a Sufi order in what purported to be posthistory. Thus, the teleology of Ismāʿili apocalypse was played out to the fullest extent in the mountainous periphery of the Persianate world, insulated from the tension with contrary trends afoot in the dynamics of Islamicate civilization.

---

89. Van Reeth 2012b, 43–45.

CHAPTER 8

The Almohad Revolution of Mahdi Ibn Tumart and the Berbers

We now come to the revolution that greatly impressed Ibn Khaldun and informed his theory of revolution. He included the analytical account of the revolution of Mahdi Ibn Tumart as "the rightly guided imam, leader of the Almohads' turn in power" (*al-imām al-mahdi sahib al-dawlat al-muwahhidin*) in the opening chapter of the *Prolegomena* (*muqaddima*) to his new science of history: To overthrow his enemies, the Lamtuna kings, also known as the Almoravids, Ibn Tumart

> called his people to their holy struggle [*jihād*] by himself and extirpated the state [*dawla*] from its bases, turning it upside down by making its highest [classes] the lowest.

So the overthrow of the Lamtuna was indeed a revolution! As for the people who followed Ibn Tumart's revolutionary leadership, Ibn Khaldun continues,

> They pledged their allegiance to him unto death, ... and got closer to God Most High by shedding their blood [i.e., the Lamtunas'] in giving effect to this mission and through partisanship [*ta'assub*] for this plea [*kalām*]: "Such was God's Sunna as fulfilled through His servants" (Q. 40:85).

The Lamtuna kings had come to power a century earlier through the Sanhāja tribes in the Maghreb in the eleventh/fifth century, but then "their tribal solidarity/partisanship [*'asabiyya*] eroded," and their hold on the peripheries of their empire weakened "until God allowed the extinction of their dynastic state and the Almohads under the leadership of Mahdi Ibn Tumart came to efface its vestiges with the force of the tribal solidarity/partisanship of the Masmuda."[1]

DRESS REHEARSAL FOR REVOLUTION: THE ALMORAVIDS' TURN IN POWER

The Berber forces that brought Ibn Tumart to power came from the Masmuda tribes of the western Sahara, and secondarily from their confederate Zanāta tribes. The Lamtuna kings they overthrew in 1147 had come to power a century earlier (in 1055) with the capture of Sijilmāsa, the capital of the Banu Khazrun of Zanāta, and they had cemented their domination with the decisive defeat of the Masmuda and the capture of their territories in 1058. The teaching of 'Abdallāh b. Yāsin (d. 1059), a religious reformer much like Ibn Tumart, was the basis of the unification of the Sanhāja tribes who had thus dispossessed the Zanāta and the Masmuda in the eleventh century and brought the Almoravids to power.

On his return journey from the Hajj, Yahyā b. Ibrāhim, a chief of one of the Juddāla branches of the Sanhāja nomads in the western Sahara, known for covering their faces with a thick veil or scarf (*lithām*), stopped in Fez to ask a renowned Muslim scholar to recommend a teacher who could bring the religion of his superficially Muslim people closer to orthodox Islam. He was given a recommendation and he took with him a Berber religious scholar from the deep southwestern Sahara near Ghana. The scholar, 'Abdallāh b. Yāsin, settled in a fortified monastery (*ribāt*) and began his teaching among the Juddāla. As soon as he had converted seventy men to his call to truth (*haqq*), he gathered them to attack and subdue the neighboring, blue-veiled tribe of Lamtuna. Together, his followers "called to truth for the redressing of injustices and the abolition of unlawful taxes ... The man who showed them this way, calling the people to the fortified monastery and to the mission for truth, was 'Abdallāh b. Yāsin." Al-Bakri gives the year 1048 for the launching of the mission and the beginning of the movement of the *murābitun* (Almoravids), so named by Yāsin on account of their conversion to his teaching in his *ribāt*. After the death of his patron, Yahyā b. Ibrāhim, however, the Juddāla, led by another religious scholar, rebelled against Ibn Yāsin, destroyed his house, and

---

1. Ibn Khaldun, 1:27, 164.

expelled him. Ibn Yāsin fled to Fez but returned to reside with the defeated Lamtuna branch, whose chief (*amir*), Yahyā b. 'Umar, was now a devout convert, and he killed all those who had risen against him among the Juddāla.[2]

Ibn Yāsin conquered the Zanāta capital, Sijilmāsa, with some two hundred Sanhāja tribesmen in 1055, and he did so a second time a year or so later. His *amir*, Yahyā b. 'Umar, died in battle in 1056, and the latter's brother, Abu Bakr, was proclaimed the new *amir* of the Almoravids in Sijilmāsa in 1058.[3] Ibn Yāsin then defeated the Masmuda tribe and conquered their territories, including the city of Aghmāt. But he was killed shortly afterward in a battle against the Barghawāta to the north in 1059.

In his brief career as a religious reformist, Ibn Yāsin sought to reenact the life pattern of the Prophet and he abolished all noncanonical taxes when he succeeded in establishing a state. More significantly, he introduced revolutionary innovations in holy warfare that were at marked variance with the military tactics of the Berbers and aimed, as Ibn Khaldun astutely perceived, at bringing them in line with those recorded for Muhammad and the rightly guided caliphs.[4] He also killed all the dogs in Sijilmāsa, where cynophagy had survived, even after the conversion of the region to Islam by the Kharijites.[5] Although some of Ibn Yāsin's idiosyncratic rulings are recorded, the period of his undisputed rule was nevertheless far too short for installing a new regime based on his doctrine.[6] He could not bring about a revolution in this short period of three or at most four years spent mainly on warfare.

After his death, the Lamtuna chief, Abu Bakr b. 'Umar, left his nephew, Yusuf b. Tāshfin, in command of the garrison in Sijilmāsa and returned to the Sahara. Writing some ten years later, al-Bakri calls him the *amir* of the Almoravids in the Sahara; his domain is described as widespread but disorderly. The city of Marrakesh was founded as the capital of the new nomadic empire under Abu Bakr, who formally appointed Yusuf b. Tāshfin his succes-

---

2. Al-Bakri 1911–13, 164–66.
3. Viguera-Molins 2010, 37.
4. Farias 1968, 812. Farias (1968, 817) further argues that Ibn Yāsin gave his movement the name *al-Murābitun* (Almoravids) because of the sense he derived from the verses of the Qur'an related to jihad that mean "the movement of those who practice the correct way of waging Holy War."
5. Farias 1968, 808–9.
6. Al-Bakri 1911–13, 169–70.

sor there in 1070. The latter was well-established in Marrakesh by 1071 and persuaded his uncle to return to the Sahara. The two rulers thus divided the Almoravid holdings between them. The southern Almoravids continued the religious character of the movement in the western Sahara under Abu Bakr (d. 1075–76) and his son, Ibrāhim. Abu Bakr appointed Imām al-Hadrami as the religious leader of the movement and successor to Ibn Yāsin, and the Almoravid father and son's zeal contributed to the Islamicization of Ghana.[7]

Far better known, however, is the history of the Almoravid Empire in the Maghreb. Yusuf b. Tāshfin conquered Fez (1070), Tangiers (1078), Algiers (1082), and Ceuta (1083). After the fall of Toledo to the Christian king of Castile, some of the alarmed Muslim local rulers and religious scholars in politically fragmented Andalusia invited him to come to their rescue, and he crossed the Straits of Gibraltar in 1086, deposed the Muslim king of Granada in 1090, and reached Lisbon in 1094.

As the Almoravid Empire expanded to include the centers of Islamic learning in the Maghreb and Andalusia, the orthodox Islam of the jurists of the Maliki school of law became its state religion, and little or no trace was left of Ibn Yāsin's more idiosyncratic doctrine and jurisprudence. During more than a third of a century of rule by the great Almoravid conqueror and consolidator, Yusuf b. Tāshfin (1072–1106), government became completely secularized, though it was committed to jihad against the Christians in Andalusia after 1086. Yusuf assumed the title of the Commander of the Muslims (amir al-muslimin), since calling himself the Commander of the Believers (amir al-mu'minin) was not acceptable to his Maliki judiciary, which reserved this title for the Abbasid caliph. Yusuf divided his nomadic patrimonial kingdom into the four provinces of Fez and Meknes in the north and Marrakesh and Sijilmāsa in the south, appointing two of his sons as his viziers in Marrakesh, one vizier in Sijilmāsa, and a nephew vizier in Meknes. His regime was thus a nomadic patrimonial monarchy, and it is not surprising that noncanonical taxes—notably, a tax on commercial transactions (qabālāt)—were reintroduced under him.[8]

7. Farias 1968, 847–61.
8. Laroui 1977, 165; Messier and Miller 2015, 98.

MAHDISM AND THE REVOLUTIONARY POWER STRUGGLE

Muhammad b. ʿAbdallāh b. Ugallid[9] was a minor chief (*amghār*) of the Hargha (Ayt Argan) branch of the Masmuda in the Sus region in the deep southwest of the Maghreb. He was known as Ibn Tumart on account of his father's surname *Tumart*, meaning "happiness" in Berber. He traveled east in search of knowledge in the second decade of the twelfth century, when he was about thirty. Although the legend has it that he met the famous Abu Hāmid Muhammad al-Ghazāli (d. 1111), he in fact met Abu Bakr al-Turtushi (d. 1126) in Alexandria and was greatly influenced by his Sunni revivalist activism under the Fatimids who ruled Egypt. Ibn Tumart returned to the Maghreb "exploding with knowledge" about the latest trends at the eastern centers of learning—namely, Ghazāli's Ashʿarite rational theology. On each stop on his way back from the east, Ibn Tumart expounded the explosive knowledge he had acquired to younger men who became his students/disciples (*talaba*). On the way back, near Bougie (Bijāya) in present-day Algeria, he met ʿAbd al-Muʾmin b. ʿAli, a notable of the Kumya branch of the Zanāta, who became his disciple and accompanied him on his return journey; they were joined in Wansharis (modern-day Ouarsenis) by Abu Muhammad ʿAbdallāh b. Mushin al Wansharisi (d. 1128), the other close disciple of Ibn Tumart who called him al-Bashir (the bringer of good news). Ibn Tumart held a conference for the *talaba* in Tlemcen, and similarly lectured to and converted *talaba* in Tunis, Mallāla, Fez, and Meknes, and his corps of student/disciples was later referred to as the *talaba* of the Infallible imam (*al-imām al maʿsum*). For them, he composed a major work on his doctrine significantly titled *Aʿazzu mā yutlab* (from the same root, *tlb*, as *talaba*) (What is most important to research!). Thus, from the beginning, the word *talaba* acquired a nuanced meaning as a special kind of student, one could say a research student, that later became distinctive in Almohad usage, as the *talaba* were corporately organized as an organ of the Almohad state and put in charge of formulating and teaching the official doctrine. *Talaba* could perhaps be translated as "research/study group."[10]

Ibn Tumart and his researchers/disciples reached Marrakesh in April 1120, where he reprimanded the sister of the Almoravid ruler, ʿAli b. Yusuf (1106–43),

---

9. Meaning "king" in the Berber language.
10. Baydhaq, 30; Ibn al-Qattān 1990, 91; Ibn Khaldun, 6:267; Fricaud 1997, 344–45, 361; Fromherz 2013, 34, 50.

for riding in public with her face uncovered, and he reportedly confronted her brother by telling him, "the Caliphate is Allah's and not yours, O 'Ali b. Yusuf!" One Almoravid jurist wanted him killed but instead he was banished and moved into a cemetery outside the walls of Marrakesh and continued his preaching for a while in that "domain of God himself" before going to Aghmāt and then fleeing south across the High Atlas. He went to the territory of the Hintāta in the Sus region at the invitation of Ismāʿil Igig, who became a disciple and a member of his assembly (al-jamāʿa), later called the Council of Ten (al-ʿashara).[11]

Ibn Tumart was well received in the Hintāta territory and recruited more followers there. He finally returned to his homeland with the Hargha, reaching Aygiliz (Aygli-n-Warghan) later in 1120. There, he built a monastery-fortress and gathered around him a crowd of students and men from different tribes, whom he taught his books, al-Murshida (The guide) and al-Tawhid (Monotheism), in the Berber language. The tribesmen he instructed reportedly considered the latter their Qur'an. According to Ibn Khaldun, his success alarmed ʿAli b. Yusuf's astrologer who predicted, on the basis of the conjunction of the two superior planets, a "king from the Berber race who will rise and will change the shape of the coinage, telling the Commander of the Muslims: 'Protect the empire from this man; he is indeed the Lord of the Conjunction and of the square dirham!'"[12] Three years later, in 1124, Ibn Tumart moved to Tinmallal (meaning "white peak" in Berber) in the Atlas Mountains, and proclaimed his mission as the apocalyptic and infallible Imam al-Mahdi. He adduced other signs of his imminent appearance, citing an apocalyptic hadith from Ibn Hanbal on the signs of the End of Time that spoke of the appearance of men whose manhood was doubtful and whose women went about cloaked but with their heads bare. This he took to refer to the Almoravids. Ibn Tumart doubtless exploited the astrologer's prediction as well, but he wanted to do more than found a new state merely as a Berber prince. Rather, he wanted to form a state on the prophetic model of his namesake, Muhammad.

In Aygiliz (Igilliz), Ibn Tumart's monastery fortress (ribāt), he frequently withdrew to a cave for ascetic practices that must have included fasting, but he

---

11. Le Tourneau 1969. 23 (citing Baydhaq, 68); Bennison 2016, 67.
12. Ibn Khaldun, 6:268–69. This is evidently an *ex eventu* prophecy, as the Almohads introduced square coins. That some astrological prophecy had been made by either side, however, does not seem unlikely.

at one time appeared at a specially organized common meal, an important tribal ritual for enhancing group solidarity through commensalism, and put salt on his hand as the symbol of the pact between those gathered and God to follow the Book of God and the Sunna of the Prophet, breaking his fast to prove that he would eat and drink as any human being, just like the rest of them, and adding "you are eating just as the prophets eat!" On a different occasion, Ibn Tumart is reported to have received the oath of allegiance from eight disciples in his cave, touching them on the head and telling them in the paraphrase of Qur'an 17:83 in the Berber language that the moment of truth had come, and that falsehood was perishing. Following the model of the Prophet, he then "migrated" with them from his *ribāt* in Aygiliz (assimilated to the Prophet's Mecca) to Tinmallal in 1124. Tinmallal (Tinmall) thus became the Almohad Medina as "the imam's abode of emigration (*dār al-hijra*)." Once there, Ibn Tumart followed the Prophet's example of receiving the general oath of allegiance (*bay'a*) under a tree. According to his secretary, eighteen named disciples (including the secretary himself as the seventh) swore their oath of allegiance, and they were "followed by the rest of the monotheists" (*muwahhidun*).[13]

The Fatimid Shi'ite idea of apocalyptic leadership (imamate) of the Mahdi, brought by two Persians fleeing persecution in the east in the first decade of the tenth century, survived the lapse of direct Fatimid rule in the Maghreb, and was appropriated by two indigenous claimants in the first half of the twelfth century: The Berber Ibn Tumart on the southwestern frontier of Islam beyond the Atlas Mountains, and the Andalusian Sufi Ibn Qasi in the southwestern regions of Andalusia.[14] Pre-Fatimid Shi'ism had, alongside Kharijism, been a major force in the conversion of the Berber tribes of the southern Maghreb, and the Idrisid rulers of Dar'a in the tenth century subscribed to the Sevener Shi'ite rite of Musā b. Ja'far, as the seventh imam. The influence of Shi'ism in the regions of Sus and Dar'a, territories of the Mahdi b. Tumart's Masmuda tribe, must have lingered into the time of Ibn Tumart. The latter's claim to the infallible imamate, if not originating from them, was oriented to the Shi'ite Berbers of the region.[15] The contemporary Fatimid Shi'ism must

---

13. Baydhaq, 40, 73.
14. As we shall see, Ibn Qasi surrendered to Ibn Tumart's successor in 1145.
15. Thus was his claim to descent from al-Hasan, which, according to Ibn Hazm, had been their qualification for the imamate since the Idrisid times. See Madelung 1977, 89.

be counted as a much stronger influence, however, as Ibn Tumart was familiar with Tartusi's anti-Fatimid activism in Egypt and must also have heard during his studies in the east of his contemporary, Hasan Sabbah's new mission (*daʿwa jadida*).

Allāhu rabbunā wa Muhammad rasulunā wa'l-mahdi imāmunā ("God is our Lord, Muhammad is our Messenger, and the Mahdi is our imam")! So goes the legend inscribed on undated Almohad coins minted under Ibn Tumart's successor, ʿAbd al-Muʾmin. A coin dated 1144 and minted by Ibn Qasi a year before he surrendered to the Almohads bears a nearly identical legend. The Andalusian's claim to Mahdihood, if it did not exist earlier, was certainly independent of the Berber Mahdi's, and his almost identical legend was superior to the Almohad's in referring to Muhammad as "our *nabi* [prophet]"—and not as a *rasul* (messenger), thus preempting the strictly correct term.[16]

Even though grafted on the bedrock of Sunni rational theology (*kalam*),[17] what the Mahdi Ibn Tumart claimed to be was indeed none other than the apocalyptic savior of the End of Time, who is by now well-known to us from Shiʿite lore. It is revealingly that in his apocryphal meeting with the great Ghazāli, the latter is most improbably said to have recognized him as the Maghrebi prince who would kill the Dajjāl and proceed to conquer Persia and Rome on the basis of his reading of the Shiʿite book of *Jafr* and the tribulations of the End of Time (*malāhim*).[18]

In one of his letters, Ibn Tumart himself reminded his followers that "the religion for which you struggle is the religion in which there is no change and no transformation until the trumpet is blown [Q. 78:18], and patience in reviving this religion is incumbent upon us."[19] The religion in question is Islam as the pure monotheism (*tawhid*) of Abraham, on account of which he calls his followers the monotheists (*muwaddihun*), or more simply, the believers (*muʾminun*). This religion was being destroyed as a result of the crass anthropomorphism (*tajsim*) and the denial of God's transcendence by the ruling

---

16. Fierro 2000a, 108–10. Muhammad was, strictly speaking, the Messenger of God; so, in the Almohad formula, Ibn Qasi's "our prophet" is more correct than "our messenger."

17. This rationalist grounding permitted, within two generations, the growth of Aristotelian philosophy to be exported as Averroism to the University of Paris

18. Goldziher 1903, 99–100.

19. On this important sign of the End of Time and several others adduced by Ibn Tumart, see chapter 2 above.

Almoravids. It was these anthropomorphist infidels, described by powerful and insulting epithets in the Berber language as *zarājina* (hypocrites), *hashm* (shame-faced) or *jushm/jushsham* (husbands of whores), who had made this present time a time of depravity, when "the knowledgeable go and the ignorant remain, the righteous go and the scum remain, the believers go and the distrustful remain!"[20] There would indeed be chaos without Ibn Tumart as the rightly guided imam and "the pillar of religion." When this imam loses his authority, "heavens will crash onto earth!" This may be taken as the prelude to the coming of God's Day of Judgment.[21]

The one added feature unfamiliar to us is the Berber identity of the Mahdi of the End of Time.[22] The coming judgment, according to the *Book of Muhammad Ibn Tumart*, will originate in the Maghreb. In a speech in 1121, Ibn Tumart claimed that our master, Muhammad, had announced the coming of

> the imam al-Mahdi, the one who will fill the earth with justice and equality, just as he shall empty it of injustice and oppression . . . The remote west will be his homeland and his time the End of Time . . .

The Mahdi, we are further told in an early Almohad source,

> will be sent by God . . . . His place will be the extreme Maghreb and his time, the End of Time: his name will be that of the Prophet . . . This is the end of the times: the name is the name, the lineage is the lineage, and the works are the works.[23]

---

20. The term *"zarājina"* is frequently used to refer to the Almoravids. Ibn al-Qattān (1990, 132) is the only source to explain it as a simile to a bird called *zarjān*, whose feathers are white but whose inside is black. The verb *zarjana*, however, means "to be prone to dissimulation and dishonesty." (I am grateful to Professor Abdellah Hammoudi for this information.) I take this to be the Berber rendering of the hypocrites (*munāfiqun*), the term used for the monotheist opposition to Muhammad in Medina in his later years (see chapter 2 above). The second word is read as *hashm* by Ibn al-Qattān and is explained with reference to the veil (*lithām*) worn by the Lamtuna men "as do modest women." De Slane reads this word in Ibn Khaldun as *jushm*, which literally means "malignant or cunning" (see Ibn Khaldun 1999, 2:272n2), and he explains it idiomatically as a slang insult referring to men whose wives are unchaste. This explanation makes good sense, since such an accusation was indeed leveled against the Almoravids, who veiled themselves while their women had their faces uncovered.

21. Cited in Fromherz 2013, 153–54.

22. Ibn al-Qattān (1990, 89) claims to have seen a letter in which Ibn Tumart said, "I am the Mahdi of the End of Time" (*ana mahdi ākhir al-zamān*), which is dated January 25, 1118/Ramadan 31, 511. See also Goldziher 1903, 100; Fromherz 2013, 183.

23. Cited in Fromherz 2013, 160, 136.

The name and the lineage referred to above are of course what the Muslim tradition required of the Mahdi as the reincarnation of Muhammad, with the same name and the same father's name. In his letter to the Almoravid inhabitants of Sus, Ibn Tumart called himself Muhammad b. ʿAbdallāh al-ʿArabi al-Qurayshi al-Hāshimi al-Hasani al-Fātimi al-Muhammadi! In the Almohad *Kitāb al-ansāb* (Book of genealogies), this Qurayshi genealogy is given alongside his Berber one. The key link in the Qurayshi genealogy is through Muhammad's daughter, Fātima: "just as Jesus son of Mary entered the offspring of Abraham through his mother, so the Mahdi entered the offspring of the Prophet through his ancestress, Fatima the Radiant in addition to his ancestor, ʿAli." The Fatimid genealogy was through Fatima's oldest son, al-Hasan, whose Idrisid descendants, as we have pointed out, had brought Shiʿism to North Africa even before the Fatimids.[24]

It is difficult to tell if Ibn Khaldun really believed in Ibn Tumart's Fatimid genealogy or pretended to do so to please his Hafsid royal patron in Tunisia who still paid lip service to the memory of the Mahdi. But he clearly and explicitly considered it sociologically ineffective and emphasized that the true force of solidarity and partisanship that propelled the Almohad movement was tribal.[25] It is equally clear from Ibn Khaldun's account, as well as all other ones, however, that Ibn Tumart devised a highly original and effective system of governance for harnessing the tribal solidarity of his Berber followers to his divine mission and the monotheist cause.

The Mahdi-Imam's Household (*dār al-imām*) was the headquarter of the nascent Almohad movement, and it included Ibn Tumart's three brothers, his sister Zaynab, and his personal servants, all of whom partook of the charisma of the holy leader as the People of the Household (*ahl al-dār*). His secretary, Baydhaq, enumerates them even before naming the disciples of the Mahdi. Once he had proclaimed his mission as the latter-day replica of the Prophet,

---

24. Baydhaq, 11–12, 22. Ibn Tumart's "Fatimid" genealogy differs significantly from that of the Fatimid dynasty, which was through Husayn, passing instead through Fatima's older son, Hasan, in order to incorporate the Idrisid dynasty through Idris b. ʿAbdallāh b. al-Hasan (d.791) as well.

25. All the Masmuda, Ibn Khaldun tells us (1:28), "became his followers, taking orders from him and his branch from the Hargha, until God completed through his mission. Know that his Fatimid genealogy was hidden ... and their following him was indeed due to their Hargha and Masmuda group solidarity. This original [sic] genealogical affiliation did not harm their group solidarity as it was unknown to those bound by it [i.e., the Hargha and the Masmuda]!"

Mahdi Ibn Tumart launched a series of raids and battles, which, like Muhammad's, were called *ghazavāt*, winning them all the way up to the Almohad capital, Marrakesh.

The growing number of nomadic recruits and the management of warfare, however, required a more formal organization. The tribal organization of Ibn Tumart's followers developed gradually and step by step. In the beginning of this state-building process, the first phase of the revolutionary power struggle in the path of God, was the Great Purge (*tamyiz*)! It is interesting to note that Baydhaq's accounts of the Great Purge and the hierarchical organization of the tribal confederation are combined under the chapter title of *tamyiz* (differentiation), a term taken to mean both the purge of the hypocrites (*munāfiqun*) from the body of true believers, and the hierarchical ranking of the latter tribesmen. The secretary also lists the emerging offices of the Mahdi's nascent state on the basis of their functional differentiation.

The purge, an important stage of the process of most revolutions, consisted in the violent elimination of those Almohad propagandists (*mubashshirun*) who were suspected of disloyalty. The leading propagandist in this group was a certain 'Abdallāh b. 'Ubaydallāh al Haskuri whom the devil had tempted to conspire against the Imam al-Mahdi.[26] Ibn Tumart then asked the divinely inspired al-Bashir al-Wansharisi to carry out the purge as he was "able to know the secret of the souls" and who "God had informed on what hypocrisy [*nifāq*] lay hidden in their souls":

> So they came tribe by tribe and were presented to al-Bashir, and he made people go to his right and to his left. Everyone he made go to his right he maintained was from the people of paradise, and no one went to his left except those who doubted the truth and the Imam al-Mahdi ... And the people on the left were set free and they knew that there was nothing for them but death and no one of them fled. And when a large number of them gathered, they were killed by relatives; the father would kill the son and the son his father and the brother his brother.[27]

In this way, the tribal obligation to avenge the blood of the victims was bypassed as they were killed by their own fathers and brothers. Furthermore, several dissident clans were gathered up and massacred.[28]

---

26. Baydhaq, 36–37.
27. Ibn al-Qattān 1990, 147–48.
28. Fromherz 2013, 65–66, 99.

During the nine or so years in Aygiliz and Tinmallal, the Mahdi Ibn Tumart thus laid the foundations of the Almohad revolutionary state. It was created and dominated by Ibn Tumart, the Infallible imam and Mahdi, who was also referred to as the Lord of the Time (*sāhib al-zamān*) regarding his temporal function as its ruler. The model was the constitution of the pristine Muslim state in Medina. Its core administrative and military organ was the Council of Ten (*al-'ashara*), consisting of Ibn Tumart's disciples among whom the essential secretarial and administrative functions were divided and who also performed as commanders in Almohad holy warfare. They were ranked according to their respective precedence in accepting the Almohad faith. After that came the assembly of the Masmuda tribes that constituted the core of Ibn Tumart's followers and holy warriors; this assembly was known as the Council of Fifty (*ahl al-khamsun/ayt khamsun*). The selection of the leaders of different branches of the Masmuda tribes who sat on the Mahdi's Council of Fifty was likewise based on their ranking according to precedence in accepting the Mahdi's teaching and in accordance with the rightly guided caliph 'Umar's principle of precedence in accepting Islam.[29] The same principle of precedence determined the placing of the tribal contingents in marching order in the battlefield.[30]

The representatives of all major Almohad tribal branches and clans were included in the Council of Fifty. This council was an adaptation of the Berber institution of the Forty (*ayt arba'in*) whose number was raised to fifty by the inclusion of the Council of Ten.[31] The Council of Fifty was the Almohad tribal parliament, just as the Forty had been that of the Berber tribal republics. A less important and presumably more representative Council of Seventy (*ahl al-sāqa*) was most likely formed after the Mahdi's death, probably by enlarging the Council of Fifty to represent new tribes affiliated with the Almohad confederation.[32]

The nonviolent differentiation within the Mahdi's tribal confederation consisted in both the ranking of the tribal units and the ranking of the

---

29. See chapter 2 above.
30. Kisaichi 1990, 86–87; Bennison 2016, 68–69.
31. Kisaichi 1990, 88, 93. This can be inferred from the fact that the oldest listings of its members mention only forty or forty-one names, and the fact that the Hafsid Council of Fifty, which was its continuation, included the ten chief shaykhs as successors of *al-'ashara*.
32. Laroui 1977, 178–79.

believers within each of them. The Hargha, the Mahdi's own branch of the Masmuda, was honored with the highest rank and called the helpers (*ansār*) of the Mahdi as analogous to the helpers of the Prophet in Medina, and the Mahdi affiliated his eighty most prominent disciples who did not belong to it by instituting brotherhood (*mu'ākhāt*) between them and the Hargha, as the Prophet had instituted brotherhood between the emigrants and the helpers during his first year in Medina. He is said to have made 'Abd al-Mu'min his own brother, which automatically affiliated him with the Hargha. He further declared the latter's tribe, the Kumya of the Zenāta, which had apparently moved south with him, as affiliated to the Hargha by right of neighborhood (*jawār*). The other seven disciples, most notably Shaykh 'Abdallāh b. Muhsin al-Bashir, who presided over the purge, were affiliated with the Hargha as brothers during the purge. Together with two other Masmuda disciples, and Baydhaq, who was atypically a Sanhāja, they constituted the Council of Ten.[33]

Three tribes were identified as emigrants (*muhājirun*) on the prophetic model, and the emigrant slaves (*al-muhājirun al-'abid*) were constituted as a quasi-tribal entity. Much more consequently, the people (*ahl*) of Tinmallal were constituted as a quasi-tribal collectivity and ranked above all tribal branches except the Hargha. To create this new collectivity in the capital of his insurgent state, Ibn Tumart had to clear it of the tribal entities he could not fully trust during the revolutionary power struggle. The Hazmira tribe of the surrounding mountain had assured him of their obedience when he moved into Tinmallal, but they continued to bear arms in the city, which made him apprehensive. When they were finally persuaded to attend one of his sermons unarmed, the Almohads who had weapons with them suddenly surrounded them, killing more than fifteen thousand Hazmira men. Ibn al-Qattān tells us that the Mahdi then

> took captive their womenfolk and their possessions as booty and he divided their land and their vineyards among his Almohad followers, and their houses were seized: to each tribe a prize![34]

A jurist from Ifriqiyya whom Ibn Tumart had appointed to the Council of Ten disapproved of the massacre, "and he was killed and crucified because he

---

33. Baydhaq, 37–43.
34. Ibn al-Qattān 1990, 139–40.

doubted the infallibility of the Imam al-Mahdi."[35] The people of Tinmallal, thus purged of elements suspected of disloyalty in the revolutionary process, were given more than twice as many representatives as the Mahdi's own Hargha tribe on the Council of Fifty, and therefore dominated that body.

The functionaries of the nascent Almohad state were ranked as holy warriors (*ghuzāt*), memorizers of the House and other memorizers (*huffāz*)—two groups that seems to have originated in the *talaba* as their younger trainees (*sighār al-talaba*). There follow the slaves of the center (*'āmmat 'abid al-makhzan*), the morality police (*muhtasabun*), including the political-ideological commissars or arbitrators (singular, *mizwār*) attached to tribal units as arbitrators and state representatives, and the party (*ahl al-hizb* [sic]), consisting of fifty men. The *talaba*, originally Ibn Tumart's research students, became the missionaries of the monotheists' state. A special corps of them appears to have been recruited exclusively from the southern Berbers and sent by the Mahdi as the *talabat al-muwahhidin* to the Masmuda tribes to indoctrinate the desert nomads. Also included among the functional components of the Mahdi's state was "the army [*al-jund*], consisting of the inhabitants of Aghmāt and other city-dwellers." As Aghmāt at the foot of the Atlas Mountains was the closest city to Tinmallal ruled by Ibn Tumart, the army was in fact the nontribal army of Almohad urban converts, whose number must have been small but must have grown with the capture of other cities after his death.[36]

Ibn Tumart's jihad state sustained by this primitive structure expanded rapidly in the 1120s, its territory reaching the region surrounding Marrakesh by 1130. Shortly after conducting the purge that made him the undisputed second-in-command, al-Bashir al-Wansharisi gathered the Almohad holy warriors, and the Mahdi conferred robes of different colors on the commanders of the tribal contingents and of the People of Tinmallal. The holy warriors confronted the Almoravid forces, comprising forty thousand foot soldiers and four hundred cavalrymen, outside Marrakesh in the Battle of al-Buhayra and were badly defeated by them. Bashir fell together with four other members of the Council of Ten who, like him, were called the martyrs of al-Buhayra. The withdrawal of divine backing indicated by this defeat made the Mahdi ill, and he died childless a few months later in Tinmallal, probably in August 1130.

---

35. Ibn al-Qattān 1990, 142.
36. Baydhaq, 46–48; Kisaichi 1990, 93, 97–98.

Before dying, however, he rode his donkey—a messianic touch in the manner of Jesus when entering Jerusalem[37]—to deliver a last sermon to his followers, promising they would conquer "Persia and the Christian lands," as predicted for the End of Time.[38]

In contrast to Ibn Yāsin, the founder of the Almoravid movement three quarters of a century earlier, Ibn Tumart was an original and fundamentalist thinker who radically rejected the Malikite orthodoxy for its immersion in derivative jurisprudence (*furu'*) at the expense of rationally accessible principles (*usul*) of religion. Instead, he advocated a return to the Qur'an and the hadith as the fundaments of Islam alongside the credo of monotheism (*'aqidat al-tawhid*) based on a rational understanding of the principles. It was incumbent on each individual believer to understand the principal tenets of religion (*usul al-din*) rationally. Indeed, sources that were contemporary with the Almohads acknowledged that Ibn Tumart initiated a rationalist rite or school of thought (*madhhab fikr*). Ibn Tumart saw his mission as the propagation of divine light, exclaiming in one instance in the Berber language to the Hintāta tribesmen: "Light, Light in the territory of the Hargha, and you, O Hintāta, are in darkness!"[39]

The Mahdi sought to reconcile his theological rationalism, for which he claimed Ghazali's authority, with heterogeneous and possibly contradictory Kharijite and Shi'ite beliefs that had deeply influenced the conversion of the Berber tribes of the Maghreb to Islam. One cannot overemphasize the fact that Ibn Tumart thought, wrote, and preached eloquently in the Berber language; indeed, properly speaking, he was a Berber thinker. From the Kharijite sources, he borrowed, inter alia, the emphasis on violent jihad (*jihād bi'l-sayf*), which he legitimized against all infidels while using his monotheistic credo as the touchstone of belief and infidelity. He thus extended the category of infidels to the "anthropomorphist" Muslims who supported the Almoravids, and at the same time eliminated the protection granted to Jews and Christians in orthodox Islam. From Shi'ism, more obviously, he took the ideas of the infallible imamate and the Mahdihood of the End of Time.[40]

---

37. As we saw in chapter 4 above, the hapless late Umayyad Caliph, Yazid III b. al-Walid, likewise rode a donkey to Damascus in 744.
38. Ibn Khaldun, 6:269–70; Kisaichi 1990, 84; Fromherz 2013, 66.
39. Ibn al-Qattān 1990, 135; Goldziher 1903; Fierro 2000b, 231.
40. Goldziher 1903, 61–62; Urvoy 1974, 20–23, 30–32; Fierro 1999, 227–28; Fierro 2010, 86.

The Mahdi's death was kept secret by his sister and four other disciples who lived in his house. One of these disciples, acting as spokesman, would from time to time appear at the door to give the Mahdi's purported orders to the monotheists who continued their warfare. This went on for some three years during which his disciples appeared to have toyed with the Shi'ite idea of a hidden imam, one who was either in concealment (*satr*) in the Ismā'ili variant or in occultation (*ghayba*) according to the Twelver variant. Meanwhile, with Bashir al-Wansharisi having fallen in battle a few months earlier, 'Abd al-Mu'min, who was thirty-five years of age at the time, had assumed command of the Almohad military forces and continued the fight against the Berbers loyal to the Almoravids in the Atlas Mountains and broke the latter's resistance, massacring two contingents belonging to the Ghumāra tribe.[41] In those years, 1130–1133, according to Ibn Khaldun's succinct account, "the disciples were apprehensive about lack of consensus and what they could expect from the wrath of the Masmuda who did not consider 'Abd al-Mu'min their kin."[42] The Mahdi's household therefore pretended the rightly guided Imam was ill but not dead, and held a meeting presided over by his sister Zaynab, until Shaykh Abu Hafs al-Hintāti (Inti) brought around the Council of Ten to accepting 'Abd al-Mu'min as the Mahdi's successor. The swearing of allegiance to the latter was then taken from the Almohad rank and file. 'Abd al-Mu'min was called as the deputy of the imam (*khalifat al-imām*);[43] his other staunch supporter, Baydhaq, testified that the Mahdi had called 'Abd al-Mu'min the "lamp of the monotheists" (*sirāj al-muwahiddin*) and designated him his successor.[44] The Mahdi is further said to have dismissed 'Abd al-Mu'min's protest that he first had to purify himself of his sins by affirming "the expurgation of your sins will be the rectification of the world [*salāh al-dunya*] at your hand!"[45]

---

41. Merad 1957, 112; Fromherz 2013, 67–68.
42. Ibn Khaldun, 6:270.
43. Ibn al-Qattān, 77.
44. Baydhaq, 56. This designation meant that he was inheriting the Mahdi's "light of guidance," which was itself an extension of Muhammad's "light of prophecy" (Brett 1999, 13). The designation *Deputy of the Imam* proved enduring and therefore strongly suggests early experimentation with the idea of the Imam in hiding or concealment. Ibn al-Qattān (1990, 77, 101, 214, 249–63) continues to use the title not only for 'Abd al-Mu'min throughout his reign but also his successors'!
45. Cited in Brett 1999, 12.

Meanwhile, the revolutionary power struggle within the Almohad insurgent state, which had already begun with Bashir's Great Purge, continued under ʿAbd al-Muʾmin as the imam's deputy alongside the jihad against the Almoravids. ʿAbd al-Muʾmin needed a further fourteen years to achieve complete victory over the Almoravids. He brought in the Zanāta tribes to the core of the Almohad fighting forces, but the Ahmohad holy warriors captured the major cities, Fez, Meknes, and Salé in 1146, and finally conquered Marrakesh after a long and hard siege in March 1147, massacring its population as well as the last youthful Almoravid ruler and his entourage.[46]

Revolutionary power struggle had continued unabated for those fourteen years. First, there were rebels who challenged ʿAbd al-Muʾmin's legitimacy as the Mahdi's successor. No sooner was the oath of allegiance to ʿAbd al-Muʾmin taken than a member of the Council of Ten, the *shaykh* of the Ganfisa tribe and commander of its contingent in the Almohad army, ʿAbdallāh b. Malwiyya, rebelled against the deputy of the imam. Even though the Ganfisa had already produced a rebel against the Mahdi, they refused to follow Ibn Malwiyya, who was consequently defeated and killed in 1133.[47] There followed the rebellion of ʿAbd al-ʿ Aziz b. Karmān from the Hargha, the Mahdi's own tribe which had always born ʿAbd al-Muʾmin resentment since Ibn Tumart had forced him upon them as a brother and now considered him a usurper.

During the following decades, in the newly conquered region to the north of the Atlas, there were several isolated rebellions of the Sanhāja Berbers against the Masmuda domination under the expanding Almohad regime in 1146, some of whose leaders were crucified in the newly conquered Fez. More significant were regional rebellions led by rival religious leaders in that and the following year. During the siege of Fez in 1146, the region of Agarsif rose against the Almohads under the leadership a thaumaturg, the Masbugh al-Yadayn (man with dyed hands). ʿAbd al-Muʾmin sent one of his generals, Yaslātan b. al-Muʿizz, to suppress the rebellion without delay[48]

The most serious resistance to the Almohad expansion came from a rival millennial charismatic leader. No sooner was the conquest of the Almoravid capital, Marrakesh, completed in 1147 than a massive uprising by a rival

---

46. Merad 1957, 114; Fierro 2010, 71; Bennison 2016, 71.
47. Baydhaq, 75, 85; Merad 1957, 115–17.
48. Baydhaq, 122–23; Merad 1957, 117–18.

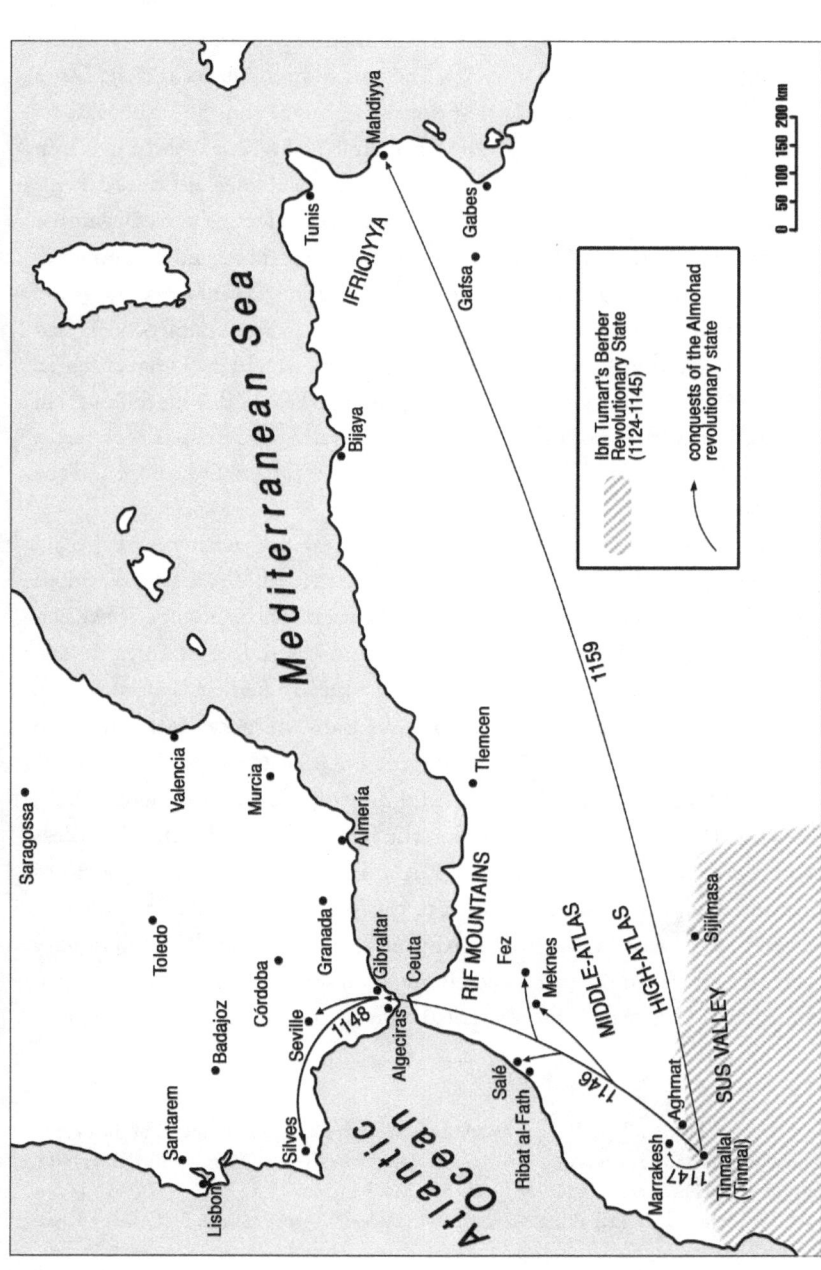

MAP 4. The Almohad revolutionary state and Empire (1124–61).

Mahdist movement under the leadership of a man who called himself Muhammad b. 'Abdallāh b. Hud and who had assumed the apocalyptic title of the Guided One (*al-hādi*) broke out in Salé and spread to Sijilmāsa and the Dar'a valley.[49] This man became known variously as Buyukandi and al-Māssi on account of the fortress/convent (*ribāt*) he had built at al-Māssa. 'Abd al-Mu'min appointed Ibn Tumart's disciple, Shaykh Abu Hafs 'Umar al-Hintāti, commander of the army sent against al-Māssi, with the defecting secretary of the last Almoravid ruler, Abu Ahmad 'Atiyya, as his vizier and second in command. The rival Mahdi or Hādi's army comprised sixty thousand infantry and seven hundred cavalry and was thus considerably larger than Ibn Tumart's army had been at the Battle of al-Buhayra. After defeating him, Abu Hafs 'Umar crucified him at the Shari'a Gate of Marrakesh and proceeded to subdue his followers in Deren and among the Haskura, who were massacred in the monastery-fortresses they controlled. 'Abd al-Mu'min himself reached Sijilmāsa and completed the suppression of the rebellion by the end of the year.[50]

Finally, there was a failed counterrevolution by the remnants of the old Almoravid regime. It broken out in Ceuta, led by its kadi, 'Ayād, who recruited the able Almoravid prince and commander, Yahyā b. 'Ali b. Ghāniya in Algeciras after its Almohad governor was expelled and killed. Ibn Ghāniya in turn put Yahyā al-Sahrāwi, an Almoravid official who had fled Fez before its fall, in charge of spreading the counter-revolution. Sahrāwi successfully turned to the disgruntled Barghawāta tribe for support and was indeed proclaimed their *amir*. Instead of seeking an alliance with the anti-Mahdist movement in Salé, however, Sahrāwi killed Hud the tailor, the father of al-Hādi. This doubtless made it easier for the Almohad Shaykh Abu Hafs to move his army north to Ceuta and quell the counterrevolution in the following year, 1147 or 1148.

Then in 1149 or 1150 came 'Abd al-Mu'min's great purge in the revolutionary power struggle, called the Confession (*i'tirāf*).[51] It was carried out by the Almohad shaykhs within their respective tribal units on the basis of the lists of names

---

49. Baydhaq gives his (real) name as 'Umar b. al-Khayyāt. The assumption of the Prophet's name was obviously necessary to sustain his claim to be the anti-Mahdi. His father, Hud, seems indeed to have been a tailor (*khayyāt*)! See Baydhaq, 107.

50. Baydhaq, 122; Ibn Khaldun, 6:274; Ibn Khaldun 1852–56, 2:181–82. I follow Ibn Khaldun's chronology.

51. Lévi-Provençal (1928, 181) and, following him, Merad (1957, 129, 131) take *i'tirāf* to mean the "recognition of the Almohad power."

of those suspected of disloyalty to them. A total of 32,730 people thus perished in the purge. The great majority of the victims were Berber tribesmen from the Hazmira, the Ragrāga, the Dakkāla, and others who had supported either the anti-Mahdist movement or the counterrevolution of Ibn Ghāniya and Sahrāwi. The victims also included 2,500 people from the Haskura of Darʿa and Sijilmāsa.[52]

By the time Ibn Ghāniya's counterrevolution was suppressed, there were Almohad garrisons in Seville, which had submitted in 1147, and several Andalusian local rulers were inviting ʿAbd al-Muʾmin to invade. Some of them significantly crossed the Strait of Gibraltar to take the pledge of allegiance to him in Salé in 1150. The annexation of Andalusia could thus not be accurately interpreted as the export of the Almohad revolution. Like that of the Almoravids before them, the empire of the Almohads was a nomadic Berber North African empire sucked into the Andalusian cities because of their high degree of fragmentation, crisscrossing loyalties, and of the constant threat of the expanding Christian kingdoms.[53]

THE ESTABLISHMENT OF PATRIMONIAL MONARCHY AND THE ALMOHAD HIERARCHY

ʿAbd al-Muʾmin b. ʿAli (d. 1163) was indeed the consolidator of the Almohad Revolution. He discarded the Almoravid regnal title of the Commander of the Muslims and assumed that of the Commander of the Believers, claiming implicitly the caliphate that, in the eyes of his Maliki subjects, legitimately belonged to the Abbasids in Baghdad. This was done slowly, however. He needed the three years between the death of the Mahdi Ibn Tumart and its acknowledgement to persuade the Masmuda Almohads to accept him as the imam's deputy in charge of holy warfare, and to admit as an affiliate his tribe, the Kumya, which was in fact a branch of the Zenāta. Baydhaq, who became his secretary and chroniclers, was careful to construct a Qurayshite genealogy for him to sustain his claim to the caliphate, which was furthermore a Fatimid genealogy matching the late Mahdi's, and indeed doubling the maternal link through an alleged ancestress, Kannuna b. Idris b. Idris.[54]

---

52. Baydhaq, 109–12 (translation 181–85); Merad 1957, 127, 131–32.
53. Bennison 2016, 74–78, 88–90.
54. Baydhaq, 22.

After the annexation of Andalusia, only Ifriqiyya, the homeland of his Kumya tribes, was left for 'Abd a-Mu'min to add to his empire, and he embarked on its conquest to complete the eastward expansion of the Almohad Empire in North Africa. The expedition against the tribes around Bougie was launched in the spring of 1153. This also provided the occasion for the onset of an intense power struggle between 'Abd al-Mu'min and Ibn Tumart's old guard—which consisted of the Hargha tribe and the people of Tinmallal and was led by his two brothers—that lasted for three years into the spring of 1156. 'Abd al-Mu'min won it and established a Berber patrimonial monarchy in the form of his dynasty that ruled the Almohad Empire for another century and was called the Mu'minid dynasty after him.

'Abd al-Mu'min had put Yaslātan b. al-Mu'izz, who was a relative of the late Mahdi and one of his household (*ahl al-dār*), in charge of the expedition alongside his own son-in-law, 'Abdallāh b. Wānudin. The two quarreled, and Yaslātan made insolent remarks about his co-commander and father-in-law before abandoning him to be killed in battle. A plot against 'Abd al-Mu'min, which involved Yaslātan as a ringleader, was said to have been discovered and foiled; it involved Ibn Tumart's two surviving brothers, 'Abd al-'Azīz and 'Isa. Yaslātan was made to disappear. At about the same time, the Hargha tribe and the people of Tinmallal rebelled. 'Abd al-Mu'im ruthlessly suppressed the rebellion. The Mahdi's brothers as its leaders were spared execution but were transported to Fez and put under house arrest. The caliph immediately went to Tinmallal to appease the survivors by distributing alms to them with largesse and enlarging the Mahdi's mosque.[55]

In 1156, 'Abd al-Mu'min made his oldest son his successor-designate, ostensibly in response to a request to do so by the tribes or people of the east, including the recently courted Banu Hilāl Arabs. He then appointed several of his younger sons as governors of the main provinces, with similarly orchestrated requests from the Banu Hilāl and the non-Masmuda "people of the west" (*gharb*)! At the same time, he took care to appoint Almohad shaykhs as advisors to each prince (*sayyid*). In reaction to this institution of monarchy, the Mahdi's brothers, 'Abd al-'Azīz and 'Isa, broke away from Fez and headed to Marrakesh to lead a rebellion to preserve the Mahdi's heritage, evidently hoping to win over its governor, Abu Hafs 'Umar b. Tafrāgin, who was another

---

55. Merad 1957, 137–41.

surviving disciple of Ibn Tumart. The latter, however, remained loyal to ʿAbd al-Muʾmin and was killed by the rebels. ʿAbd al-Muʾmin, who had held his investiture ceremony outside the capital and in the provincial city of Salé, rushed to Marrakesh, quelled the rebellion, and massacred the rebels, including Ibn Tumart's brothers. Various tribes rose up against ʿAbd al-Muʾmin's measures and were put down in the following two years. The Almohad revolutionary movement was thus hijacked by the founder of the new Muʾminid Berber dynasty that belonged to the Kumya tribe of the Zanāta, which now replaced the Masmuda as the main support base of the Almohad regime. The Masmuda realized that the Almohad Revolution was no longer theirs. In 1157, ʿAbd al-Muʾmin sealed the appropriation of the revolution by a visit to the fortress-monastery of the Mahdi Ibn Tumart. In fact, he was buried there in the Mahdi's tomb after his death in 1163.[56]

The institution of monarchy went hand in hand with a measure of centralization of government, which was aided by the continuous admission of former Almoravid officials. ʿAbd al-Muʾmin was probably the first ruler in the Maghreb to order land registration in 1160. The Almohad armies were transformed by the inclusion of all sorts of professional soldiers, Arab tribesmen, and Christian contingents from Andalusia, and one does not hear much more of Ibn Tumart's holy warriors (*ghuzāt*). The Almohads also created an efficient postal service in their empire. The centralization of the Muʾminid patrimonial monarchy completed the change in the meaning of jihad from revolutionary power struggle against internal enemies to a Muslim holy war against the Christians. This change had begun with the annexation of Andalusia and was completed in the final stage of the conquest of Ifriqiyya in 1159, which was presented as the jihad to liberate the Mahdiyya from the Normans of Sicily—curiously, the city founded by the Fatimid and not the Almohad Mahdi.[57]

The revolutionary break with the past was celebrated under ʿAbd al-Muʾmin by issuing unprecedented square coins that bore no date, most likely to indicate the coming of a new era, and ʿAbd al-Muʾmin continued to perform the call to prayer according to Ibn Tumart's new formula while "correcting" the *qibla* direction of the mosques in the cities he conquered. As the supreme commander of the Almohad holy war after the fall of Bashir al-Wansharisi

---

56. Le Tourneau 1956; Merad 1957, 143–53, 160.
57. Le Tourneau 1969, 61; Fierro 2010, 85; Bennison 2016, 86–87.

and the death of the Mahdi, he created the Almohad Empire in North Africa and proceeded to annex Andalusia at the behest of repeated requests from its threatened Muslim inhabitants. The administrative needs of the Almohad Empire could no longer be met by the Council of Ten, as they had been under the Imam al-Mahdi.

'Abd al-Mu'min already had a group of *talaba* from Aghmāt with him as he fled from the battlefield at al-Buhayra in 1130, and he most probably organized the *talaba* as ideological commissars in Tinmallal between 1133 and 1147. Furthermore, he gave the *huffāz*, originally the memorizers of the Mahdi's works, administrative assignments. Once he conquered Marrakesh and made it the capital of his revolutionary jihad state in 1147, he set up the *talaba* of the capital (*al-hadar*), which was also called the *talaba* of the court/royal presence (*al-hadra*) with the establishment of monarchy, assigned to his permanent service under a shaykh with his own budget. He later divided the *talaba* corps into the itinerant *talabat al-safar*, most likely under the direction of an official called the *mizwār al-talaba*, and the *talaba* of the center (*al-makhzan*) under a shaykh, also call the head (*ra'is*) of the *talaba*. The itinerant *talaba* included the group that retained the Mahdi's designation of *talabat al-muwahhidin*, but they continued to be assigned only to the branches of the Masmuda tribe. 'Abd al-Mu'min also set up a college (*madrasa*) for training the *huffāz* in Marrakesh. In 1152–53, 'Abd al-Mu'min distributed contingents of soldiers in Marrakesh for doctrinal/ideological training among the *talaba* and the *huffāz*. Furthermore, he dictated the creed (*'aqida*) in the Berber language to the scribes as the official statement of the Mahdi's teaching, and he provided copies for discussion sessions organized by the *talaba* among the tribes and in the cities throughout the empire.[58]

In short, as the deputy of the imam al-Mahdi, 'Abd al-Mu'min had developed the institutions of *talaba* and a similar group of militant clerics called the *huffāz* into agencies of government, thereby building the unique structure of the Almohad ideological state, alongside which he instituted a Berber monarchy in his own dynasty. He thus created the equally unique dual structure of the Almohad imperial caliphate in North Africa and Andalusia,

---

58. Urvoy 1974, 20; Urvoy 2005, 747–49; Kisaichi 1990, 94; Fricaud 1997, 348–56, 362. Confirmation that the original language was the Berber can also be found in some translation infelicities.

consisting of the Mu'minid dynastic state, on the one hand, and the Almohad hierocracy or hierarchy, on the other.[59]

The establishment of the Berber monarchy in the Mu'minid dynasty also had a major impact on the evolution of other Almohad institutions. 'Abd al-Mu'min entrusted the education of the sons (*abnā'*) of the regime to the college for the *huffāz* in Marrakesh.[60] This decision must have changed the curriculum of the *huffāz* college, and it at any rate quickly transformed it into the school for training the administrative cadre of the Almohad Empire. The sons of the shaykhs of the Council of Ten and the Council of Fifty, who were referred to by the title of *sayyid* (master), were trained there, creating, through generations, new categories of *sayyids* and *shaykhs* of the *huffāz* and grand guardians (*kibār al-huffāz*). The meaning of the term *huffāz* itself changed imperceptibly from the original "memorizers" to a linguistically alternative meaning of "guardians." The college in Marrakesh accordingly educated members of the ruling elite of the Almohad Empire, teaching them the official doctrine and state ideology, while at the same time training a cadre of ideological commissars to supervise and organize the *talaba* in the provincial cities and tribal areas.

The *talaba* of the court/capital, *talaba al-hadar/hadra*, underwent a very different institutional evolution. Instead of being incorporated into the Almohad hierocracy, it was secularized as a long-term consequence of Ibn Tumart's commitment to rational theology. The *talaba al-hadra* at the caliphal court comprised the regime's theoreticians and held frequent sessions for debate (*mudhākira*) at the court in the presence of 'Abd al-Mu'min (1133–63) and his successor, Abu Ya'qub Yusuf (1163–84). Indeed, the *talaba al-hadar/hadra* gradually became an advisory body to the Almohad caliphs, and its great shaykhs were given occasional commissions and even took part in the caliphs' military expeditions. The number of its members was predictably small— twenty-eight at one time—but these members came to constitute a royal academy housing the intellectual elite of the Mu'imid dynasty.

In line with its primary function as a royal academy, the *talaba al-hadra* held regular sessions debating major issues that were attended by the Almohad

---

59. Bonine 1990; Fierro 200b, 230–31.
60. Compare to the *abnā' al-dawla* created by the Abbasid Revolution and discussed in chapter 5 above.

caliphs, 'Abd al-Mu'min, Abu Ya'qub Yusuf, and Abu Yusuf Ya'qub al-Mansur (1184–99). After the conquest of Andalusia, 'Abd al-Mu'min took an interest in these intellectual debates, and he frequented the philosopher Abu Bakr Muhammad b. Tufayl, who became the physician and advisor of his son, Abu Ya'qub, himself the governor of Seville for seven years before ascending the throne. Ibn Tufayl arranged a private audience with Abu Ya'qub to introduce to him a younger philosopher capable of disseminating the philosophy of Aristotle: Abu'l-Walid Muhammad b. Ahmad Ibn Rushd (d. 1198), who soon became known to the Latins as Averroes. Ibn Rushd belonged to a distinguished family of kadis of Cordoba and he inherited that office himself. Furthermore, he became Abu Ya'qub's physician after Ibn Tufayl's resignation in 1182. We find Ibn Rushd attending the debating sessions of the court *talaba* in the company of his royal patron in 1172, and again in 1182.[61]

Abu Ya'qub Yusuf not only took an interest in the intellectual debates of the court *talaba* and led them at times but was also well-read and keenly interested in philosophy and sought the company of "theoretical thinkers" (*ahl 'ilm al-nazar*) such as Ibn Tufayl and Ibn Rushd.[62] He cautiously promoted public discussion of the relation between religion and philosophy, and in the 1170s he commissioned Ibn Rushd, through Ibn Tufayl who was still his physician, to write commentaries on the works of Aristotle. In his *Commentary on Plato's* Republic, Ibn Rushd praised Abu Ya'qub Yusuf as his royal patron and a philosopher king, while proposing as the foremost task of a philosopher king the education of his subjects. This would make him the best ruler, given his theoretical knowledge. Abu Ya'qub tried to live up to this ideal and was acclaimed by the historian al-Marākishi as the only true Berber king. According to Ibn Rushd's own theory, which later came misleadingly to be called the theory of double truth and was propagated by the Latin Averroists, religion and philosophy can be reconciled as theoretical and allegorical interpretations, respectively, of the same truth. Ibn Rushd was the greatest thinker produced by the Almohad regime in association with its royal academy. He also wrote a major treatise on jurisprudence as the kadi of Cordoba and the foremost Almohad jurist.[63]

    61. Puig 1992, 246; Fricaud 1997, 372.
    62. al-Marākishi as cited in Hourani 1967, 11.
    63. Averroes 1967, 62, 11, 17; Butterworth 1975, 125; Fierro 1999.

Ibn Rushd was certainly aware of Ibn Tumart's endorsement of allegorical interpretations in his rational demonstration of the unity of God. With the caliph Abu Ya'qub's encouragement, Ibn Rushd found the time ripe to promote his famous theory of prophecy as an allegorical interpretation by means of powerful imagery that was effective in swaying the masses to the truth. In order to demonstrate that the Divine Law (*shari'a*) makes the study of philosophy obligatory in his *Decisive Treatise (fasl al-maqāl) on the Harmony of Religion and Prophecy*, Ibn Rushd replaced the primitive rationalism of the Ash'arite theology of Ghazāli and Ibn Tumart with his own advanced argument, according to which rational demonstration through logic in philosophy, on the one hand, and persuasion through rhetoric in allegorical interpretation of religion, on the other, were alternative methods for reaching the truth. His argument that "the study of the books of the ancients is obligatory by [God's] Law" because they open "the door of theoretical study which leads to the truest knowledge of Him" was certainly consistent with Ibn Tumart's teaching that the principles of religion could only be understood by rational proof. In fact, Ibn Rushd sought to demonstrate this consistency by ending the *Decisive Treatise* with the praise of the Almohad rule through which God had bestowed many benefits on those "who had trodden the path of study and sought to know the truth." This was done

> by summoning the masses to a middle way of knowing God the Glorious, [a way] which is raised above the low level of the imitators of authority [*muqallidin*] . . . and by drawing the attention of the elite to their obligation to make a thorough study of the principles of religion.[64]

The denunciation of imitating authorities in derivative legal norms (*taqlid*) and the endorsement of the obligation to study the principles of religion by reason in this final passage are pure Ibn Tumart. It can even be further argued that the Averroist double epistemology of different modes of expression of truth for the masses and the elite was consistent with Ibn Tumart's principle of differentiation (*tamyiz*) that served as the basis for the creation of an Almohad hierarchy charged with the guidance of the masses!

However this may be, the Mu'minids never disbanded the distinctive institutions of the Almohad hierocracy and the doctrinal/ideological state.

---

64. Averroes 1967, 48, 71 (translation slightly modified).

Their Berber patrimonial monarchy in fact coexisted with the Almohad hierocracy, resulting in the regime's distinctive dual structure of power. The duality of patrimonial monarchy and Mahdist revolutionary Almohadism persisted to the end, although with constant tension between the two components. For instance, the Ahmohad shaykhs gained the upper hand in the court *talaba*/royal academy in a debating session in 1196 or 1197 that was presided over by the vizier who was the nephew of the Tumartian grand shaykh Abu Hafs 'Umar al-Hintāti, and leveled accusations of heresy against the venerable kadi of Cordoba, which secured his banishment. This banishment did not, however, last long, and Ibn Rushd was recalled to Marrakesh shortly before his death in 1198.[65]

The preponderantly Berber Almohad political/ideological state retained its vitality into the thirteenth century, producing such important figures as the historian Ibn al-Qattān, whose father was the *ra'is al-talaba*, and Ibn Sāhib al-Salāt, whose history of the Almohad movement bore a significant title clearly meant to perpetuate the doctrinal/ideology heritage of the Mahdi: *al-minn bi'l-imāma 'la'l-mustas'afin bi-an ja'alahum Allāh a'imma wa ja'alahum wārithin* (The bounty through the imamate on the disinherited, consisting in God's making them the leaders, and making them the inheritors). The title contained the paraphrase of verses 7:137 and 275 from the Qur'an, and it was clearly intended to demonstrate the divine sanction behind the Almohad Revolution led by an infallible Imam al-Mahdi

The duality of the Berber monarchy and the Almohad hierarchy was replicated throughout the structure of domination in the Almohad Empire: The Ahmohad shaykhs (*shuyukh al-muwahhidin*) versus the Mu'minid nobility (*sādāt al-mu'minin*); the grand guardians versus the local/tribal *huffāz*; and the *talaba* of the court and the local/tribal Almohad *talaba*. Not even the late Mu'minid caliph al-Ma'mun (1227–32), who abandoned al-Mahdi's doctrine and massacred a number of Almohad shaykhs, could dismantle the hierarchy. In fact, the Almohad shaykhs in Tinmallal survived the overthrow by the Mu'minids in Marrakesh for six years, lasting up to 1275.[66]

---

65. Fricaud 1997, 362, 375–79; Fierro 2010, 76–81.
66. Fierro 2010, 79–81.

THE CONSEQUENCES OF THE BERBER
REVOLUTION OF THE MAHDI B. TUMART

The foremost consequence of Ibn Tumart's Berber revolution was to deepen the Islamicization of the Berber tribes that had been begun by the Kharijites and continued by the Idrisids, the Fatimids, and the Almoravids. Although the earlier Kharijite and Shi'ite conversion waves left discernible traces in Ibn Tumart's thought, his doctrinal synthesis within the framework of Ash'arite rational theology was original and compelling. Its revolutionary impact was, however, not owing to its originality but to Ibn Tumart's genius in creating the institutions of the student/researchers (*talaba*) and the memorizers (*huffāz*), which were manned overwhelmingly by Berbers, to disseminate and preserve his teaching of monotheism. The consequent regime that consolidated his institutional innovations under his successor created the distinctive Almohad regime that survived him by almost a century and a half.

Secondly, Ibn Tumart took an important step in giving legitimacy to and institutionalizing Berber authority of chieftains, the *ugallid* and the *amghār*. Despite Ibn Tumart's ingenious coupling of tribal and religious solidarity, which so impressed Ibn Khaldun, this attempt to institutionalize the forms of Berber authority caused some tension with the Mahdist charismatic authority, tension that was eventually resolved by his successor, 'Abd al-Mu'min, in favor of a patrimonial Berber monarchy. More consistent and less fraught with tension was Ibn Tumart's innovative extension of the Berber institution of the Parliament of Forty (*ayt arba'in*) into the Almohad councils, especially the Council of Ten and the Council of Fifty.

The third consequence of the Almohad Revolution, and its most important one in world history, was the rehabilitation of Greek philosophy in general and of Aristotle in particular. The rehabilitation of philosophy and the rational sciences, after the severely debilitating attack by Ibn Tumart's intellectual hero, Abu Hāmid al-al-Ghazāli, was Ibn Rushd's greatest achievement for the Islamicate civilization, and, as I have argued, should be considered a long-term consequence of the Almohad Revolution. Ibn Rushd is known as the greatest refuter of the influential refutation of philosophers by al-Ghazāli. Paradoxical though this may appear to be, this represented the end stage of the developmental path opened by Ibn Tumart's insistence on grounding his creed of monotheism squarely on the rational understanding of the principles of religion. If Ibn Tumart's creed was rightly considered the foundation of a school of thought (*madhhab fikr*), then Ibn Rushd's philosophy would indeed be its culmination. Within the Islamicate civilization, Ibn Khaldun's *Prolegomena*, which develops Ibn Rushd's typology of political philosophy into the new science of history and was written in the fourteenth century in a Hafsid successor state to the Almohad Empire, can also be seen as one of the long-term consequences of the Almohad Revolution. The intercivilizational long-term consequence of the revolution of the Almohad school of thought was arguably greater than that within the Islamicate civilization. Through the latter, the heritage of Aristotle was transmitted to Western Europe, and the Latin Averroists dominated the University of Paris within a generation, paving the way for one of its Dominican professors, Thomas Aquinas, to commission the translation of the remaining works of Aristotle from the Greek, most notably the *Politics*, which had never been translated into Arabic, and to secure the reception of Aristotle by the Catholic Church.

CHAPTER 9

The Development of Islamicate Conceptions of Revolution

Revolutions worthy of the name are not only memorable events in world history, but they also generate concepts to perpetuate their memory. The French Revolution of 1789 gave birth to the modern concept of revolution itself. The revolutions considered in this book likewise generated general conceptions of major transformation of the political order. As the memory of these revolutions was constructed and reconstructed by historians, so the general conceptions of revolution evolved and were intermingled. This chapter therefore traces the emergence and development of the Islamicate conceptions of revolution through the fourteenth century against the background of the ancient conception of the transfer of divinely granted sovereignty or world domination from one empire to the next that can be dated back to the birth of apocalyptic messianism.

As we have seen, the term *fitna* (dissension) was used in reference to the three civil wars of the first centuries of Islam. Its strongly pejorative connotation, however, contrasts sharply with the positive connotations of the modern concept of revolution. By contrast, the connotations of the term *dawla*, which originally meant "revolution" or the "turn" in power, was given an entirely positive meaning during the time of the Abbasid Revolution and it implied divine sanction. But it lost its original revolutionary connotations with the consolidation of the Abbasid imperial authority and acquired the meaning of (rule by a) dynasty and "the state."[1] There is, however, a third term for revolution that corresponds to the

---

1. Bernard Lewis (1972 [1993]) discussed these terms but concluded that neither was comparable to the modern concept of revolution as a radical sociopolitical change, making the

Latin *revolutio* in that it originally meant the revolution of the stars in astronomy but came to be used by historians in the West as *revolutio regni* to denote a major convulsion in the kingdom. The corresponding Arabic term, *inqilāb*, meaning revolution in modern Persian and Turkish (though no longer in modern Arabic), in fact dates back to the eighth century and was used to explain fundamental changes in society and polity.[2]

THE APOCALYPTIC IDEA OF TRANSFER OF SOVEREIGNTY IN ANTIQUITY

The transfer of sovereignty, as the rise and fall of empires and nations, and similarly expressed in the idea of *dawla* (rotation in world domination), was a common theme in antiquity. The best place to start the search for it is the book of Daniel, the Old Testament book with the largest number of Old Persian loan words. Its second chapter, dated to the mid-third-century BCE, synthesizes the Hellenistic idea of succession of empires from Greek historiography with the Persian idea of the four ages of increasingly debased metals preceding the advent of the Zoroastrian millennial savior in *Bahman Yasht*, which ages are taken to represent the four empires of Babylonia, Media, Persia, and Macedonia.[3] In Daniel chapter 7, which is dated to the inception of the Maccabean Revolution and marks the emergence of historically oriented apocalypticism, "Daniel" replaces metals by monstrous beasts in his symbolic representation of empires as kingdoms of men, as compared to the coming

---

idea of social revolution as a fundamental change in the social and political order inconceivable in Islam. The evidence presented in this chapter shows this *not* to be the case. Lewis largely missed the link between *dawla* as domination or empire of nations and *inqilāb*, the key concept of political astrology meaning fundamental religio-political change to be discussed here. The same is true of Mottahedeh (1980, 185–86), who offers a perceptive analysis of *dawla* as "divinely granted turn in power," but does not link it to the term termed *inqilāb* used in the astronomical explanation of major shifts in the divinely granted turn in power. Furthermore, neither author indicates the persistence of the sense of precariousness underlying the conception of dynastic change, accompanied as it usually was by socioeconomic devastation, which made possible the continued use of *dawla* to mean the transfer of sovereignty.

2. Koselleck 1985, 43–46. It is in this sense that, as late as 1788, Edward Gibbon (1932, 1:1; 2:521) speaks of the decline and fall of the Roman Empire, the rise of Islam, and the Turkish conquest of Constantinople as revolutions.

3. Momigliano (1987) 1994.

Kingdom of God.[4] Thus, in Daniel's dream of the four beasts of the apocalypse, we read:

> I saw, coming on the clouds of heaven, as it were a son of man. He came to the One most venerable[5] and was led into his presence· On him was conferred rule [šolṭān], honor and kingship [malḵū]· His rule is an everlasting rule· (7:13–14)

The One most venerable then said:

> The fourth beast is the fourth kingdom [malḵū] on earth, different from all other kingdoms. (7:23)

From this kingdom will rise eleven iniquitous kings, the last of whom will be destroyed. The text in Daniel (7:27) continues:

> And kingship [malḵūṯā] and rule [šolṭānā] ... will be given to the people of the holy ones of the Most High, whose kingship [malḵūṯ] is eternal, and whom all empires [singular, šolṭānā] shall serve and obey.[6]

The idea of the everlasting kingship of God Most High becomes central in the Qur'an: "Verily God's is the Kingship of Heavens and the Earth" (Q. 3:189, 5:20, 7:157, 24:42, 42:48, 45:26, 48.14). "His is the kingdom" (mulk) (Q. 64:1).[7] Therefore, he grants it to and withdraws it from any son of Adam as he wishes:

> Say: "O God, possessor of kingship, Thou givest kingship [mulk] to whom thou wilt, and thou seizest kingship from whom thou wilt ... (3:26) Indeed God chose Adam and the House of Abraham and the House of 'Imrān [Moses's father] above all beings ... (3:31)

The ethico-theistic notion of transfer of sovereignty in the book of Daniel was thus transmitted to Islam in an apocalyptic context. I have argued that the apocalyptic battle (milḥamah) of the last book of Daniel [= ardig-e bozorg,

---

4. The chapter is in Aramaic because of its dependence on the much older ch. 2.
5. Or, the Ancient of Days, whom Widengren identified with Zurvan, the Mazdean deity of time.
6. The term sulṭān, the Arabic cognate for šolṭān, is accordingly given the meaning of "authority" in the Qur'an, is often qualified as clear or manifest (mubin), and is granted by God to Moses (Q. 4:152, 11:96, 40:23, 51:38), to his brother Aaron (Q. 23:45), and to other prophets as proof of their divine mandate.
7. In contrast to the kingdom of God in Christianity, which is not of this world.

"the great war" of Zoroastrian apocalypticism],[8] in which God places the archangel Michael at the head of a heavenly host, influenced the Qur'an's apocalyptic conception of the Battle of Badr, in which (according to the earliest commentaries) God sends down three hundred angels (Q 3:120), headed by Michael and Gabriel· It is in the context of that precarious first Muslim victory that God speaks of different nations' turn in rule:

> Such days we turn out in turn [nudāwilhā, from dwl, the root of the concept of dawla (turn in rule/domination)] among peoples! . . . so that God may prove the believers and blot out the infidels. (Q. 3:134–35)

We meet the same idea in another verse (Q. 7:34): "To every nation a term; when their term comes, they shall not put it back by a single hour nor put it forward."

A millennium after the rise of Islam, the apocalyptic transfer of sovereignty was recovered by the Fifth Monarchy Men of the Puritan Revolution in England, so called because they identified with the people of a God (in the above-cited Daniel 7:27) "whose kingship is eternal, and whom all empires shall serve and obey.[9]

It is interesting to note that we also find another term for revolution resulting from wrongdoing or tyranny in the Qur'an. After assuring those who are oppressed (zulimū') of divine help, the final verse of sura 26 gives them the assurance that "the oppressors shall surely know by what overturning they will be overturned [ayya munqalibi yanqalibun]" (Q. 26:228). The infinitive for both these terms is inqilāb, which hereby acquires an ethical, normative connotation. We do, however, find the term without the implication of a value judgment in a poem by an eyewitness about the civil war between the sons of Caliph Hārun al-Rashid, al-Amin, and al-Ma'mun (811–13), which is described as the inqilāb al-zamān (revolution of the days).[10]

---

8. See chapters 1 and 2 above, and see further Shapira 2013, 40n1.

9. Meanwhile, a somewhat similar notion of *translatio imperii* prevailed in Western Christianity that was, however, not apocalyptic but secular. It was applied to the establishment of Constantinople as the new Rome in Late Antiquity (Al-Azmeh 2014, 18–31). With the rise of the Catholic Church, the notion of *translatio imperii* became constitutionalized with the famous early medieval forgery, the "Donation of Constantine" as the deed of transfer of *imperium* to the bishop of Rome as the "vicar of Christ." The alleged transfer even included the right to appoint consuls and patricians and served as the transfer of the empire from the "Greeks" to the Germans. The final historicization and secularization of *translatio imperii* took place in the fourteenth century by imperial ideologues such as Marsiglio of Padua (d. 1342). (Ullman 1965)

10. Tabari, 3:805.

In the Syriac sources from the mid-seventh century, the rise of a Muslim empire is seen as "the victory of the sons of Ismael, who empowered and subdued these two empires [the Roman and the Persian] [and] came from God." As Bishop Isho'ayhb III of Adiabene (d. 659) stated, it was "the Arabs, to whom God has at this time given the rule [šolṭānā] over the world." The Synod of May 676 accordingly dated its canons to the year 57 of "the rule of the Arabs" (šolṭānā d-tayyāye).[11]

In the Persianate world more generally, the transfer of world domination came to mean the transfer of the divinely granted turn in power from the Persians to the Arabs. To the eleventh-century bureaucrat and historian, Bayhaqi (d. 1077/470), the transfer of sovereignty clearly meant that "the Arabs' turn in power (dawlat)—may it last forever—came and invalidated the tradition [rusum] of the Persians ['ajam]." There was more to Bayhaqi's political thought, however. In his search for a secure foundation for a new science of history, he came to peg the pattern of history on a political ethic. I have elsewhere cited his remarkable formulation of the Islamicate theory of the two powers, which remained definitive for the medieval period and beyond. He is equally remarkable, however, for elaborating the normative theory of revolution (which is at the same time an ethic of accountability) based on the notion of divinely ordained transfer of royal power.

ISLAM'S SOCIAL REVOLUTION AND ITS PERSIANATE SELF-CONCEPTION

We find two different ideas of revolution emerging from of Islam's social revolution, the Hashemite or Abbasid Revolution discussed in chapters 5 and 6. The first was a deterministic theory of revolution in earthly kingdoms as a natural phenomenon, which has received little or no attention in the secondary literature on the subject. The idea had Indian origins, was developed in late-Sasanian Iran, and was absorbed into astronomical theories in the early Abbasid period. It was the central concept of the theory of the astral determination of rotation of dynasties, nations, and religions in power that can be called political astrology. The term for "revolution" in this theory was *inqilāb*, though it is often used in conjunction with *dawlat* as the divinely ordained

---

11. Hoyland 1997, 187, 196.

turn in power. Both terms were used to describe the Khurasanian uprising against the Umayyads or the Hashemite Revolution.

The second conception of revolution is a normative one and it is found in the subsequent Arabic and Persian literature on statecraft and political ethics. It explains revolution as the consequence of the moral decay of the ruler and his failure to uphold justice and the principles of government. According to this second theory, the revolutionary upheaval and transfer of divinely ordained turn in power from one dynasty, nation, or religion to another dynasty or nation results from the failure to maintain the prosperity of the kingdom through the justice of the king. The two conceptions are complementary and mutually supportive.

The earliest expression of the normative conception used for a deliberately revolutionary purpose dates from the Hashemite Revolution and is found in a rousing speech given by the Hashemite revolutionary commander, Qahtaba b. Shabib (d. 749),[12] to his revolutionary army on its march toward Kufa, delivered on the eve of the conquest of Gorgan in July 748:

> Men of Khurasan, this land belonged to your forefathers before you, and they were given victory over their enemies on account of their justice and righteous manners, until they changed and became unjust.... God Most High was enraged with them and took away their authority [sultān] and gave the humblest nation [umma] on earth under them [i.e., the Arabs] domination over them; the latter took their land and their women and stole their children. The latter nation ruled with justice and remained faithful to the covenant for a while... [but] then they changed and went astray and became oppressive in their rule, and the people of piety and righteousness among the offspring of the Prophet became fearful. Therefore [God] has empowered you against them [i.e., the Arabs turned oppressive].... And God will give you victory over them."[13]

The Abbasid Revolution opened the path for the development of the Islamicate civilization by incorporating a very different conception of revolution, one formulated in terms of natural science and soon applied to the Abbasid Revolution itself. It was a deterministic theory of revolution in earthly kingdoms as a natural phenomenon in a world ruled by stars. The idea had Indian

---

12. He was a settled, Persian-speaking, Arab Khurasanian His given name was Ziyād. (See Sharon 1978, 445.) Qahtaba's speech was undoubtedly in Persian even though it is recorded in Arabic by Tabari, since it precedes the writing of Persian as a literary language in the Arabic alphabet.

13. Tabari, 2:2005.

origins, was developed in late-Sasanian Iran, and was absorbed into the astronomical theories of Māshā'allāh and Abu Mash'ar Balkhi in the early Abbasid period. It was the central concept of the theory of the astral determination of major turns of dynasties, nations, and religions in power.[14]

Astronomy had been brought to Iran and Central Asia centuries earlier and had been well received there. The Zurvanite tendencies in particular developed astrological fatalism in the last centuries of Sasanian era.[15] Given this astrological preoccupation in late-Sasanian culture, it is not surprising that Indian astronomy, too, attracted the attention of scholars who, during Khosrow I's reign, translated the most advanced works in the field, works that were used for compiling the tables of the royal astronomical treatise known as the *Zij-e shāhi.* The Iranian appropriation of Indian astronomy was not passive but involved a distinctive innovation that sharpened its political edge into the Sasanian theory of astral determination of the rise and fall of dynasties. It amounted to "the theory that history is the unfolding of the influences of periodically recurring Saturn-Jupiter conjunction."[16]

Zoroastrianism, meanwhile, developed a millennial motif whose revolutionary potential was realized a decade after Khosraw I's death, albeit briefly. Bahrām Chubin (javelin), the scion of a Parthian royal family and the chief Sasanian commander and war hero, who had personally slain the Great Khāqān of the eastern Turks, rose in the east against Hormozd IV and proceeded to the famous Dezh Rōyēn (bronze fort) in the region of Bukhara. He then marched to Iran, captured Ctesiphon, and crowned himself king, striking coins with his effigy in the years 590 and 591 (years 1 and 2 of his reign). Ardashir, the founder of the Sasanian Empire, was at the time placed five hundred years after Zoroaster, and Bahrām's propagandists said he was rising five hundred years after Ardashir—that is, at the close of the millennium of Zoroaster, as the expected savior king, Kay Bahrām Varjāvand. He himself proclaimed the overthrow of the Sasanian dynasty, whose ancestor Ardashir was of lowly birth, and the restoration of the Parthian dynasty of his own

---

14. Arjomand 2012.

15. They considered the twelve signs of the Zodiac as beneficent and the seven planets as commanders of evil, which "oppress all creation and deliver it over to death," and they believed destiny and character alike to be determined by the constellation of stars at the moment of birth (Zaehner 1961, 206).

16. Pingree 1963, 242, 245.

ancestors.[17] Bahrām Chubin's millennial revolution was, however, cut short by foreign military intervention as Hormozd's son, Khosraw II, who had escaped to Byzantium, returned with a Roman army of forty thousand men to defeat him. This failed revolution nevertheless engendered the apocalyptic expectation of the return of the hero from the bronze fort, which, as we saw in chapter 6, motivated the uprising of Abu Muslim's Zoroastrian follower, Sonpādh, in 755.

According to Zoroastrian cosmogony recorded in the ninth century, the millennium of Zoroaster is marked by the appearance of the first of the three millennial saviors. That is to say, Ushēdar, the son of Zoroaster, who had two forerunners or helpers that are themselves heroes who save the land of Iran from its enemies and demons (with historic echoes of the invasion of Iran by the Greeks and ultimately the Arabs) and thus prepare the material world for his appearance. When the world is turned upside down and "slaves will walk in the path of nobles; the horseman will become a man on foot; and the man on foot a horseman," a savior king, Kay Wahrām (Bahrām), and an immortal hero, Pishyōtan, will appear to save Iran from chaos and cleanse it of the Xyōns (Turks/Hephthalites), the Romans ("demons with parted hair"), and the Tāzigs (Arabs). Kay Wahrām would rise from the East with uplifted white banners and blaze forward to the land of Iran. The savior of the second millennium, Ushēdar-Māh, is a purely mythical figure, as is the universal savior of the third and final millennium, Sōshyānt.

Muslim astronomy developed from the Khosrow's royal tables, as well as from the other Indian astronomical tables known as the Zij Hind-Send. From the very beginning, the Sasanian theory of astral determination of major historical upheavals gave this astronomy a keen historicopolitical angle. This aspect was developed into a distinctive Muslim science for the prediction of the predetermined future. This science for the astral determination of political upheavals was elaborated with the hindsight of the Abbasid Revolution. It adopted the Sasanian astrological techniques for predictions of dynastic change on the basis of the *Zij-e shāhi*, on which Zoroastrian millennialism was superimposed.[18] The extant statements of this theory date from the eighth and ninth centuries and are the work of Māshā'allāh, the Jewish astrologer who, together with the Zoro-

---

17. Ferdawsi 1995/1374, 9:29–32.
18. Kennedy and Pingree 1971, vi–viii, 75; Pingree 1968, 6–13.

astrian astrologer Nawbakht and the latter's compatriot, 'Omar b· Farrokhān, cast the horoscope for the foundation of the new city of peace (*madinat al-salām*, Baghdad) in 762· It was elaborated in a famous treatise by Māshā'allāh's disciple, Abu Mash'ar Balkhi, who died at the age of over a hundred in 886·

Māshā'allāh wrote a tract on *Conjunctions and the Shifting of the Years*, which highlighted the epochal significance of the conjunction of Saturn and Jupiter in every triplicity and offered predictive advice to political astrologers:

> When a rising man [*qā'em*] rises [to rule], know the year in which he rises, and be informed of what I determine for you concerning the matter of kings. The matter of kings is known from the Sun, Saturn, Jupiter, and Mars. The Sun gives the years, and these planets sometimes increase them and sometimes decrease them.[19]

A generation later, Abu Ma'shar Balkhi moved from his native Balkh in Central Asia to Baghdad where his circle of associates and disciples grew, overlapping with the network of scholars engaged in translations from the Greek, including Ptolemy's *Almagest*, and philosophical neophytes centered around the famous House of Wisdom/Philosophy (*ḥikma*). In *The Book of Religions and Empires*, Abu Mash'ar classified different conjunctions of the "superior planets," Saturn and Jupiter, in terms of their frequency, which is inversely related to the magnitude of change they bring about in human affairs. Here the term for "empire" is *dawla*, which, like "turn in power," comes to mean empire or world domination in the sense of the four sovereignties/empires of the book of Daniel. The conjunction of Saturn and Jupiter occurs in the spring tropical sign of the Zodiac once every 960 solar years (conveniently close to the one thousand lunar years equated with the Zoroastrian millennium), once every 240 years with the shift from one triplicity to another, and once every twenty years in each sign. To these, he added the conjunction of the two inauspicious planets, Saturn and Mars, once every thirty years, and two other conjunctions. He used the theory of conjunctions to explain the transfer of empire from one nation or religious community to another (once every 960 years) as well as the changes of dynasties within each empire.

Abu Mash'ar did not see his political astrology as incompatible with the lore of statecraft and its political ethic. On the contrary, he thought the influence of the planets worked through the disappearance of justice and

---

19. Yamamoto and Burnett 2000, 2:546 (translation 547, slightly modified).

prosperity of the ruling dynasty and the appearance of corruption and disobedience among its subjects. Nor was there any obstacle to the combination of the conception of government in statecraft and political ethic and that of revolution in historical/political astrology. Nor, for that matter, did the emergent philosophy in Baghdad find Abu Mash'ar's astrological theory incompatible with the normative one. On the contrary, in a tract titled *The Empire (dawla) of the Arabs and Its Duration*, the philosopher Ya'qub b. Ishāq al-Kindi (d. 866), who was one of Abu Mash'ar's students, applied the theory to all the civil wars and revolutionary upheavals of Islamic history, including the fairly recent militarization of caliphal government with the recruitment of Turkish praetorian slaves (*mamluks*), whose horoscope he cast for the year 212 (at least a decade earlier than seems warranted historically).[20]

Another ninth-century practitioner of political astrology, Ibn Abi Tāhir Tayfur (d. 893), followed up on Māshā'allāh's calculations on the rise of Islam and the Arab empire as determined by the shift of triplicity on March 19, 571, and other horoscopes, to demonstrate that the conjunction of Saturn and Jupiter at the vernal equinox in March 749 had determined "the shift [*tahwil*] in the Conjunction of the Arabian empire to the Hashemite Imams," which he described as "the general revolution in religion and the state" (*al-inqilāb al-kulli fi'l-din wa'l-mulk*).[21] We may anachronistically take this proto-Persianate notion as the definition of a great revolution.

Apocalyptic numerological speculations had thus continued from ancient times. It was this political astrology that became the most respected science of prediction of the heavenly predetermined future revolutions in world domination, and thus stimulated numerous apocalyptic uprisings throughout Islamic history. We only need to remember the widely cast horoscope of the shift of triplicity at the vernal equinox of the year 809 to realize that the maturation of the science of political astrology had much to do with the civil war of 809–13, which brought the era of Islamic political apocalypticism to a close. Political astrology played an important role in the history of the chiliastic Isma'ili movement.[22]

---

20. Yamamoto and Burnett 2000, 2:10–12, 68–71, appendix III.
21. Ibn Abi Tāhir Tayfur n.d., folio 60a.
22. Astrological speculations were by no means particular to heterodoxy. On the contrary, they were common to all Muslims. The news of the Mongol invasion of northern Iran, for instance, inspired apocalyptic oracles about the destruction of Cairo at the tenth Conjunction of the Earthly Triplicity in 1226 (Arjomand 1998, 267).

Furthermore, as we saw in chapter 7, the theorists of the Fatimid Revolution who wrote the great tenth-century Isma'ili encyclopedia, the *Epistles of the Brethren of Purity*, adopted the prevailing historical/ political astrology: changes in the sovereignty of the dynastic houses (*ahl bayt*) and civil wars occur at the conjunctions of Saturn and Jupiter every twenty years, changes in world domination from one nation to another at the shifts from one triplicity to another every 240 years, and the greatest revolutions of all, changes in religion by the great prophet-lawgivers, occur every 960 (solar) years, or every (lunar) millennium, at the great conjunction of Saturn and Jupiter at the shift back to the initial triplicity of the signs of fire. The Brethren of Purity took a further step to reconcile this duodecimal system of the Zodiac with the heptads of the Judeo-Christian sacred history. The Prophet is made to say: "The life of this world is seven thousand years; I have been sent in the last of these millennia." Each millennium—that is, 960 solar years—is divided into two complete cycles, each consisting of four 120-year quarters of ascension, apogee, decline, and clandestinity. The term *qā'em* (riser/rising man) is given a new apocalyptic meaning by the Isma'ili religious metaphysic. Each 120-year quarter cycle is inaugurated by a *qā'em*, who is followed by six imams. The seventh imam who completes the heptad is the *qā'em* of the next quarter-cycle. The *qā'em* of the Resurrection would be expected at the end of the millennium of Muhammad, which is the final millennium. In short, the *Epistles* deftly combined the political astrology of Abu Mash'ar with the normative theory propounded by Qahtaba in the course of the Hashemite Revolution to buttress the Ismā'ili apocalyptic world history as the cyclical turn of the seven messianic Qa'ims·

Muslim political astrology as the theory of astral determination of revolutions in world history thus provided a conception of gradations of revolution, the highest grade of which was surely meant as a major change in the social and political order, which is just what we mean by the terms "great revolution" and "social revolution" today. Furthermore, modern revolution constitutes an act of foundation legitimating the regime installed by it. In the same way, the conjunction of stars that caused the revolution according to political astrology legitimated the new turn in power of the dynasty (*dawla*) it instituted by astral revolution. The key term, Lord of the (auspicious) Conjunction (*sāhib-qirān*) for the founder of the dynasty, performed just this function and was thus among the motivating factors in a major revolutionary cycle in the Persianate world after the Mongol invasion.

As we have seen, the two conceptions of revolution, the deterministic and the normative, are complementary. Their mutual articulation and reconciliation represented the Islamicate understanding of human agency within the framework of cosmic laws. Bayhaqi applied the notion of divinely ordained transfer of power he found in the Qur'an to the empire of his Ghaznavid patrons: "God, since the creation of Adam, had decreed that kingship be transferred from one religious polity [*ummat*] to another and from one group to another . . . 'Say, O God, possessor of kingship [*mulk*], thou give sovereignty to whomever thou will and take it away from whomever thou will!' (3:26)." Bayhaqi then adds: "Thus one must know that when God's decree removes the robe of kingship [*mulk*] from one group and places it on another, there is divine wisdom and general interest [*maslahat-e 'āmm*] in this for people on this earth."[23]

Bayhaqi knew well the astronomical explanation of major shifts in divinely granted turn in power, termed *inqilāb* and *dawla* alternately. The persistence of the sense of precariousness underlying the conception of dynastic change, accompanied as it usually was by socioeconomic devastation, made possible the continued use of *dawla* also to mean the transfer of sovereignty as it was acquiring the meaning of the state.[24]

THE MAHDIST REVOLUTIONS IN NORTH AFRICA AND THE MAGHREBI CONCEPTION OF REVOLUTION

The Ismā'ili encyclopedists, the Brethren of Purity, incorporated the state-of-the art political astrology into their own millennial idea of revolution that was included in the official ideology of the Fatimid Empire after the conquest of Egypt and Syria in the latter part of the tenth century. In the second half of the eleventh century, while the Fatimid caliphs propagated their ideology through an elaborate bureaucratic apparatus in Cairo that sent out missionaries to shrinking Abbasid domains in Iraq and the rising Seljuq Empire farther east, the Seljuq sultans reacted by supporting the Abbasid caliphate in Baghdad and sustaining the so-called Sunni restoration. Abu Hāmid Muhammad al-Ghazāli (d. 1111), a major architect of this restoration in the east, coupled

---

23. Bayhaqi 1977/1376, 2:1017.
24. Bayhaqi 1997/1376, 1:153; Waldman 1980, 60–61; Arjomand 2010, 234.

his refutation of the Ismāʿili doctrine on behalf of the Abbasid caliph with the development of the Persianate political ethic that informed Bayhaqi's theory of the two powers for the benefits of the Seljuq sultans.

Meanwhile, the Normans had wrestled Sicily from Fatimid rule, and the Christian *Reconquista* in Andalusia was in full force. Abu Bakr Muhammad b. al-Walid al-Tartushi, a Sunni thinker who was displaced from eastern Andalusia to Syria under Fatimid rule and died in Alexandria in 1136 (520 AH), followed the great Ghazāli in reviving the Persianate political ethic and statecraft in *Sirāj al-Muluk* (The lantern of the kings) in a clear, albeit implicit, challenge to the reigning Fatimid ideology. One of Tartushi's followers, Muhammad b. Zafar al-Siqilli (d. 1170 or 72), was a similarly displaced Muslim from Sicily who also drifted across the Mediterranean to the Fatimid domains. Ibn Zafar, who was discovered as a Muslim Machiavelli by his modern Sicilian compatriots, Michele Amari (in 1852) and Gaetano Mosca (in 1936), never adjusted to the life of an exile and died in misery in Syria. He did, however, return to Sicily briefly and dedicated a book to one of the remaining emirs there that is remarkable for drawing on the medieval Persianate political ethic and statecraft for his advice to rulers on how to suppress rebellions and avoid a revolutionary overturn. Ibn Zafar's Machiavellian advice on the control and suppression of mass uprising was given a strikingly appropriate title, *Sulwān al-mutāʿ fi ʿudwān al-atbāʿ* (Consolation for the ruler during the hostility of the subjects)—a title that stands in sharp contrast to those in the advice literature or the so-called mirrors for princes. Although we have no idea how many Muslim princes read his book or heeded his advice, we must note it for its insight into the perceptions of the severely menaced Maghrebi ruling elite in this period of revolutionary turmoil.[25]

The Sicilian Ibn Zafar used the two principles of Persianate statecraft—namely, ruling with justice and maintaining the social hierarchy, to generate a theory of rebellion and to recommend as the remedy to it a combination of repression by force and exercise of benevolent justice. To Ibn Zafar, the maintenance of the social hierarchy means keeping each individual within his estate

---

25. In my opinion, Ibn Zafar's editors go too far in crediting him with a theory of revolution (Kechichian and Dekmejian 2003, 80–87). The theoretical import of his tract—namely, the precept that the ruler should avoid alienating the subjects in the middle ranks of the social hierarchy who could become leaders of the masses and incite them to uprising—is in fact included in our Aristotelian-Paretan model of Integrative Revolution.

and preventing the admixture of different classes of subjects. "This is why monarchs strictly restrain their subjects, each within the limits of his own social stratum, to prevent uprisings." Political turmoil begins when one or some members of the second estate, whose discontent arises from "the arrogance engendered by a long period of prosperity," assume the leadership of the "masses in a state of excitement and tumult."[26] The masses or the populace constitute the third estate of the subjects "that always supports those who advocate causes without questioning either their words or their actions."[27]

It is interesting to note that to support his argument, Ibn Zafar adduces the testament attributed to Ardashir, the leader of the Sasanian Revolution in the early third century, the revolution that established the Sasanian Empire in Iran, and all the more so because Ardashir's testament is cited in the story of a rebellion among the subjects of an Indian king that forced him to flee his capital and take refuge in a frontier fortress. The rebellion was incited by the agents of Ardashir's descendant, Khosraw Anushirvān, and the wise Indian counselor who reminding the satrap who commanded the Persian occupying army during the rebellion of Ardashir's theory of justice as the basis of kingship paid with his life for this admonishment. The injustice of the Persian occupying forces, however, eventually enabled the besieged Indian king to regain the loyalty of his subjects by demonstrating his commitment to the principles of royal justice and thus to quell the rebellion![28]

The Hashemite Revolution began on the eastern periphery of the lands of the Umayyad caliphate and integrated the Persianate world into Islam and gave birth to the theory of astrally determined revolution that was acted out by the Fatimid messianists a century and a half later. The Almohad Revolution, by contrast, began on the remotest and least integrated western periphery of the Muslim world and resulted in the Islamicization and integration of the Berber tribes of the Maghreb. As we have saw in chapter 8, Mahdi Ibn Tumart saw his goal as a revolution, and it is therefore worth spelling out his conception of revolution further. His goal of establishing the absolute transcendence of God against the anthropomorphism of the Almoravids required a revolutionary transformation of their sociopolitical regime. Their anthro-

26. Ibid., 243–44.
27. Ibid., 259.
28. Ibid., 260–61. On Ardashir and the Sasanian Revolution, see Arjomand 2019, ch. 6.

pomorphism made them wrongdoers and oppressors, whose revolutionary overthrow, as Ibn Tumart reminded his followers in his oldest extant exhortation, is enjoined by the Qur'an (26:228): "The oppressors shall surely know by what overturning they will be overturned." He even wrote a letter to the Almoravid ruler 'Ali b. Yusuf warning him of the same coming God-ordained revolution, ending it with the citation of the same verse. The revolutionary struggle was indeed "the *jihād* against the infidels," among whom Ibn Tumart emphatically included nominal "anthropomorphist" Muslims, waged by "your brethren in the religion of God and the Sunna of his Messenger."[29]

Ibn Tumart's Qur'anic conception of revolution did not generate an autonomous sociological theory of revolution, any more than did the Persianate conception developed by Bayhaqi. The theory came from Aristotle and was developed by Ibn Khaldun, who was heir to the Andalusian philosophical tradition developed under the second Almohad ruler, Abu Ya'qub Yusuf (1163–84).

In chapter 8, we met the great Andalusian philosopher, Abu'l-Walid Muhammad Ibn Rushd (Averroes) (d. 1198), who was close to the second Almohad caliph, Abu Ya'qub Yusuf, through the physician, Ibn Tufayl (d. 1185), and who succeeded the latter in that post after his death. The Almohad monarch commissioned Ibn Rushd to publicize philosophy with commentaries on Aristotle's works. When it came to political philosophy, Ibn Rushd wrote a commentary on Plato's *Republic* as Aristotle's *Politics* was not translated into Arabic. In his commentary on Plato's *Republic*, Ibn Rushd discussed the Greek notion of revolutionary transformation as change in the constitution of the polity from one type to another and applied the Aristotelian typology to the decay of regimes in Muslim Spain as lapses from timocracy to oligarchy, and from democracy to tyranny. This was an attempt to shore up the Greek typology of political regimes and did not fit the Andalusian cases he had in mind. Theoretical innovation came with another thinker from the Maghreb, 'Abd al-Rahmān Ibn Khaldun (d. 1406), who criticized Averroes precisely for not seeing that timocracy was a bad definition for the urbanized nobility of Muslim Spain who, as a result of sedentarization, had lost the group solidarity on which honor was based.

Ibn Khaldun's theory of the cycles of rise, senility and disintegration of dynastic states is well known in itself, though not its conscious Greek deriva-

---

29. Baydhaq, 2, 4, 11.

tion.[30] In fact, he explicitly discussed Aristotle's rhetoric and political science as the two branches of knowledge closest to his new positive science of history It is as a good, empirically minded Aristotelian that Ibn Khaldun explains cyclical change in terms of the structural properties of historical Muslim polities, which are grounded in a dual social organization· The social structure he portrays consists of urban centers of civilization and tribal peripheries· Its political order rests on two distinct elements: ruling authority or monarchy (*mulk*) and the instrument for gaining it is group solidarity (*'asabiyya*)· According to Ibn Khaldun, both these elements are generated in tribal societies, but they become separated with the complexity of civilization· Monarchy is transferred to the urban centers, while group solidarity is sustained and reproduced only in the tribal periphery A cyclical motion of rise and fall of tribally originated dynastic states is generated by the interaction between the centers of civilization, in which group solidarity is weakened by education and law-abiding, and the tribal societies of the periphery, where strong group solidarity is constantly reproduced· It is important to note that Ibn Khaldun's term I have translated as "dynastic state" is none other than the above-mentioned *dawla*, the term for revolution in the sense of turn or rotation in power that first gained currency in reference to the Abbasid Revolution and later came to mean the state (whose turn in power was divinely ordained—the claim made by all dynastic states)·

In short, Ibn Khaldun offered as a structural precondition of dynastic change, the endemic translocation of ruling authority or monarchy and group solidarity between the nomadic periphery and the sedentary centers in a dual social structure. He also paves the way for a theoretical move from dynastic change to revolution by considering the *superimposition* of new religiously (or by modern extension, ideologically) based solidarity upon existing, tribal group solidarity. A religious cause and movement, therefore, needs group solidarity if it is to succeed:

> Religious mission cannot materialize without group solidarity. This is so because any mass [political] undertaking by necessity requires group solidarity . . .

The prophets and religious reformers who fail are precisely those who do *not* recognize the significance of group solidarity. Those who succeed, are the

---

30. Dale 2006.

ones who do.³¹ As we saw in chapter 8, Ibn Khaldun took two notable examples of the revolutionary combination of tribal solidarity and religion from the history of the Berbers in his native Maghreb· He showed how the urban-educated religious reformers, the Almoravid leader, 'Abd Allāh b· Yasin (d·1059), and the Almohad leader, the Mahdi Ibn Tumart (d· 1130), unified the Berber tribes by their religious teaching and preaching on the periphery and established puritanical empires of virtue in North Africa and Spain· Ibn Khaldun thus brings in religion explicitly to explain the major cases of dynastic change, which approximate our modern concept of revolution· One of his relevant chapters is titled "the [dynastic] states with broad domination and great ruling authority have their origin in religion, be it either prophethood a calling to God·"

Furthermore, the Almoravid and Almohad cases illustrate that the victory of revolutions beginning in the nomadic periphery is slow. The revolutionaries advance from their remote stronghold gradually with a series of attacks on governmental forces. The end comes after a long time with the military defeat of the dynasty and the capture of its capital and other major cities. The revolt against the dynastic state begins in a remote tribal periphery with the religious leaders who have mobilized the group solidary of the tribesmen. Their victory does not come suddenly but after many indecisive battles until senility takes hold of the ruling dynasty, resulting in the weakening of its group solidarity and a sharp decline in its military and fiscal power.

Ibn Khaldun was heir not just to Greek political philosophy but also to ancient learning more generally. He found the ancient notion of transfer of world domination from one nation to another missing in Muslim historiography, expect in the work of the great Mas'udi, and made it fundamental to his new science of history, rendering it as "transformation of the conditions of nations and races with changes in eras and the passage of time." The nations of the ancient world, the old Persians, Assyrians, Nabataeans, the Tubbas, the Israelites, and the Egyptians had their empires and distinctive institutions. "Then came the later Persians [the Sasanian Empire], the Romans and the Arabs, and these conditions were transformed and through them the customs underwent a revolution [*inqalabat*]." Then follows the most interesting and

---

31. Khaldun, 1:9–42, 143–44 (translation 1:77–83, 168–71, 275–76); Mahdi 1957, 125, 157; Dale 2006, 435–38.

critical point in the description of the rise of Islam as the revolution that initiated the Arabs' divinely ordained turn in power. This shows Ibn Khaldun's theoretical originality in reinterpreting the ancient notion of transfer of sovereignty:

> Then came Islam through the turn in power of the Mudar [*bi-dawla mudar*]—the northern Arabian tribes including Muhammad's Quraysh—and thus transformed [*inqalabat*] all the conditions [of the earlier nations], undergoing yet another revolution [*inqilābatan*].[32]

These, then, are the essentials of the Khaldunian type of revolution. It begins in the periphery with a militarized solidary group that is united by a religious cause. The key factor for explaining the failure of the regime and the success of the insurgents is differential solidarity. The urban base of the regime lacks social cohesion while the already strong group solidarity of the insurgents is strengthened by a unifying religious cause.

I have applied Ibn Khaldun's theory as a type of Integrative Revolution throughout this book, especially to the very revolution that directly inspired his theory—namely, the Almohad Revolution. The implication should be clear: the effort to understand the causes and consequences of the Mahdist revolution in the Maghreb by its greatest historian, Ibn Khaldun, drawing on the political philosophy of Averroes, the third-generation product of the Almohad school of thought, made a lasting contribution to the general theory of revolution.[33]

---

32. Khaldun, 1:29, 167.
33. See further, Arjomand 2019, introduction.

Concluding Remarks

This study in historical sociology has sought to broaden the horizons of Islamic scholarship by developing a comprehensive comparative sociological framework for messianism and its revolutionary consequences. The apocalyptic motivation of revolutionary action is here conceived as a driving force of history but one that collides with structural social and political conditions, as well as with the historical contingencies that channel its revolutionary impetus and affect the direction of its unfolding. Apocalyptic messianism has accordingly been developed as a cultural ideal type for the motivation to revolutionary social action, supplemented by a structural typology of revolutions drawn from world history that models their clustered causes and consequences.

The models we have so far had for revolution are almost exclusively the historical experience of the West in modern times. My structural ideal types are, by contrast, derived from world history through a systematic assessment of the historical experience of other civilizational zones or world regions. They therefore extend the sociological models of revolution systematically by the comparative method and thus broaden our theoretical horizon. To the comparative structural typology or revolutions, we can now add a geographical dimension. All our revolutions begin with intense religiopolitical mobilization in a relatively small area: The Yathrib oasis (Medina) in Mohammad's Constitutional Revolution, the Marv oasis in the Hashemite Revolution, the Kutāma lands in Ifriqiyya in the Fatimid Revolution, and the Masmuda lands around the Sus Valley to the south of the High Atlas Mountains in the

Almohad Revolution.[1] With the consolidation of the revolution in each and every case, the intense revolutionary mobilization is channeled into warfare and conquests that create vast empires. The Muslim empire of conquest was thus created after the unification of Arabia by Muhammad's successors: Abu Muslim's revolutionary armies poured out from Marv eastward to the border of China and westward to Egypt. The Fatimid armies under the Mahdi first extended southward to Sijilmasa and eastward to the Mediterranean coast, where they built Mahdiyya, and then, under al-Mu'izz after intense mobilization owing to the Dajjāl's rebellion, they went farther eastward to Egypt, where the latter built Cairo, and thence to Syria and Arabia, stopping short of overthrowing the Abbasid caliphate in Iraq. The Almohad revolutionary armies under 'Abd al-Mu'min crossed the Atlas Mountains northward to create the Almohad Empire in the Maghreb and Andalusia.[2]

Combining these two sets of ideal types, that of political messianism and those of revolution, I have labeled Muhammad's Constitutive Revolution "realized messianism," underlining the distinctive consequence of its messianic motivation as well as its constitutive role in setting the process and structural pattern for the cycle of three major revolutions in the Islamicate civilization. Using two sets of ideal types instead of one is intended to show how messianism inflected Islam's sociopolitical revolutions and was at the same time channeled by the sociopolitical structure of Muslim societies.

Muhammad's Constitutive Revolution institutionalized the struggle in the path of God, jihad, as the prototypical process of revolution in world history and the pattern to recur in every subsequent Islamicate revolution examined in this book. Muhammad's revolution was also constitutive in that it constituted Islam as a universalist religion of salvation. The revolutionary struggle in the path of extension of the House of Islam (*dār al-islām*) and its intensive penetration of Muslim societies was yet a second process to be replicated by each subsequent Mahdist revolution concurrent with a new wave of Islamicization at its crust. The Abbasid, the Fatimid, and the Almohad revolutions each occurred as the critical component of a new waves of Islamicization on the peripheries of the Muslim empire of conquest: the conversion of Khurasa-

---

1. See maps 1–4. The areas of initial intensive mobilization are shaded in maps 2, 3, and 4.
2. See the campaign arrows in maps 2, 3, and 4.

nian *mawālī* in the Hashemite Revolution, and of the North African Berber tribes in the Fatimid and Almohad revolutions.

To summarize my typological approach to messianism and revolution, what is most remarkable is that the Khaldunian structural model of revolution fits all these cases, just as it does the Maccabean uprising: they are all revolutions from the peripheries of empires—namely, the Judaean periphery of the Seleucid Empire, the Arabian periphery of the Persian, Roman, and Ethiopian empires, and the Khurasanian, Ifriqiyya, and south-Maghrebi peripheries of the Muslim empire. However, the Khaldunian model of revolution was modified to incorporate the conflict between nomads and intellectuals in the process of revolution into the macrostructural dynamics of Ibn Khaldun's model, using his own metaphor, of the transformation of the nomadic wolf founding dynastic states into urban sheep—princes debilitating by civilization. This modification is pioneered for the case of the Fatimid Revolution in chapter 7.

The reconceptualization of the process of revolution is not, however, confined to the Khaldunian ideal type of revolution but is required for all of them. Let me recapitulate the theoretical import of the concept of process in relation to messianism and revolution. The liminality of the revolutionary moment of enthusiasm stimulated by apocalyptic messianism undergoes structuration in the process of revolution consisting of the revolutionary power struggle in the short run and revolutionary constitutional politics in the long term. The teleology of the revolution then unfolds within the sociopolitical structures of our comparative typologies that trace the causes of millennially motivated revolutions to their consequences. An important original contribution of this study is to develop the century-old crude notion of revolutionary process, and put it in a comparative and historical context for the first time. Doing so means relating the process of revolution not only to the integrating but also the centralizing consequences of revolution suggested by our Tocquevillean ideal type, as modified in an earlier study to highlight the role of elites dispossessed by the concentration of power in the dynastic state in providing the leadership of revolutionary movements. In the case of the millennially motivated Mahdist revolutions, the generic process of centralization of power overlaps with the specific process of routinization of messianic charismatic authority. In modern revolutions this process ends with centralizing power in the state the revolutionaries initially sought to destroy. In all our cases of premodern Mahdist revolutions in the Islamicate civilization, by contrast, the routinization of messianic charisma by its conversion to royal charisma of lineage concurrently with the centralization of power takes the form of establishing a strong imperial monarchy: the monarchy of the Quraysh in the Umayyad caliphate, the imperial monarchies/caliphates of the Abbasids in the east, the Fatimid dynasty in North Africa and Syria, and the Mu'minid dynasty in the Maghreb and Andalusia.

The main and most remarkable finding of this book, however, is the close association between Islam as a world religion and the messianically motivated integrative cycle of revolutions in the first six centuries of its history. The cycle begins with the conversion of Arabia to Islam by Muhammad and his first two successors and continues after a century with waves of both extensive and intensive Islamicization of the peoples—non-Arab subjects—of the Muslim empire of conquest first on its eastern and then on its western peripheries.

Just as with their peripheral location in the imperial structure of authority, the teleologies of our Mahdist revolutions are also closely related, though not identical. There is a progression from the universalization of messianism from the nativistic revolution in Judaea to the universalist features of the Abrahamic religions of salvation that ends with Muhammad's Constitutive Revolution. Thereafter, we have a repeating epicycle of Islamic revolutions recapitulating the universalized experience of messianism under a subsequent Mahdi as Muhammad redivivus repeating the Prophet's formative revolutionary struggle in the path of God.

In our comparative framework, Mahdism has been analyzed as a member of the family or type of apocalyptic messianism. The apocalyptic dimension of Mahdism consisted in the expectation of the End of Time and the intense motivation to revolutionary action in liminal time and space generated by this expectation. The messianic dimension of Mahdism consisted in acting in obedience to a Mahdi as Muhammad redivivus and engaging in the absolute politics of the revolutionary moment of enthusiasm under his charismatic leadership. Time and again we have met the replication of the prophetic model—the life of Muhammad, his name, migration, and struggle in the path of God—in each one of the subsequent successful revolutions discussed (and for that matter in the failed Mahdist uprisings not discussed).

The search for the messianic motivation of Muhammad's revolutionary action is arguably the most original contribution of this study. Its origins were discovered in the religious Judaic reaction to Hellenization during the Maccabean revolt in the mid-second century BCE that gave birth to the book of

Daniel and the Dead Sea Scrolls. These scriptures were in fact well known to the Jews of Medina in the seventh century, who acted as a direct conduit for the Qumran messianism. The location of seventh-century Arabia on the triple periphery of empires led to a further original finding concerning the rise of Islam. It is possible that the Qumran apocalyptic messianism was conveyed through early Muslims of the so-called first hijra to Ethiopia who may have brought the Ethiopian book of Enoch back with them. What is more certain, however, is the critical input of Manichaeism from Mesopotamia and the Persian Empire to the east through the sixth-century heresy of Mazdak. The same focus on Mesopotamia and its religious culture helped us identify the obscure Sabeans the Qur'an mentions as a salvation-oriented community of monotheists alongside the Jews and the Christians.

The teleology of realized messianism, however, differs from case to case. It had far-reaching consequences in the case of Muhammad's Constitutive Revolution; it meant the creation of Islam as a world religion and the foundation of its community of believers (*umma*). The consequences of realized messianism were more limited in the cases of the Mahdist revolution and amounted to the appropriation of apocalyptic titles of Qa'im, Mansur, Mahdi, and Hādi by successive Abbasid caliphs, and of Mahdi, Qa'im, and Mansur by the Fatimid caliphs. The assumption of these millennial titles was part of the process of the routinization of charisma of the messianic revolutionary leader for the legitimation of patrimonial monarchy. The routinization of the charisma of Mahdi Ibn Tumart into the charisma of lineage of the Almohad caliphs occurred without any appropriation of messianic titles, since these were already claimed by the rival Mahdis who had been suppressed by 'Abd al-Mu'min, who had founded his own new patrimonial dynasty.

The epicycle of the revolutions of the Muslim empire of conquest from the eighth century onward can metaphorically be thought of as the export of the Constitutive Revolution of Islam. Chronologically, this sets the demolition of the Isma'ili mountain fortresses in 1256 and the conquest of Baghdad and the overthrow of the Abbasid caliphate by the Mongol army in 1258 as the terminal point of our inquiry. The thirteenth century and the first half of the fourteenth century are marked by a striking absence of millennial revolution. This period is distinguished by the Mongol invasion and the formation of a Turko-Mongolian type of nomadic empires of conquest politically, and by the massive spread of Sufism on the religious front. Sufism at this stage must have taken the wind off the sails of revolutionary millennialism, or at any rate did not fan them. It was not until the late fourteenth and early fifteenth century that we witness the transformative impact of Shi'ite apocalyptic messianism on popular Sufism in the form of millennial revolutionary movements. Millennial Mahdism then reappears in Sufi garb, motivating engagement in intense this-worldly struggle against Turko-Mongolian domination. Innerworldly Sufi mysticism is then transformed into the absolute messianic politics of the here and now. The post-Mongol Sufi Mahdism appears in a different world, however, the Persianate world of the Turko-Mongolian nomadic empires, and to understand that would require a different book.[3]

The present book, however, is complete in achieving its stated goal—namely, the critical examination of the formative historical experience of a vast world region shaped by the Islamicate civilization. As such, it should enable us to revisit the timely issues of messianism and modern political religions and thereby give us a better understanding of the apocalyptic politics and its current vicissitudes in Islam—a world religion with a greater potential than any for regenerating political messianism.

---

3. See Arjomand 2022.

ABBREVIATIONS

ENCYCLOPEDIAS

EI   *Encyclopaedia of Islam.* Rev. ed. 11 vols. Leiden: E.J. Brill, 1954–2002.
EIr   *Encyclopaedia Iranica.* 14 vols. 1982–2007. http://www.iranicaonline.org.

JOURNALS

BSOAS	*Bulletin of the School of Oriental and African Studies, London*
IJMES	*International Journal of Middle East Studies*
JAOS	*Journal of the American Oriental Society*
JESHO	*Journal of the Economic and Social History of the Orient*
JIS	*Journal of Islamic Studies*
JJS	*Journal of Jewish Studies*
JNES	*Journal of Near Eastern Studies*
JPS	*Journal of Persianate Studies*
JRAS	*Journal of the Royal Asiatic Society*
JSAI	*Jerusalem Studies in Arabic and Islam*
Lincei	*Accademia Nazionale dei Lincei. Rendiconti Morali*
MW	*Muslim World*
REI	*Revue des Études Islamiques*
RHR	*Revue de l'Histoire des Religions*
RSO	*Rivista degli Studi Orientali*
SI	*Studia Islamica*

PRIMARY SOURCES

1QH	The Thanksgiving Hymns. In G. Vermes, *The Dead Sea Scrolls in English*, 189–236.
1QpHab	Commentary on Habakkuk. In G. Vermes, *The Dead Sea Scrolls in English*, 336–39.
4 Ezra	Metzger, B. M., ed. "The Fourth Book of Ezra." In *The Old Testament Pseudepigrapha*, edited by J. H. Charlesworth, 517–59. Vol 1. New York: Doubleday, 1983.
4Q171	Commentary on Psalms. In G. Vermes, *The Dead Sea Scrolls in English*, 348–52.
4QMMT	Qimron, E., and J. Strugnell, eds. *Qumran Cave 4*. Vol. 5, *Misqat Ma'aśe ha-Torah*. Oxford: Clarendon Press, 1994.
Aghāni	al-Isfahāni, Abu'l-Faraj. *Kitāb al-Aghānī*. Cairo: Matba'at Dār al-Kutub al-'Arabīyah.
Akhbār D	al-Duri, 'A.-'A., and 'A.-J. al-Mutallabi, eds. *Akhbār al-dawla al-'Abbāsiyya wa fihi akhbār al-'Abbās wa waladihi*. Beirut: Dār al-Ṭalī'ah li-al-Ṭibā'ah wa-al-Nashr, 1971.
Akhbār T	al-Dinawari, Abu Hanifa Ahmad b. Dawud. *Akhbār al-tiwāl*. Edited by 'A. 'Amir. Cairo: Wāzarat al-Thaqāfah wa-al-Irshād al-Qawmī, al-Iqlīm al-Janūbī; al-Idārah al-'Āmmah lil-Thaqāfah, 1960.
Ansāb	al-Baladhuri, Ahmad b. Yahya b. Jabir. *Ansāb al-Ashrāf*. The bibliographic information for the individual volumes used in this study is as follows:
	Vol. 2, parts 1 and 2. Edited by W. Madelung. Beirut: Deutsches Orient Institut (in consignment with Klaus Schwarz Verlag Berlin), 2003.
	Vol. 3. Edited by 'A.-'A. Al-Duri. Beirut: Deutsches Orient Institut (in consignment with Klaus Schwarz Verlag Berlin), 1978.
	Vol. 4, part 2. Edited by 'A.-'A. Al-Duri and 'I. 'Uqla. Beirut: Deutsches Orient Institut (in consignment with "Klaus Schwarz Verlag Berlin, 2001.
	Vol. 5. Edited by S. D. Goitein. Jerusalem: Magnes, 1935.
	Vol. 6, part B. Edited by Khalil 'Athamina. Jerusalem: Institute of Asian and African Studies/Hebrew University of Jerusalem, 1993.
Baydhaq	al-Baydhaq, Abu Bakr al-Sanhāji. *Kitāb Akhbār al-Mahdi*. In *Documents inédits d'Histoire Almoahade*, edited and translated by E. Lévi-Provençal, 1–133 (Arabic text), 75–224 (French translation). Textes arabes relatifs à l'histoire de l'Occident musulman. Paris: P. Geuthner, 1928.

CD	Damascus Document. In G. Vermes, *The Dead Sea Scrolls in English*, 95–113.
Epistles	*Rasā'il Ikhwān al-Safā' wa-Khillān al-Wafā'*. 4 vols. Cairo: Maṭba'at al-'Arabīyah, 1928.
Fihrist	Ibn al-Nadim, Muhammad b. Ishāq. *Al-Fihrist*. Edited by Y. A. Tawil. Beirut: Dar al-kutub 'Ilmiyya, 2010.
Fragmenta	*Fragmenta historicorum arabicorum, et quidem pars tertia operis / Kitábo 'l-Oyun wa 'l-hadáïk fi akhbári*. 1871. Edited by M. J. de Goeje. Leiden: E. J. Brill.
Iftitāh	Qādi al-Nu'mān b. Muhammad. *Risāla iftitāh al-da'wa*. Edited by W. al-Qādi. Beirut: Dār al-Thiqāfa, 1970.
Life	A. Guillaume. *The Life of Muhammad: A Translation of Ibn Ishaq's Sirat Rasul Allah*. Oxford: Oxford University Press, 1955. (Page references to the original Arabic text of Ibn Ishāq's *Sira* are given in the margins of Guillaume's translation.)
Maqātil	Abu'l-Faraj al-Isfahāni. *Maqātil al-ṭālibiyyīn*. Cairo: n.p., 1949/1368.
Muqaffa'	'Abdallāh b. al-Muqaffa'. *Risāla fi'l-sahāba*. Translated by Ch. Pellat as *"Conseilleur" du Calife*. Paris: Maisonneuve et Larose, 1976.
Muruj	al-Mas'udi, Abu'l-'Ali b. al-Husayn. *Muruj al-Dhahab wa Ma'ādin al-Jawhar*. Edited by Ch. Pellat. 11 vols. Beirut: Publications de l'Université Libanaise, 1970.
OTP	Charlesworth, J. H., ed. *The Old Testament Pseudepigrapha*. 2 vols. New York: Doubleday, 1983.
Tabari	al-Tabari, Muhammad b. Jarir. *Ta'rikh al-rusul va'l-muluk*. Edited by M. J. de Goeje. 15 vols. Leiden: E. J. Brill, 1879–1901/1985–2000.

The annotated English translation is *The History of al-Tabari*. SUNY Series in Near Eastern Studies. Edited by Ehsan Yarshater. 40 vols. Albany: State University of New York Press, 1985–2002. The bibliographic information for the individual volumes used in this study is as follows:

Vol. 21. *The Victory of the Marwānids*. Translated by M. Fishbein. 1990.

Vol 25. *The End of Expansion*. Translated by Kh. Y. Blankinship. 1989.

Vol. 26. *The Waning of the Umayyad Caliphate*. Translated by C. Hillenbrand. 1987.

Vol. 27. *The 'Abbāsid Revolution*. Translated by J. A. Williams. 1985.

Vol. 28. *'Abbasid Authority Affirmed*. Translated by J. D. McAuliffe. 1995.

	Vol. 29. *Al-Mansur and al-Mahdi*. Translated by H. Kennedy. 1990.
Tanbih	al-Masʿudi, Abu'l-ʿAli b. al-Husayn. *Al-Tanbih wa'l-ishrāf*. Edited by M.J. de Goeje. Leiden: E.J. Brill, 1894. Reprint 1967.
Tarjuma	Sādiqi, J.M., ed. *Tarjuma-ye Tafsir-e Tabari*. 8 vols. in 4. Tehran: Tūs, 1993.

REFERENCES

'Abbās, I., ed. 1988. *'Abd al-Ḥamīd ibn Yaḥyā al-kātib wa mā tabqā min rasā'ilihi wa rasā'il Sālim Abi'l-'Alā'*. Amman: Dār al-shurūq.
Abbott, N. 1967. *Studies in Arabic Literary Papyri II: Qur'ānic Commentary and Tradition*. Chicago: University of Chicago Press.
'Abdallāh b. al-Muqaffa'. 1976. *Risāla fi'l-saḥāba*. Translated by Ch. Pellat as *"Conseilleur" du Calife*. Paris: Maisonneuve et Larose, 1976.
Abel, F. M. 1952. *Histoire de la Palestine*. 2 vols., Paris: Gabalda.
Agha, S. S. 1997. "A Viewpoint of the Murji'a in the Umayyad Period." *JIS* 8 (1): 1–42.
———. 2003. *The Revolution Which Toppled the Umayyads: Neither Arab nor 'Abbāsid*. Leiden: E. J. Brill, 2003.
Aguadé, J. 1979. "Messianismus zur Zeit der frühen Abbasiden: Das Kitāb al-Fitan des Nu'aim ibn Hammād." PhD diss., Eberhard-Karls-Universität, Tübingen.
Ahlwardt, W. 1883. *Anonyme Arabische Chronik*. Greifswald: Selbstverlag.
Al-Azmeh, A. 2007. *The Times of History: Universal Topics in Islamic Historiography*, Budapest: Central European University Press.
———. 2014a. *The Emergence of Islam in Late Antiquity: Allah and his People*. Cambridge: Cambridge University Press.
———. 2014b. *The Arabs and Islam in Late Antiquity: A Critique of Approaches to Arabic Sources*. Berlin: Gerlach Press.
———. 2018a "Paleo-Islam: Transfigurations of Late Antique Religion." In *A Companion to Religion in Late Antiquity*, edited by J. Lőssl and N. J. Baker-Brian, 345–68. Oxford: Wiley Blackwell.
———. 2018b. "Implausibility and Probability in Studies of Paleo-Qur'anic Genesis." In *Islam in der Moderne, Moderne in Islam*, edited by F. Zemmin, J. Stephan and M. Corrado, 15–40. Leiden: E. J. Brill.
———. 2019. "Pagan Arabs, Arabian Prophecy, and Monotheism." Review of *Islam and its Past: Jahiliyya, Late Antiquity, and the Qur'an*, edited by Carol Bakhos and

Michael Cook. *Marginalia Review*, March 1, 2019. https://themarginaliareview.com/pagan-arabs-arabian-prophecy-monotheism/.

Amir-Moezzi, M.-A. 1992. *Le Guide divin dans le Shi'isme original: Aux sources de l'ésotérisme en Islam*. Paris: Lagrasse.

———. 2006. "Considérations sur l'expression Din 'Ali." In *La religion discrete: croyances et pratiques spirituelles dans l'islam* shi'ite, 19–47. Paris: Librairie Philosophique J. Vrin.

———. 2016. "Muhammad le Paraclet et 'Ali le Messie: Nouvelles remarques sur les origins de l'Islam et de l'imamologie shi'ite. " In *L'Ésotérisme Shi'ite: Ses sources et ses prolongements*, edited by M. A. Amir-Moezzi, M. De Cillis, D. de Smet, and O. Mir-Kasimov, 19–54. Turnhout: Brepols.

Amir-Moezzi, M. A., M. De Cillis, D. de Smet, and O. Mir-Kasimov, eds. 2016. *L'Ésotérisme Shi'ite: Ses sources et ses prolongements*. Turnhout: Brepols.

Anthony, S. W. 2012. "The Mahdi and Treasures in Tāleqān." *Arabica* 59:459–83.

Arjomand, S. A. 1984. *The Shadow of God and the Hidden Imam: Religion, Political Organization and Societal Change in Shi'ite Iran from the Beginning to 1890*, Chicago: University of Chicago Press.

———. 1994. "'Abd Allah ibn al-Muqaffa' and the 'Abbasid Revolution." *Journal of Iranian Studies* 27 (1–4): 9–36.

———. 1998. "Islamic Apocalypticism in the Classical Period." In *The Encyclopedia of Apocalypticism*, edited by B. McGinn, 238–83. Vol. 2. New York: Continuum.

———. 2000. "Ġayba." *EIr* 10:341–44.

———. 2001. "Perso-Indian Statecraft, Greek Political Science and the Muslim Idea of Government." *International Sociology* 16 (3): 455–73.

———. 2003. "Medieval Persianate Political Ethic." *Studies on Persianate Societies* 1:3–28.

———. 2007. "Islam in Iran. vi. The Concept of Mahdi in Sunni Islam" *EIr* 14: 134–36.

———. 2009. "The Constitution of Medina: A Socio-legal Interpretation of Muhammad's Acts of Foundation of the *Umma*." *IJMES* 41 (4): 555–75.

———. 2010. "Legitimacy and Political Organisation: Caliphs, Kings and Regimes." In *The New Cambridge History of Islam*, edited by R. Irwin, 225–73. Vol. 4, *Islamic Cultures and Societies to the End of the Eighteenth Century*. Cambridge: Cambridge University Press.

———. 2012. "The Conception of Revolution in Persianate Political Thought." *JPS* 5 (1): 1–16.

———. 2014. "Crystallization of Islam and the Developmental Paths in the Islamicate Civilization." In *Social Theory and Regional Studies in the Global Age*, edited by S. A. Arjomand, 203–20. Albany: State University of New York Press.

———. 2019. *Revolution: Structure and Meaning in World History*. Chicago: University of Chicago Press.

———. 2022. *Revolutions of the End of Time: Apocalypse, Revolution, and Reaction in the Persianate World*. Leiden: E. J. Brill.

al-Ashʿarī al-Qummī, Saʿd b. ʿAbd Allah. 1963. *Kitāb al-Maqālāt wa'l-Firaq*. Edited by M. J. Mashkur. Tehran: n.p., 1963.
———. 2021. "Manichaeism as a World Religion and its influence on Islam." *JPS* 14:1–2.
Asmussen, J. P., ed. and trans. 1975. *Manichaean Literature: Representative Texts Chiefly from Middle Persian and Parthian Writings*. Delmar, NY: Scholars Facsimiles & Reprints.
ʿAtwān, H. 1980. *Sīrat al-Walīd b. Yazīd*. Cairo: Dār al-Maʿārif.
Averroes. 1967. *On the Harmony of Religion and Philosophy (Kitāb faṣl al-maqāl)*. Translated by G. F. Hourani. London: Luzac.
al-Azdi, Yazid b. Muhammad. 1967, *Tārīkh al-Mawṣil*. Edited by ʿA. Habiba. Cairo: n.p..
Bahār, M.-T. 1935. Introduction to *Tārikh-e Sistān*, لو – ۱. Tehran: n.p.
al-Baydhaq, Abu Bakr al-Sanhāji. 1928. *Kitāb Akhbār al-Mahdi*. In *Documents inédits d'Histoire Almoahade*, translated and edited by E. Lévi-Provençal, 1–133 (Arabic), 75–224 (French). Paris: Librairie Orientaliste.
Baker, K. M. 2013. "Revolution 01." *Journal of Modern European History* 11 (2): 187–219.
al-Bakri. 1911–13. *Kitāb al-masālik wa'l-mamālik (Description de l'Afrique septenoriale)*. Edited and translated by M. G. De Slane. Algiers: n.p.
al-Baladhuri, Ahmad b. Yahya b. Jabir. 1935–2002. *Ansāb al-Ashrāf*. Vols. 2–6. (Please see the abbreviations for each volume's full bibliographic details.)
Balʿami, Abu ʿAli. 1987/1366. *Tārikhnāma-ye Balʿami*. Edited by M. Rawshan. 3 vols. Tehran: Nashr-e Naw.
Baneth, D. Z. H. 1971. "What Did Muhammad Mean When He Called His Religion Islam? The Original Meaning of *Aslama* and Its Derivatives." *Israel Oriental Studies* 1:183–90.
Barthold, W. (1928) 1968. *Turkestan down to the Mongol Invasion*. Translated by H. A. R. Gibb. Reprint. London: Luzac.
Bashear, S. 1997. *Arabs and Others in Early Islam*. Princeton, NJ: Darwin Press.
———. 2004. "Hanifiyya and Hajj." In *Studies in Early Islamic Tradition*, XIV: 1–21. Jerusalem: Max Schloessinger Foundation.
Bates, M. 2003. "Khurasani Revolutionaries and al-Mahdi's Title"." In *Culture and Memory in Medieval Islam: Essays in Honour of Wilferd Madelung*, edited by Farhad Daftary and Josef W. Meri, 279–317. London: I. B. Tauris.
Bayhaqi, Abu'l-Fazl Mohammad b. Hosyan. 1997/1376. *Tārikh-e Bayhaqi*. Edited by M. Dāneshpazhuh. 2 vols. Tehran: Hirmand.
Bazargan, M. 1976/1335, 1981/1360–98. *Sayr-e tahavvol-e Qur'an*. Vol 1. Tehran: Qalam. Vol. 2. Tehran: Sherkat-e Enteshār.
Benkheira, M. 2013. "Onomastique et religion: à propos d'une réforme du nom propre au cours des premiers siècles de l'Islam." In *Les non-dits du nom' Onomastique et documents en terre d'Islam: Mélanges offerts à Jacqueline Sublet*, edited by C. Müller and M. Roiland-Rouabbah, 319–56. Damascus: n.p.

Bennison, A. K. 2016. *The Almoravid and Almohad Empires*. Edinburgh: Edinburgh University Press.

Bernheimer, T. 2006. "The Revolt of 'Abdallāh b. Mu'āwyia: A Reconsideration through the Coinage." *BSOAS* 69 (3): 381–93.

Berquist, J. L. 1995. *Judaism in Persia's Shadow*. Minneapolis: Fortress Press.

Bickerman, E. 1947. *The Maccabees*. New York: Schocken Books.

———. 1979. *The God of the Maccabees*. Translated by H. R. Moehring. Leiden: E. J. Brill.

———. (1935) 1980. "La Carte séleucide de Jérusalem." In *Studies in Jewish and Christian History*, 44–85. Part 2. Leiden: E. J. Brill.

Bidez, J., and F. Cumont. 1938. *Les Mages hellénisés*. 2 vols. Paris: Les Belles Lettres.

Bijlefeld, W. A. B. 1969. "A Prophet and More Than a Prophet? Some Observations on the Qur'anic Use of the Terms 'Prophet' and 'Apostle.'" *MW* 59 (1): 1–28.

Biruni, Abu Rayhān Muhammad b. Ahmad. 1879. *The Chronology of Ancient Nations: An English Version of the Arabic Text of the* Athâr-ul-Bâkiya *of Albîrûnî, or "Vestiges of the Past," Collected and Reduced to Writing by the Author in A.H. 390–1, A.D. 1000*. Translated and edited by C. E. Sachau. London: W. H. Allen.

Bishop, E. 1958. "The Qumran Scrolls and the Qur'an." *MW* 48 (3): 223–36.

Blankinship, Kh. Y. 1988. "The Tribal Factor in the 'Abbasid Revolution'." *JAOS* 108 (4): 589–602.

———. 1994. *The End of the Jihad State: The Reign of Hisham ibn 'Abd al-Malik and the Collapse of the Umayyads*. Albany: State University of New York Press.

Blenkinsopp, J. 1981. "Interpretation and the Tendency to Sectarianism." In *Jewish and Christian Self-Definition*, edited by E. P. Sanders, 1–26. Vol. 2. Philadelphia: Fortress Press.

Bligh-Abramski, I. 1988. "Evolution versus Revolution: Umayyad Elements in the Abbasid Regime." *Der Islam* 65:226–43.

Bolshakov, O. G. 1998. "Central Asia under the Early 'Abbasids." In *History of Civilizations of Central Asia*, edited by S. M. Asimov and C. E. Bosworth, 25–40. Paris: UNESCO.

Bonine, M. 1990. "The Sacred Direction and City Structure: A Preliminary Analysis of the Islamic Cities of Morocco." *Muqarnas* 7:50–72.

Boyce, M. 1979. *Zoroastrians: Their Religious Beliefs and Practices*. London: Routledge.

———. 1984. "On the Antiquity of Zoroastrian Apocalyptic." *BSOAS* 47 (1): 57–75.

Boyce, M., and F. Grenet. 1991. *A History of Zoroastrianism*. Vol. 3. Leiden: E. J. Brill.

Bravmann, M. M. 1972. *The Spiritual Background of Early Islam: Studies in Ancient Arab Concepts*. Leiden: Brill.

Brett, M. M. 1994. "The Mim, the 'Ayn, and the Making of Ismā'ilism." *BSOAS* 57:25–39.

———. 1996. "The Realm of the Imam: The Fatimids in the Tenth Century." *BSOAS* 59:431–49.

———. 1999. "The Lamp of the Almohads: Illumination as a Political Idea in Twelfth-Century Morocco." In *Ibn Khaldun and the Medieval Maghrib*, 1–27. London: Ashgate Variorum.

———. 2001. *The Rise of Fatimids*. Leiden: E.J. Brill.

———. 2017. *The Fatimid Empire*. Edinburgh: Edinburgh University Press.

Brown, P. 1971. *The World of Late Antiquity, AD 150–750*. London: Thames & Hudson.

Browne, E. G., 1902. *Literary History of Persia*. 4 vols. London: T. Fisher Unwin.

Busse, H. 1991. "Jerusalem in the Story of Muhammad's Night Journey and Ascension." *JSAI* 14:1–40.

Butterworth, Ch. 1975. "New Light on the Political Philosophy of Averroes." In *Essays on Islamic Philosophy and Science*, edited by G. Hourani, 118–27. Albany: State University of New York Press.

Cahen, C. 1961. "La Changeante portée sociale de quelques doctrines religieuses." In *L'Élaboration de l'Islam*, 5–22. Paris: Presses Universitaires de France.

———. 1963. "Points de vue sur la 'Révolution Abbaside.'" *Revue Historique*: 292–337.

Calder, N. 1993. *Studies in Early Muslim Jurisprudence*. Oxford: Clarendon Press.

Canard, M. 1952. "L'Autobiographie d'un chambellan du Mahdî 'Obeidallâh le Fâtimide." *Hespéris* 39:280–329.

Casanova, P. 1911. *Mohammed et la fin du monde*. Paris: Paul Guethner.

———. 1924. "Idris et 'Ouzair." *Journal Asiatique* 205:357–60.

Chabbi, J. 1997. *Le Seigneur des tribus*. Paris: Noêsis.

Charlesworth, J. H. 1983. *The Old Testament Pseudepigrapha*. 2 vols. New York: Doubleday.

Chelhod, J. 1955. *Le Sacrifice chez les Arabes*. Paris: Presses Universitaires de France.

———. 1962. "Mythe chez les Arabs." *L'Homme* 2 (1): 66–90.

Cohn, N. 1957. *The Pursuit of the Millennium: Revolutionary Messianism in Medieval and Reformation Europe and its Bearing on Modern Totalitarian Movements*. London: Weidenfeld and Nicolson.

Collins, J. J. 1975. "The Mythology of Holy War in Daniel and the Qumran War Scroll: Point of Transition in Jewish Apocalyptic." *Vetus Testamentum* 25:596–612.

———. 1984. *The Apocalyptic Imagination: An Introduction to the Jewish Matrix of Christianity*. New York: Crossroads.

———. 1985. "Daniel and His Social World." *Interpretation: A Journal of Political Philosophy* 39 (2): 131–43.

———. 1991. "Genre, Ideology and Social Movements in Jewish Apocalypticism." In *Mysteries and Revelations: Apocalyptic Studies since the Uppsala Colloquium*, edited by J. J. Collins and J. H. Charlesworth, 11–32. *Journal for the Study of the Pseudepigrapha*. Supplement Series 9. Sheffield: Sheffield Academic Press.

———. 1993. *Daniel: A Commentary on the Book of Daniel*. Minneapolis: Fortress Press.

———. 1995. *The Scepter and the Star: The Messiahs of the Dead Sea Scrolls and Other Ancient Literature*. New York: Doubleday.

———. 1997. *Apocalypticism in the Dead Sea Scrolls*. London: Routledge.

Colp, C. 1983. "Development of Religious Thought." In *The Cambridge History of Iran*, edited by E. Yarshater, 819–65. Vol. 3, part 2, *The Seleucid, Parthian and Sasanian Periods*. Cambridge: Cambridge University Press.

———. 1984–86. "Das Siegel der Propheten." *Orientalia Suecana* 33–35:71–83.

Conrad, L. 1991. "Syriac Perspectives on Bilād al-Shām during the 'Abbasid Period." In *Bilād al-Shām during the 'Abbasid Period*, edited by M. A. al-Bakhit and R. Schick, 1–44. Amman: History of Bilād al-Shām Committee.

Cook, D. 2002. *Studies in Muslim Apocalyptic*. Princeton, NJ: Darwin Press.

Cook, M. 2000. *Commanding Right and Forbidding Wrong in Islamic Thought*. Cambridge: Cambridge University Press.

Cottaruzza, M. 2018. "Political Religion, Apocalypticism, and the End of History: Some Considerations." In *The Apocalyptic Complex: Perspectives, Histories, Persistence*, edited by N. al-Baghdadi, D. Marno, and Matthias Riedl, 203–20. Budapest: Central University Press.

Crone, P. 1980. *Slaves on Horses: The Evolution of the Islamic Polity*. Cambridge: Cambridge University Press.

———. 1987. *Meccan Trade and the Rise of Islam*. Princeton, NJ: Princeton University Press."

———. 1989. "On the Meaning of the 'Abbasid Call to *al-Rida*." In *The Islamic World: Essays in Honor of Bernard Lewis*, edited by C. E. Bosworth, C. Issawi, R. Savory, and A. L. Udovitch, 95–111. Princeton, NJ: Darwin Press.

———. 1991. "Mawla." *EI* 6:874–82.

———. 1993. "Al-Muhallab b. Abi Sufra." *EI* 7:357.

———. 1994a. "The First-Century Concept of *Hiǧra*." *Arabica* 41:352–87.

———. 1994b. "Were the Qays and Yemen of the Umayyad Period Political Parties?" *Der Islam* 71:1–57.

———. 1998. "The 'Abbasid Abnā' and Sāsānid Cavalrymen." *JRAS*, Series 3, 8 (1): 1–19.

———. 2007. "Quraysh and the Roman Army: Making Sense of the Meccan Leather Trade." *BSOAS* 70 (1): 63–88.

———. 2010. "The Religion of the Qur'ānic Pagans: God and the Lesser Deities." *Arabica* 57 (2): 151–200.

———. 2012. *The Nativist Prophets of Early Islamic Iran: Rural Revolt and Local Zoroastrianism*. Cambridge: Cambridge University Press.

———. 2013. "The Book of Watchers in the Qurān." In *Exchange and Transmission across Cultural Boundaries: Philosophy, Mysticism, and Science in the Mediterranean World*, edited by H. Ben-Shammai, S. Shaked, and S. Stroumsa, 16–51. Jerusalem: Israel Academy of Sciences and Humanities.

Crone, P., and M. Cook. 1977. *Hagarism: The Making of the Islamic World*. Cambridge: Cambridge University Press.

Crone, P., and M. Hinds. 1986. *God's Caliph: Religious Authority in the First Century of Islam*. Cambridge: Cambridge University Press.

Cumont, F. 1909. "La plus ancienne géographie astrologique." *Klio* 9:263–73.

———. 1931. "La fin du monde selon les mages occidentaux." *RHR* 104:29–96.
Daftary, F. 1990. *The Ismā'ilis: Their History and Doctrines*. Cambridge: Cambridge University Press.
———. 2003. "Hasan Sabbāh." *EIr* 12:34–37.
———. 2018. "The Early Ismaili Imamate: Background to the Establishment of the Fatimid Caliphate." In *The Fatimid Caliphate: Diversity of Traditions*, edited by F. Daftary and S. Jiwa, 10–21. London: I. B. Tauris.
Dale, S. F. 2006. "Ibn Khaldun: The Last Greek and the First *Annaliste* Historian." *IJMES* 38 (3): 431–51.
Dancy, J. C. 1972. *The Cambridge Bible Commentary: The Shorter Books of the Apocrypha*. Cambridge: Cambridge University Press.
Daniel, Elton L. 1979. *The Political and Social History of Khurasan under Abbasid Rule, 747–820*. Minneapolis: Bibliotheca Islamica.
———. 1996. "The 'Ahl al-Taqādum and the Problem of the Constituency of the Abbasid Revolution in the Merv Oasis." *JIS* 7 (2): 150–79.
———. 1997. "Arabs, Persians, and the Advent of the Abbasids Reconsidered." *JOAS* 117 (3): 452–548.
Daryaee, T. 1999. "The Coinage of Queen Bōrān and Its Significance for Late Sāsānian Imperial Ideology." *Bulletin of the Asia Institute*, n.s., 13:77–82.
Davenport, G. L. 1971. *The Eschatology of the Book of Jubilees*. Leiden: E. J. Brill.
De Blois, F. de 1986. "The Abu Sa'idis or So-called 'Qarmatians' of Bahrayn." *Proceedings of the Seminar for Arabian Studies* 16:13–21.
———. 1995. "The 'Sabians' (*Sābi'un*) in Pre-Islamic Arabia." *Acta Orientalia* 56:39–61.
———. 2002. "Naṣrānī, (Ναζωραῖος) and ḥanīf (ἐθνικός): Studies on the Religious Vocabulary of Christianity and of Islam." *BSOAS* 65 (1):1–30.
———. 2011. "Islam in the Arabian Context." In *The Qur'ān in Context: Historical and Literary Investigations into the Qur'ānic Milieu*, edited by A. Neuwirth, N. Sinai, and M. Marx, 615–24. Leiden: Brill.
De Goeje, M. J. 1886. *Mémoire sur les Carmathes du Bahraïn et les Fatimides*. Leiden: E. J. Brill.
De la Vessière, É. 2007. *Samarcande et Samarra: élites de l'Asie centrale dans l'empire abbaside*. Paris: Association pour l'avancement des études iraniennes.
Dennett, D. C. 1939. "Marwān ibn Muhammad: The Passing of the Umayyad Caliphate." PhD diss., Harvard University.
———. 1950. *Conversion and the Poll Tax in Early Islam*. Cambridge, MA: Harvard University Press.
Denny, F. M. 1977. "*Umma* in the Constitution of Medina." *JNES* 36 (1): 37–47.
De Smet, D. 2016. "Les racines docéiste de l'imamologie shi'ite." In *L'Ésotérisme Shi'ite: Ses sources et ses prolongements*, edited by M. A. Amir-Moezzi, M. De Cillis, D. de Smet, and O. Mir-Kasimov, 87–112. Turnhout: Brepols.
Dimant, D. 1994. "Apocalyptic Texts at Qumran." In *The Community of the Renewed Covenant*, edited by E. Ulrich and J. VanderKam. Christianity and Judaism in Antiquity, vol. 10. South Bend, IN: Notre Dame University Press.

———. 1995. "The Qumran Manuscripts: Content and Significance." In *Time to Prepare the Way in the Wilderness: Papers on the Qumran Scrolls by Fellows of the Institute for Advanced Studies of the Hebrew University, Jerusalem, 1989–1990*, edited by D. Dimant and L. Schiffman, 23–58. Studies on the Texts of the Desert of Judah, vol. 16. Leiden: E. J. Brill.

al-Dinawari, Abu Hanifa Ahmad b. Dawud. 1960. *Akhbār al-tiwāl*. Edited by 'A. 'Amir. Cairo: Wāzarat al-Thaqāfah wa-al-Irshād al-Qawmī, al-Iqlīm al-Janūbī; al-Idārah al-'Āmmah lil-Thaqāfah.

Donner, F. M. 1981. *The Early Islamic Conquests*. Princeton, NJ: Princeton University Press.

———. 1986. "The Formation of the Islamic State." *JAOS* 106 (2): 283–96.

———. 1993. "The Growth of Military Institutions in the Early Caliphate and Their Relation to Civilian Authority." *Al-Qantara: Revista de Estudios Árabes* 14: 311–26.

———. 1998. *Narrative of Islamic Origins: The Beginning of Islamic Historical Writing*. Princeton, NJ: Darwin Press.

———. 2008a. Introduction to *The Expansion of the Early Islamic State*, edited by F. M. Donner, xiii–xxi. London: Ashgate Variorum.

———. 2008b. "The Qur'an in Recent Scholarship: Challenges and Desiderata." In *The Qur'an in Its Historical Context*, edited by G. S. Reynolds, 29–50. London: Routledge.

———. 2010. *Muhammad and the Believers at the Origins of Islam*. Cambridge, MA: Belknap Press of Harvard University Press.

Dostal, W. 1991. "Mecca before the Time of the Prophet—attempt of an Anthropological Interpretation." *Der Islam* 68 (2): 193–231.

Drijvers, H. J. W. 1974. "Mani und Bardisan." In *Mélanges d'Histoire des Religions offerts à Henri-Charles Puech*, 461–69. Paris: Presses Universitaires de France.

Du Bois, J.-D. 2016. "La figure du prophète dans la religion manicheéenne." In *L'Ésotérisme Shi'ite: Ses sources et ses prolongements*, edited by. M. A. Amir-Moezzi, M. De Cillis, D. de Smet, and O. Mir-Kasimov, 113–25. Turnhout: Brepols.

Duchesne-Guillemin, J. 1979. "Cor de Yimā et trompette d'Isrāfīl." *Comptes rendus de l'Académie des Inscriptions* 5:539–49.

al-Duri, 'A.-'A. 1981. "Al-Fikra al-mahdiyya bayn al-da'wa al-'abbāsiyya wa'l-'aṣr al-'abbāsial-awwal." In *Studia Islamica and Arabica: Festschrift for Ihsān 'Abbās*, edited by Wadād al-Qāḍi, 123–35. Beirut: American University of Beirut.

al-Duri, 'A.-'A., and 'A.-J. al-Mutallabi, eds. 1971. *Akhbār al-dawla al-'Abbāsiyya wa fihi akhbār al-'Abbās wa waladihi*. Beirut: Dār al-Ṭalī'ah li-al-Ṭibā'ah wa-al-Nashr.

Eckhardt, B. 2016. "The Seleucid Administration of Judea, the High Priesthood and the Rise of the Hasmoneans." *Journal of Ancient History* 4 (1): 57–87.

Eddy, S. K. 1961. *The King is Dead: Studies in the Near Eastern Resistance to Hellenism*. Lincoln: University of Nebraska Press.

Elad, A. 1995. "Aspects of the Transition from the Umayyad to the 'Abbasid Caliphate." *JSAI* 19:89–112.

———. 2000. "The Ethnic Composition of the 'Abbasid Revolution: A Reevaluation of Some Recent Research." *JSAI* 24:246–326.
Enayat, H. 1977. "An Outline of the Political Philosophy of Rasā'il of the Ikhwān al-Safā'." In *Ismā'ili Contributions to Islamic Culture*, edited by S. H. Nasr, 25–49. Tehran: Imperial Iranian Academy of Philosophy.
Eqbāl, 'A. (1927/1306) 2003/1382. *Sharh-e hāl-e 'Abdallāh Ibn al-Muqaffa'*. Tehran: Asātir.
———. 1933/1312. *Khāndān-e Nawbakhti*. Tehran: Tahuri.
Erder, Y. 1990. "The Origins of the Name Idris in the Qur'ān: A Study of the Influence of Qumran Literature on Early Islam." *JNES* 49 (4): 339–50.
———. 1994. "The Karaites' Sadducee Dilemma." *Israel Oriental Studies* 14: 195–226.
Farias, P. F de Moraes. 1968. "The Almohads: Some Questions Concerning the Character of the Movement During its Periods of Closest Contact with the Western Sudan." *Bulletin de l'Institut Fondamental d'Afrique Noire* 29B: 794–878.
Ferdawsi, Abu'l-Qāsem. 1995/1374. *Shāhnāma*. Moscow ed. 9 vols. Tehran: n.p.
Fierro, M. 1996. "On Al-Fātimi and Al-Fātimiyyun." *JSAI* 20:130–61.
———. 1999. "The Legal Policies of the Almohad Caliphs and Ibn Rushd's *Bidāyat al-Mujtahid*." *Journal of Islamic Studies* 10 (3): 226–48.
———. 2000a. "Le Mahdi Ibn Tûmart et al-Andalus: l'élaboration de la légitimité almohade." *Revue du monde musulman et de la Méditerranée* 91:107–24.
———. 2000b. "Spiritual Alienation and Political Activism: The Ġurabā' in al-Andalus during the Sixth/Twelfth Century." *Arabica* 47 (2): 230–60.
———. 2010. "The Almohads (524–668/1130–1269) and the Hafsids (627–932/1229–1526)." In *The New Cambridge History of Islam*, edited by M. Fierro, 66–105. Vol. 2, *The Western Islamic World: Eleventh to Eighteenth Centuries*. Cambridge: Cambridge University Press, pp.
Finkelstein, L. 1989a. "The Men of the Great Synagogue (*circa* 400–170 B.C.E.)." In *The Cambridge History of Judaism*, edited by W. D. Davies and L. Finkelstein, 229–44. Vol. 2, *The Hellenistic Age*. Cambridge: Cambridge University Press.
———. 1989b. "The Pharisaic Leadership after the Great Synagogue (170 B.C.E.-135 C.E.)." In *The Cambridge History of Judaism*, edited by W. D. Davies and L. Finkelstein, 245–77. Vol. 2, *The Hellenistic Age*. Cambridge: Cambridge University Press.
Fletcher, M. de Gogorza. 1988–89. "The Anthropological Context of Almohad History." *Hespéris-Tamuda* 26–27:25–51.
Flint, P. W. 1995. "The Prophet Daniel at Qumran." Paper presented at the Annual Convention of the American Academy of Religion in Philadelphia, PA.
Flusser, D. 1972. "The Four Empires in the Fourth Sibyl and the Book of Daniel." *Israel Oriental Studies* 2:148–75.
———. 1982. "Hystaspes and John of Patmos." In *Irano-Judaica: Studies Relating to Jewish Contacts with Persian Culture Throughout the Ages*, edited by Sh. Shaked, 12–75. Jerusalem: Ben-Zvi Institute.

Foss, C. 2010. "Muʿāwiya's State." In *Money, Power and Politics in Early Islamic Syria: A Review of Current Debates*, edited by John Haldon, 75–96. Farnham: Ashgate.
Fowden, G. 1993. *Empire to Commonwealth: Consequences of Monotheism in Late Antiquity*. Princeton, NJ: Princeton University Press.
———. 2001. "Varieties of Religious Community." In *Interpreting Late Antiquity: Essays on the Postclassical World*, edited by G. W. Bowersock, P. Brown, and O. Grabar, 82–106. Cambridge, MA: Harvard University Press.
———. 2014. *Before and After Muhammad: The First Millennium Refocused*. Princeton, NJ: Princeton University Press.
Fragmenta historicorum arabicorum, et quidem pars tertia operis / Kitābo 'l-Oyun wa 'l-hadāïk fi akhbári. 1871. Edited by M. J. de Goeje. Leiden: E. J. Brill.
Fricaud, É. 1997. "Les *talaba* dans la société almohade." *Al-Qantara* 18:33–87.
Fromherz, A. J. 2013. *The Almohads: The Rise of an Islamic Empire*. London: I. B. Tauris.
Gabrieli, F. 1935a. "Al-Walīd ibn Yazīd. Il califfo e il poeta." *RSO* 15:1–64.
———. 1935b. *Il Califfato di Hishâm: Studi di storia omayyade*. Alexandria: n.p.
Garcia Martinez, F. 1988. "Qumran Origins and Early History: A Groningen Hypothesis." *Folia Orientalia* 15:113–36.
———. 1992. *Qumran and Apocalyptic: Studies on the Aramaic Texts from Qumran*. Leiden: E. J. Brill.
Gardizi, Abu Saʿid ʿAbd al-Hayy b. Zahhāk. 1984/1363. *Tārikh-e Gardizi*. Edited by ʿAbd al-Hayy Habibi. Tehran: Donya-ye Ketāb.
Gibbon, E. 1932. *The Decline and Fall of the Roman Empire*. 2 vols. New York: Modern Library.
Gignoux, P. 1974. "La Signification du voyages extra-terrestre dans l'eschatologie mazdéenne." In *Mélanges d'Histoire des Religions offerts à Henri-Charles Puech*, 63–69. Paris: Presses Universitaires de France.
Gil, M. 1987. "The Medinan Opposition to the Prophet." *JSAI* 10:65–96.
———. 1992. "The Creed of Abu ʿĀmir." *Israel Oriental Studies* 11:9–57.
Gilliot, C. 1998. "Les 'Informateurs" juifs et chrétiens de Muhammad." *JSAI* 22:86–124.
———. 2006. "Creation of a Fixed Text." In *The Cambridge Companion to the Qurʾān*, edited by J. D. McAuliffe, 41–58. Cambridge: Cambridge University Press.
Goldziher, I. 1877. *Mythology among the Hebrews and Its Historical Development*. Translated by R. Marineau. London: Longmans, Green.
———. (1888) 1971. *Muslim Studies / Muhammedanische Studien*. Edited by S. M. Stern. 2 vols. London: George Allen and Unwin.
———. 1903. *Le Livre de Muhammad ibn Tumart, Mahdi*. Algiers: n.p.
———. 1920. *Die Richtungen der islamischen Koranauslegung*. Leiden: E. J. Brill.
Goitein, S. D. 1968. *Studies in Islamic History and Institutions*. Leiden: E. J. Brill.
Goldstein, J. A. 1975. "The Tales of the Tobiads." In *Christianity, Judaism and Other Greco-Roman Cults: Studies for Morton Smith at Sixty*, edited by J. Neusner, 85–123. Part Three: *Judaism before 70*. Leiden: E. J. Brill.
———. 1976. *I Maccabees*. New York: Doubleday.

———. 1983. *II Maccabees*. New York: Doubleday.
———. 1987. "How the Authors of 1 and 2 Maccabees Treated the 'Messianic' Promises." In *Judaisms and Their Messiahs at the Turn of the Christian Era*, edited by J. Neusner, W. S. Green, and E. S. Frerichs, 69–96. Cambridge: Cambridge University Press.
———. 1989. "The Hasmonean Revolt and the Hasmonean Dynasty." In *The Cambridge History of Judaism*, edited by W. D. Davies and L. Finkelstein, 292–351. Vol. 2, *The Hellenistic Age*. Cambridge: Cambridge University Press.
Goodwin, J. 2005. "Revolutions and Revolutionary Movements." In *Handbook of Political Sociology: States, Civil Societies, and Globalization*, edited by T. Janoski, R. Alford, A. Hicks, and M. A. Schwartz, 404–22. Cambridge: Cambridge University Press.
Grabar, O. 2005. *Early Islamic Art, 650–1100: Constructing the Study of Islamic Art*. Vol. 1. Variorum Collected Studies Series. Abingdon: Ashgate.
Grossman, M. 2002. *Reading for History in the Damascus Document: A Methodological Method*. Leiden: E. J. Brill.
Guillaume, A. 1955. *The Life of Muhammad: A Translation of Ibn Ishaq's Sirat Rasul Allah*. Oxford: Oxford University Press, 1955.
Haddad, Y. Y. 1974. "The Conception of the Term Dīn in the Qurʾān." *MW* 64:114–23.
Halm, H. 1996a. *Empire of the Mahdi*. Leiden: E. J. Brill.
———. 1996b. "The Ismaʿili Oath of Allegiance (*ʿahd*) and the Sessions of Wisdom (*majālis al-ḥikma*) in Fatimid Times." In *Medieval Ismaʿili History and Thought*, edited by F. Daftary, 91–115. Cambridge: Cambridge University Press.
Hamdani, A. 1979. "An Early Fatimid Source." *Arabica* 26:62–75.
Hamdani, A., and F. de Blois. 1983. "A Re-examination of al-Mahdi's Letter to the Yemenites on the Genealogy of the Fatimid Caliphs." *JRAS*, Series 3, 32:173–207.
Hasson, I. 1991. "Les *Mawālī* dans l'armée musulmane sous les premiers Umayyads." *JSAI* 14:176–213.
Hawting, G. R. 1978. "The Significance of the Slogan." *BSOAS* 41 (3): 453–63.
———. 1987. *The First Dynasty of Islam: The Umayyad Caliphate AD 661–750*. Carbondale: Southern Illinois University Press.
———. 1993. "Mukhtār b. Abī ʿUbayd." *EI* 7:521–24.
Heidemann, S. 2011. "The Evolving Representation of the Early Empire and Its Religion on Coin Imagery." In *The Qurʾān in Context: Historical and Literary Investigations into the Qurʾānic Milieu*, edited by A. Neuwirth, N. Sinai, and M. Marx, 149–96. Leiden: E. J. Brill.
Hengel, M. 1974. *Judaism and Hellenism: Studies in their Encounter in Palestine during the Early Hellenistic Period*. Philadelphia: Fortress Press.
———. 1989. "The Interpretation of Judaism and Hellenism in the Pre-Maccabean Period." In *The Cambridge History of Judaism*, edited by W. D. Davies and L. Finkelstein, 167–228. Vol. 2, *The Hellenistic Age*. Cambridge: Cambridge University Press.
Hilali, A. 2010. "La Palimpseste de Sanʿa et la canonization du Coran. Nouveaux éléments." *Cahiers du Centre Gustave Glotz* 21:443–48.

Hinds, M. 1971a. "Kufan Political Alignments and their Background in the Mid-Seventh Century A.D." *IJMES* 2:346–67.

———. 1971b. "The Banners and Battle Cries of the Arabs at Siffin (657 AD)." *Al-Abhāth*: 3–42.

———. 1972. "The Murder of the Caliph 'Uthmān." *IJMES* 3:450–69.

Hinnells, J. R. 1973. "The Zoroastrian Doctrine of Salvation in the Roman World: A Study of the Oracle of Hystaspes." In *Man and His Salvation: Studies in Memory of S. G. F. Brandon*, edited by E. J. Sharpe and J. R. Hinnells, 125–48. Manchester: Manchester University Press.

Hodgson, M. G. S. 1955a. "How Did the Early Shi'a Become Sectarian?" *JOAS* 75 (1): 1–13.

———. 1955b. *The Order of Assassins: The Struggle of the Early Nizârî Ismâ'îlîs against the Islamic World*. The Hague: Mouton.

———. 1974. *The Venture of Islam: Conscience and History in a World Civilization*. Chicago: University of Chicago Press.

Horbury, W. 1998. *Jewish Messianism and the Cult of Christ*. London: SCM Press.

———. 2003. *Messianism among the Jews and Christians: Twelve Biblical and Historical Studies*. London: T&T Clark.

Hourani, G. F. 1967. Introduction to *Averroes on the Harmony of Religion and Philosophy*, 1–43. London: Luzac.

Hoyland, R. G. 1997. *Seeing Islam as Others Saw It*. Princeton, NJ: Darwin Press.

———. 2001. *Arabia and the Arabs: From the Bronze Age to the coming of Islam*. London: Routledge.

———. 2006. "New Documentary Texts and the Early Islamic State." *BSOAS* 3:395–416.

Hulgård, A. 1998. "Persian Apocalypticism." In *The Encyclopedia of Apocalypticism*, edited by J. J. Collins, 39–83. Vol. 1, *The Origins of Apocalypticism in Judaism and Christianity*. New York: Continuum.

Humphreys, R. S. 1991. *Islamic History: A Framework of Inquiry*. Princeton, NJ: Princeton University Press.

al-Husayni, M. B. 1969. "Shi'ār al-khawārij 'ala'l-nuqūd al-islāmiyya." *Al-Maskūkāt* 2 (1): 32–35.

Hutter, M. 2005. "Manichaeism: Manichaeism in Iran." In *Encyclopedia of Religion*, edited by L. Jones, 5659–62. Vol. 8. 2nd ed. Detroit: Macmillan Reference.

Ibn Abi Tāhir Tayfur. n.d. Untitled. British Library Oriental MS. Add. 7473.

Ibn al-Nadim, Muhammad b. Ishāq. 2010. *Al-Fihrist*. Edited by Y. A. Tawil. Beirut: Dar al-kutub 'Ilmiyya.

Ibn al-Qattān, Hasan b. 'Ali. 1990. *Nuzum al-jumān li-tartīb mā salafa min akhbār al-zamān*. Beirut: Dār al-Gharb al-Islāmi.

Ibn A'tham al-Kufi. *Kitāb al-futuh*. n.d. 9 vols. Beirut: Dār al-Kutub al-'ilmiyya.

Ibn Ishāq, Muhammad. 1858. Kitāb *Sirat Rasul Allāh: Das Leben Muhammed's nach Muhammed Ibn Ishâk; bearbeitet von Abdel-Malik Ibn Hischâm*. Edited by F. Wüstenfeld. 2 vols. Göttingen: Dieterichsche Universitäts-Buchhandlung.

Ibn Khaldun, Abū Zayd 'Abd al-Raḥmān ibn Muḥammad. 1967. *The Muqaddimah*. Translated and edited by F. Rosenthal. 3 vols. Princeton, NJ: Princeton University Press.

———. 1992. *Kitāb al-'ibar (Tārikh Ibn Khaldun)*. 6 vols. Beirut: Dār al-kubu al-'Ilmiyya.

Ibn Qutayba, 'Abdallah b. Muslim. 1983. *'Uyūn al-Akhbār*. 4 vols in 2. Beirut: Dār al-Kutub al-'ilmiyya.

———. 1999. *Histoire des Berbères et des dynasties musulmanes de l'Afrique Septentrionale*. Translated by W. M. de Slane. Edited by Paul Casanova. 4 vols. Paris: Paul Geuthner.

Ibn Sa'd, Muhammad. 1904–28. *Kitāb al-Ṭabaqāt al-Kabir*. Edited by E. Mittwoch and E. Sachau. 9 vols. Leiden: E. J. Brill.

Ibn Tahir al-Baghdadi, Abu Mansur Abd al-Kahir. (1935) 1978. *Moslem Schisms and Sects (al-Farq bayn al-firaq)*. Part 2, translated by A. S. Halkin. Philadelphia: Porcupine Press.

Imhof, A. 2011. "The Qur'an and the Prophet's Poet: Two Poems by Ka'b b. Mālik." In *The Qur'ān in Context: Historical and Literary Investigations into the Qur'ānic Milieu*, edited by A. Neuwirth, N. Sinai, and M. Marx, 389–403. Leiden: E. J. Brill.

al-Isfahāni, Abu'l-Faraj. 1927. *Kitāb al-Aghānī*. Cairo: Matba'at Dār al-Kutub al-'Arabīyah.

———. 1949/1368. *Maqātil al-ṭālibiyyīn*. Cairo: n.p.

al-Istakhri, Ibrahim b. Muhammad al-Farsi. 1927. *Masālik al-Mamālik*. Edited by M. J. de Goeje. Leiden: E. J. Brill.

Ivanow, W. 1933. *Two Early Ismaili Treatises*. Bombay: n.p.

———. 1948. *Studies in Early Persian Ismailism*. Bombay: n.p.

Izutsu T. 1964. *God and Man in the Koran: Semantics of the Koranic Weltanschauung*. Tokyo: Keio Institute of Cultural and Linguistics Studies.

Ja'far b. Mansur al-Yaman. 1952. *Kitābu 'l kashf of Ja'far b. Manṣūri 'l Yaman*. London: Oxford University Press.

al-Jāhiz, Abū 'Uthmān 'Amr b. Baḥr. 1932/1851. *Al-Bayān wa'l-tabyīn*. Edited by Ḥasan al-Sandūbī. 3 vols. Cairo: Maktabat al-Tijāriyya.

al-Jahshiyārī, Muhammad b. 'Abdus. 1938. *Kitāb al wuzarā' wa'l-kuttāb*. Edited by Mustafā al-Saqqā. Cairo: n.p.

Jambet, C. 1990. *La grande résurrection d'Alamût: les formes de la liberté dans le shi 'isme ismaélien*. Lagrasse: Verdier.

Jeffery, A. 1938. *The Foreign Vocabulary of the Qur'an*. Baroda: Oriental Institute.

Jeremias, G. 1963. *Der Lehrer der Gerechtigkeit*. Göttingen: Vandenhoeck & Ruprecht.

Jones, J. M. B. 1957. "The Chronology of the *Maghāzī*—a Textual Survey." *BSOAS* 19:245–80.

Judd, S. 2008. "Reinterpreting al-Walid b. Yazid." *SAOS* 128 (3): 439–58.

Juvayni, 'Alā' al-Din 'Atā-Malik. 1911. *Tārikh-i Jahān-gushā*. Edited by M. Qazvini. 3 vols. Leiden: E. J. Brill.

Kaegi, W. E. 1992. *Byzantium and the Early Islamic Conquests*. Cambridge: Cambridge University Press.

al-Kalbī, Hishām b. Muhammad b. al-Sā'ib. 1924. *Kitāb al-asnām*. Edited by Ahmad Zaki Pasha. Cairo: n.p.

Karev, Y. 2002. "La politique d'Abū Muslim dans le Māwarā'annahr: Nouvelles données textuelle et archéologiques." *Der Islam* 79:1–46.

Kassis, H. E. 1983. *A Concordance of the Qur'ān*. Berkeley: University of California Press.

Kechechian, J. A., and R. H. Dekmejian, eds. 2003. *The Just Prince: A Manual of Leadership; Including Sulwān al-mutā' fi 'udwān al-atbā'* (*Consolation for the Ruler during the Hostility of the Subjects*) *by Muhammad ibn Zafar al-Siqqilli*. London: Saqi.

Kennedy, E. S., and D. Pingree. 1971. *The Astrological History of Māshā'allāh*. Cambridge, MA: Harvard University Press.

Kennedy, H. 1981a. *The Early Abbasid Caliphate*. London: Croom Helm.

———. 1981b. "Central Government and Provincial elites in the early 'Abbāsid Caliphate." *BSOAS* 44 (1): 26–38.

al-Khatīb al-Baghdādi, Ahmad b. 'Ali. 1931. *Tārīkh Baghdād*. Vol. 13. Cairo: Maktabat al-Khānjī.

Khoury, R. G. 1983. "Sources islamiques de la '*sira*.'" In *La Vie du prophête Mahomet*. Paris: Presses Universitaires de France.

Kisaichi, M. 1990. "The Almohad Social-Political System or Hierarchy in the Reign of Ibn Tumart." *Memoirs of the Research Department of the Toyo Bunko* 48:81–101.

Kister, M. J. 1962. "'A Booth like the Booth of Moses . . .': a Study of an Early *Hadith*." *BSOAS* 25:150–55.

———. 1965. "Mecca and Tamim (Aspects of their Relations)." *JESHO* 8:113–63.

———. 1968a. "Al-Hira: Notes on its Relations with Arabia." *Arabica* 15:143–69.

———. 1968b. "Al-tahannuth: An Inquiry into the Meaning of a Term." *BSOAS* 31:223–36.

———. 1972. "Some Reports concerning Mecca: From Jāhiliyya to Islam." *JESHO* 15:61–93.

———. 1979. "On the Wife of the Goldsmith of Fadak and her progeny: A Study in Genealogical Tradition." *Muséon* 92:321–30.

———. 1980. "*Labbayka allāhumma, labbayka . . .*: On a Monotheistic Aspect of a Jāhiliyya Practice." *JSAI* 2:33–57.

———. 1981. "'O God, tighten Thy grip on the Mudar . . .: Some Socio-Economic and Religious Aspects of an Early *Hadith*." *JESHO* 24:242–73.

———. 1984. " . . . illā bihaqqihi . . . A Study of an Early Hadith." *JSAI* 5:33–52.

———. 1986. "The Massacre of the Banu Qurayza." *JSAI* 8:61–96.

———. 1994. "Social and Religious Concepts of Authority in Islam." *JSAI* 18:84–127.

———. 2002. "The Struggle against Musaylima and the Conquest of Yamāma." *JSAI* 27:1–56.

Knibb, M. A. 1978. *The Ethiopic Book of Enoch*. 2 vols. Oxford: Clarendon Press.

Kochnev, Boris. 2001. "Les Monnaies de Muqanna." *Studia Iranica* 30:143–50.

Koenen, L. 1981. "From Baptism to the Gnosis of Manichaeism." In *The Rediscovery of Gnosticism*, edited by B. Layton, 734–56. Vol. 2, *Sethian Gnosticism*. Leiden: E.J. Brill.

Kohlberg, E. 1997. "Sulaymān b. Surad." *EI* 9:826–27.

Koselleck, R. 1985. *Futures Past: On the Semantics of Historical Time*. Translated by Keith Tribe. Cambridge, MA: MIT Press.

Kropp, M. 2008. "Beyond Single Words: *Mā'ida—Shaytān—jibt* and *ṭāghut*: Mechanisms of Transmission into the Ethiopic (Gəʿəz) Bible and the Qur'ānic Text." In *The Qur'ān in its Historical Context*, edited by G.S. Reynolds, 204–16. London: Routledge.

Kosmin, P. 2014. *The Land of the Elephant Kings: Space, Territory, and Ideology in the Seleucid Empire*. Cambridge, MA: Harvard University Press.

———. 2016. "Indigenous Revolts in 2 Maccabees: The Persian Version." *Classical Philology* 111 (1): 32–53.

al-Kulayni, Abu Ja'far Muhammad b. Ya'qub. 1957–60/1377–79. *Al-Kāfi*. Edited by 'A.-A Ghaffari. 8 vols. Tehran: Enteshārāt-e 'elmiyya-te Eslāmiyya.

Kurd 'Ali, Muhammad. 1913. *Rasā'il al-bulaghā': tahtawii 'alā mā 'urifa li-'Abd Allāh ibn al-Muqaffa'*. Cairo: Dār al-Kutub al-'Arabīyah al-Kubrā.

Lammens, H. 1910. "Le 'Triumvirat" Abou Bakr, 'Omar et Abou 'Obaida." *Mélanges de la Faculté Orientale de l'Université St. Joseph de Beirut* 4:113–44.

Landes, R. 2018. "The Varieties of Millennial Experience." In *The Apocalyptic Complex: Perspectives, Histories, Persistence*, edited by N. al-Baghdadi, D. Marno, and Matthias Riedl, 3–34. Budapest: Central University Press.

Lapidus, I.M. 1972. "The Conversion of Egypt to Islam." *Israel Oriental Studies* 2:248–62.

Laroui, A. 1977. *The History of the Maghrib: An Interpretive Essay*. Princeton, NJ: Princeton University Press.

Lassner, J. 1980. *The Shaping of 'Abbasid Rule*. Princeton, NJ: Princeton University Press.

———. 1986. "Abu Muslim, son of Salit: A Skeleton in the 'Abbasid Closet?" In *Studies in Islamic History and Civilization in Honor of D. Ayalon*, edited by M. Sharon, 97–104. Jerusalem: Cana.

———. 1989. "The 'Abbasid *Dawla*: An Essay on the Concept of Revolution in Early Islam." In *Tradition and Innovation in Late Antiquity*, edited by F.M. Clover and R.S. Humphreys, 247–70. Madison: University of Wisconsin Press.

Lecker, M. 1993. "Idol Worship in Pre-Islamic Medina (*Yathrib*)." *Le Muséon* 106: 331–46.

———. 1994. "Kinda on the Eve of Islam and during the *Ridda*." *JRAS* 3 (43): 333–56.

———. 1995a. "Wāqidi's Account of the Status of the Jews of Medina: A Study of a Combined Report." *JNES* 54:15–32.

———. 1995b. "Judaism among Kinda and the *Ridda* of Kinda." *JAOS* 115:635–50.

———. 1997a. "Zayd b. Thabit, 'a Jew with Two Sidelocks': Judaism and Literacy in Pre-Islamic Medina (Yathrib)." *JNES* 56 (4): 259–73.

———. 1997b. "Siffin." *EI* 9:552–56.

———. 2002. "The Levying of Taxes for the Sassanians in Pre-Islamic Medina." *JSAI* 27:109–26.

———. 2004. *The "Constitution of Medina": Muhammad's First Legal Document*. Princeton, NJ: Darwin Press.

———. 2010. "Glimpses of Muhammad's Medinan Decade." In *The Cambridge Companion to Muhammad*, edited by J. E. Brockopp, 61–79. Cambridge: Cambridge University Press.

———. 2014. "Three Parties for a Single Pact." *Oasis* 19:100–106.

Leehuis, F. 1988. "Origins and Early Development of the *tafsīr* Tradition." In *Approaches to the History of the Interpretation of the Qur'ān*, edited by A. Rippin, 13–30. Oxford: Oxford University Press.

Le Tourneau, R. 1956. "Du Mouvement almohade à la dynastie mu'minide: la révolte des frères d'Ibn Tumart de 1153 à 1156." In *Mélanges d'histoire et d'archéologie de l'occident musulman offertes à G. Marçais*, 111–16. Paris: n.p.

———. 1969. *The Almohad Movement in North Africa in the Twelfth and Thirteenth Centuries*. Princeton, NJ: Princeton University Press.

Lévi-Provençal, E. 1928. " L'Histoire des Almohades d'Abu Bakr b. 'Ali as-Sanhāǧi, surnommé Al-Baidak." In *Documents inédits d'Histoire Almoahade*, 75–225. Paris: Paul Geuthner.

Lewis, B. 1953. "An Apocalyptic Vision of Islamic History." *BSOAS* 13:308–38.

———. 1968. "The Regnal Titles of the First Abbasid Caliphs." In *Dr. Zakir Husain Presentation Volume*, edited by Tara Chand, 13–22. New Delhi: Crescent.

———. (1972) 1993. "Islamic Concepts of Revolution." In *Islam in History: Ideas, People, and Events in the Middle East*, 311–20. Chicago: Open Court.

Lowick, N. M. 1979. "Une Monnaie 'Alide d'al-Basrah date de 145 H (762–3 après J.-C.)." *Revue Nu mismatique* 6:218–24.

MacKenzie, D. N. 1979. "Mani's Šābuhragān." *BSOAS* 42:500–534.

———. 1980. "Mani's Šābuhragān." *BSOAS* 43:288–310.

Madelung, W. 1965. *Der Imam al-Qāsim ibn Ibrāhīm und die Glaubenslehre der Zaiditen*. Berlin: De Gruyter.

———. 1977. "Some Notes on Non-Isma'ili Shi'ism in the Maghrib." *Studia Islamica* 44:87–97.

———. 1981a. "'Abd Allāh b. al-Zubayr and the Mahdi." *JNES* 40 (4): 291–305.

———. 1981b. "New Documents Concerning al-Ma'mun, al-Fadl b. Sahl and 'Ali al-Rida." In *Studia Islamica and Arabica: Festschrift for Ihsān 'Abbās*, edited by Wadād al-Qādi, 333–46. Beirut: American University of Beirut

———. 1982. "The Early Murji'a in Khurasan and Transoxania and the Spread of Hanafism." *Der Islam* 59 (1): 32–39.

———. 1986a. "Has the *Hijra* Come to an End?" *REI* 54:225–37.

———. 1986b. "Apocalyptic Prophesies in the Umayyad Age." *Journal of Semitic Studies* 31 (2): 141–85.

———. 1988. *Religious Trends in Early Islamic Iran*. New York: Bibliotheca Persica.

———. 1989. "The *Hāshimiyyāt* of al-Kumayt and Hashimi Shi'ism." *SI* 70:5–26.
———. 1996. "The Fatimids and the Qarmatis of Bahrayn." In *Medieval Isma 'ili History and Thought*, edited by F. Daftary, 21–73. Cambridge: Cambridge University Press.
———. 1997a. *The Succession to Muhammad: A Study of the Early Caliphate*. Cambridge: Cambridge University Press.
———. 1997b. "Hamdān Qarmat and the Dā'i Abu 'Ali." *Proceedings of the 17th Congress of the Union européenne desarabisants st islamisants*, 115–24. St. Petersburg, August 21–26.
———. 2003 "A Treatise on the Imamate of the Fatimid Caliph al-Mansur bi-Allāh." In *Texts, Documents and Artefacts: Studies in Honor of D. S. Richards*, edited by C. F. Robinson, 69–77. Leiden: E. J. Brill.
Madelung, W., and P. E. Walker. 2000. *The Advent of the Fatimids: A Contemporary Shi'i Witness*. London: I. B. Tauris and the Institute of Ismaili Studies.
———. 2011. "The *Kitāb al-Rusum wa'l-izdiwāj wa'l-tartib* Attributed to 'Abdān (d. 286/899): Edition of the Arabic Text and Translation." In *Fortresses of the Intellect: Ismaili and Other Islamic Studies in Honor of Farhad Daftary*, edited by Omar Alí-de-Unzaga, 103–66. London: I. B. Tauris.
Mahdi, M. 1957. *Ibn Khaldun's Philosophy of History: A Study in the Philosophic Foundation of the Science of Culture*. London: Routledge.
Mannheim, K. 1978. *Ideologie und Utopie*. 6th ed. Frankfurt: Verlag G. Schulte-Bulmke.
Marquet, Y. 1972. "Les Cycles de la souraineté selon les Épîtres des Ikhwān al-safā'." *SI* 36:47–69.
Marsiglio of Padua. 1993. *Defensor minor and De Translation Imperii*. Translated and edited by C. J. Nederman. Cambridge: Cambridge University Press.
Mashkur, M. J. 1948/1327. "Sonb ād." *Pashutan* 1 (7): 31–34.
al-Mas'udi, Abu'l-'Ali b. al-Husayn. (1894) 1967. *Al-Tanbih wa'l-ishrāf*. Reprint. Leiden: E. J. Brill.
———. *Muruj al-dhahab wa ma'din al-jawhar*. Edited by Ch. Pellat. 11 vols. Beirut: Publications de l'Université Libanaise.
Merad, A. 1957. "Abd al-Mu'min et la conquête d'Afrique du Nord." *Annales de l'Institut d'Études Orientales* 15:110–63.
Messier, R. A., and J. A. Miller. 2015. *The Last Civilized Place: Sijilmasa and Its Saharan Destiny*. Austin: University of Texas Press.
Miles, G. C. 1938. *The Numismatic History of Rayy*. New York: American Numismatic Society.
———. 1957. "Some Arab-Sasanian and Related Coins." *American Numismatic Society Museum Notes* 7:187–209.
———. 1959. *Excavation Coins from the Persepolis Region*. New York: American Numismatic Society.
Millar, F. 1978. "The Background to the Maccabean Revolution: Reflections on Martin Hengel's Judaism and Hellenism." *JJS* 29:1–21.
Minqāri, Nasr b. Muzāhim [al-Minqāri al-Tamimi al-Kufi]. 1884. *Waq'at Siffin*. Tehran: n.p.

Momigliano, A. 1975. *Alien Wisdom: The Limits of Hellenization.* Cambridge: Cambridge University Press.
———. (1987) 1994. *Essays on Ancient and Modern Judaism.* Edited by Silvia Berti. Translated by Maura Masella-Gayley. Chicago: University of Chicago Press.
Monnot, G. 1975. "L'histoire des religions en Islam, Ibn al-Kalbī et Rāzī." *RHR* 188:23–34.
Morony. M. G. 1984. *Iraq after the Muslim Conquest.* Princeton, NJ: Princeton University Press.
Mosca, P. G. 1986. "Ugarit and Daniel 7: A Missing Link." *Biblica* 67:496–517.
Moscati, S. 1947. "La Rivolta di ʿAbd al-Ǧabbār contro il califfo al-Mansūr." *Lincei* 8 (2): 613–15.
———. 1949. "Studi su Abu Muslim." I and II. *Lincei* 8 (4): 323–35; 474–95.
———. 1950a. "Studi su Abu Muslim." III. *Lincei* 8 (5): 89–105.
———. 1950b. "Per una Storia dell'Antica Šīʿa." *RSO* 30:251–57.
———. 1952. "Il Testamento di Abū Hāšim." *RSO* 27:28–46.
Mottahedeh, R. P. 1975. "The ʿAbbāsid Caliphate in Iran." In *The Cambridge History of Iran,* edited by R. N. Frye, 57–89. Vol. 4, *From the Arab invasion to the Saljuqs.* Cambridge: Cambridge University Press.
———. 1980. *Loyalty and Leadership in an Early Islamic Society.* Princeton, NJ: Princeton University Press.
Murphy-O'Connor, J. 1974. "The Essenes and their History." *Revue Biblique* 81:215–44.
———. 1976. "Demetrius I and the Teacher of Righteousness (I *Macc.*, x, 25–45)." *Revue Biblique* 83:400–420.
al-Murtadā, al-Sayyid. 1907/1325. *Amālī al-Sayyid al-Murtadā.* Cairo: n.p. Reprint, Qom 1982/1403.
Nagel, T. 1970. "Bericht über den Aufstand von Muhammad b. ʿAbdallah." *Der Islam* 46:227–62.
———. 1972. *Untersuchungen zur Entsehung des Abbasidischen Kalifates.* Bonn: Selbstverlag des Orientalischen Seminar der Universität.
Narshaji, Abu Bakr Muhammad b. Jaʿfar. 1972/1351. *Tārikh-e Bukhārā.* Edited by Mudarris Razavi. Tehran: Bunyād-e Farhang-e Irān.
Nebes, N. 2011. "The Martyrs of Najrān and the End of the Himyar." In *The Qurʾān in Context: Historical and Literary Investigations into the Qurʾānic Milieu,* edited by A. Neuwirth, N. Sinai and M. Marx, 27–59. Leiden: E. J. Brill. Neusner, J. 1963. "Parthian Political Ideology." *Iranica Antiqua* 3:40–59.
Neuwirth, A. 2003. "Qurʾan and History—a Disputed Relation: Some Reflections on Qurʾanic History and History in the Qurʾan." *Journal of Qurʾanic Studies* 5 (1): 1–18.
———. 2006. "Structure, Linguistic and Literary Form." In *The Cambridge Companion to the Qurʾān,* edited by J. D. McAuliffe, 97–114. Cambridge: Cambridge University Press.
———. 2011. "The House of Abraham and the House of Amram: Genealogy, Patriarchal Authority and Exegetical Professionalism." In *The Qurʾān in Context: His-*

torical and Literary Investigations into the Qur'ānic Milieu, edited by A. Neuwirth, N. Sinai and M. Marx, 499–531. Leiden: E. J. Brill.
Nevo, Y., and J. Koren. 1990. "The Origins of the Muslim Descriptions of Jāhilī Muslim Sanctuary." *JNES* 49:23–44.
———. 2003. *Crossroads to Islam: The Origins of the Arab Religion and the Arab State.* New York: Prometheus Books.
Newby, G. D. 1971. "Observations about an Early Judaeo-Arabic." *Jewish Quarterly Review* 61:212–21.
———. 1988. *A History of the Jews of Arabia.* Columbia: University of South Carolina Press.
Nezām al-Molk. 1962. *Siyar al-Moluk (Siyāsat-nāma).* Edited by H. Darke. Tehran: Bank-e Melli.
Nickelsburg, G. W. E. 1982. "The Epistle of Enoch and the Qumran Literature." *JJS* 33:333–48.
———. 1987. "Salvation without and with a Messiah: Developing Beliefs in Writings Ascribed to Enoch." In *Judaisms and Their Messiahs at the Turn of the Christian Era*, edited by J. Neusner, W. S. Green, and E. S. Frerichs, 49–68. Cambridge: Cambridge University Press.
———. 1991. "The Apocalyptic Construction of Reality in 1 *Enoch*." In *Mysteries and Revelations: Apocalyptic Studies since the Uppsala Colloquium*, edited by J. J. Collins and J. H. Charlesworth, 51–64. *Journal for the Study of the Pseudepigrapha.* Supplement Series 9.
Nöldeke, T. (1860) 1909–1938. *Geschichte des Qorāns.* Revised by F Schwally, G. Bergsträsser, and O. Pretzl. Leipzig: T. Weicher.
———. 1910. "Lehnwörter in und aus dem Äthiopischen." In *Neue Beiträge zur semitischen Sprachwissenschaft*, 31–66. Strassburg: Verlag Karl J. Trübner.
Noth, A. 1994. *The Early Arabic Historical Tradition: A Source-Critical Study.* Edited by Lawrence I. Conrad. Translated by Michael Bonner. Princeton, NJ: Darwin Press.
———. (1968) 2008. "Isfahān-Nihāwand: A Source-Critical Study of Early Islamic Historiography." In *The Expansion of the Early Islamic State*, edited by F. M. Donner, 247–62. London: Ashgate Variorum.
Nuʿaym ibn Hammād al-Marwazi. 1991. *Kitāb al-Fitan.* Edited by S. Zakkār. Mecca: al-Maktabah al-Tijārīyah.
Omar, F. 1969. *The ʿAbbasid Caliphate, 132/750–170/786.* Baghdad: n.p.
———. 1976. *ʿAbbasiyyat: Studies in the History of the Early ʿAbbasids.* Baghdad: University of Baghdad.
Parsons, T. 1966. *Societies: Evolutionary and Comparative Perspectives.* Englewood Cliffs, NJ: Prentice-Hall.
Pellat, Ch. 1976. "*Conseilleur*" *du Calife.* Paris: Maisonneuve et Larose.
Pingree, D. 1963. "Astronomy and Astrology in India and Iran." *Isis* 54:229–46.
———. 1968. *The Thousands of Abu Maʿshar.* London: Warburg Institute.
Pirenne, H. 1925. *Medieval Cities: Their Origins and the Revival of Trade.* Translated by Frank D. Halsey. Princeton, NJ: Princeton University Press.

———. 1937. *Mahomet et Charlemagne*. Paris: Félix Alcan.
Pizzorno, A. 1994. *Le Radici della Politica Assoluta e altri Saggi*. Milan: Feltrinelli.
Puech, E. 1994. "Messianism, Resurrection, and Eschatology at Qumran and in the New Testament." In *The Community and the Renewed Covenant: The Notre Dame Symposium on the Dead Sea Scrolls*, edited by E. Ulrich and J. VanderKam. Christianity and Judaism in Antiquity, vol. 10. South Bend, IN: Notre Dame University Press.
———. 1996. "246.4Qapocryphe de Daniel ar." *Qumran Cave 4* 17 (3): 165–84.
Puech, H.-Ch. 1972. "Le Manichéisme." In *Histoire des Religions*, 523–645. Vol. 2, La formation des religions universelles et les religions de salut dans le monde méditerranéen et le Proche-Orient: Les religions constituées en Occident et leurs contrecourants. Paris: Gallimard.
Puig, J. 1992. "Materials on Averroes's Circle." *Journal of Near Eastern Studies* 51 (4): 241–60.
al-Qāḍi, Wadād. 1993a. "The Earliest 'Nābita' and the Paradigmatic 'Nawābit.'" *SI* 78:27–61.
———. 1993b. "Early Islamic State Letters: the Question of Authenticity." In *The Byzantine and Early Islamic Near East*, edited by A. Cameron and L. I. Conrad, 215–76. Princeton, NJ: Darwin Press, 1993.
———. 1994. "The Religious Foundation of Late Umayyad Ideology and Practice." In *Saber Religioso y Poder Politico: Actas del simposio internacional, Granada, 15–18 octubre 1991*, 231–75. Madrid: Agencia Española de Cooperación Internacional.
Qāḍi al-Nuʿmān b. Muhammad. *Risāla iftitāh al-daʿwa*. Edited by W. al-Qāḍi. Beirut: Dār al-Thiqāfa, 1970.
Qimron, E., and J. Strugnell, eds. 1994. *Qumran Cave 4. Vol. 5, Misqat Maʿaśe ha-Torah*. Oxford: Clarendon Press.
Rabin, C. 1957. *Qumran Studies*. Oxford: Oxford University Press.
Rad, G. von. 1967. *The Message of the Prophets*. San Francisco: HarperCollins.
Rahman, F. 1976. "Pre-Foundations of the Muslim Community in Mecca." *SI* 43: 5–24.
———. 1980. *Major Themes of the Qurʾan*. Minneapolis: Bibliotheca Islamica.
Rasāʾil Ikhwān al-Ṣafāʾ wa-Khillān al-Wafāʾ. 1928. 4 vols. Cairo: Maṭbaʿat al-ʿArabīyah,
Reeves, J. C. 1994. "Jewish Pseudepigrapha in Manichaean Literature: The Influence of the Enochic Library." In *Tracing the Threads: Studies in the Vitality of Jewish Pseudepigrapha*, edited by J. C. Reeves, 173–204. Atlanta: Scholars Press, 1994.
Reid, S. B. 1989. *Enoch and Daniel: A Form Critical and Sociological Study of the Historical Apocalypses*. BIBAL Monograph Series 2. North Richland Hills, TX: BIBAL Press.
Retsö, J. 2003. *Arabs in Antiquity: Their History from the Assyrians to the Umayyads*. London: RoutledgeCurzon.
———. 2011. "Arabs and Arabic in the Age of the Prophet." In *The Qurʾān in Context: Historical and Literary Investigations into the Qurʾānic Milieu*, edited by A. Neuwirth, N. Sinai, and M. Marx, 281–92. Leiden: Brill.

Reynolds, G. S. 2001. "Jesus, the Qā'im and the End of the World." *RSO* 75 (1–4): 55–86.
Robertson Smith, W. (1889) 1972. *The Religion of the Semites: The Fundamental Institutions*. New York: Schocken Books.
Robin, Ch. 2000. "Les 'filles de Dieu' de Saba á la Mecque: Reflexions sur l'agencement des patheons dans l'Arabie ancienne." *Semitica* 50:113–92.
Robinson, Chase F. 2004. "The Conquest of Khuzistan: A Historical Reassessment." *BSOAS* 67:14–39.
Rodinson, M. (1961) 1971. *Mohammed*. Translated by Anne Carter. New York: Pantheon Books.
Rotter, G. 1982. *Die Umayyaden und der zweite Bürgerkrieg (680–692)*. Wiesbaden: Steiner.
Rubin, U. 1975. "Pre-Existence and Light: Aspects of the Concept of Nur Muhammad." *Israel Oriental Society* 5:62–119.
———. 1985. "The 'Constitution of Medina': Some Notes." *SI* 52:5–23.
———. 1990. "*Ḥanīfiyya* and Ka'ba." *JSAI* 13:85–112.
———. 1995. *The Eye of the Beholder: The Life of Muhammad as Viewed by Early Muslims*. Princeton, NJ: Darwin Press.
———. 2001 "Muhammad." In *Encyclopedia of the Qur'an*, edited by J. D. McAuliffe, 3:440–58. Oxford: Oxford University Press.
Rudolph. K. 1983. "Wellhausen als Arabist." *Sitzungsberichte der Sächsischen Akademie der Wissenschaften zu Leipzig* 123 (5): 5–57.
Sadeghi, B. 2011. "The Chronology of the Qur'ān: A Stylometric Research Program." *Arabica* 58:210–99.
Sadeghi, B., and U. Bergmann. 2010. "The Codex of a Companion of the Prophet and the Qur'ān of the Prophet." *Arabica* 57 (4): 343–436.
Sadeghi, B., and M. Goudarzi. 2012. "San'ā' I and the Origins of the Qur'ān." *Der Islam* 87:1–129.
Sadighi, Gh.-H. 1938. *Les Mouvements religieux iraniens au IIè et au IIIè siècle de l'hégire*. Paris: Les Presses modernes.
Schacht, J. 1963. "Sur l'expression 'Sunna du Prophète." In *Mèlanges d'orientalisme offerts à Henri Massé*. Tehran: n.p.
Sakhnini, 'I. 1998. *Al-'Abbāsiyūn fī sanawāt al-ta'sīs*. Beirut: al-Mu'assis al-'Arabiyya.
Saleh, W. A. 2010. "The Arabian Context of Muhammad's Life." In *The Cambridge Companion to Muhammad*, edited by J. E. Brockopp, 21–38. Cambridge: Cambridge University Press.
Sarkisyanz, M. 1955. *Russland und der Messianismus des Orients*. Tübingen: Mohr.
Schaper, J. 2007. "The Persian Period." In *Redemption and Resistance: The Messianic Hopes of Jews and Christians in Antiquity*, edited by M. Bockmuehl and J. C. Paget, 3–14. London: T&T Clark.
Schiffman, L. H. 1989. *The Eschatological Community of the Dead Sea Scroll*. Atlanta: Scholars Press.

Seidensticker, T. 2011. "Sources for the History of Preislamic Religion." In *The Qur'ān in Context: Historical and Literary Investigations into the Qur'ānic Milieu*, edited by A. Neuwirth, N. Sinai and M. Marx, 293–321. Leiden: E.J. Brill.

Sellwood. D. 1983. "Numismatics: Minor States in Southern Iran." In *The Cambridge History of Iran*, edited by E. Yarshater. Vol. 3, part 11, *The Seleucid, Parthian and Sasanian Periods*.

Serjeant, R. B. 1978. "The *Sunnah Jāmi'a*, Pacts with the Yathrib Jews, and the *Tahrim* of Yathrib: Analysis and Translation of the Documents Comprised in the So-called 'Constitution of Medina.'" *BSOAS* 41 (1): 1–42.

———. 1982. "The Interplay between Tribal Affinities and Religious (Zaydi) Authority in the Yemen." *Al-Abhāth* 30:11–48.

Severus. 1947. *History of the Patriarchs of the Coptic Church of Alexandria*. Edited and translated by B. Evetts. Vol. 3, *Agathon to Michael I (766)*. Paris: Firmin-Didot.

Shaban, M. 1970. *The 'Abbasid Revolution*. Cambridge: Cambridge University Press.

Shacklady, H. 1986. "The 'Abbasid Movement in Khurāsān." *Occasional Papers of the School of Abbasid Studies* 1:98–112.

Shaked, Sh. 1969. "Esoteric Trends in Zoroastrianism." *Proceedings of the Israel Academy of Sciences and Humanities* 3:175–221.

———. 1972. "Qumran and Iran: Further Considerations." *Israel Oriental Studies* 2:433–46.

———. 1987. "Paymān: An Iranian Idea of Contract." In *Transition Periods in Iranian History*, edited by Ph. Gignoux, 217–40. Actes du Symposium de Freibourg-en-Brisgau. Leuven: Association pour l'avancement des études iraniennes.

Shapira, D. D. Y. 2013. "Banners, Spears, Black Raiders and Byzantines: Some Textual Notes on Late Sasanian and Post-Sasanian Zoroastrian Apocalyptic Texts." *JPS* 6:39–63.

Sharon, M. 1978 "Kahtaba." *EI*. 2nd ed. Vol. 4, 445–47.

———. 1983. *Black Banners from the East: The Establishment of the Abbasid State; Incubation of a Revolt*. Jerusalem: Magnes Press.

———. 1984. "The Development of the Debate around the Legitimacy of Authority in Early Islam." *JSAI* 5:121–41.

———. 1986. "Military Reforms of Abu Muslim, their Background and Consequences." In *Studies in Islamic History and Civilization in Honor of D. Ayalon*, edited by M. Sharon, 105–43. Jerusalem: Cana.

———. 1990. *Revolt: The Social and Military Aspects of the 'Abb'āsid Revolution*. Jerusalem: Max Schloessinger Memorial Fund.

Shoemaker, S.J. 2014. "The Reign of God Has Come: Eschatology and Empire in Late Antiquity and Early Islam." *Arabica* 61 (5): 514–58.

Shoufani, E. S. 1973. *Al-Riddah and the Muslim Conquest of Arabia*. Toronto: University of Toronto Press.

Simon, R. 1991. "Allah or God? The Semantic and Religious Meaning of 'Allah' on the Eve of Islam and in the Qur'ān." *Acta Classica Universitatis Scientiarum Debreceniensis* 27:129–34.

Sinai, N. 2011. "The Qur'an as Process." In *The Qur'ān in Context: Historical and Literary Investigations into the Qur'ānic Milieu*, edited by A. Neuwirth, N. Sinai and M. Marx, 407–39. Leiden: E. J. Brill.
Sohm, R. (1888) 193. *Outlines of Church History*. London: Macmillan.
Sourdel, D. 1954. "La Biographie d'Ibn al-Muqaffa'." *Arabica* 1:307–23.
———. 1959. *Le Vizirat 'Abbaside de 749 à 936*. 2 vols. Damascus: n.p.
Stern, S. M. 1983. *Studies in Early Isma'ilism*. Jerusalem: Magnes Press.
Stroumsa, G. G. 1986. "'Seal of the Prophets': The Nature of a Manichaean Metaphor." *JSAI* 7:61–74.
———. 2003. "A Nameless God: Judaeo-Christian and Gnostic Theologies of the Name.'" In *The Image of the Judaeo-Christians in Ancient Jewish and Christian Literature*, edited by Peter I. Tomson and Doris Lambers-Petry, 230–43. Tübingen: Mohr.
Suermann, H. 2011. "Early Islam in the Light of Christian and Jewish Sources." In *The Qur'ān in Context: Historical and Literary Investigations into the Qur'ānic Milieu*, edited by A. Neuwirth, N. Sinai and M. Marx, 135–48. Leiden: E. J. Brill.
al-Tabari, Muhammad b. Jarir. 1879–1901/1985–2000. *Ta'rikh al-rusul va'l-muluk*. Edited by M. J. de Goeje. 15 vols. Leiden: E. J. Brill.
Talmon, J. L. 1952–60. *The Origins of Totalitarian Democracy*. 2 vols. London: Secker & Warburg.
———. 1960. *Political Messianism—The Romantic Phase*. London: Secker & Warburg.
Tcherikover, V. 1959. *Hellenistic Civilization and the Jews*. New York: Atheneum.
Teixidor, J. 1997–98. "Antiquités sémitiques." *Annuaire du Collège de France*: 713–35.
Tilly, Charles. 1978. *From Mobilization to Revolution*. Reading, MA: Addison-Wesley.
Tocqueville, A. 1955. *The Old Régime and the French Revolution*. Translated by S. Gilbert. New York: Doubleday.
———. 1959. *The European Revolution and Correspondence with Gobinau*. Edited and translated by John Lukacs. New York: Doubleday Anchor.
Tora-Niehoff, I. 2011. "The 'Ibād of al-Hira: An Arab Christian Community in Late Antique Iraq." In *The Qur'ān in Context: Historical and Literary Investigations into the Qur'ānic Milieu*, edited by 135–A. Neuwirth, N. Sinai, and M. Marx, 323–447. Leiden: E. J. Brill.
Tucker, W. F. 1975. "Bayān b. Sam'ān and the Bayāniyya: Shi'ite Extremists of Umayyad Iraq." *MW* 65 (4): 241–53.
———. 1977. "Abu Mansur al-'Ijil and the Mansuriyya: A Study in Medieval Terrorism." *Der Islam* 54:66–76.
———. 1980. " 'Abd Allah Ibn Mu'āwiya and the Janahiyya: Rebels and Ideologues of the Late Umayyad Period." *SI* 51:39–57.
Ullmann. W. 1965. *A History of Political Thought: The Middle Ages*. London: Penguin Books.
Ulrich, E., and J. Vanderkam, eds. 1994. *The Community of the Renewed Covenant: The Notre Dame Symposium on the Dead Sea Scrolls*. Christianity and Judaism in Antiquity, vol. 10. South Bend, IN: University of Notre Dame Press.

Urvoy, D. 1974. "La Pensée d'Ibn Tumart." *Bulletin des Études Orientales* 27:19–44.
———. 2005. "Les Professions de Foi d'Ibn Tumart." In *Los Almhades: Problemas y Perspectivas*, edited by Patrice Cressier, Maribel Fierro, and Luis Molina, 739–52. Madrid: Consejo Superior de Investigaciones Cientificas.
———. 1995. *The Dead Sea Scrolls in English*. 4th ed. London: Penguin.
Van Arendonk, C. 1978. "Khashabiyya." *EI* 4:1086–87.
VanderKam, J. 1984. *Enoch and the Growth of an Apocalyptic Tradition*. Catholic Biblical Quarterly Monograph Series 16. Washington, DC: Catholic Biblical Association of America.
———. 1994. "Messianism in the Scrolls." In *The Community of the Renewed Covenant: The Notre Dame Symposium on the Dead Sea Scrolls*, edited by E. Ulrich and J. Vanderkam. Christianity and Judaism in Antiquity, vol. 10. South Bend, IN: Notre Dame University Press.
Van Ess, J. 1970. "Les Qadarites et la Ġaylānīya de Yazid III." *SI* 31:269–86.
———. 1978. "Discours à rebours de l'histoire de Muʿtazilisme." *REI* 56 (2): 59–128.
———. 1991–97. *Theologie und Gesellschaft in 2. und 3. Jahrhundert Hidschra*. 6 vols. Berlin: De Gruyter.
Van Henten, J. W. 2007. "The Hasmonean Period." In *Redemption and Resistance: The Messianic Hopes of Jews and Christians in Antiquity*, edited by M. Bockmuehl and J. C. Paget, 15–28. London: T&T Clark.
Van Reeth, J. M. F. 2012a. "Who is the 'Other' Paraclete?" In *The Coming of the Comforter: When, Where and to Whom? Studies on the Rise of Islam and Various Other Topics in Memory of John Wansborough*, edited by C. Segovia and B. Lourié, 432–52. Piscataway, NJ: Gorgias Press..
———. 2012b. "Melchisédech, le propète éternel selon Jean d'Apamée et le monarchianisme musulman." *Oriens Christianus* 96:8–46.
———. 2016. "La Robe blanche des serviteurs de dieu: ʿAdi b. Zayd, le Coran, Bardésane et al-Muqannaʿ." In *L'Ésotérisme Shiʿite: Ses sources et ses prolongements*, edited by M. A. Amir-Moezzi, M. De Cillis, D. de Smet, and O. Mir-Kasimov, 221–67. Turnhout: Brepols.
Van Vloten, G. 1892. "Ueber einige bis jetzt nicht erkannte Münzen aus der letzten Omeijadenzeit." *Zeitschrift der Deutschen Morgenlandischen Gesellschaft* 46 (3): 441–44.
———. 1894. *Recherches sur la Domination arabe, le Chiʿitisme et les Croyances messianiques sous le Kalifat des Omayades*. Amsterdam: n.p.
———. 1898. "Zur Abbasidengeschichte." *Zeitschrift der Deutschen Morgenländischen Gesellschaft* 53 (2): 213–26.
Veccia Vaglieri, L. 1949. "Le vicendi del Kharijismo in epoca abbaside." *RSO* 24: 31–44.
———. 1952. "Il conflitto ʿAli-Muʿāwiya e la secessione khārijgita riesaminati alla luce di fonti ibādite." *Annali de l'Istituto Universitario Orientali di Napoli*, n.s., 4:1–94.
Velji, J. A. 2016. *An Apocalyptic History of the Early Fatimid Empire*. Edinburgh: Edinburgh University Press.

Vermes, G. 1992. "The Oxford Forum for Qumran Research Seminar on the Rule of War from Cave 4 (4Q285)." *JJS* 43:85–90.

———. 1995. *The Dead Sea Scrolls in English*. 4th ed. Penguin: London.

Viguera-Molins, M. 2010. "Al-Andalusia and the Maghrib (from the Fifth/Eleventh Century to the Fall of the Almoravids)." In *The New Cambridge History of Islam*, edited by M. Fierro, 21–47. Vol. 2, *The Western Islamic World: Eleventh to Eighteenth Centuries*. Cambridge: Cambridge University Press.

Villeneuve, F. 2010. "La Résistance des cultes bétyliques d'Arabie face au monothéisme: De Pau à Barsauma à Muhammad." In *Le Problème de la christianisation du monde antique*, edited by H. Inglebert, S. Destephen, and B. Dumézil, 219–31. Paris: Picard.

Voegelin, E. 1952. *The New Science of Politics*. Chicago: University of Chicago Press.

Wacholder, B. Z. 1978. "The Letter from Judah Maccabee to Aristobulus: Is 2 Maccabees 1:10b-2:18 Authentic?" *Hebrew Union College Annual* 49:89–133.

———. 1983. *The Dawn of Qumran: The Sectarian Torah and the Teacher of Righteousness*. Cincinnati: Hebrew Union College Press.

Walker, P. E. 2006. "The Relationship between Chief *Qāḍi* and Chief *Dāʿi* under the Fatimids." In *Speaking for Islam: Religious Authority in Muslim Societies*, edited by G. Krämer and S. Schmidtke, 70 –94. Leiden: E. J. Brill.

———. 2014. "The Role of the Imam-caliph as Depicted in Official Treatises and Documents Issued by the Fatimids." In *The Study of Shiʿi Islam*, edited by F. Daftary and G. Miskinzoda, 411–32. London: Institute of Ismaili Studies, 2014.

Wansbrough, J. 1977. *Quranic Studies: Sources and Methods of Scriptural Interpretation*. Oxford: Oxford University Press.

———. 1978. *The Sectarian Milieu: Content and Composition of Islamic Salvation History*. Oxford: Oxford University Press.

al-Wāqidi, Muhammad b. ʿUmar. 1966. *The Kitāb al-maghāzi*. Edited by M. Jones. 3 vols. London: Oxford University Press.

Watt, W. M. 1953. *Muhammad at Mecca*. Oxford: Oxford University Press.

———. 1956. *Muhammad at Medina*. Oxford: Oxford University Press.

Weber, M. 1952. *Ancient Judaism*. Translated by H. H. Gerth and D. Martindale. New York: Free Press.

———. 1978. *Economy and Society*. Edited by G. Roth and C. Wittich. 2 vols. Berkeley: University of California Press.

Wellhausen, J. 1883. "Mohammedanism." In *Encyclopaedia Britannica*. 10th ed. 26: 544–65.

———. 1899. "Prolegomena zur ältesten Geschichte des Islams." In *Skizzen und Vorarbeiten* 6:1–160. Berlin: Georg Reimer.

———. (1878) 1957. *Prolegomena to the History of Ancient Israel*. Translated by J. Sutherland Black and A. Menzies. New York: Meridian Books.

———. (1897) 1961. *Reste arabischen Heidentums*. Berlin: De Gruyter.

———. (1902) 1963. *The Arab Kingdom and Its Fall*. Translated by M. G. Weir. Beirut: Khayyat.

———. 1975a. "Muhammad's Constitution of Median." Translated by W. Behn. In *Muhammad and the Jews of Medina*, edited by A.J. Wensinck, 128–38. Freiburg: Klaus Schwarz Verlag.

———. 1975b. *The Religio-Political Factions in Early Islam*. Edited by R.C. Ostle and S.M. Walzer. Amsterdam: North Holland.

Wheeler, B.M. 1999–2000. "'This is the Torah that God Sent down to Moses': Some Early Islamic Views of the Qur'ān and Other Revealed Books." Graeco-Arabica 7–8:571–604.

Whelan, E. 1998. "Forgotten Witness: Evidence for the Early Codification of the Qur'ān." *JOAS* 118 (1): 1–14.

Widengren, G. *The Great Vohu Manah and the Apostle of God: Studies in Iranian and Manichaean Religion*. Uppsala: Uppsala Universitets Årsskrift.

———. 1950. *The Ascension of the Apostle and the Heavenly Book*. Uppsala: Uppsala Universitets Årsskrift.

———. 1955. *Muhammad, the Apostle of God, and his Ascension*. Uppsala: Uppsala Universitets Årsskrift.

———. 1974. "La Sagesse dans le Manichéisme." In *Mélanges d'Histoire des Religions offerts à Henri-Charles Puech*, 501–15. Paris: Presses Universitaires de France.

Widengren, G., A. Hultgård, and M. Philonenko. 1995. *Apocalyptique iraniennne et dualism qumrânien*. Paris: Maisonneuve.

Winston, D. 1966. "The Iranian Component in the Bible, Apocrypha, and Qumran: A Review of the Evidence." *History of Religions* 5:183–216.

Wurtzel, C. 1978. "The Coinage of the Revolutionaries in the Late Umayyad Period." *American Numismatic Society Museum Notes* 23:161–99.

Yamamoto, K., and Ch. Burnett, eds. and trans. 2000. *Abu Ma'šar on Historical Astrology: The Book of Religions and Dynasties on Great Conjunctions*. 2 vols. Leiden: E.J. Brill.

al-Ya'qubi, Ahmad b. Wahb b. Wādih. 1960. *Tārīkh al-Ya'qūbī*. 2 vols. Beirut: Dār Sādir.

Yarshater. E. 1983. "Iranian Common Beliefs and Worldviews." In *The Cambridge History of Iran*, edited by E. Yarshater, 343–58. Vol. 3, part 2, *The Seleucid, Parthian and Sasanian Periods*. Cambridge: Cambridge University Press.

———. 1985–2002. *The History of al-Tabari*. SUNY Series in Near Eastern Studies. Edited by Ehsan Yarshater. 40 vols. Albany: State University of New York Press.

Yusofi, Gh.-H. 1989/1368. *Abu Moslem, sardār-e khorāsāni*. Tehran: Kitabha-ye Jibi.

Zaehner, R.C. 1961. *The Dawn and Twilight of Zoroastrianism*. New York: G.P. Putnam's Sons.

Zakeri, M. 1995. *Sāsānid Soldiers in Early Muslim Society: The Origins of 'Ayyārān and Futuwwa*. Wiesbaden: Harrassowitz.

Zarrinkub, 'A.-H. 1975. "The Arab Conquest of Iran and Its Aftermath." In *The Cambridge History of Iran*, edited by R.N. Frye, 1–56. Vol. 4, *From the Arab invasion to the Saljuqs*. Cambridge University Press, pp.

———. (1964/1343) 1984. *Tārīkh-e Irān ba'd az eslām*. Tehran: Amir Kabir.

Zaryāb-Kho'i, 'A. 1989/1368. *Bazmāvard*. Tehran: 'Elmi.

INDEX

A'azzu mā yutlab, 266
Abān b. Yazid b. Muhammad b. Marwān, 161
Abbasid Revolution, 14–15, 173–223
    Arabist and Persianist, 25–29
    historiography of 24–30
'Abd Allāh (worshipper of Allāh), 95
'Abd al-'Aziz b. Karmān, 278
'Abd al-'Aziz b. Tumart, 282
'Abd al-Jabbār b. 'Abd al-Rahmān al-Azdi, 28, 185, 209–10
'Abd al-Malik b. Marwān (Umayyad caliph), 132, 144–47
'Abd al-Mu'min b. 'Ali (Almohad caliph), 266, 269, 274, 277–86, 289, 313
'Abd al-Muttalib, 95, 220
'Abd al-Rahmān (worshipper of Rahmān), 95
'Abd al-Rahmān al-Fihri, 143–44
'Abd al-Rahmān b. 'Awf, 118
'Abd al-Rahmān b. Muhammad b. al-Ash'ath, 175
'Abd al-Rahmān b. Muljam al-Murādi, 129
'Abd al-Rahmān b. Muslim. See Abu Muslim al-Khurāsāni
'Abd al-Rahmān b. Rustam, 189
'Abd al-Samad b. 'Ali, 195
'Abd al-Shams, 95
'Abd al-'Uzza, 95
'Abdallāh b. 'Abbās, 120, 124, 129
'Abdallāh b. 'Ali al-Saffāh, 157–58, 171, 183–88
'Abdallāh b. al-Hasan, 181, 209, 211–17, 224
'Abdallāh b. Ja'far al-Sādiq, 229, 251
'Abdallāh b. Mas'ud, 118, 139
'Abdallāh b. Malwiyya, 278
'Abdallāh b. Mu'āwiya, 27, 163–69, 173, 190
'Abdallāh b. Muhammad b. Ismā'il, 235
'Abdallāh b. 'Ubaydallāh al Haskuri, 272
'Abdallāh b. Ubayy, 105
'Abdallāh b. 'Umar I, 122
'Abdallāh b. 'Umar II 'Abd al-'Aziz, 158, 163, 181
'Abdallāh b. Wānudin, 282
'Abdallāh b. Yāsin, 263–64
'Abdallāh b. al-Zubayr. See Ibn al-Zubayr, 'Abdallāh
'Abdallāh II (Aghlabid amir), 247
'Abdallāh the Elder (Ismā'ili leader), 228–29
'Abdān, Abu Muhammad (Ismā'ili leader), 228–29, 233–36, 239–42
abnā' al-dawla (sons of the [Abbasid] revolution), 189, 196, 208n6
Abraha, 78, 101
Abraham: ancestor of the Arabs, 75, 87, 103–4, 107, 234, 261, 271
    the Book (suhuf) of, 85–86
    the first Muslim, 75, 103, 254, 269
    the hanif, 85–86
    House of, 98n74, 111–12, 125–26, 243–44, 293
absolute politics, 3–4, 12–13, 89, 312–14
Abu 'Abdallāh al-Shi'i, Husyan b. Ahmad b. Zakariyā', 232, 241–51, 254, 259
Abu 'Amr b. al-'Alā', 222
Abu 'Āmir, 78
Abu 'Awn, 'Abd al-Malik b. Yazid, 180, 185–87, 210

346 ◆ INDEX

Abu Bakr al-Siddiq (the second rightly-guided caliph), 95, 112–15
Abu Bakr Muhammad b. al-Walid al-Tartushi, 303
Abu Bakr b. ʿUmar, 264
Abu Ayyub al-Muriyāni al-Khuzi, 196
Abu Dāwud Khālid b. Ibāhim, 179, 195, 197, 209
Abu Dharr al-Ghifāri, 120
Abu Hafs ʿUmar al-Hintāti (Inti), 277, 280, 288
Abu Hafs ʿUmar b. Tafrāgin, 282
Abu Hanifa, 156, 174–75, 177
Abu Hāshim, al-Hasan b. Muhammad b. al-Hanafiyya, 139
Abu Hātim al-Rāzi, 242
Abu Humayd al- Marwarrudhi, 196
Abu Ishāq Khālid b. ʿUthmān, 191
Abu Khālid, 209
Abu Mansur Muhammad b. Ahmad, 217
Abu Mashʿar Balkhi, 297, 299–301
Abu Muhammad al-Sufyāni, 143n61, 157, 161, 166
Abu Musā al-Ashʿari, 119
Abu Musā al-Sarrāj, 153
Abu Muslim al-Khurāsāni, 153, 167–68, 174–97, 206–8, 174
Abu Muslimiyya, 206–10
Abu Qays b. al-Aslat, 85
Abu Saʿid b. Bahrām al-Jannābi, 229, 233, 241–42
Abu Salama al-Khallāl, 170n65, 180–87, 190, 192
Abu Sanbar, 244
Abu Sufiyān, 109, 132
Abu Tāhir Suleymān al-Jannābi, 242–44
Abu Tālib, 89, 91, 98, 164
House of, 218
Abu Yaʿqub Yusuf (Almohad caliph), 285–87, 305
Abu Yusuf Yaʿqub al-Mansur (Almohad caliph), 286
Abu ʿUbayda b. al-Jarrah, 113
Abu Yazid (Kharijite rebel), 253–54
Abu Zakariā, 241
Abuʾl-ʿAbbās ʿAbdallāh (Abbasid caliph), 181–82
Abuʾl-ʿAbbās Muhammad b. Ahmad, 232, 247–49, 251
Abuʾl-Dawāniq. *See* al-Mansur Abu Jaʿfar ʿAbdallāh
Abuʾl-Jahm b. ʿAtiyya, 171, 180–81, 184–85, 191
Abuʾl-Qāsim ʿIsā b. Musā, 233
Abuʾl-Sarāyā, 226
Abuʾl-Shalaghlagh Muhammad (Ismāʿili leader), 233, 239
Abuʾl-Walid ʿUmayr b. Hāniʾ, 158
Abwāʾ, 212–13
acceptable one, the. *See* al-ridā
Acra, 42, 53, 65
Agarsif, 278
Agha, Said Salih, 26
Aghlabids, 246–48, 251–52
Aghmāt, 264, 267, 275, 284
Ahbār (hoberim), 82, 139
ahl al-bayt (Household of the Prophet), 159n29, 164
ahl al-khamsun (ayt khamsun), 273
ahl khurāsān (people of Khurasan), 25
ahl al-sāqa, 273
Ahmad, 9, 74, 88, 95n63, 100
Ahvaz, 133, 164, 170, 214, 216, 228
ʿĀʾisha, Mother of the Faithful, 79, 122–27, 130, 133
ʿajam (dumb, Persian), 189, 203, 260, 295
Akhbār al-Dawlat al-ʿAbbāsiya, 25–26
ākhir al-zamān. *See* End of Time
Alamut, 259–60
al-ʿashara (Almohad Council of Ten), 267, 273
al-Aswad al-ʿAnsi, 113–14
Al-Azmeh, Aziz, 18, 21–22n52
Alcimus (Jakim), 59–62
Alexander the Great, 33, 37, 39
al-hādi (the rightly guided), 214–17, 280, 313
ʿAli b. Abi Tālib, ʿAli al-Aʿlā, 95, 117–31
ʿAli b. al-Fadl, 232–33
ʿAli b. Muhammad, 227
ʿAli b. Musā al-Ridā, 227–28
ʿAli b. Yusuf (Almoravid amir), 266–67
ʿAlids, 209, 212, 224–26
al-Kumait b. Zayd, 164
Allāh, 17–18
Allāh al-Rahmān (Merciful God), 101
Almohad Revolution, 262–90
  Berber dimension of, 30–31, 289
  as Mahdist revolution, 30–31
Almohadism, as *madhhab fikr* (school of thought), 276, 290
Amari, Michele, 303
amghār (Berber minor chief), 266, 289
amir al-muʾminin (Commander of the Believers), 110, 118, 183, 226, 265

amir al-muslimin (Almoravid Commander of the Believers), 110
'Āmir b. Dubāra, 167–69, 178, 184
'Āmir b. Ismā'il, 185–86
'Ammār b. Yāsir, 118
'Amr b. 'Adi, 77
'Amr b. al-'Ās, 117, 124, 129
'Amr b. al-Hamiq, 119
Amr b. 'Ubayd, 156
Anabaptists, 5
Ancient of Days, 50
Animal Apocalypse, 53–54, 56
ansār (Helpers), 112–13, 117–18, 122–24, 133, 274
'Ans, 114
Antioch-at-Jerusalem, 40, 42
Antiochus III, 36, 39
Antiochus IV Ephiphanes, 38–43
Anushirvān, 227, 304
Apocalypse of Weeks, 49
apocalypticism: apocalyptic mentality, 3–4, 33–34
  motivation of revolutionary action, 3–4, 12–13, 88–101, 312–13
  and otherworldly eschatology, 11, 71–72, 88, 104–5
  and transfer of sovereignty, 292–95. *See also* mahdism; messianism; millennialism
Aquinas, Thomas, 290
Arabia, political unification of, 8–10, 75, 106–15
Arab Khurasanians, 178, 183
Arabian Peninsula, 76*map*, 79; periphery of three empires, 75–88
  pre-Islamic religions of, 76–87
Arabism, 145, 223
'Arafāt, 218
ardig-e buzurg (the great war), 71, 293–94
Ardashir (Sasanian king), 221, 297, 304
Aristotle, 14n26, 33, 218n23, 286, 289–90, 305
Aristotelian-Paretan revolution. *See* Integrative Revolution, Aristotelian-Paretan
Artaxerxes I, 35
'asabiyya: as group solidarity, 306
  as tribal factionalism, 50–61, 164, 262
Asad al-Qasri, 152
Asāwira, 136
Ass of the Jazira. *See* Marwān II
Atlas Mountains, 167–68, 275–78, 309–10
Averroes. *See* Ibn Rushd
Averroists, Latin, 286, 290

Aws, 80, 105
Aws Allāh, 85
Awzā'i, 158
Aygiliz (Igilliz ,Aygli-n-Warghan), 267–68, 273
ayt arba'in (Almohad Parliament of Forty), 273, 289
Azāriqa, 133–34

Baal Shamim, 42
bāb (gate [to the imam]), 231
bāb al-abwāb (Fatimid office), 232, 255
Baghdad, 25, 28, 222, 225–26
Bahman Yasht, 292
Bahrām Chubin, 297
Bahrain, 241–45
Bajila, 152
al-Balādhuri, 200
Balkh, 152, 176–79, 185, 221
Banu al-Asbagh, 239
Banu Hāshim, 15, 26, 112, 126, 142, 164, 174, 190, 211–12
Banu Hilāl, 282
Banu Khazrun, 263
Banu al-'Ullays, 239
Banu Qurayza, 108
Banu Umayya, 112, 118, 130
Baqliyya, 243n48
Barāz-banda, 210
Bardaisan, 77
Barghawāta, 264, 280
Barmak, 152
Barmakis, 221
Barqalitus. *See* Paraclete
bashir (bringer of good news), 89, 91
Bashmur, 186
Basra, 119, 123–24, 129, 133, 137, 158
Bassām b. Ibrāhim, 190–91
Battle of Bākhamrā', 216
Battle of Badr, 106–7, 142, 175n6, 294
Battle of al-Buhayra, 275, 280
Battle of Marj Rāhit, 132, 143
Battle of Qādisiyya, 118
Battle of Talas, 191
Battle of the Camel, 124, 127
Battle of the Trench, 108–9
Battle of Siffin, 125–27, 129, 131
Battle of Uhud, 78–79
Battle of Zāb, 76*map*, 171, 178, 185, 194
Bayhaqi, Abu'l-Fadl 292, 295, 302–3, 305
Bazargan, Mehdi, 22

Beh-Āfarid, 196n69
Ben Sira, 39
Berber rebellion of 738, 155–56
betyls/baetyls, 80
Bilga family, 41
Biruni, Abu Rayhān, 84, 91–92, 210, 242
Bishop Isho'ayhb III of Adiabene, 295
Book of Enoch, Ethiopic, 34, 79, 98, 313
Book of Idols, 79
Book of Mazdak, 221
book of Revelation (Apocalypse of John), 11
Book of the Giants, 82
Book of Watchers, 98
Bougie (Bijāya), 266, 282
boulé (Seleucid assembly), 38
Brethren of Purity. *See* Ikhwān al-Safā'
Brett, Michael, 30–31
Buddha, 92
Bukayr b. Māhān, 186
Bukhara, 179, 210, 297
Busir, 185–86

Calder, N., 20
caliphal absolutism, 218–22
caliphate, early elaborations of the idea, 112, 120–24, 134, 149
Casanova, Paul, 18
Centennium, 140
Ceuta, 265, 280
Chabbi, Jacqueline, 21
charismatic authority: of the Prophet, 100–101, 116, 119, 248
of the Qa'im-Mahdi, 139–44
as replication of Muhammad's, 139, 182, 269
routinization into the charisma of lineage, 9, 253–58, 312–13
routinization and centralization of power, 9, 311–13
chiliasm. *See* millennialism
Christianity, 76–77, 79, 81–83, 87
Mesopotamian Gnostic, 73, 76–77, 91, 99, 140–41
Chronicle of 819, 184
civil wars: first, 117–31
second, 15, 24, 131–39, 150
third, 149–72
City of David, 42
City of Peace (Baghdad). *See Madinat al-salām*
Coele-Syria, 38

Cohn, Norman, 6
Commentary on Plato's Republic, 286, 305
Communism, 5–6
Companions of the Cave, 140
Companions of the Cloak (*ashāb al-kisā'*), 245n55
Companions of the Prophet, 117–27
constitutional politics. *See* revolution, consequences, constitutional politics
Conversion to Islam. *See* Islamicization
Cook, Michael, 19–20
Cordoba, 286
Countercaliphate of Ibn al-Zybayr, 133–34
counterrevolution, 134, 144
Marwanid, 144–47
Crone, Patricia, 19–20
Ctesiphon, 297
Cyrus, 34, 64

Da'ā'im al-islām, 254, 256
Dadhoyeh, al-Muqaffa', 153
dahid (strike)!, 25, 186, 197
dā'ī (missionary), 234, 239, 255–56
dā'ī al-du'āt (Fatimid chief missionary), 256
Dajjāl (Antichrist), 140, 142–43
Dakkāla, 281
Damascus Document, 56
Daniel, Book of, 33, 44–47, 50–56
Danielic apocalyptic, 7, 46–47
influence on the Dead Sea Scrolls, 46–47, 71–72
Persian influence on, 46
on the Qur'an, 73, 99–100
dār al-hijra (abode of migration), 8, 74, 233, 239, 244, 247, 249, 254, 268
Dar'a, 281
Darius I, 34
da'wa thāniya (Second Mission), 227
da'wat-e jadid (New Mission), 259
dawla (turn In power), 24, 148, 165, 200, 237, 242, 247, 255, 262, 291–94, 298, 300–302, 306, 308
Dawraq, 164
Dāwud b. 'Ali (Abbasid), 152, 182, 216n19
Daylam, 208, 225, 228, 260
Day of Judgment/Resurrection (*yawm al-din*), 11, 13, 96, 98, 104, 111, 159, 230, 270
Dead Sea Scrolls, 7, 13, 34, 71, 92n.52, 313
dehqāns, 30, 152, 179, 196, 216
Demetrius I (Seleucid king), 61
Demetrius II (Seleucid king), 65

Decisive Treatise (fasl al-maqāl) on the Harmony of Religion and Prophecy, 287
Deren, 280
Dezh Rōyēn (bronze fort), 297
Dhakwāniyya, 157, 167
Dhu Nuwās, 141
diwān al-jund (army registry), 150
Dome of the Rock, 146, 216
dōrēsh ha-Torah, 98
dual power, 60–61, 128, 192–200, 205

Ecbatana, 61
Elephant Sura, 78
Elijah, 72
Elkasaites, 77
empires, 9, 22n52
   apocalyptic transposition of, 55, 74, 98, 293
   Achaemenid, 33–37
   Almohad, 284–88
   Byzantine (Roman), 9, 24, 146
   as context for the rise of Islam, 76*map*, 75–88
   Ethiopian, 76–79
   Fatimid, 252–58
   Sasanian, 9, 75–78, 114, 307
End of Time, 9, 11, 13, 45–47, 55, 71, 82, 88–89, 95–109, 141, 248, 267, 270, 276, 312
Enoch, Epistle of, 44, 47–49
Enoch, Similitudes of, 71–72, 88
Epistles of the Brethren of Purity and Friends of Fidelity (Rasā'il ikhwān al-safā' wa khillān al-wafā'), 234–38, 249–50, 256, 300–301
eschaton (end), 11, 44–45, 49–50, 54, 70, 104
Eschatological theodicy, 104–5
Essenes, 4, 19, 45, 48, 62, 65, 67–73
   differentiation from Hasidic movement, 61–62, 67–68
   later offshoots in Arabia, 81–82
Estakhr, 165, 148
Ethiopia, 9, 24, 76, 78–79, 83, 313
   colonies in Arabia, 76*map*
European Revolution of 1848, 2
Ezra, 35–36, 38, as the messenger of God, 99
Ezra, the fourth book of, 98

Fars, 27, 134, 138, 145, 164–67, 183–86, 201, 214, 216, 229
Fascism, 5–6
Fatimid Revolution, 224–61
   Berber dimension of, 265
   historiography of, 30–31

Fatimids, origins of the term: *al-fātimiyun, al-fawātim*, 240. See also Ismāʿili Shiʿa
Fatima the Radiant (*fātima al-zahrā'*), 271
Fazlur Rahman, 22
fidā'i, 259
Fifth Monarchy Men, 294
fitna (dissension, civil war), 74. See civil wars
Firuz the Daylamite, 113
frašo kereti (renewal of the world), 11, 34, 97, 270
fratarakā i yazdān (commanders of the gods), 38
French Revolution of 1789, 2, 4, 6, 10, 291
Friends of God (*auliyā'Allāh*), 231, 234–36
fryštg/freštag, 93–94
Fustāt, 119, 129

Gabriel, Archangel, 55, 93, 99–100, 106, 294
Ganāva, 229, 241
Ganfisa, 278
Gerlich, Fritz, 5
Geschichte des Qorans, 16
ghārāt (raids), 129
Ghazāli, Abu Hāmid Muhammad, 266, 269, 276, 287, 289, 303
Ghassān, 80
Ghatafān, 114
ghayba (occultation), 139, 208, 225, 246
Ghaylān al-Dimashqi, 158–59
Ghulāt. See Shiʿa, "extremist"
Ghumāra, 277
Gibraltar, Straits of, 269, 281
Goldziher, Ignaz, 16–17, 19
God's deputy (*khalifat Allāh*), 121, 123, 145–46, 160, 164, 168, 218
Granada, 265
Great Resurrection, the, 258–61
Greatest Tribulation (*al-malhama al-ʿuzma/al-kubra*), 142
Great Tribunal of the Pharisees, 43

Habakkuk Commentary (*pesher*), 58, 62–63, 66
Habiba b. Abu Sufyān, 79
Hafs b. al-Walid al-Hadrami, 160
Haft Bāb-e Sayyiduna (The seven gates of our Lord), 260
Hagarism, 19, 21
Haggi, 34
Hajj, 84–85, 110, 192, 234, 263
al-Hajjāj b. Yusuf al-Thaqafi, 144–46, 155, 174–79

ḥakam (judge-arbiter), 8, 105, 107
Halakhic Letter, 59, 67, 69, 83
Hamā', 229
Hamdān Qarmat, 227–35
Hammādah bt. Muʿāwiya, 213
Hamid b. Yahya al-Kātib, 153–54
Hamrā', 136
hanif talbiya, 85
Hanifa, 113, 115
Hanifiyya-Sābi'a (Hanif-Converts), 83–88, 92, 313
Hanukkah, 53
Hargha (Ayt Argan), 266–67, 274–78, 282
al-Hārith b. Nawfal, 181n22
al-Hārith b. Surayj, 156, 174–79
Harran, 86n22, 151–52, 166, 168, 171, 195
Harura, 128
Hārun al-Rashid (Abbasid caliph), 221, 225–26
al-Hasan b. ʿAli, 129, 131
Hasan al-Basri, 139
Hasan al-ʿAskari, 227–28, 232, 235
Hasan al-Harsh, 226
Hasan b. Farah b. Hawshab b. Zādān, 229
Hasan b. Muʿāwiya, 139, 213
al-Hasan b. Qahtaba, 188
Hasan II b. Mohammad b. Bozorg-Omid, 259
Hasan Sabbāh, 256–59, 269
Hashemite movement: Hāshimiyya, 26, 200–201, 210–11, 212n14, 213, 216, 218, 221–22
Hashemite Revolution, 25–26, 173–92, 197–98, 205, 213, 216–17, 224, 295–96. *See also* Abbasid Revolution
"*Hāshim, yāri!*" (Help, O Hashim!), 210
Hāshim b. Hakim: al-Muqannaʿ, 210
Hāshimiyya (Abbasid capital before Baghdad), 28, 197
Hāshimiyyāt, 164
hasid, 47
Hasidic synagogue, 44
Hasidism (ancient), 47–48, 51–57, 60–63
Hasidim-Maccabean revolutionary coalition, 63
Haskura, 280–81
Hasmonians, 65, 68–69
al-Husayn b. ʿAli b. al-Nuʿmān, 256
hawāriyun, 93
Hawting, G. R., 20
hayra (perplexity), 228
Hazmira, 274–75, 281
Heavenly Tablets, 44, 48

Hellenization, 37–44
  revolutionary coalition against, 47–49, 51–56, 60–62
Hellenizer (*meshummad*) as apostate, 43
Hereafter (*ākhira*), 104
higher criticism, 16–19
hijra, 74, 83, 105–6, 313
Hims, 157, 159, 161–62
Himyar, 83, 142, 175
Hintāta, 267, 276
al-Hira, 9, 75, 77–78, 82–84, 105, 190, 193, 199
Hishām b. ʿAbd al-Malik (Umayyad caliph), 148–53
Hour (*al-sāʿa*), the, 13, 74, 89, 91, 94, 96–98, 104, 225, 253, 294
House of ʿAbbās, 200–205, 211
House of Absalom, 63
House of David, 10, 112
House of Hashmonay, 68
Hoyland, Robert, 21
Hudaybiyya, Truce of, 109
huffāz (Almohad), 275
Hujr b. ʿAli al-Kindi, 135
Hülegü, 256
Hulwan, 165, 207
Humayd al-Marwarrudhi, 196
Humayd b. Qahtaba, 195, 200
hunafā'/sābi'un. *See* Hanifiyya-Sābi'a
Hunayn, 109
Husayn al-Ahwāzi, 228
al-Husayn b. ʿAli, 133, 135
  "revenge of," 136
hyperdeconstruction, 19–23
Hystaspes, Oracle of, 37, 64

Ibadi Khawārij, 191n49, 214*map*
Ibn Abi Tāhir Tayfur, 300
Ibn al-Kalbi, 78–79, 83
Ibn al-Muqaffaʿ, ʿAbdallāh, 192, 200–205, 220
Ibn al-Nadim, 77, 86
Ibn al-Zubayr, ʿAbdallāh, 132–37
Ibn Hamdān, 243
Ibn Harmah, 218
Ibn Hawshab, 229–36, 244, 253
Ibn Hazm, 99
Ibn Ishāq, 91, 94, 218, 222–23
Ibn Khaldun, Abd al-Rahman, 14n27, 305
Ibn Kathir, 23
Ibn Moshkān, 190
Ibn al-Qattān, 274, 288
Ibn Qutayba, 78

Ibn Rushd, Abu'l-Walid Muhammad b. Ahmad, 286, 305
Ibn Sa'd, 95, 100
Ibn Sāhib al-Salāt, 288
Ibn Tufayl, Abu Bakr Muhammad, 286, 305
Ibn Zafar al-Siqilli, Muhammad, 303–4
Ibn Tabātabā. *See* Muhammad b. Ibrāhīm
Ibrāhīm II (Aghlabid amir), 247
Ibrāhīm al-Imam (Abbasid), 181, 209
Ibrāhīm b. Mālik al-Ashtar, 136–37, 144
Ibrāhīm b. Maymun al-Sā'igh, 177
Idris, 98
Idrisid dynasty, 216
Ifriqiyya, 31, 189, 241, 244, 247–50, 252, 274–75, 282–83, 309–11
Ikjān, 245–47, 249–51
Imām al-Hadrami, 265
Imamate, 149
  as charismatic leadership, 207, 266
  concealed (*satr*), 234–35
  theory of, 204, 254–58
imam-caliph, 255–58
Imam-Mahdi
Imam-Mahdi-Qa'im, 239, 255
inqilab, inqilāb al-zamān (revolution of the days), 292, 294, 295
Interpreter of the Law (Torah), 57–58, 70, 98
Iranians, 28–30, 137–38
Integrative Revolution, 13–14, 18, 74
  Aristotelian-Paretan, 14n26, 24–26
  Khaldunian, 14, 28–30, 302–8
  rise of Islam as its prototype, 308
irjā', 174
'Isā b. 'Ali (Abbasid), 184, 191–95, 198–201
'Isā b. Māhān, 191
'Isā b. Musā (Abbasid), 194, 196
'Isā b. Tumart, 282
Isfahan, 27, 137, 165, 169, 207, 243–44
Ishāq b. Muslim al-'Uqayli, 171
Ishāq the Turk, 208
Ishmael, 84, 87, 90, 120
Ishmaelites, 19
islām (submission [to God]), 103–4, 110
Islamicate civilization, 23–24, 31, 88, 110, 115, 147, 223, 290
Islamicization: of Ghana, 265
  of Ifriqiyya, 30
  by the Khawārij, 134, 146, 268, 276
  of Khurasan, 173–79, 206–11
  of the Magreb, 289–90, 310
Islamic Revolution of 1979 in Iran, 6–7

Ismā'il Igig, 267
Ismā'il b. Ja'far, 251
Ismā'il b. Khālis al-Qasri, 163
Ispahbadh Khurshid, 208
Isrāfil, 106
Izutsu, Toshihiko, 22

Ja'd b. Dirham, 162
Ja'far b. Hanzala, 197
Ja'far b. Abi Tālib, 79
Ja'far b. Muhammad al-Sādiq, 190–91, 212
Jābir al-Ju'fi, 229
Jacobinism, 4, 6
Ja'far b. Mansur al-Yaman, 254
Jafnids, 176
Jahm b. Safwān, 156
Jahmiyya, 177
Jahwar b. al-Marrar al-'Ijli, 208
jamā'a (community), 131
Jason, son of Simon the Just, 40–42, 60n92
Jazira, 137, 151, 161, 168, 171, 188, 198, 239
Jehoshaphat, 36
Jesus: the anointed (*masih*), 92, 94
  Second Coming of, 139–40, 142, 182
  son of Mary, 90–94, 99, 102, 171, 276
Jesus of Splendor, 94
Jewish oral law, 20
Jibal, 165
jihād (holy struggle), 10, 74, 89, 115, 118, 144, 234, 247, 262, 265, 275–76, 283–84, 305, 310
  emergence of, 105–11
  and *hijra*, 105–6
  as the prototype of revolutionary process in history, 310
John bar Penkaye, 138
John Hyrcanus, 68–69
Jonathan Maccabee, 61–68
Jose b. Joezer, 44, 60
Josephus, 48, 68, 71, 81, 85
Jubilees, book of, 47–48, 53, 56, 67
Judaism, 47, 73, 83, 101
  in Arabia, 7–8, 13, 81–88, 313
  Karaite, 81
  Max Weber on ancient, 3, 7, 9
  non-rabbinical, 9, 13, 67
  non-rabbinical in Arabia, 81, 93n57, 97
  Second Temple/postexilic Judaism, 9, 35, 47
Juddāla, 263
Judaean Desert, 56, 67, 69–70

Judas Maccabee, 50, 52–58, 62
Juday' al-Kirmāni, 177–79
Judith, 52–53

Ka'ba, 80, 84, 216, 243
Ka'b al-Ahbār, 82, 99, 139, 141
Ka'b b. 'Abdah, 118
Ka'ba, 132, 216
kāfirkūbāt (infidel-smashers), 136, 178, 190
kairotic time, 5, 8–12, 101
Kalb, 132–33
Kalila wa Dimna, 221
Kannuna b. Idris b. Idris, 281
Karaites, 82
Karbala, 133
Kawād, 77
Kay Bahrām (Wahrām) Varjāvand, 297
Kaysān b. Abi 'Amra, 136–38
Kaysāniyya, 136–39, 144, 224
Khadija, 90
Khālid b. 'Abdallāh al-Qasri, 151–55
Khālid b. al-Walid, 83, 114–15
Khālid b. Barmak, 185, 221
Khālidiyya, 209
khalifa. See caliphate
Khashabiyya (club-wielders), 136, 145
Khawārij (secessionists), 29, 120, 125–30, 133–34, 144–46, 264
Khāzim b. Khuzayma al-Tamimi, 190–91
Khazraj, 80, 105
Khosraw I, Anushirvān, 75, 77–78, 105, 114, 297
Khosraw II, 298
Khurasan, 74, 118, 145, 147, 173–92
Khurramiyya (neo-Mazdakis), 84
Khuzā'a, 80
Kiā Bozorg-Omid, 259
Kināna, 80
Kinda, 78
al-Kindi, Ya'qub b. Ishāq, 300
kingdom of Aksum, 77. *See* Empires, Ethiopian
Kister, M.J., 21
Kitāb al-rushd wa'l-hidāya (Book of righteousness and guidance), 231
Kitāb al-Rusum wa'l-izdiwāj wa'l-tartib (Book of norms, pairing, and order), 213
Kufa, 24, 119–23, 128, 133–38, 173
Kumait b. Zayd, 164
Kumya, 266, 274, 281–83
Kutāma, 244–53, 309–10

Kuthayyar 'Uzza, 139, 164
kuttāb (secretaries), 15, 221

Lakhmid, 175, 176*map*
Lammsar, 259
Lamtuna, 262–64, 270
Last Day (*yawm al-ākhir*)
Lāt, 80
Late Antiquity thesis, the, 23–24
Law (Torah) of Moses, 35, 38
Leontopolis, 64–65
Lecker, Michael, 21
Liar (*daggāla*), 62–63, 140
Lord of All Beings (*rabb al-'ālamayn*), 103
Lord of the Time (*sāhib al-zamān*), 241
Lord of the West (*sahib al-maghrib*), 193

Maccabean Revolt, 34
  as nativistic revolution in Judaea, 43–44, 51–53
  religious background, 34–51
  revolutionary power struggle, 50–69
Maccabean temple-state, 61–69
Madā'in, 51, 134
Man of the Birthmark (*sāhib al-shāma*), 24–41
Man of the She-Camel (*sāhib al-nāqa*), 240
madinat al-mansur (City of the Victor), 216
madinat al-nabiy (City of the Prophet), 8
madinat al-salām (City of Peace), 216, 222, 299
al-mahdi (the rightly-guided), 13
  myth of as Muhammad redivivus, 10, 13, 139
al-Mahdi bi'llāh (Fatimid caliph), 250
Mahdi Ibn Tumart, 30, 262, 266–81, 305
Mahdism, 1–2, 9, 11, 280–81, 302, 306, 308
  apocalyptic, 139–44, 211–16
  as charismatic messianic leadership, 13, 111–12, 207
  realized, 107–16, 216–19, 252–58, 281–89
  Shi'ite, 9, 139–44. *See also* millennialism; Qa'im-Mahdi
Mahdist revolutions, 31, 135–38, 144, 216, 231–32, 236, 311–12
  and conversion to Islam, 310–11. *See also* Islamicization
Mahdiyya, 253, 283, 310
majālis al-hikma, 256
Major Themes of the Qur'an, 22
Makhul b. Abi Muslim, 158
malāhim (apocalyptic battles), 142,
Mālik al-Ashtar al-Nakha'I, 118–21

Mālik b. Haytham al-Khuzāʿī, 196
Malik Yazdāq, 261
Mallāla, 266
mamluks (praetorian slaves), 300
al-Maʾmun (Abbasid caliph), 86n38, 288, 294
Manāt, 80
Māni: of Light, 77, 92–93
  as the Messenger of Jesus Christ, 94
  as the Paraclete, 92–94
  as the Seal of the Prophets, 90, 92
Manichaeism, 7, 9, 13, 72, 76–78, 82, 85, 91–92, 97, 100, 151, 313
Manichaean-Mazdakites (*zanādiqa*), 78, 211
Manichaean Prophetology, 13, 88–89, 92–94
al-Mansur, Abu Jaʿfar ʿAbdallāh (Abbasid caliph), 28n74, 183, 219–20
Mansur al-Yaman, 175
al-Mansur biʾllāh (Fatimid caliph), 252
Mansur b. Jumhur al-Kalbi, 157–59, 166–67
Mansur of the Himyar, 142
Mannheim, Karl, 5
Manuhmed/Manvahmed, 94
al-Marākishi, 286
Marcion, 77
Marrakesh, 265–67, 272, 275, 278–88
Marw, 150–51, 177
Marwān al-himār (Marwān the Ass). See Marwān II
Marwān I b. al-Hakam, 132, 143
Marwān II b. Muhammad (Umayyad caliph), 29, 143, 151–52
Marx, Karl, 2, 4
Marxism-Leninism, 2, 3–5
Masbugh al-Yadayn, 278
Māshāʾallāh, 297, 299
Masih b. al-Hawāri, 164
Masmuda, 263–68, 273–78, 281–84, 309
al-Māssa, 280
Master of the Revolution/Mission (*sāhib al-dawla/daʿwa*), 153, 174
Masʿudi, 162, 164
Maškilim, 45–47, 54–56, 64–66, 72, 81–82
Matatron, 82
Mattathias, 51–52
Mawāli (non-Arab clients), 18, 24–27, 133–34
  as an estate, 131–32, 150, 219–23
Mawsil, 137
Mazdaean religion, 11, 24, 76–77, 97
Mazdak, 77, 207, 210, 313
Mazdakites, 77–78, 84

Mecca, 8, 84–90, 133–34
  conquest of, 109–10
Medina, 8, 16–17, 74–78, 81–118, 122–24, 130–33
  Constitution of, 81n18, 108–11, 123n15
Meknes, 265–66, 278
Melkizedek, 91–92, 95, 260–61
Men of the Great Synagogue, 36, 43
Menelaus, 41–42, 53, 59–60
Messiah (the anointed one), 10–11, 34, 70, 94, 95n63, 98–99, 111–15
Messenger of God (*rasul Allāh*), 8, 74, 77, 90–94, 104, 107, 134, 176, 269
Messianic Rule, 71
messianism, 1–6
  apocalyptic, 3–4, 7, 69–73, 104
  as charismatic leadership, 11, 100–101, 106–19, 248
  emergence as an evolutionary universal, 10–11
  Mahdism as a form of, 1, 10–13,
  Marxism-Leninism as, 2,
  and modern myth of revolution, 2,
  as the origin of revolutionary transfer of sovereignty, 291–95
  otherworldly transpositions of, 72, 88–89
  political, 1–6, 104, 212, 225, 310, 314
  realized, 9–10, 16, 104–5. See also millennialism
Michael, archangel, 55–56, 93, 99, 106, 294
Mila, 247
milhamah, 71, 100, 293
millennialism, 5–6
  Buddhist, 6,
  Christian, 5–6
  Russian Orthodox, 6
  Shiʿite, 6–7, 299–300
Mithridates, I, 61
Modein, 51
Mosca, Gaetano, 303
Muʿāwiya b. Abu Sufyān, 124–31
Mubashshir, 91
mubashshirun) (Almohad propagandists), 272
Mubayyida (the whites), 209–10
Mudar, 29, 80, 150, 308
Mughiriyya, 224–25
muhājir, 105–6, 274
al-Muhallab b. Abi Sufra, 138
muhammad (the praised one), 9
  corresponding to Manuhmed/Manvahmed, 94

Muhammad b. ʿAbdallāh b. Hud, 280
Muhammad b. ʿAbdallah b. al-Hasan, the Mahdi, 28, 211–16
Muhammad b. ʿAbdallāh, the Messenger of God, 8–10, 74–111
  House of the Prophet, 26–28, 111, 120, 125–26, 130–31, 142, 147, 159, 167–69, 179–82, 184, 249–53, 258
  Messenger of the Lord of All Beings, 104
  the Paraclete (Ahmad), 74, 88
  the Prophet of the Gentiles (*nabi al-ummi*), 74, 88, 90, 1000, 107
  the Prophet/Messenger of the *malhima*, 100, 106
Muhammad b. ʿAli (Abbasid), 152–53
Muhammad b. ʿAli al-Misri al-Khurāsāni al-Akhbāri, 217
Muhammad b. Abi Bakr, 117, 125, 129
Muhammad b. Abi Hudhayfa, 112
Muhammad b. al-Ashʿath b. Qays, 138, 184
Muhammad b. al-Hanafiyya, 134–37, 139
Muhammad b. Ibrāhim, 226
Muhammad b. Idris, 216
Muhammad b. Ismāʿil, 228, 233, 235, 239–40, 246, 251, 254
Muhammad b. Jaʿfar (Talibid), 170
Muhammad b. Jaʿfar al-Dibāj, 226
Muhammad b. Khālid al-Qasri, 169–70, 180, 184
Muhammad b. Sul, 184, 189–90, 200
Muhārib b. Musā, 165
al-Mukhtār b. Abi ʿUbayd al-Thaqafi,, 24, 135–41, 143–44
Mukhtāriyya, 136
muʾākhāt (pact of brotherhood), 8, 106, 274
al-Muʿizz biʾllāh (Fatimid caliph), 252–58, 310
multiple sovereignty, 128, 133, 157–58, 192–200, 205
muʾmin (believer), 81
Muʾminid dynasty, 282–85, 287–88, 312
munāfiqun (hypocrites), 79, 270n20, 272
Munahhemanā, 94
al-Muqannaʿ. See Hāshim b. Hakim
Muqātil b. Sulaymān, 222
murābitun (Almoravids), 263
Murjiʾite rebellion, 173–79
  its millennialism, 175–76
Musʿab b. al Zubayr, 133, 137
Musā al-Kāzim, 225
Musā b. Kaʿb, 178
Musaylima b. Habib, 113–15

Muslimiyya (or Abu Muslimiyya)
Muʿtazila, 158–59
muwahhidun (monotheists), 269. See Almohads

nabi (prophet), 8, 74, 92–93, 102, 107, 269
nadhir (warner), 89
Nāfiʿ b. Azraq, 133–34
Nahravan, 129
Najada b. ʿĀmir, 133
Najadāt, 133
Najran, 79, 83
Nasafi, 244
al-nafs al-zakiyya (the Pure Soul). See Muhammad b. ʿAbdallah b. al-Hasan, the Mahdi
Nāser Khosraw, 241
Nasr b. Sayyār, 150–51, 157–58,
Nawbakht, 218
Nayzak, 192, 196–97
Nazarenes (*nasārā*), 81–83
Nazoraeans (Ναζωραῖοι). See Nazarenes
Negus (*najāshi*), 78–79
Nehemiah, 35–36
Nesa, 178
Nishapur, 207, 242
Nisibin, 195
Nizāri Ismaʿilis, 258–61
Nöldeke, Theodor, 16, 19
Noth, Albrecht, 18–19

Oman, 189, 191
Onias III, 41, 46, 59–60
Onias IV, 59–60, 62n99, 63–64
Origins of Muhammadan Jurisprudence, 17

Paraclete, 9, 13, 74, 88–94, 100, 261
Parsons, Talcott, 11
Peasant rebellions, 5, 187n57
Penitents (*tawwābun*), 135–36
People of Equality and Justice, 159, 174
People of the Book (*ahl al-kitāb*), 81, 86, 88
People of the Good (*ahl al-khayr*), 231, 249–52, 256
Persian Sibyl, 36–37
Persis (Fars), 36–38, 43n37
Pharisees, 44–45, 48, 51, 59–60, 66–68, 72, 83
Phineas, 51–52
Pishyōtan, 140
Pirenne, Henri, 23
Pirenne thesis, the, 23–24

political, the, 33
  heteronomy under messianism, 3–4, 34
politics of absolute end. *See* absolute politics
Prolegomena (muqaddima), 262
Prolegomena to the History of Israel, 17
prophecy, 8–10
  and the End of Time, 9, 72, 88–89, 95–96
  ex eventu, 225, 253, 267
  Muhammad's, 101–5
prophets, 9, 34, 74, 90–93, 110
  the gentile prophet (*al-nabiyy al-ummi*), 74, 90, 100. See also *nabi*
Ptolemies of Egypt, 36
Ptolemy Philometor, 62n99, 64
political religion, 3–6

Qadariyya, 149, 156–62, in relation to Khairi-jte and Shi'ite trends, 158–59
Qadi al-Nu'mān, 245, 247, 254–56, 258
qa'em/qāim (the standing or living one), 140–41
Qahtaba b. Shabib, 169–70
al-Qāhir (Abbasid caliph), 217
qā'im āl Muḥammad, 224
al-Qā'im bi-Amr Allāh (Fatimid caliph), 253
Qa'im of the Resurrection (*qiyāma*), 229, 259–60
Qa'im-Mahdi, the, 13, 139–44, 205
  as the Greatest Proof (*hujja*) of God, 230
  and the Second Christ (*al-masih al-thāni*), 229
Qahtāni, 141–42, 175
Qarmatis (Carmatians), 229, 242–45
Qairawan, 246
Qatari b. Fujā'a, 134, 146
Qays, 29, 132n37, 150, 154–55, 163
Qays b. al-Aslat, 85
Qays b. Sa'd b. 'Ubāda, 123–24
Qinnasrin, 166
Qumran, 4, 19, 45, 56,
  apocalyptic messianism of, 7, 67, 69–73
  community in the Judaean desert, 67–73
  influence on Islam, 73, 88, 312–13. See also Essenes
qur'ān (recitation), 87, 96, 131
Qur'an, apocalyptic verses, 96–99, study of, 10, 17, 19–23
Qur'anic Studies, 19
Qur'ān readers (*qurrā'*), 111
  and the First Civil War, 118–31
Quraysh, 80, 85, 105–13, 118, 131–32, 142, 308
  the caliphate of, 131–32, 223, 312

Qutayba b. Ghurak, 179
Qutayba b. Muslim al-Bāhili, 145

Rabi'a, 29, 163, 188–89
Radwa Mountains, 139
Ragrāga, al-Rahmān, 101–2
Raita, 171, 183n29
al-ridā (the acceptable one), 134, 165, 175
  from the House of the Prophet, 26, 167, 178, 180, 184, 218, 246
raj'a (return of the dead), 139
Raqqada, 247–50
Rāwandiyya 191, 210
Rayy, 137, 157, 165, 184, 187, 207–8, 215, 222, 242
Rebellions on the periphery of empire, 75–88, 155–56, 173–92
Revolution, 1–15, 120
  apocalyptic motivation of, 3–4
  causes, 3–4, 13, 117, 148
  and centralization of power, 15, 22n52, 216–19
  consequences of constitutional politics of, 12–13, 15, 116–17, 311
  conception of Marxist-Leninist revolution, 2–5
  conception of Maghrebi revolution, 302–8
  conception of Persianate revolution, 31, 295–302
  export of, 111–12, 145, 178–79, 256–58, 281, 313
  ideal-types (models) of, 13–15
  ideal-type (model) of Aristotelian-Paretan Revolution, 14n26
  ideal-type (model) of Constitutive Revolution, 14n25, 116; in Arabia, 8–10, 75, 107–8
  ideal-type (model) of Integrative Revolution, 13–14, 18
  ideal-type (model) of Khaldunian Revolution, 14n27, 302–8
  ideal-type (model) of Tocquevillian, 14–15, 18
  Mahdist revolutions, modern myth of, 2, 4, 12, 291
  and messianism, 1–5, 9–13, 310–14
  motivated by value-ideas, 4, 12, 272, 290
  and nativism, 36–38, 51–69, 206–11
  and political quietism, 4, 294
  process of revolutionary power struggle, 12, 51–68, 105–11, 192–200, 228–51, 266–83, 311
Sasanian Revolution, 76, 304

Tocquevillian Revolution, 14–15, 148. See also Abbasid Revolution; Fatimid Revolution; Hashemite Revolution; Mahdist revolutions
Rubin, Uri, 21
Risāla fī'l-sahāba (Essay on the companionship), 201
Riyāh b. 'Uthmān al-Murri, 213
Robertson Smith, W., 16
Rusāfa, 151, 153, 166
Rustamid dynasty, 189

Sabaeans (sābi'un), 86n38, 88, 313. See also Hanafiyya-Sābi'a
Sabaean Book, the, 86
sābiqa (precedence), 112, 273
Sa'd b.Abi Waqqās, 122
Sa'd b. 'Ubāda, 112
Sadducees, 48, 58, 65, 68
as latter-day Karaites 81–82. See also Zadokite
saddiqin, 81–82
Sadeghi, Behman, 21
al-saffāh (the blood-shedder, also the generous), 142–43
al-Saffāh (Abbasid caliph). See 'Abdallāh b. 'Ali; Abu'l-'Abbās 'Abdallāh
Sahrāwi, 280
Sa'id b. al-Husayn, a.k.a. Abu Muhammad 'Abdallāh, 239, 241
Sa'id b. Jubayr, 164
Sajjāh b. Aws, 115
Saktān, 245
Saladin (Salāh al al-Din al-Ayyubi), 254
Salamiyya, 229, 232–33, 239–41, 249
Sālih b. 'Ali (Abbasid), 186
Sālim b. 'Abd al-Rahmān, 153
Salm b. Qutayba b. Muslim al-Bāhili, 170
Sāmān, 152
Samanid dynasty, 84
San'ā, 114
San'ā' palimpsest, the, 21
Sanhāja, 261–64, 274, 278
Sarjun b.Mansur, 146
Sarkisyanz, Manuel, 6
al-Sayyid al-Himyari, 140
Sawād (black land) of Kufa, 229, 242
sayyids (Almohad), 285
Sayr-e tahavvol-e Qur'an, 22
Schacht, Joseph, 16–17, 19; School of Oriental and African Studies of the University of London (SOAS), 20, 30

Seal of the Prophets (khātam al-nabiyyin), 89–90
Second Coming of Christ, the, 91, 243
Second Temple, 35, 47
Secular religion. See political religion
Seleucid Empire, 11, 33–42
Seleucids, 7, 36–39, 52
Seleucus, 36
Sefidhanj, 174
Šelikhā, 92–93
Seljuq Empire, 258–59, 302–3
Sepid-jāmagān. See Mubayyida
Shaban, M.A., 25
Shāh-Āfarid, 155
Shahrazur, 180
Shāpuragān, 92
Sharik b. Shaykh al-Mahri, 179
Shi'a: Extremist (ghulāt), 137, 139–40, 224–25
  Imami (Twelver), Imamiyya, 30, 140, 213, 222, 225–32, 255–56
  Ismā'ili, 30–31, 216, 224–61
  Sevener, 226, 229, 235, 251
  Zaydi, 30, 225–28
shaykhs (Almohad), 285
shirk (associationist polytheism), 80
Shurā (electoral council), 118, 122, 134, 159–60, 175, 181
Sirāj al-Muluk (The lantern of the kings), 303
sirāj al-muwahiddin (the lantern of the monotheists), 277
Sibawayh, 222
Sijilmasa, 241–42, 249, 263–65, 280–81, 310
Simon Maccabee, 62–63, 68–69
Simon the Just (high priest), 38–39
Sira, of the prophets and kings, 204
Sistan, 135, 145
Soghdia, 179–80, 210
Sonpādh, 207–8, 298
Sons of Zadok, 53, 57–60, 63–65, 70, 82
Spouter of Lies. See Liar (daggāla)
Sōshyānt, 298
State, the. See Structure of Domination
structure of domination, 1
  pre-Islamic Arabia, and the three empires of Median caliphate, 112–16, breakdown of, 117, 19
  Abbasid, Almohad, Fatimid, 252–58
  mahdistic, of the Seleucid Empire in Judaea, 34–42, its crisis and breakdown, 51–69
  Marwanid, 133–34, 149–56, breakdown of, 26, 165–66, 169–72

revolutionary state, 245, 257map, 273–75, 279map, 284. See also dual power and sovereignty
Sudayf b. Maymun, 190
Sufyān b. Muʿāwiya al-Muhallabi, 164
al-Sufyāni, 143
Sulaymān b. Habib al-Muhallabi, 170
Sulaymān b. Hishām, 155–68, 190
Sulaymān b. Kathir, 187–88, 197
Sulaymān b. Surad al-Khuzāʿī, 135–36
Sunna, 125–26, 128, 131, 161, 175, 204
Sunni Islam: formation in sectarian context, 126–31
Sus valley, 309–10
Susa, 38–39
Sybilline Oracles, 63–64

Tabari, 23, 84, 162
Tabaristan, 208
Tabuk, 110
Tadmur, 190
Tāʾif, 80, 85
Tahart, 189
talaba (Almohad), 266, 275,
Talman, Jacob, 5–6
Tinmallal, 267–68, 273–75, 282–84, 288
Tilly, Charles, 133
tamyiz (the Almohad Great Purge), 272, 288
Tocqueville, Alexis de, 2
Trotsky, Leon, 128
Talha b. ʿUbaydallāh, 117–18, 121–27, 130
Talha b. Khuwaylid, 113
Tamim, 29, 175
Tamiyya, 225
Tawazur, 245
Taxo, 50
Tayyʾ, 114
Teacher of Righteousness, 57–58, 60–70, 83
Temple Scroll, 57–58, 65, 70
Testament of Moses, 50
Thaqif, 80
Tlemcen, 266
Toledo, 265
Tobiad family, 41

Ugallid, 266, 289
ʿuluj (infidel hulks), 189
ʿUmar b. ʿAbd al-Khattāb al-Fāruq (second rightly-guided caliph), 95, 110–15
ʿUmar II b. ʿAbd al-ʿAziz, 154
Umayya b. Abiʾl-Salt, 85

ʿUmayr b. Hāniʾ, 158
umma community of believers, 31, 75, 101 formation in Medina, 75, 107–8
Umm Salama (Abbasid), 171
Umayyads. See Banu Umayya
Ushēdar-Māh, 298
ʿUthmān al-Kirmāni, 179
ʿUthmān b. ʿAffān (rightly-guided caliph), 113, 117–24, 149
ʿUzayr, 99

Voegelin, Eric, 5–6

Wahb b. Munabbih, 142
al-Walid II b. Yzid b. ʿAbd al-Malik, (Umayyad caliph), 149–56
Wansbrough, John, 19–20, 22, 30
Wansharis, 266
Wansharisi, Abu Muhammad ʿAbdallāh b. Mushin (al-Bashir), 266, 272
Wāqifiyya, 225, 235, 246
Waraqa b. Nawfal, 90
Wars of Apostasy (*ridda*), 113–14
Wāsil b. ʿAtāʾ, 158
Weber, Max, 3, 5–7, 12, 131, 228, 252
Wellhausen, Julius, 17–19, 24–26
Wicked Priest, the, 60–62, 66–67
Wohu Manah, 94

"*yā Mansur amit,*" 142, 210
"*yā Muhammad, ya mansūr!*" 142
Yahyā b. ʿAbdallāh, 228
Yahyā b. ʿAli b. Ghāniya, 280–81
Yahyā b. Ibrāhim, 263
Yahyā b. Khālid al-Barmaki, 221
Yahyā b. ʿUmar, 264
Yahyā b. Zacharia, 239
Yahyā b. Zayd b. ʿAli, 27, 168
Yahweh, 11, 35, 53, 55, 103; as the God of heaven, 46
Yaman, 29, 150, 154, 175, 177
Yaslātan b. al-Muʿizz, 278, 282
Yathrib, 8
Yazid III (Umayyad caliph), 149–69, 175
Yehud (Achaemenid province), 35
Yemen, 232–33
Yusuf b. Tāshfin, 264–65
Yusuf b. ʿUmar al-Thaqafi, 155–61

Zachariah, 34
Zadok, sons of, 57–58, revolutionary program of, 65–69

Zadokite high priests of Jerusalem, 38—39, 41, 59–60
al-Zahhāk b. Qay al-Shaybāni, 168–69
Zakarōye b. Mehōye, 233, 239–40
Zanāta, 263–64, 278, 283
zandiq, 77–78. *See also* Manichaean-Mazdakites
Zanj (rebellion of black slaves), 227
Zayd b. ʿAli b. al-Husayn, 142, 149, 152, 159, 163, 173, 180, 208
Zayd b. ʿAmr b. Nufayl, 84, 90
Zayd b. Musā (zayd al-nār), 226
Zerubbabel, 35
ZiyādaT Allāh III (Aghlabid amir), 247
Zoroaster, 92, 208, 244, 297–98
Zoroastrian apocalyptic, 11, 34, 38, 58, 64, 70–71
Zoroastrianism, 76, 80
al-Zubayr b. ʿAwwām, 117–18, 122–30

Founded in 1893,
UNIVERSITY OF CALIFORNIA PRESS
publishes bold, progressive books and journals
on topics in the arts, humanities, social sciences,
and natural sciences—with a focus on social
justice issues—that inspire thought and action
among readers worldwide.

The UC PRESS FOUNDATION
raises funds to uphold the press's vital role
as an independent, nonprofit publisher, and
receives philanthropic support from a wide
range of individuals and institutions—and from
committed readers like you. To learn more, visit
ucpress.edu/supportus.

www.ingramcontent.com/pod-product-compliance
Lightning Source LLC
Chambersburg PA
CBHW030518230426
43665CB00010B/668